LAMENT
FOR AN
OCEAN

Justice Denied: The Law versus Donald Marshall

Unholy Orders: Tragedy at Mount Cashel

Rare Ambition: The Crosbies of Newfoundland

The Prodigal Husband: The Tragedy of
Helmuth and Hanna Buxbaum

The Judas Kiss: The Undercover Life of Patrick Kelly

LAMENT FOR AN OCEAN

The Collapse of the Atlantic Cod Fishery
A True Crime Story

Michael Harris

M&S

Cloth edition published 1998
Updated trade paperback edition published 1999

Canadian Cataloguing in Publication Data

Harris, Michael, 1948-
Lament for an ocean : the collapse of the Atlantic cod fishery :
a true crime story

Includes index.
ISBN 0-7710-3960-3

1. Cod fisheries – Atlantic Coast (Canada).   2. Cod fisheries –
Economic aspects – Newfoundland.   3. Fishery policy – Canada.
4. Fishery policy – Newfoundland.   I. Title.   II. Title: Collapse of the
Atlantic cod fishery.

SH351.C5H375 1999   338.3´727633´0916344   C99-931849-7

We acknowledge the financial support of the Government of Canada
through the Book Publishing Industry Development Program for
our publishing activities. Canadä

We further acknowledge the support of the Canada Council for the Arts
and the Ontario Arts Council for our publishing program.

Set in Bembo by M&S, Toronto
Printed and bound in Canada

McClelland & Stewart Inc.
The Canadian Publishers
481 University Avenue
Toronto, Ontario
M5G 2E9

1 2 3 4 5   03 02 01 00 99

For my grandfather William Tilley, 1894-1968,
who left Newfoundland in the Great Depression, never to return.
On his deathbed, he asked for partridge berries.

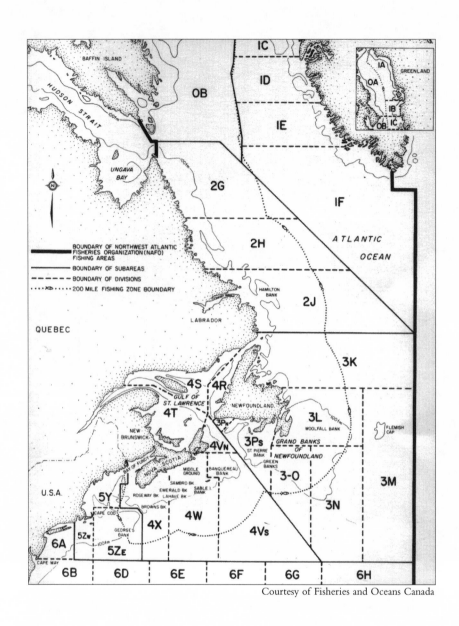

Courtesy of Fisheries and Oceans Canada

Two-Hundred-Mile Fishing Zone
and NAFO Fishing Boundaries

Contents

"What we have is not an adjustment problem, but the most wrenching societal upheaval since the Great Depression. Our communities are in crisis. The people of the fishery are in turmoil."

> – Earle McCurdy, president of the Fish, Food, and
> Allied Workers union, in *Atlantic Fisherman*

"If I were an Atlantic premier, I'd sue the feds. If I were a fisherman or a processor, I'd launch a class-action lawsuit. Heads should be rolling in Ottawa."

> – Silver Donald Cameron, *The Globe and Mail*

I

NOBODY'S WATERS

It was the other shot that was heard around the world. The 50-calibre machine-gun bursts from the *Cape Roger*, three in all, marked the first time since Confederation that Canada had fired on another country in defence of the national interest. When the order came to open fire, the officers aboard the fisheries patrol vessel were so taken aback, they asked that the command be repeated. The fateful words crackled once more over the ship's radio: an initial burst was to be fired over the bow of the Spanish trawler *Estai*, the next rounds into her screw sixty seconds later if she refused to stop. After warning the Spanish captain to move his crew forward, Captain Newman Riggs nodded to Bernie Masters, who adjusted the sights on the *Cape Roger*'s heavy gun and sucked in a deep breath as his finger squeezed the trigger.

This "act of war," as it would soon be called, was perpetrated against an unarmed fishing vessel by the nation that had invented peacekeeping, in the name of conserving a fish most Canadians had never heard of, and until very recently, most fishermen treated as an unwanted by-catch: the suddenly controversial turbot.

For four nerve-wracking hours in the afternoon of March 9, 1995, the *Estai* had done its best to elude three Canadian patrol vessels, two from the Department of Fisheries and Oceans (DFO), the other from the Canadian Coast Guard. The ships had been pursuing the *Estai* for suspected illegal turbot fishing off Newfoundland's Grand Banks. There were even allegations that the vessel had a secret hold containing twenty-five tonnes of contraband American plaice. In an attempt to outrun its pursuers, Captain Enrique Davila González had ordered his men to cut the *Estai*'s nets, worth $80,000. Anything was better than having the contents of the *Estai*'s hold, bulging with undersized fish, revealed.

Canada had been preparing for this moment for several weeks. The federal fisheries minister, Brian Tobin, first raised the prospect of using force to end chronic overfishing off Canada's east coast in a full cabinet meeting. Prime Minister Jean Chrétien had agreed to the discussion and must have been surprised that Tobin's idea hadn't died a quick death around the cabinet table. What the prime minister didn't know was that his enterprising fisheries minister had already successfully lobbied his colleagues, some of whom had rejected their own departmental advice to side with Tobin.

The Justice Department recommended against seizing foreign fishing vessels in international waters because the relevant law was either muddy, non-existent, or favoured the Spanish; the RCMP opposed the use of force because of civil liabilities it feared might arise out of an armed confrontation; the Department of National Defence rejected Tobin's gunboat diplomacy against a NATO ally.

But opposition from the mandarins didn't stop Justice Minister Allan Rock, Solicitor-General Herb Grey, or Defence Minister David Collenette from backing Tobin. After the cabinet meeting that laid the groundwork for confronting the Spanish on the high seas, a grudgingly impressed prime minister buttonholed his fisheries minister to compliment him on his private manoeuvring. There was no such praise, grudging or otherwise, from Foreign Affairs Minister André Ouellet. From start to finish in what would become known as the Turbot War, he and his department remained bitterly opposed to raising a fist to a friend over something as "inconsequential" as fish stocks.

The crew of the *Estai* was on tenterhooks as the Canadian vessels closed in. The prospect of a catastrophic collision in the dense fog and rough, icy seas of the northwest Atlantic was bad enough, but the 50-calibre bursts had taken the sea chase to an unacceptable level of risk. Just before 5:00 p.m. Ottawa time, González put a stop to the dangerous game of cat and mouse he'd been playing with the three Canadian ships. When the *Estai* finally gave up, a team of armed Canadian fisheries officers in orange survival suits, led by Frank Snelgrove, scrambled aboard, seized the ship, and placed her captain under arrest.

The Spanish crew had fended off two previous boarding attempts. Earlier on that raw March day the RCMP had tried to board the *Estai* using hooks and ladders. The crew had repulsed them by uncoupling their grappling gear. It was a bad moment for the Mounties. They might always get their man, but not necessarily their fisherman. When they tried to get back into their Zodiac, it capsized, sending the boarding party into the ocean and their Uzi submachine guns to the bottom. Ultimately, it took seven DFO officers to do what the RCMP could not.

During the unsuccessful boarding attempts, the Spanish fishermen got a hint of what was to come. Eyewitnesses amongst the *Estai*'s crew claimed that one of the officers had brandished a weapon and pointed it at them. The Spaniards were dumbfounded. Manuel Nogeira, a thirty-five-year-old crew member who had been fishing the Grand Banks since he was fourteen, stated the Spanish case as well as any diplomat: "We are not stealing. These are nobody's waters."

While Canadian authorities were taking charge of the *Estai*, the prime minister was in Winnipeg attending a Liberal Party fund-raiser. Jean Chrétien had authorized the use of force by Canadian fisheries officers in the showdown on the Grand Banks. The previous evening, he had spoken by telephone with Jacques Santer, the president of the European Commission (which manages the European Union's policies and trade relationships) in an eleventh-hour bid to avoid an armed confrontation. A deal was struck: negotiating teams from both sides would meet in Brussels to defuse the escalating crisis. But Chrétien insisted on one condition: Spanish trawlers would have to observe a sixty-day moratorium on all turbot fishing in the disputed zone while the talks proceeded. When he learned the next day that the Spanish fleet had resumed fishing, Chrétien had given the green light to the use of force. Risky as it was, it was better than watching yet another fish stock make the one-way trip to commercial extinction.

The order to stop the *Estai* by force was issued after a meeting at 200 Kent Street in the Ottawa headquarters of the DFO. At the meeting were Brian Tobin's deputy minister, Bill Rowat; Gordon Smith, undersecretary of state at Foreign Affairs; and Jim Bartleman, an international affairs expert from the Prime Minister's Office. Tobin convened the meeting a few hours into the sea chase, not knowing whether the Spanish vessel would eventually stop of her own accord. When it became obvious she intended to keep running, Tobin called in Max Short. A former fishermen's union executive, Short knew the wharf and human nature better than anyone else in the room.

"If they get away, it will be a great victory for them," Short said. "If we catch them, it'll tear the heart, the guts, and the soul out of them. Pursue the sons of bitches all the way to Spain."

Tobin produced the already drafted order to stop the *Estai*, by force if necessary, and everyone present signed it, including a surprised and reluctant Gordon Smith. The command was passed on to the DFO headquarters in Newfoundland, where fisheries officer Sandy Hollett was standing by to coordinate the mission.

Although no one in the country knew it, Canada was virtually on a war footing. Tobin had requested and received full naval support for the *Estai* mission, including the deployment of submarines. Manning the command centre in Halifax was Admiral

Gary Garnett, whose job it would be to direct naval firepower if the need arose. But with the submarines giving Canada the strategic advantage, it was unlikely that push would come to shove.

Nor were there likely to be any surprises, as the government was intercepting all messages to the Spanish fleet. (It was from one of these intercepted communications that Canada first learned that the Spanish referred to Brian Tobin as "El Bandito.") The chief of defence staff, John de Chastelain, attended every cabinet meeting during the *Estai* affair, and the Department of National Defence (DND) had a representative at every DFO strategy session. In the informal parlance of official Ottawa, it was "elephant-shit stuff."

The *Estai* was part of Spain's enormous global fishing fleet, an armada of ten thousand vessels, more boats than the fleets of the other fourteen countries of the European Union combined. Her home port was the Galician coastal city of Vigo, the heart of the Spanish fishing industry. Throughout the vessel's ordeal, José Suarez-Llanos, spokesman for the Vigo Ship Owners Co-operative, which owned the *Estai*, sat glued to the satellite telephone. As the heart-stopping pursuit came to an end, he and his colleagues heard the captain's last words just before the *Estai* was seized: "*Estan escalando!*" They're climbing up!

Spanish diplomats learned of the seizure during an informal social call at the Portuguese embassy in Ottawa. They immediately fired off two official protests to the Canadian government, complaining that the capture of their vessel amounted to an act of piracy on the high seas. Although Canada took a different view, many thought it was a strange way to settle a fishing dispute between friends. As John Wright, the senior vice-president of the Angus Reid polling group later put it, what Canada had done amounted to an act of "green Ramboism."

There was a little more to it than that. The *Estai* was suspected of breaking a freshly minted Canadian law designed to prevent another catastrophe like the one that had closed Newfoundland's fabled cod fishery in 1992, throwing forty thousand Atlantic

Canadians out of work and permanently clouding their future. The Coastal Fisheries Protection Act permitted Canadian enforcement officers to arrest so-called "flag-of-convenience" foreign vessels on the high seas when they were suspected of breaking international fishing agreements. By being registered in Panama, for example, a Spanish trawler could break fishing regulations with impunity since that country was not a member of the Northwest Atlantic Fisheries Organization (NAFO).

Canada's legislation was also intended to reflect the reality that certain fish stocks "straddle" the 200-mile national limit, meaning that domestic conservation efforts could be nullified when the fish moved farther offshore into the nets of foreign fleets. The turbot was one of those stocks. The deep-water flatfish is found all along the continental shelf, from Davis Inlet in the north to the southern Grand Banks. In its southern habitat, the turbot regularly migrates beyond the 200-mile limit.

DFO scientists had long understood that fish are not uniformly distributed over the rich fishing grounds off Newfoundland, but congregate where the shelf breaks into the so-called Nose and Tail of the Banks. The catches in those areas are much higher than their size would indicate. In fact, the Tail of the Grand Banks is known as a "nursery" for juvenile cod, American plaice, and yellowtail flounder, species that regularly move beyond Canada's 200-mile limit.

The new law to protect these straddling stocks had received unanimous parliamentary approval in June 1994. It was amended on March 3, 1995, to include the Spanish and Portuguese fleets, the bad boys of the international fishing community. Canadian officials had concluded that if they waited for diplomacy to settle the fishing dispute, or a favourable judicial ruling at the Hague, the fight to save the turbot would be purely academic.

While Spain fumed, Newfoundlanders cheered the swashbuckling action of Canada's fisheries minister, forty-year-old Liberal MP Brian Tobin. His bold initiative triggered a burst of nationalism usually reserved for Stanley Cup hockey teams and Olympic gold medallists. Thousands of people lined the docks in St. John's, waving provincial flags and lustily cheering the veteran Newfoundland MP as they awaited the arrival of the *Estai* under a brilliant March sun. The powerful Fish, Food, and Allied Workers union (FFAW) was out in full force, converging on the dock in the same yellow school buses so often used in the past to bring fishermen to protests against the federal government.

In a rare show of national unity, the rest of the country applauded along with Newfoundland. An Angus Reid poll showed that nine out of ten Canadians approved of Tobin's actions. Eighty-seven per cent of Atlantic Canadians supported the government's tough line against Spain, and in the rest of Canada support for the arrest of the *Estai* ranged from 84 per cent in Quebec to an astonishing 94 per cent in Manitoba and Saskatchewan. It was about as patriotic as Canadians ever get. On March 27, 1995, during a supply stop at a Canadian Forces base in Winnipeg, a Spanish air force jet was plastered with pro-Tobin decals. A military spokesman told reporters with a smile that he doubted the vandals would be brought to justice.

Allan Gotlieb, Canada's former ambassador to the U.S.A., called the *Estai* affair "our Gulf War." Doffing its hat to Ottawa's grit, CBC's "Saturday Afternoon at the Opera" ended its March 11 program with a selection from *The Pirates of Penzance*, dedicated to Brian Tobin and his plucky buccaneers. Even the *Globe and Mail*, which had just one correspondent on the East Coast to cover the four provinces of Atlantic Canada, ran a front-page story about the first salvo in the Turbot War. Not everyone took it quite so seriously. The *Vancouver Sun* responded with a page-one recipe for the endangered flatfish.

Heavy ice delayed the *Estai*'s arrival in St. John's for nearly three days. Still, emotions were high when the Spanish vessel, gleaming white in the bright March sun, finally came through the Narrows under Canadian escort and tied up in St. John's Harbour. Spanish and Portuguese fishermen had been traditionally welcomed in

Newfoundland when they needed vessel repairs, provisions, or medical help for sick or injured crew members. But with their own cod fishery destroyed and closed, Newfoundlanders were in no mood to tolerate overfishing by anyone, including old friends. Captain González and José Luis Pardos, Spain's ambassador to Canada, were vigorously jostled as they were escorted through the throng of angry fishermen on their way to the Duckworth Street law courts. An egg struck a German diplomat accompanying the Spaniards through the boisterous crowd.

A total of four EU diplomats ran the gauntlet with Pardos and González. Alfred Siefer-Gaillardin, France's ambassador to Canada, explained that the show of solidarity was necessary to remind Canada that when it harassed Spanish vessels, it was rousing a sleeping giant; the entire European Union.

Just a day after the seizure of the *Estai*, the EU's swift and pre-dictable response was widely reported around the world. At an emergency meeting in Brussels on March 10, 1995, the fifteen-nation Union denounced Tobin's action as lawless, reckless, and totally unacceptable. It warned that unless the situation was imme-diately redressed, there would be serious damage to the historically good relations between Canada and Europe. The Spanish took more practical action. They dispatched warships, promising they wouldn't hesitate to protect their fishing fleet from further acts of piracy by Canada.

Europe's sabre-rattling realized the worst fears of Canada's min-ister of foreign affairs. André Ouellet was vacationing in Mexico when the *Estai* was arrested, and he was bombarded at his hotel with updates on the showdown from his worried staff. Before leaving Canada, Ouellet had informed the prime minister that he was totally opposed to the confrontationist strategy crafted by Tobin and a passionate coterie of DFO officials, who were every bit as sanguine about standing up to the Spanish as their minister.

Ouellet and his officials favoured a diplomatic resolution of the dispute, the traditional policy of successive Canadian governments of both political stripes. He deeply resented what he took to be the dangerous jingoism of his colleague from Newfoundland. The prime minister managed to find the humour in the situation. Walking out of the House of Commons, he quipped to one of Tobin's aides, "Your Brian thinks he is Napoleon."

Tobin's apparent hot-headedness was anything but an aberration of traditional Canadian policy. In 1979, Ottawa had seized nineteen American tuna boats for illegally fishing off Canada's west coast. In June 1994, Tobin had slapped a $1,500 fee on U.S. salmon fishermen navigating the coastal waters of British Columbia, successfully forcing the Americans to resume talks on a badly needed Pacific salmon treaty. In August 1994, he had also ordered the seizure of two U.S. scallopers illegally fishing in Canadian waters.

The American vessels were arrested beyond the 200-mile limit, touching off an international incident that never hit the mainland press. American ambassador Jim Blanchard delivered a blunt message to Tobin, who had acted without approval from either the prime minister or Foreign Affairs. "Blanchard told me that Teddy Kennedy was going nuts. We had twenty-four hours to return the vessels or else. I said, 'Or else what, Jim? You'll go to war?'" Tobin's brinkmanship paid off. Before the scallopers were released, the Americans recognized Canada's jurisdiction over Icelandic scallops, tacitly accepting the Law of the Sea's provisions for so-called sedentary species. This action was in keeping with Canada's fierce protection of the longest coastal territory in the world. As Allan Gotlieb put it: "It's a mysterious dimension of the Canadian psyche. We've always been very conciliatory and emphasized arbitration on other matters, but when it comes to coastal waters and territorial issues, we've always felt we needed to take unilateral action."

The bitter disagreement over tactics between Ouellet and Tobin became so serious that it eventually led to a tense meeting in the Prime Minister's Office. The clerk of the privy council was present in case resignations were offered or demanded. Tobin now acknowledges that the turbot crisis came perilously close to ending his political career. "Let's just say that things got sufficiently interesting that on a couple of occasions I shredded my private ministerial papers," he says. "I was way out on a limb on this one and there were quite a few people trying to cut it off."

On March 12, Captain González and the *Estai* were formally charged with fishing for a straddling stock in contravention of Canada's new Coastal Fisheries Protection Act. The *Estai*'s master was also charged with failing to "bring about" when ordered, throwing a net overboard, and wilfully obstructing a fisheries officer. After posting $8,000 for bail, Captain González was released.

Spain bristled, declaring that there would be no negotiations about fish quotas until the *Estai*, which had been fishing off the Grand Banks for five straight months, was released. Emma Bonino, the tough-talking EU Commissioner for Fisheries, agreed that the seizure of the trawler on the high seas was a "flagrant violation of international law."

Brian Tobin was a worthy opponent for Bonino. The former member of the "Rat Pack" was just as fiery as Bonino and had once been thrown out of the House of Commons for calling then prime minister Brian Mulroney a liar. But Bonino sensed she had the upper hand. Aware that 35 per cent of Canada's gross national product depended on trade with the EU (fishing accounts for just I per cent of GNP), Bonino hinted darkly at sanctions against Canada for its act of "organized piracy." It was a threat that had always worked in the past and it appeared to be working again.

Three days later, the *Estai* was released from Canadian custody after posting a $500,000 bond. At 8:30 p.m. on the evening of March 15, she steamed out through the Narrows and began the long voyage back to Vigo. The opening battle of the Turbot War had gone to Canada. It had not been an easy victory. The security service didn't rule out a foreign assassination attempt on Canada's fisheries minister, and as a precautionary measure, Tobin sent his family out of the country on a Florida vacation.

In the first blush of victory, Brian Tobin was able to take the moral high ground of enforcing the quota cuts made by the regulatory body responsible for the fishery on the high seas. In an era when awareness of ecological devastation was at an all-time high, it was a powerful argument: "We will not tolerate non-compliance with the proper decisions of the Northwest Atlantic Fisheries Organization," Tobin declared.

The Northwest Atlantic Fisheries Organization, NAFO, was founded in 1978, a year after Canada unilaterally declared its 200-mile offshore economic zone. With headquarters in Dartmouth, Nova Scotia, NAFO acts as a forum for international cooperation in scientific research, management, and conservation of fish stocks beyond Canada's zone. Each September, its members hold meetings to set the total allowable catch (TAC) for the upcoming fishing year, and to assign national quotas out of the overall allocation.

Fifteen "contracting parties" belonged to NAFO at the time of the Turbot War: the European Union, Bulgaria, Cuba, Denmark, Iceland, Japan, Korea, Norway, Poland, Romania, Russia, Estonia, Latvia, Lithuania, and Canada. Like many international organizations, NAFO has no shortage of lofty objectives, but few means of realizing them. This is particularly true when a dispute arises. A member country could opt out of the fisheries plan merely by objecting to any of the organization's decisions. After taking that unilateral step, they would no longer be bound by NAFO rules and regulations and could, in effect, set their own quotas.

By the late 1980s, the European Community (as the EU was then known) was objecting to most of its NAFO quotas, a tactic that effectively loosed the Spanish factory-freezer trawler fleet on NAFO-regulated waters off Canada's east coast. There were many ways of circumnavigating NAFO's attempts at regulation. Fish were dumped at sea, transferred to other vessels, or landed in third-country ports to conceal evidence of NAFO infractions. Under international law, legal authority to control fishing vessels was vested in the country of registry. It looked good on paper, but prosecutions by the country of registry either never took place or were impossible to follow up. When it came to the high seas, it was every ship for itself, and the consequences for the living resource the fishermen so relentlessly pursued were catastrophic.

Both Canadian and Russian research surveys had shown a phenomenal decline in turbot stocks dating from the early 1980s, reflected by catch-rates that were in sharp decline both within and outside Canada's 200-mile zone. In February 1994, Canadian researchers discovered that the stock off Labrador and eastern Newfoundland had dropped by a staggering two-thirds from the biomass survey of 1991. There was also a preponderance of young fish in the remaining stock. The news could not have been worse. The female turbot has to be at least ten years old before it can spawn. With few large, mature fish of breeding age, the species could easily be wiped out by fishing fleets looking for a species to replace the once-abundant cod.

There was nothing mysterious about the devastation of the fish also known as Greenland halibut. Until June 1994 there had been no catch restrictions on turbot outside Canada's 200-mile zone, largely because no one was interested in catching it. But as cod catches plummeted, foreign vessels switched their fishing effort to the unprotected turbot. In a matter of months, the fish the Spanish call *palometa* went from being a species no one wanted to the largest commercial groundfish stock off eastern Canada. In a frighteningly short period of time, turbot was fished to the brink of commercial extinction.

To prevent a repeat of the cod fiasco, Canada asked NAFO to set a turbot TAC for the first time in the organization's history. In a show of good faith to other NAFO members, Tobin slashed the turbot quota in Canadian waters by 75 per cent, even though fishermen from Newfoundland and Quebec had also turned to the turbot fishery as a way of coping with the 1992 cod moratorium.

NAFO's scientific council met on June 29, 1994, and decided that conservation measures were in order to protect the turbot. At the organization's annual September meeting in Dartmouth, Tobin pressed for controls on turbot catches outside the Canadian economic zone. Canada's conservation arguments carried the day.

NAFO delegates accepted a drastic cut in the total allowable turbot catch, from 60,000 to just 27,000 tonnes.

Gaining a consensus on conservation was the easy part. NAFO members next had to divide the reduced quota among several fish-hungry national fleets. On February 1, 1995, the delegates to NAFO met in Brussels. Ottawa's ace in the hole was Brian Tobin. Although technically barred from the meeting, Tobin waited outside for more than four hours while the delegates yelled and screamed at one another over who would get the biggest share of the reduced turbot quota.

Canada's aim was to garner enough support around the table to carry the day against the Europeans in a vote. When Korea looked like it was siding with the EU, Tobin's deputy minister, Bill Rowat, escorted the member back to Canada's delegate room for a chat with his minister. Tobin was blunt: Canada–Korea relations were on the line; if the Koreans couldn't vote with Canada, they had better abstain. Poland was offered "a little bit of silver hake" off British Columbia in return for supporting Canada's position on the East Coast, an offer that was all the more attractive since Tobin had cancelled their hake contract for supporting the Europeans on a previous NAFO matter. The Japanese could be counted on because they would do anything to protect their lucrative tuna contract in Canadian waters. "We were, in effect, buying their votes. But, hey, that's the real world of international negotiations," one Canadian negotiator said.

At the end of an abrasive three days, with Tobin pacing like a tiger in the back rooms and Bill Rowat watching like a hawk as the votes were tallied, the result was finally announced. Canada was awarded 60 per cent of the total quota, the EU just 12.6 per cent. The vote ratifying the allocation was six to five, with two abstentions. For the first time in NAFO's history, the delegates failed to reach a consensus on the annual fishing plan, but Canada had outsmarted the Europeans and won.

"My heart was pounding," Bill Rowat remembers. "The Spanish negotiator went nuts when we won. 'You're not going to kick us off the Nose and the Tail of the Banks,' he shouted. The Spanish deputy fisheries minister was sitting behind me, glaring. From the look on his face, he could have spit on me."

By any standard, it was a bitter defeat for the high seas foreign fleets. During the previous three years, the fifteen countries of the EU (now seventeen) had officially taken 50,000 tonnes of turbot and were now reduced to just 3,400 tonnes for 1995. By contrast, Canada had caught only 3,000 tonnes of turbot in 1994 but would now be getting about 60 per cent of the 1995 quota of 27,000 tonnes. Angered by their paltry quota, several EU members formally objected to NAFO's allocation and unilaterally set their own quota to match what Canada had been given.

The stage was set for confrontation.

In the months leading up to the arrest of the *Estai*, Brian Tobin was under intense pressure in Newfoundland to do something about the forty or so Spanish vessels that continued to trawl for the last commercially viable groundfish stock in international waters off the Grand Banks. There were threats and insults on all sides, but federal officials felt powerless to regulate the Spanish and Portuguese beyond the 200-mile zone. On the high seas, fish had always been a so-called common property resource, owned by no one and there for the taking by any vessel that could catch it.

FFAW president Earle McCurdy wanted Ottawa to bring in regulations that would permit Canadian fisheries officers to arrest Spanish and Portuguese vessels suspected of plundering the stock. Bud Hulan, then Newfoundland's fisheries minister, backed the union's demand. In a province where people who had lived off the sea for four hundred years were now forbidden to jig a cod for their table, no one could understand how the federal government could stand by and watch the foreigners catch the last fish.

A consummate populist, Brian Tobin sniffed the wind and decided it was time to show solidarity with his constituents. In mid-February 1995, he spoke at the tenth annual conference of the Inshore Fishermen's Improvement Committee in Clarenville,

Newfoundland. He told the raucous, foot-stomping crowd exactly what they wanted to hear: Ottawa could not, and would not, allow the EU to wipe out the turbot the way it had the cod and other groundfish stocks off Newfoundland.

"It was the EU use of the Northwest Atlantic Fisheries Organization objection procedure in the late 1980s that led to the moratoria on flatfish and cod on the Tail of the Grand Banks," Tobin thundered.

It was arguable history but excellent politics. For a minister who had inherited a fisheries portfolio with its major sector closed down for the foreseeable future, Tobin was wildly popular. As he once quipped to a reporter, "There's no fish, so I can afford to do the right thing." Newfoundlanders sensed a fight in the offing and they believed Brian Tobin was the "bucco" who would give the foreigners a black eye.

Tobin did his best to live up to his billing. A month after his Clarenville speech, he dispatched a patrol fleet and helicopters to inspect foreign vessels fishing outside Canada's 200-mile zone, threatening to board ships suspected of violating NAFO's turbot allocation. Canadian submarines were also at sea to help the DFO track foreign trawlers in the area. If matters came to a head, at least no one could say that they hadn't seen it coming.

During a stormy, two-hour meeting between officials from Canada and the EU on March 3, 1995, Ottawa officially requested a sixty-day moratorium on turbot fishing while the quota question was discussed. When EU officials played for more time, Canada unexpectedly put their feet to the fire. As he was leaving the meeting that Friday night, Gordon Smith's executive assistant at Foreign Affairs informed the EU officials from the doorway that the Governor General had just given royal assent to an amendment to the Coastal Fisheries Protection Act. It was now illegal for Spanish and Portuguese vessels to fish straddling stocks, including turbot, contrary to NAFO conservation rules. The EU officials were stunned and asked permission to remain in the room to discuss Canada's ultimatum. Everyone realized the potential for a violent confrontation. Tiny Iceland had almost come to war with British fishermen and warships in 1976 over the protection of fish stocks. A year later, the Argentine navy injured Soviet and Bulgarian fishermen when they fired on them during the arrest of nine trawlers inside their 200-mile zone. In the same year, a Burmese gunboat sank a Thai fishing boat and captured another. But would peace-loving Canada take things that far? The EU officials had forty-eight hours to agree to the joint moratorium or face the consequences. Their answer came five hours before the deadline: a unanimous no.

Emma Bonino laid down the law. She said that the Union wanted to avert a trade war with Canada, but if a European boat was seized, the EU would be forced to take "vigorous action." As expected, Newfoundlanders applauded Tobin's aggressive stand. Obliquely referring to the political in-fighting he faced in Ottawa, the minister joked with reporters about how he was handling the pressure of squaring off against the Europeans and some of his own colleagues: "I'll either hang in or be hanged."

Having given fair warning, the government wasted no time declaring its intentions. On March 6, Tobin announced that Canada would seize the "pirate ships" that were illegally fishing for turbot off the Grand Banks. Uncertain if he was bluffing, the EU made a conciliatory gesture. On Tuesday, March 7, the Spanish and Portuguese fleets ceased fishing, although poor weather on the Grand Banks may have had as much to do with the stoppage as diplomacy. Portugal's maritime affairs minister, Eduardo Azevedo Soares, again pleaded that the dispute be settled by diplomats, not destroyers. Two days later, the EU vessels boldly resumed fishing and Tobin seized the *Estai*. The Spanish fishermen were outraged. One captain offered to take "the maniac" Tobin out to sea to show him that there were more fish on the Grand Banks now than there had been five years before.

For days after the seizure of the *Estai*, the political temperature continued to rise. The EU pulled out of a scientific cooperation agreement with Canada that was about to be signed and threatened to boycott the June 1995 Group of Seven summit in Halifax.

The country calling for the harshest measures was the one most affected by what had happened. Spain demanded immediate sanctions against Canada for machine-gunning its vessel in international waters and confirmed that it had dispatched warships to join the fishing fleet off the Grand Banks. Javier Solana, Spain's foreign minister, suggested on nationwide radio that Canadians would soon need visas to visit his country. He also warned that Canada would shortly find itself defending its act of war at the World Court in The Hague.

André Ouellet's worst fear appeared to be coming to pass: an armed confrontation with an old ally that could lead to trade embargoes and even the loss of life. On March 10, 1995, the same day that a Spanish frigate, *Vegia*, steamed out of port headed for the Grand Banks, Canada summoned the EU's ambassadors to the Department of Foreign Affairs. There, Dr. José Luis Pardos formally handed Spain's official protest over the *Estai* affair to Canada's undersecretary of state for foreign affairs, Gordon Smith.

Spain's reaction to the *Estai* affair wasn't all righteous indignation and diplomacy. The Spanish informed the Department of National Defence that they would fire on any Canadian boarding party that tried to stop any of their vessels from fishing in international waters. Brian Tobin was at a dinner party in New York hosted by Canada's ambassador to the United Nations when he got the news. After discovering that the DND had replied to the Spanish threat with the scant phrase "message received," Tobin was outraged. He and his officials already knew that the DND backed André Ouellet and Foreign Affairs in the Turbot War. In fact, the DND had produced a handbook outlining what they were prepared to do if Canada and Spain came to blows. A copy was soon leaked to the DFO. "Basically what it came down to was this," one insider said. "You guys [DFO] do the rough stuff, and if things go wrong, we'll swab the decks of the blood."

Tobin cornered UN Ambassador Robert Fowler and told him to get back to his former friends in the DND and make clear that when a foreign nation threatens to fire on Canadians, the armed forces have to do better than merely acknowledge their bellicosity. Fowler complied.

While politicians on both sides pawed the ground and tried not to blink, a more scholarly assessment of the crisis was taking place behind the scenes. Manuel do Carmo Gomes of Lisbon University observed that the *Estai* affair was being distorted by patriotic half-truths on both sides. The author of a book about fish assemblages and food webs on the Grand Banks, Gomes's opinion carried weight in Europe and North America.

Gomes believed that the dispute was more about politics than principles. Newfoundlanders had been facing turmoil since the cod collapse in 1992, and the Canadian government badly wanted to show them that it was vigorously conserving all remaining stocks. In fact, Gomes argued, Canada deserved most of the blame for what had happened, not only to invaluable cod stocks, but also to American plaice and other species that had been almost fished out.

It had been Canadian scientists who had miscalculated fish stocks during the 1980s, which in turn had led to years of disastrously high quotas inside Canada's jurisdiction. When the facts finally emerged, Ottawa had waited three fateful years before taking action. To the Portuguese academic, it looked like Tobin was trying to blame the Europeans for a domestic disaster brought on by Canadian fisheries mismanagement.

Since Canada had had exclusive jurisdiction over 90 per cent of the disputed zone for eighteen years, Gomes's argument was not easily dismissed. Was the world really to believe that having wiped out several species inside its 200-mile zone, Canada was now the champion of conservation in the 10 per cent of the Grand Banks it didn't control?

"Instead of facing their responsibilities, the government of Canada spent too much effort blaming the foreign fleets fishing outside their 200-mile limit for the depletion of cod. But one only has to look at a map to see how much of the Grand Banks is within and outside the Canadian Economic Zone to realize those arguments are crap," Gomes fumed.

The author was no kinder to his own countrymen. He dismissed claims by Portugal and Spain that the turbot stock was in good shape and accused the two countries of spreading self-serving falsehoods when they insisted that they had always respected NAFO catch limits. In fact, the Spanish fleet had a reputation for ignoring quotas wherever its unwanted fleet showed up. When Namibia gained independence in 1990, one of the new government's first acts was to expel the Spanish fleet for fishing out the country's once-rich hake stocks. The Spanish factory-trawler fleet then headed for the Nose and Tail of the Grand Banks. (Interestingly, both Spain and Portugal were excluded from fishing in European waters for ten years as a condition of joining the EU in 1986.) By a conservative estimate, the Spanish were taking 50,000 tonnes of turbot a year just outside Canada's 200-mile limit.

Even Greenpeace Spain supported Canada's position, agreeing that European overfishing of the straddling turbot stocks on the Grand Banks could lead to an environmental disaster. The conservation organization asked Spain's fisheries minister to admit responsibility for stock depletion in the northwest Atlantic and urged him to respect NAFO catch limits. In making its request, Greenpeace pointedly reminded the government that Spain had routinely exceeded these limits for years.

Both Gomes and Greenpeace were closer to the truth than either party directly involved in the international standoff. The Turbot War, draped in nationalism and self-interest passed off as principle, was the old, sad story of the fishery. Governments rarely took regulatory action if it meant throwing fishermen out of work. When the fish disappeared, they merely shifted the blame elsewhere and sent the fleet after "alternate" species. Canada, Portugal, and Spain had all played key roles in wiping out the ocean's incredible, though not inexhaustible, bounty on the Grand Banks. Patriotic myths aside, everyone who made their living from the sea knew there were no clean hands in the fishery.

★

Instead of destroying Brian Tobin's career, the Turbot War sent it into the political stratosphere. After seizing the *Estai*, Tobin walked into the House of Commons to a standing ovation that even included the members of the separatist Bloc Québécois. The very first question on the Turbot War had been planted with Lucien Bouchard in a private meeting he held with Tobin before Question Period. The Bloc had not yet figured out that there was a carefully crafted national-unity element to the federal government's fish strategy *vis à vis* the Spanish. The Quebec referendum had been called for that autumn and the Liberals correctly reasoned that a strong show of Canadian sovereignty could only help the federalist cause. As the minister took his seat, fellow Liberals called out, "Academy Award." In a blatant appeal to emotion, Tobin told the nation that the *Estai* had been netting baby and juvenile fish in contravention of international law.

The facts were firmly on his side. Ninety-eight per cent of the *Estai*'s catch was under sixty centimetres, far too small to have spawned. Even more dramatic, 70 per cent could fit in the palm of the minister's hand. "That's a baby. That's a juvenile," he roared to the approval of Canadians unfamiliar with NAFO regulations.

Spain quickly pointed out that there was no NAFO-established minimum size for turbot. As the Spanish minister of agriculture, fisheries and food, Luis Atienza, told the *Financial Times*, "One can hardly be accused of breaking a non-existent rule."

Technically correct, Atienza's defence was doomed in a world where ecology had become a religion. As the details of what the Spanish had been doing on the Grand Banks began to unfold, support for Canada's "green Ramboism" soared. Fisheries officers who had searched the *Estai* found two sets of logbooks recording her catch, each reporting different numbers. Outside the Commons, Tobin said that one book appeared to have been prepared for NAFO inspectors and the world, the other for the captain's employer.

On March 16, the nets cut by the crew of the *Estai* in their effort to outrun Canadian authorities finally arrived in St. John's. *The Vandvoort*, a vessel from the fleet of Fishery Products International in Newfoundland, found the severed nets in 1,200 metres of water. RCMP forensics experts in Halifax matched the nets to cables removed from the *Estai*. Just as Brian Tobin had predicted, their mesh was smaller than NAFO regulations allowed. Instead of the regulation 130 millimetres, the mesh on the the *Estai*'s nets was a mere 114 millimetres. Compounding the infraction, the nets had an interior liner that was even tighter – a scant 80-millimetre mesh. With that combination, few fish in the *Estai*'s path could escape.

Within a few hours of the nets being brought ashore, the *Teleost*, a $30-million DFO marine research vessel, steamed to the Nose and Tail of the Grand Banks to assess the remaining turbot stocks. Tobin later announced that evidence from the *Estai*, coupled with Canadian research data, indicated that the stock was now too fragile to sustain a commercial fishery.

In the heady days after the arrest of the *Estai*, Brian Tobin told the press that Canada would take "whatever enforcement measures are necessary" to preserve fragile turbot stocks on the Grand Banks, including the arrest of more Spanish vessels. But when five Spanish ships resumed fishing for turbot just outside the disputed zone after the *Estai* was released, the minister didn't follow through on his tough talk. He explained his apparent reversal by saying that he couldn't ask unarmed fisheries inspectors to board foreign vessels on the high seas in a confrontational atmosphere where they might be taken hostage.

Behind the scenes, diplomats on both sides were quietly taking control. With the release of the *Estai* on March 15, Canada eased back into its more familiar role of international negotiator. The prime minister said that Canada had made its point by seizing the ship and now offered to consider "redistributing" her share of the turbot quota among EU members as Spain had demanded. But there was a price: in return, Canada would insist on much stricter enforcement of NAFO fishing regulations on the high seas.

The reasons for this strategic sidestep were legal and diplomatic. Although Tobin had used Canada's Coastal Fisheries Protection Act to justify the arrest of the *Estai* beyond Canada's 200-mile limit, international law had not yet solidified around the complex jurisdictional issues involved. The new Canadian legislation was based on provisions of the United Nations Convention on the Law of the Sea (UNCLOS) drafted in 1982, which dealt with the protection of straddling and migratory fish stocks. A draft agreement for implementation of the provisions was tabled in August 1994 at UN headquarters in New York, but the agreement was still unsigned at the time of the *Estai*'s arrest. Until it was officially adopted, Canada's case at the World Court remained seriously flawed.

Nevertheless, the Canadian government had reason to be optimistic about its case. UNCLOS had tentatively stated that distant-water fleets, such as Spain's, had to cooperate with coastal states to conserve and manage stocks that migrate in and out of territorial waters. Nations with long-distance fishing fleets, such as the EU countries, Japan, China, and Korea, opposed mandatory conservation measures. Countries such as Canada, Iceland, Norway, Argentina, Peru, New Zealand, and Indonesia, which had experienced the devastation caused by foreign fleets off their shores, wanted a binding treaty that would enforce international conservation rules. The Canadian position was greatly strengthened when the United States, Russia, and many island states in the Pacific supported mandatory conservation.

The Canadian position found allies because the *Estai* affair was being repeated all around the world. If something wasn't done, it was only a matter of time before countries would be going to war over fish. In September 1994, an Anglo–Spanish trawler was arrested by Britain's Royal Navy for a suspected breach of fishing regulations. In August of the same year, the French navy arrested a Spanish trawler for carrying undersized fish. Again in August, five Spanish vessels attacked four French trawlers, wounding one French fisherman in the ensuing fire fight.

As fate would have it, the fifth UN Conference on Straddling Fish Stocks and Highly Migratory Fish Stocks was scheduled for the end of March 1995 in New York. Canada had been making "back-channel" diplomatic progress, and Paul Lapointe, Canada's fisheries envoy to the UN, worried that the Turbot War might hurt or even scuttle negotiations for a UN treaty on straddling stocks. If a diplomatic agreement could be reached, it would provide a legal way out of the quarrel that Canada was currently trying to win by force. Given the diplomatic sensitivities involved, March was the wrong month to unleash boarding parties on other nations' vessels.

In the talks leading up to the conference, Canada made it clear that it hadn't abandoned the use of force on the high seas, only refined it. Two Canadian patrol vessels were being equipped with special "warp-cutters," designed to be towed behind a fisheries patrol vessel and to hook the heavy, steel cables that attach a fishing net to a trawler, then sever them at a depth that didn't endanger the lives of crew members on board either ship. While the talks continued, Canadian fisheries officers began manoeuvres on the Grand Banks to learn how to use this made-in-Newfoundland answer to incorrigible fish pirates. Madrid wasn't overly impressed. The Spanish believed that Canada "didn't have the balls" to cut fishing nets on the high seas, as secret intelligence sources duly reported to Ottawa.

On Sunday March 26, 1995, while diplomats from sixty countries were arriving in New York to attend the crucial UN conference, Canadian officers tried to board the Spanish ship *Verdel*, which had been fishing for turbot on the Nose of the Grand Banks. Instead of stopping, the *Verdel* hauled its nets and took off at high speed. To facilitate its escape the ship's captain also called on a Spanish warship, the *Vegia*, to confront the Canadians. The *Vegia* steamed to the area and cut across the bow of the *Cape Roger* at the dangerous distance of fifty feet. Undeterred, the Canadian ship and three other patrol vessels gave chase for forty-five minutes until heavy fog made pursuit too risky. Unlike the confrontation with the *Estai*, no shots were fired. The incident prompted other Spanish vessels to stop fishing, eliciting a colourful broadside from Brian Tobin: "Sunday for the Spanish fleet, given that they're no longer fishing, is a day of rest versus a day of arrest, and I'm sure they prefer the rest."

Chrétien again backed his minister's use of force. He had little choice. Tobin made a powerful presentation to cabinet, using intelligence reports that clearly showed that all twenty Spanish ships in the zone were continuing to misreport their catch and use illegal net liners. Tobin's deputy minister, Bill Rowat, had spent five years in the Privy Council Office and knew that every morning the keeper of secrets and information, euphemistically known as the legal counsel, held bilateral meetings with the clerk of the privy council, Jocelyn Bourgon. The intelligence reports that Ward Alcock had passed on during Rowat's time in the PCO were available to all ministers of government, though few used them. Rowat knew what to ask for, and Tobin put the reports to devastating effect in arguing the need to take action against the Spanish. The clerk, the most powerful public servant in the country, had only one word of advice for Rowat. "I hope you know what you're doing," she said.

There was another reason Chrétien supported his fisheries minister. When it became obvious that Spanish vessels had moved back into the disputed zone and were again violating NAFO regulations, Brian Tobin laid his job squarely on the line. Either the government supported his policy of conservation-by-force against unscrupulous fish pirates, or the prime minister could explain Tobin's resignation from cabinet.

In a hastily called early morning cabinet meeting attended by ten ministers and the chief of defence staff, a dispute arose about whether or not there was a quorum to approve Tobin's demand for action against the Spanish. The prime minister broke the logjam. "When I say there's a quorum, there's a quorum," he announced. A reluctant John de Chastelain, gold cane and all, was given the rules of engagement by cabinet. The chief of defence staff was to take "every necessary action" to prevent the Spanish from fishing on the Nose and Tail of the Grand Banks. To protect Canadian personnel and vessels, the prime minister instructed his defence minister, David Collenette, to inform the Spanish of the gravity of the situation: If Spanish frigates uncovered their guns, the Canadian navy would sink them. Chrétien made it clear that Canada was still prepared to cut nets and arrest trawlers if the Spanish persisted in violating NAFO quotas.

After the captain of the Spanish trawler *Pescamaro Uno* refused to allow DFO officials to conduct an onboard inspection, the DFO braintrust in the Kent Street bunker decided to cut the vessel's nets. Because hockey legend Don Cherry had praised the government for taking a firm hand with the Spanish, Bill Rowat called "Hockey Night in Canada" to let Cherry know that more "rock 'em, sock 'em" fisheries policy was on the way. While Tobin weighed the risks of more diplomatic roulette, one of his Newfoundland advisers, Max Short, used a phrase he would repeat throughout the Turbot War: "Jesus Christ, minister, it's just another inch off your cock." The *Sir Wilfred Grenfell* went to work with its warp-cutters, sending the *Pescamaro Uno*'s nets to the bottom. Cherry loved it, and the *Toronto Sun* headline had readers laughing: "Tobin Cuts Their Nets Off."

Spain failed to see the humour. In the port city of Vigo, 100,000 angry citizens demonstrated to defend the right of their distant-water fleet to harvest the Grand Banks as they saw fit. On March 27, 1995, Spain's minister of foreign affairs, Javier Solana, summoned the Canadian ambassador in Madrid to protest formally the continuing harassment of Spanish trawlers.

Behind the scenes, Gordon Smith was conducting feverish negotiations with the EU. Spain agreed that the total catches would have to be gradually diminished; what she could not accept was that the Spanish fleet would bear the brunt of the reduced turbot quota. "The issue is not how much is being fished, but who fishes," Solana declared, reminding everyone that the Grand Banks were discovered in part by Spanish navigators. "Therefore, we feel we are in our own right to fish there."

No one was surprised when Brian Tobin rose at the UN conference and insisted that his decision to stop Spanish overfishing beyond Canada's 200-mile zone was made solely to preserve the last commercially viable groundfish stock in the northwest Atlantic.

Just as predictable was Emma Bonino's rejoinder: The issue was not conservation, but Canada's violation of international law.

The Europeans stuck to the position that the most important issue on the table was not turbot, but the fact that Canada had resorted to piracy when it seized the *Estai* on the high seas. It was a solid argument. Unless ships are believed to be involved in slavery, terrorism, or drug trafficking, international law expressly forbids the search and seizure of vessels in international waters. The Europeans suspected that the real purpose behind the unprecedented Canadian law was not conservation, but a unilateral fish-grab. By refusing to refer the dispute to the World Court, Canada was, in effect, acknowledging that its legal case was fatally flawed – or so the Europeans believed.

By the time Canada and Spain collided at the UN, everyone mistakenly believed that the Turbot War had entered a public relations phase. Bonino and Tobin spoke back-to-back before the General Assembly. "Where is the net?" Bonino asked. "No one has seen the net." Canada's fisheries minister had a surprise in store for her. After his speech, Tobin walked out of the UN building to a throng of waiting reporters. "You want to see the net?" he said. "Follow me." Using a tactic that had worked well for environmental groups such as Greenpeace, Tobin led the press to a barge on New York's East River, across from the United Nations buildings. Wearing life jackets, he and Newfoundland premier Clyde Wells took the journalists by boat across the river to show them the *Estai*'s 3,150-kilogram net, complete with its undersized liner designed to catch "baby" turbot. It had taken three days to truck the enormous net to New York, where it was hoisted by a crane for all the world to see. Reporters were shocked at the size of the seventeen-storey net that Tobin called "an ecological monstrosity." Tobin also provided the media with photographs of the tiny fish found in the hold of the *Estai*. Some were no longer than a cigarette. "We're down now finally to one last, lonely, unloved, unattractive little turbot clinging on by its fingernails to the Grand Banks of Newfoundland," Tobin lamented.

Despite his ludicrous metaphor, Tobin's message was gobbled up by the world media. His colourful hyperbole and gleeful denunciation of his opponents only enhanced his reputation as a master communicator.

While Tobin and Bonino duked it out in public, talks between Canadian and EU officials soldiered on in private. In a move designed to increase the pressure on Tobin and the prime minister, Madrid followed through on its earlier threat to file a case against Canada at the World Court in The Hague. Scrappy to the end, Tobin reminded the world that the turbot would be long gone by the time the court decided which nation had the law on its side. His knack of getting the big shapes right made him an easy winner in the war for the hearts and minds of ordinary people.

Cracks began to appear in the ranks of the European Union. Britain announced that it would not back EU sanctions against Canada, and even vetoed a joint communiqué protesting Canadian actions. Old alliances began to reassert themselves. Canadian flags went up in coastal communities in Britain in support of the seizure of the *Estai* and Canada's hard line against the Spanish.

British fishermen complained that there wasn't enough Brian Tobin in their own fisheries minister, the conciliatory Michael Jack. Angry British fishermen in Plymouth had set off orange smoke flares and pelted Jack with flour because they believed he had been overly generous in allowing Spain access to European fishing grounds. Nor had the fishermen forgotten that in February 1995, Spanish fishermen in the Bay of Biscay had surrounded British trawlers and cut their nets. The Conservative government in Britain was under heavy public pressure to support Canada more vigorously against the hated Spanish.

With the issue of migratory stocks unresolved at the UN, the diplomatic venue shifted back to the talks between Canada and the EU. By the end of March, a negotiated end to the Turbot War was within reach. In return for an offer of an increased share of the turbot quota, Spain and Portugal were seriously considering new conservation measures in the northwest Atlantic, including the possibility of allowing a neutral observer on every fishing vessel to control overfishing.

But Emma Bonino wasn't prepared to leave the ring without landing a few heavy blows herself. In an attempt to knock Brian Tobin off his moral pedestal, she issued a nine-page statement condemning Canada's own destructive fishing practices. She reminded the world that despite the cod moratorium, Canada had allowed so-called recreational fishermen to catch an estimated 20,000 tonnes of cod. Bonino also pointed out that Canada had engaged in the same destructive fishing practices it had condemned in the Spanish and Portuguese – high-grading, discarding, and dumping of immature and non-targeted fish at sea. She drew particular attention to the fact that the collapse of Newfoundland's invaluable cod stock took place long after Canada extended its jurisdiction in 1977.

The point was as embarrassing as it was obvious.

While the diplomats haggled, the consequences of the Turbot War were being felt well beyond the fishery. As of April 1, 1995, all Canadian citizens visiting Spain were required to carry visas. A Canadian family living in England became the first private citizens to feel the bite of the new policy. When they showed up at the Birmingham International Airport to take their holiday flight to the Canary Islands, they were not allowed to board the aircraft without visas. When they asked for an $1,800 refund on their cancelled trip, the travel company refused.

The public mood in Spain was turning ugly. On April 6, three thousand Spanish fishermen pelted the Canadian embassy in Madrid with dead fish and eggs. The outburst followed reports that Canadian patrol vessels had confronted two Spanish trawlers that had resumed fishing in the disputed area of the Grand Banks. Police in riot gear formed a cordon in front of the embassy, and Canadian officials hastily hauled in the Canadian flag to prevent demonstrators from burning it. The protesters, who looked remarkably like their boisterous counterparts in Newfoundland, shouted, "*Piratas!*" *Pirates!* at Canadian diplomats watching uneasily from the embassy's windows.

The head of the Vigo Ship Owners Co-operative said that unless Spain got a turbot quota of 18,600 tonnes a year, fifteen hundred fishermen and eight thousand related workers would lose their jobs. The protesters had spent the night travelling from Vigo to the Spanish capital to protest the turbot quotas that Canada was demanding. One of them was Captain González, who had become a national hero in the wake of the *Estai* affair. While the demonstrators jeered and sang, González accused the Spanish government of failing to defend the rights of its own fishermen. He said that Canada's real motive was to become "a pirate of the twenty-first century" by seizing control of the entire continental shelf off its eastern shores.

With their citizens in a nationalistic frenzy, it was difficult for the negotiating team of either country to retreat from its original position. Polls in Spain showed that 92 per cent of the population believed that Canada was the villain of the Turbot War, the same as the percentage of Canadians who believed that Spain was the fish pirate and that Brian Tobin had done the right thing.

Events at sea continued to threaten the sensitive negotiations. The captain of the trawler *Ana Maria Gandon* told fellow Spaniards via ship-to-shore radio that two Canadian patrol boats had tried to board his vessel in heavy rain on April 5. When that failed, they tried four times to cut his nets, again without success.

There was also a complaint from a Spanish captain that a Canadian patrol vessel had broken from the fog at full speed, passing within a few feet of the Spanish trawler. The incident touched off an angry exchange between the captain of the trawler and the captain of the Spanish frigate that was supposed to be protecting the fishing fleet. When the warship's captain radioed that he was on his way, the skipper of the trawler, still shaking from the near miss with the Canadian patrol vessel, replied, "Yes, and when you get here, I'll be in my cabin changing my shorts."

In Ottawa, Brian Tobin claimed that Canadian authorities were merely trying to identify the Spanish trawlers. "We caught them with their nets down and they panicked. And they pulled them in in a big hurry and scurried out of the zone," he said. He suggested that it was time for Spanish captains to calm down. "We've considered shipping Prozac out by helicopter," he joked.

But the near ramming had actually taken place. It was, as one insider describes it, "one of those scenarios of psychological warfare played out during the turbot crisis that we could never officially acknowledge."

There was one other necessary deception the Tobin gang perpetrated. When reporters were allowed into DFO headquarters during the standoff between Canada and Spain, they were encouraged to turn their cameras on the monitors that showed the position of Canadian vessels on the Grand Banks. Knowing that the Spanish would be watching the media's broadcasts, the DFO played fast and loose with the numbers and positions of Canadian ships to keep the European fish pirates looking over their shoulder.

Although tempers had flared over these latest incidents, both sides remained at the negotiating table. Meanwhile, it was full steam ahead for the public relations campaign. Royce Frith, Canada's High Commissioner to Britain, visited Cornwall to take more Canadian flags to the fishermen who had been flying the Maple Leaf in support of their Canadian counterparts. Frith's office had received over fifteen hundred calls, letters, and faxes supporting what Brian Tobin and the Canadian government were doing.

The only setback for Canada in the media war with the Europeans came when British television reported that Newfoundlanders were killing seals for their penises. Seal penises are a prized aphrodisiac in China, as well as an ingredient in traditional medicines. Remembering how the International Fund for Animal Welfare had closed down the annual Newfoundland seal hunt with a relentless, worldwide media campaign, Tobin wasted no time in responding to the potentially damaging story. He told the press that the DFO frowned on the killing of seals for their sex organs and vowed to punish anyone who tried to profit from such a destructive and inhumane practice.

Tobin's stock continued to soar. When the PMO conducted private polling, it found that it had a new superstar in its feisty fisheries minister. Even in Quebec, Tobin was a hit with more than 80 per cent of the population, a love affair that continued long after he left federal politics to become premier of Newfoundland.

For a month after the capture of the *Estai*, Premier Clyde Wells had been urging Newfoundlanders to be patient during the difficult negotiations between Canada and the EU. But by April 12, he too was publicly accusing the Spaniards of dragging out the talks so that their fifteen trawlers could continue pillaging turbot stocks on the Grand Banks.

Wells knew that the Spanish were catching an estimated 250 tonnes of turbot each week and had long since surpassed the 1995 quota of 3,400 tonnes set for the EU by NAFO.

The normally tight-lipped politician told the *Globe and Mail*, "We simply can't just stand by and watch the Spanish thumb their noses at the entire world. . . . They keep on being arrested in other parts of the world for their bad fishing practices. The whole world should know how irresponsible the Spanish fishing practices are, and if the European community cannot restrain them, Canada is going to have to move to do so."

The stumbling block to a settlement was the same one that had left NAFO divided and impotent in the first place: Everyone agreed that conservation was necessary, but the Spanish and the Portuguese would not accept how the reduced quota was divided. Since they were the only EU members fishing for turbot off Canada's shores, the negotiation came down to the need to accommodate Spain. (Although Portugal caught significant amounts of turbot, its catch was sold to the Spanish.)

Spain demanded that EU vessels get half of the 27,000-tonne quota set by NAFO. In the give and take of the negotiations, Spain dropped its demand to 12,000 tonnes, triggering a counter-proposal from Gordon Smith that the EU and Canada get 10,000 tonnes apiece. While the diplomats sparred, the scene on the Grand Banks was ominous: Seventeen EU trawlers fished in the disputed area under the protection of two Spanish frigates, which were in turn watched by six patrol ships from the DFO and the Coast Guard, backed up by warships and submarines from the Canadian navy.

Under tremendous pressure in Newfoundland to stop foreign overfishing on the Grand Banks, Tobin accused the Spanish of trying to sabotage the talks. He finally persuaded his Liberal colleagues that the only way of breaking the impasse was another show of force. On April 16, Easter Sunday, fisheries officers got the order to board and seize other Spanish vessels fishing in the disputed zone.

Although it was never reported, Canada came within twenty minutes of a shooting war with Spain. The Canadian military had picked up a conversation from the Spanish in which the possibility of refuelling their fighter jets over the Atlantic was openly discussed. That way, Spanish fighters could be used in what Madrid was referring to as its "Falklands." What the Spanish did not know was that Canadian destroyers were under orders to sink any Spanish warship as soon as it uncovered its guns.

The best peacemaker turned out to be the weather. With a fierce gale battering the northwest Atlantic, the captain of one of the Spanish frigates moved several hundred miles away from the disputed zone to ride out the storm. It was a prudent move, as the ship he was commanding was too small for the weather conditions. The Canadian navy and the Coast Guard had been concerned that the Spanish vessel would sink and had been poised to rescue her as the ultimate public relations coup of the Turbot War.

With a poor strategic position and one of its warships far from the theatre of operations, the EU accepted a deal just moments before the first Canadian boarding parties headed for the Spanish fleet. When Tobin and his advisers received word of the deal in the

DFO's Kent Street headquarters, the tension of just a few moments earlier turned to giddy relief.

It was port and cigars all around.

From Canada's point of view, the centrepiece of the agreement was a new commitment to conservation in the disputed areas of the Grand Banks. Spain agreed to independent onboard inspectors on all fishing vessels, increased satellite surveillance of ships at sea, and greater rights for Canadian inspection of EU vessels both on the high seas and in port. But it would be the EU that decided when Canadian inspectors would be allowed to board a ship suspected of breaking the rules. And if the ship had indeed violated NAFO regulations, it would still be up to its home country to mete out the punishment.

The Spanish negotiating team spun the deal as a success for Madrid. Canada gave up 6,000 tonnes of its turbot quota, raising the EU's quota from 12.6 to 40 per cent, or 10,000 tonnes in 1995. The Spanish also wanted Canada to repeal the March 1995 amendment to the Coastal Fisheries Protection Act that had been used to extend its fisheries regulations over the straddling stocks on the Grand Banks. Officials at Foreign Affairs were prepared to bend on this point, but Brian Tobin was not. Instead, Spain was merely dropped from the list of countries covered by the legislation. It was a token concession, since there was nothing to prevent Ottawa from putting Spain back on the list if she ever again overfished.

Canada also agreed to return the 130 tonnes of turbot on board the *Estai* to the Vigo Ship Owners Co-operative, a cargo worth $350,000. All charges of illegal fishing against the *Estai*'s owners were dropped, and Canada paid back the bond and bail money posted by the Spanish for the release of the trawler and her captain.

When the final details were agreed to a month later after a three-day, secret session, a patter of applause could be heard coming from the negotiating room. NAFO had agreed to adopt the rules negotiated between Canada and the EU. The Turbot War was officially over.

In Europe, Greenpeace and British fishermen hailed the deal as a victory for ecology and a black eye for destructive Spanish fishing practices. The British industry hoped that Canada's success with the EU would inspire Britain to help its own troubled fishery. The Canadian situation had highlighted problems that Spain was causing all over the world. On April 14, the day before the EU struck its deal with Canada, the Spanish trawler *Chimbote* had been arrested near the Scilly Isles off southwestern England on suspicion of illegal fishing. As the vessel was escorted into Plymouth, local fishing boats flying Canadian flags joined the flotilla.

Other countries took heart from Canada's victory over Spain. During negotiations for a new fishing agreement with the EU, Morocco demanded drastic cuts in Spanish quotas off its coastal waters. With everyone trying to play the "Canadian card," tempers flared in Galicia region among fishermen who were tired of being portrayed as the villains of the world fishery. On May 19, near Algeciras in Spain, fifty of them hijacked a Dutch truck travelling from Morocco to the Netherlands, forcibly dumping half of its ten-tonne cargo of prawns.

The Spanish fishermen felt betrayed and humiliated by the EU and their own government. As industry spokesman Reinaldo Iglesias put it, "Jesus Christ was sold for thirty coins . . . but in this case, you could say we were sold out for a plate of fish." Iglesias predicted that 80 per cent of the eight thousand jobs in the Galician deep-sea fishing industry would be lost. Within two years, he sourly predicted, the Spanish distant-water fleet would set sail into history. At word of the accord, morale on the Spanish vessels still fishing off the Canadian coast hit rock bottom. The Spanish frigate captain who had left the disputed zone to ride out the storm was relieved of his command when his vessel docked in Cadiz. Spanish honour had taken a hard blow and someone had to pay for it.

In Newfoundland and Labrador, a province that had been asked to put its hope for the future in conservation, no one was happy about giving part of the Canadian quota to Spain. Still, FFAW president Earle McCurdy expressed general support for the agreement. "It gives us some hope that the kinds of bitter medicine we're choking down may bring about a cure because there's some control finally in this area."

Brian Tobin was at dockside in St. John's to greet the DFO and Canadian Coast Guard vessels as they returned from their mission of policing the Spanish fleet. He personally thanked each of the 160 crew members for a job well done under stressful conditions. The merger of the Canadian Coast Guard with Fisheries and Oceans had just come into effect under Tobin's stewardship, and their collaboration during the fisheries dispute had been a ringing success. Leo Strowbridge, a strapping fisheries officer who epitomized the strong, silent type, was singled out for special thanks.

"If you want to know why the Spanish were frightened half to death, I sent them a picture of Leo with a scowl on his face!" an emotional Tobin said to one of the forty-two men who had stood ready to do their duty for the past six weeks.

As Newfoundland's favourite son and his family strolled along the quay visiting the ships, the crowd applauded, shook his hand, and asked for autographs. One observer commented that Tobin was acting as though it was "the greatest victory since VE day fifty years before." In a way, it was.

Back in Ottawa, senior DFO mandarins watched as a new star was born in the "natural ruling party." Wheels within wheels began turning, to showcase the young man who was suddenly being touted as a possible successor to the prime minister. Unreported in all the glory of Brian Tobin's international political success was that a number of senior staffers in the DFO had put their careers on the line to back their minister. In fact, the Turbot War came down to this: In the name of doing what they passionately believed was the right thing, an entire department of the federal government had conducted a successful rebellion against the gentlemen's club of official Ottawa. It was a high crime against protocol for which their opposite numbers in Foreign Affairs would not forgive them.

On May 7, 1995, the weather improved enough off the Newfoundland coast for the transfer of Canadian fisheries observers to the twenty-four Spanish and Portuguese vessels still fishing for turbot on the Nose and Tail of the Grand Banks, four hundred kilometres out to sea. The new regulations were being put to the test.

On April 28, the *Mayi Cuatro* had severed its own net after being boarded by DFO officers. Although it was not made public at the time, the DFO chartered a Canadian fishing vessel, the *Atlantic Dorothy*, which found the *Mayi Cuatro*'s net two days later. The net, which had smaller mesh than regulations allowed, was quietly sent to Spain as evidence of a serious breach of NAFO conservation measures.

The EU ordered the *Mayi Cuatro* to return to Spain with its hold closed so that it could be inspected by European officials. One of them later said that the ship's action was "totally irresponsible" and had jeopardized the operations of the entire fleet. A few days later, the Spanish government suspended the licence of the *Mayi Cuatro* after it determined that her net had a liner with a 76-millimetre mesh, nearly half as small as NAFO regulations allowed.

Old habits died hard. A month after the *Mayi Cuatro* incident, a boarding party from the Canadian destroyer *Nipigon* found eleven tonnes of turbot that were not recorded in the log of the Spanish trawler *Patricia Nores*. The vessel had been fishing just outside Canada's 200-mile zone. The contraband catch was stowed in a secret compartment concealed by boxes piled in front of its hatchway. The boarding party found the hold only because a sharp-eyed officer noticed that the refrigeration unit for the area was turned on. The fisheries observer who was already onboard the Spanish trawler had missed the concealed hold.

Inspectors from the EU were called in to confirm the discovery and the Spanish government officially agreed with the findings. A month later, the European fishing commissioner announced that the *Patricia Nores* would face a charge in a Spanish court of illegal fishing. A fish pirate had been caught and punished, but more important, the Europeans had accepted Canada's evidence.

By the end of July 1995, the threat of huge fines and the presence of neutral observers on foreign vessels accomplished what years of diplomacy never had. Catches fell by half. The trawlers couldn't make enough money to justify the long and expensive trip to the Grand Banks and many left for other fishing grounds. There were now only thirteen EU vessels fishing in international waters off Newfoundland. The number of Spanish trawlers alone dropped from twenty to just six.

It was a dramatic turnaround from the height of the Turbot War, when there were forty-seven ships, mostly from Spain and Portugal, on the Grand Banks. At the same point in the summer of 1993, there had been a stunning sixty-two trawlers vacuuming these once rich waters. Brian Tobin was the lion of the season for pulling off what no fisheries minister before him had dared to attempt and what former fisheries minister John Crosbie had mocked him for even suggesting.

But there was one belated voice raised in opposition to Tobin's handling of the Turbot War. Speaking to the European parliament at Strasbourg, Parti Québécois international affairs minister Bernard Landry denounced Canada's handling of the incident as "a deplorable diplomatic failure." The PQ had finally figured out how critically important Ottawa's spirited defence of Canada's fisheries jurisdiction was to the pending national-unity battle. With the Québec referendum only months away, the separatists did an about-face at Strasbourg.

"We were very disappointed to see our country reduced to opening fire on fishing vessels of friendly countries," Landry said in a speech that was delivered partly in Spanish. He assured the dozen major European politicians in the audience that a sovereign

Québec would handle things differently. "I pledge to you that a sovereign Québec will be a partisan of the most peaceful and legal resolution of fishing conflicts."

It was a far cry from the standing ovation that the Bloc Québécois had given Brian Tobin in the House of Commons, but that didn't stop Jacques Parizeau from insisting that the separatists had not flip-flopped on the issue; in politics as in war, truth is the first casualty.

Canada's fisheries minister was still sufficiently worked up about the Turbot War that he made plans to exhibit the *Estai*'s nets at the Central Canadian Exhibition in Ottawa in mid-August for its 600,000 visitors to see. The huge net was strung across the rafters at the Aberdeen Pavilion to accompany a DFO exhibit detailing the capture of the *Estai* and the need for fisheries conservation.

Spain called Tobin's plan "an act of serious offence" to a friend and ally of Canada. The Spanish ambassador accused the Canadian government of trying to manipulate Canadian public opinion "to the detriment of Spanish fishermen and relations between the Canadian and Spanish peoples." The diplomat said that he was "astonished and outraged" by Canada's decision to make a circus exhibit out of the *Estai*'s nets.

Spanish pride was spared further insult. The night before the Exhibition opened, the federal government ordered workers to remove the *Estai*'s nets from the rafters. Ottawa paid the Exhibition $50,000 for leaving so glaring a hole in one of their key pavilions.

It was not the diplomats, though, but the fishermen who had the last word. "In five hundred years we haven't fished all the resources," an old Spanish captain remarked. "But Canada, in the last fifteen years, says there is no more cod, no plaice, there's no turbot, there's no nothing. For us, that's really difficult to believe."

Considering the once legendary abundance of the Grand Banks, who would have believed it possible to empty the sea?

2

THE CROWDED SEA

The myth of inexhaustible bounty was born early. On June 24, 1497, a Venetian adventurer acting for Henry VII stepped ashore in the New World and raised banners for the King of England and the Pope. A little over a month later "the great admiral," John Cabot, was fêted in the streets of Bristol for his remarkable discovery. Among the giddy tales of Cabot's voyage, one stood out. It was reported to the Duke of Milan that "the sea there is swarming with fish, which can be taken not only with the net, but in baskets let down with a stone."

In 1501 the Company of Adventurers to the New Found Lands was chartered to exploit the newly discovered fishing grounds. Although they felt like trailblazers, they were actually following in the distant wake of others. Five hundred years earlier, the Norse had established a settlement at L'Anse aux Meadows (now a world heritage site), on Newfoundland's Great Northern Peninsula. But it was Cabot's discovery that opened the island to European development.

One of the first to follow Cabot was Gaspar Corte-Real of Portugal, whose statue stands on a promontory in front of Confederation Building in St. John's, gazing towards the harbour's famous

Narrows. In 1500, Corte-Real landed there and christened the island Terra del Rey de Portugal. With the rise of mercantilism in the sixteenth century, there was sufficient investment money available to exploit distant markets to supply Europe's rapidly growing cities. The discovery of vast new fish stocks off the shores of Newfoundland fuelled a spectacular growth in the European economy. While Cortés and Pizarro were making Spain Europe's wealthiest nation with spoils from Mexico and Peru, Captain John Smith, who pioneered the English fishing settlements in Maine, wisely predicted that fish would become a greater source of treasure than all the gold and silver looted by the Conquistadors.

By 1520, Newfoundland's coasts were being fished by the French, English, Portuguese, and Spanish Basques, although it was primarily the French and Portuguese who developed the early fishery. England was slower to exploit Newfoundland waters because it had established fishing interests in Iceland, which had the advantage of being closer to British ports. It was not until 1580, when the Danes levied licence fees on foreign vessels fishing off Iceland, that England switched its overseas fishing effort to the Grand Banks.

In the early days, fish was harvested exclusively from inshore waters. It was then split, dried, and salted directly on the island's pebble beaches or on wooden platforms known as flakes. Unlike heavy, cumbersome barrels of pickled beef and pork, salt cod was easily transported and could be kept almost indefinitely, important advantages on long voyages to market. Salt cod was a popular and relatively cheap source of protein, especially in Roman Catholic countries, where the consumption of meat was forbidden for 166 days of the year. As the northern European herring stocks began to disappear in the mid-sixteenth century, the markets in southern Europe increasingly turned to cod for protein, driving up demand and prices for the mainstay of the Newfoundland fishery.

Over time, two distinct types of fishery developed; the Banks or deep-sea fishery, and the coastal or inshore fishery. One of the key differences between them was the length of the fishing season: the

Banks fishery could be prosecuted for most of the year, while the coastal effort was possible only in the summer months when the cod migrated inshore and the weather permitted the use of small boats to harvest them.

Each participant in the new fishery took a distinctive approach to processing its catch. By 1550, the French had developed the "wet" fishery, catching cod a hundred miles or more offshore, where it was salted and barrelled at sea. This method of curing the catch commanded a higher price in the markets of Paris than hard-dried cod, although the Bretons and French Basques continued to produce "dry" salt cod for both the domestic and foreign market. Lacking the salt reserves of the French, Spanish, and Portuguese, British fishermen developed their own method of preserving the catch, the so-called "English Cure," using a minimum of the precious mineral.

From the very beginning of the Newfoundland shore-based industry, quality was a problem. The lightly salted, hard-dried product that was prized around the tables of Europe required considerable processing skills, and some fishermen rushed the curing of their catch. The main problem was the water content. To dry the fish properly, the air temperature had to be between 16 to 27 degrees Celsius and the relative humidity below 76 per cent. A light wind was another necessary part of the drying process. If the correct procedure wasn't followed and the water content remained too high, the fish would begin to deteriorate on the long voyage to market. Sometimes producers tried to pass off fish that had been semi-cured to save work in what was a labour-intensive process. Since there were no uniform standards among buyers, the quality of salt cod fluctuated from season to season, sometimes the best in the world, sometimes so poor it had to be dumped.

In contrast, Norwegian merchants sent collection vessels to gather fresh cod from the fishermen who caught it off the coast of Iceland. The captains of these collection vessels then personally supervised the curing process and rigidly maintained high standards. As early as 1829, the British Foreign Office was made aware that in the important market of Madrid, Norwegian cod was considered a better quality product than Newfoundland salt fish.

Slow to adjust to the demands of a more discriminating market, Newfoundland saw its salt cod trade with Spain, Portugal, and Italy gradually supplanted by the superior product from Norway and France. Having lost its pre-eminent position in the markets of Barcelona, Oporto, and Genoa, Newfoundland turned to Brazil, with its large Roman Catholic population and preferential trading agreement with Britain, to make up the lost business. By the outbreak of the First World War, Brazil was Newfoundland's biggest customer, buying 30 per cent of Newfoundland's salt cod production.

For almost a hundred years after the discovery of the Grand Banks fishery, cod was treated as a common property or international resource. In practice, though, England and France dominated it by the end of the sixteenth century, each sending about one hundred and fifty ships every spring for the annual fishing season. On August 5, 1583, Sir Humphrey Gilbert sailed into St. John's Harbour and took formal possession of the island on behalf of his monarch, Elizabeth I. On the return voyage to England, Gilbert died when his ship went down in a fierce storm during a fateful journey he had spent reading Sir Thomas More's startling new book, *Utopia*.

The adventurers passed into history; the fishing effort endured. Each year, fleets from the West Country in England carried lightly salted shore-cured cod back to London, where it was shipped to Spain and exchanged for manufactured goods and Spanish currency, which were in turn taken back to England. The ships were then reprovisioned for the long and expensive trip to the distant fishing grounds and the lucrative cycle of mercantilism began again.

Newfoundland cod made huge fortunes for English fish merchants and paid for their spectacular mansions in Devon and Dorset. It was not angels or lions that were carved into their massive stone fireplaces, but the creature that made such ostentatious wealth possible, the magnificent cod. By the beginning of the seventeenth century, one of England's principal sources of wealth was fish from the northwest Atlantic, just as Captain Smith had predicted.

The resource was still abundant. A discourse on Newfoundland published in London told of the cod being so thick by the shore "that we heardlie have been able to row a boate through them." The English fished from Cape Bonavista to Cape Race. Over the long hours of the historical clock, a few permanent communities sprang up on the rugged island.

War was the inspiration for settlement. During extended hostilities with Spain between 1656 and 1659, the English lost a thousand fishing vessels. To avoid capture by the Spanish fleet, fishermen began to stay on the island year-round. The first official settlement in Newfoundland was near Cupids on Conception Bay in 1610. Sir John Guy established the short-lived colony ten years before the Pilgrims arrived in Plymouth. Guy arrived from Bristol with thirty-nine hopeful colonists, who built houses and cleared land only to discover that the soil was too poor to support farming. Four of them didn't survive their first Newfoundland winter.

The English fishing merchants were just as happy that the colony failed. They saw land grants and tenants as a threat to the aggressive exploitation of the fishery and used their political influence in England to discourage permanent settlement in Newfoundland. Their goal was to make sure that nothing interfered with their unfettered use of the shoreline. In 1671, cutting wood or building near the shore was strictly prohibited. Legal authority rested with the "captains of the harbour" or the first master who arrived from England in the spring to begin fishing. By the end of the seventeenth century, scattered settlement was allowed, but just enough to uphold England's claim to the island. Any meaningful form of civil government was actively discouraged.

During the European wars of the late seventeenth century, Newfoundland was both a prize and a pawn. The Dutch attacked St. John's in 1665, but they were so moved by the poverty of the people that they didn't burn the settlement as was the custom of the day. Pierre Le Moyne d'Iberville, a soldier-adventurer born in New France, was considerably less compassionate. He captured the town in 1696 and terrorized coastal settlements up and down the Avalon Peninsula. Before he was through, d'Iberville had murdered two hundred people and put thirty-six settlements to the torch. The attacks continued until France lost her protracted war with England.

The 1713 Treaty of Utrecht halted the French fishery along the south coast of Newfoundland. In return for removing her settlers, France negotiated fishing rights from the western end of the Strait of Belle Isle southward to Cape Bonavista, a stretch of coast known as the French Shore. Under the Treaty of Paris that ended the Seven Years War in 1763, France gained the islands of St. Pierre and Miquelon off the south coast, but surrendered her claim to the vast, unsettled territory of Labrador to the English.

By 1750, Newfoundland had 8,225 residents: fourteen years later, the number had doubled. Preoccupied with the American Revolution, the British migratory fishery in Newfoundland declined, its fishermen too worried about falling into the hands of press gangs or pirates to make the long voyage to and from the fishing grounds. As a result, the colony got its first, heady taste of independence. A new merchant class sprang up that built "plantations" with stages and warehouses of their own to exploit the fishery locally. At the end of the seventeenth century, most residents still returned to England for the winter, but now they left behind caretakers to make repairs and ready the "fishing rooms" for the spring season. These caretakers, joined by the occasional deserter from a ship or failed colonist, became the first permanent Newfoundlanders. They were eventually joined by the merchants themselves, who remained on the island to protect their growing investments and to build St. John's first elegant houses from the profits of cod. The number of migrant fishermen still grew in the postwar periods, depressing profits for Newfoundland's resident fishermen and entrepreneurs. But an irreversible trend had begun and the resident fishermen eventually forced the migratory fishermen out of business. By 1795, Newfoundland fishermen outnumbered their migratory counterparts from the West Country by five to one.

The Napoleonic Wars that dragged on for nearly twenty years destroyed the last vestiges of the migratory fishery. By 1815, Newfoundland was no longer what William Knox described as "a great ship moored near the Banks during the fishing season for the convenience of English fishermen," but a thriving colony with over forty thousand residents. Local entrepreneurs threw off their British overlords and became buyers and exporters of their own salt fish. With economic independence came the demand for political freedom. Newfoundlanders agitated for a government that would promote local interests over those of the British merchants of the West Country who had made their fortunes here. Political maturity was a slow but sure process. In 1817, the colony got its first year-round governor, in 1824, a constitution, and finally in 1832, representative government. By 1815, many of the residents of the island were native-born, and the place throbbed with a new nationalism. Inspired by growing freedom and confidence, the belief took hold that strangers had been sucking the vitals of the country dry for too long and it was time for Newfoundlanders to steer their own ship.

In the early nineteenth century, twenty thousand Irish immigrants came to Newfoundland to escape poverty and famine. They signed a bond with a sailing master, which committed them to pay for their passage with future earnings in the colony. In practice, it was the colonial employer who repaid the captain, and then transferred the debt to the servant's account. Since servants had to buy everything from their employers at inflated prices, this arrangement was a form of vassalage. No matter how hard the servants worked, their debt grew. The open hostility that still lingers between the merchant and the labouring classes in Newfoundland has its origin in this early abuse.

After the Napoleonic Wars, most commercial activity was centred in St. John's, although outports like Harbour Grace and

Brigus remained important because of the annual seal hunt and the Labrador fishery. The outports produced world-renowned skippers such as Bob Bartlett, who captained the *Roosevelt* on Admiral Robert Peary's expeditions to the Arctic in 1905 and 1908.

Most outports survived on a combination of the inshore cod fishery and subsistence agriculture. The entire family worked to support the household, growing vegetables, making hay, and gathering berries and wood. The men caught the fish, but it was the women and children who handled the backbreaking task of curing it. The local merchant extended credit to fishermen so that they could buy supplies for the summer fishery. The fisherman eventually paid his bill in salt cod at the end of the season. Poverty or prosperity depended on the catch, and there were many seasons when debt to the merchant went unpaid and a family's winter provisions were reduced to the bare necessities.

The market for salt fish was strong, mostly because it was cheaper than meat in southern Europe, Brazil, and the Caribbean. In Italy in 1889, for example, beef was forty to fifty cents a pound, salt fish only twelve cents. An agent would arrange for the sale of the fish when it arrived at market, and set up payment through a London bank. Newfoundland vessels would return with cargoes of Barbadian rum or salt from Spain, occasionally stopping in England to offload cotton for the booming British textile industry.

The very abundance of the Newfoundland fishery often produced gluts of cod that drove down the price of the finished product. There were different grades of fish depending on the cure, the weather, and the individual producer's expertise. The lowest grade was sent to the sugar plantations in the West Indies as cheap food for slaves and its sale was prohibited in any other market. (Slavery was not abolished in Spain's New World colonies until 1880.) Barter was the common form of payment, in which sugar, molasses, and rum would be traded for salt cod.

Since the price was always set in distant markets, fishermen never knew in advance how much they would receive for their catch. It was only after the trans-Atlantic telegraph cable was successfully laid in 1866 that any timely financial information was relayed from European markets. Thirty-five years later that would all change when the Italian inventor Guglielmo Marconi received the first wireless message from Cornwall, England, from his perch on Signal Hill, high above the city of St. John's.

The abundance of the fishery was a mixed blessing. Without any other local industry or large-scale agriculture, Newfoundland was almost entirely dependent on the sale of dried and salted cod to unregulated foreign markets. Since the colony had to import nearly all its provisions, feast could turn to famine if prices dropped, the fish didn't arrive, or someone else caught them.

From the fishery's dazzling beginnings, foreign competition was a fact of life in Newfoundland. The 1814 Treaty of Paris confirmed French fishing rights along the French Shore from Cape St. John to Cape Ray. By the end of the nineteenth century, the French were responsible for over a quarter of all catches off Newfoundland. This windfall was deeply resented by the merchants of St. John's. As they saw it, Imperial authorities were using the colony's stunning resources to seal international agreements, and worse, to support a fish-marketing rival. Whether it was Britain or Canada, Newfoundland has always been in more danger from her dancing partners than from her rivals in the fishery.

As the towns of Conception Bay and Trinity Bay grew, local fishermen began sailing their schooners to Labrador for the summer fishery. By the 1890s, 46 per cent of the total Newfoundland catch was taken off Labrador. Salt fish was still the main export, but Newfoundland faced stiff competition from Norway, France, and Iceland.

In the 1880s, the French and the Norwegians began making changes to suit the demands of their markets in southern Europe. They exported in smaller bales and would call at several ports to deliver the required product, including very small orders. By comparison, Newfoundland exporters insisted on selling their entire cargo in one port. They also demanded immediate payment in sterling, drawn on London banks, while their competitors readily accepted local currency and gave credit for three months.

Despite all the hardships of being a one-industry island, Newfoundland's year-round population ballooned from 19,000 in 1803 to 250,000 by the outbreak of the First World War. But while the population increased more than ten-fold, the total salt fish exports merely doubled. The numbers told a grim story: The per capita production had declined disastrously in just over a hundred years. There were too many fishermen chasing too few fish.

The major exception to Newfoundland's dangerous dependency on cod was sealing. It would be difficult to overestimate the importance of the annual seal hunt to the Newfoundland economy of the nineteenth century. Until the end of the eighteenth century, the hunt was largely land-based; but once schooners set sail for the ice, it was transformed into an industry that would become almost as important to the Newfoundland economy and way of life as the massive cod fishery. During the Napoleonic Wars, Newfoundland exported salt cod worth £600,000 annually. The export of seal products was worth anywhere from £20,000 to £60,000 a year. But by 1844, only twenty years later, sealing produced over a third of Newfoundland's total exports. In 1857, 370 ships and 13,600 men went to the ice and the seal hunt was worth an astonishing £425,000. An estimated eighteen million animals were taken between 1800 and 1860.

Despite harsh working conditions and meagre earnings, sealing gave Newfoundland families something the cod fishery did not – hard cash. That meant a lot when shopping in the company stores. If you used cash, you paid one price, but if you only had vouchers, you paid more. The highest crew share during the steamer era was $303 per man, paid in 1866 to the men of the ss *Retriever*. Between 1900 and 1913, when the catches were in sharp decline, the average share per man was only about $41 for a two-month voyage to the Front. Even though sealers had to pay for their own boots and travel to St. John's (many walked from the outports to meet their ships), what was left still amounted to a small fortune by the standards of the day.

By the second half of the nineteenth century, it was obvious that the seal herds were being overhunted. In 1860, only 20 per cent of the 292 vessels that took part in the seal hunt made a profit. By the last two decades of the century, the harvest was less than half of what it had been in the 1830s and 1840s. As the new century began, seal products accounted for less than one-tenth of the value of Newfoundland's total exports. Important as it had once been, the seal hunt could no longer postpone the inevitable pressure on the inshore fishery and its amazing stock of cod.

As the seal hunt declined, so did the Labrador fishery, which was beset with quality and marketing problems in an increasingly competitive industry. As long as salt fish was taken to market in sailing ships, it was a seller's market with small cargoes arriving irregularly. But when steamships began carrying fish to Europe in the 1880s, large shipments would often arrive within days or even hours of those of the competition. The resulting fish gluts drove down prices and it was suddenly a buyer's market. In their rush to outdo the competition and get to market first, Newfoundland fish merchants competed mercilessly against one other. All too often they did this by shipping fish that weren't fully cured, compounding the quality problem that had dogged the Newfoundland fishery for generations.

Cutthroat competitiveness and a lack of cooperation among merchants prevented the establishment of a marketing board that could have set quality standards. Meanwhile, technical innovation was reshaping the whole industry. At first, fishermen had used single lines with baited hooks to catch cod. These were later replaced by bultows, long lines from which hundreds of baited hooks were suspended. But it was the invention of the cod trap in the 1870s that most dramatically changed the inshore fishery. Vast schools of cod in pursuit of caplin were guided into the trap by a net. The fishermen then closed the opening and crowded the cod together by hauling in the trap. The catch was then scooped out with fishforks. If the cod came inshore, and a whale or an iceberg didn't ruin the net, the cod trap could be an extremely productive way of fishing.

The decline of the seal hunt and the Labrador fishery put relentless pressure on the Grand Banks cod stocks. From 1880 to 1910 the number of boats and fishermen in Newfoundland dramatically increased, largely because there were so few employment alternatives. The 1911 census showed that almost 44,000 men and 23,000 women worked in the fishery. By comparison, just 2,800 men worked in lumbering, and fewer than 2,300 in mining. Unlike the Labrador or Banks fishery, which required a significant capital investment, it didn't take a lot of money to enter the inshore fishery. Even when tough times drove the larger companies into bankruptcy, families that had ruled out emigrating to Boston or Toronto stayed with the inshore fishery.

The increase in the number of fishermen meant smaller landings. In 1888, a fisheries commission was appointed in Newfoundland to study the problems that were threatening to overwhelm the one-industry island. A Norwegian, Adolph Nielson, was hired as superintendent of fisheries. His mandate was to find a suitable site in one of the bays on Newfoundland's east coast for a fish hatchery. Nielson established a cod hatchery at Dildo and in six years, 832,929 million eggs were hatched and planted in the waters of Trinity Bay. In 1895 there were reports of an abundance of cod in the bay, while neighbouring Conception and Bonavista bays were comparatively empty. Twenty-three lobster hatcheries were also established. When illness forced Nielson to return to Norway in 1897, the Newfoundland government withdrew funding and closed the hatcheries.

In addition to the problem of declining stocks, Newfoundland also lacked the capital to modernize its largest industry. Cod traps, seines, gill-nets, and trawls all made their appearance in Newfoundland, yet the fishery remained an almost exclusively inshore effort. Between 1889 and 1894 the Banks fishery declined from 330 vessels to a mere 58. Although there were fluctuations that saw prices go up in time of war, revolution, or worldwide shortages, the price for Newfoundland cod had sharply declined by 1914.

Sometimes the fish mysteriously failed to migrate inshore. There was a widespread catch failure in 1817, another in 1868, and yet another in 1885, just when the Norwegian and French fisheries were expanding. The French subsidized their fleet, allowing them to become important salt fish exporters. Under a government bonus system, every man outfitted for the Newfoundland fishery received a bounty of fifty francs and he received a further twenty-franc bounty for each quintal (roughly fifty kilograms) of salt cod he produced. Because of this subsidy, French salt cod drove down the price of its Newfoundland counterpart to the point where the Newfoundland shippers could not compete in European markets.

At the best of times, fishing for a living was a precarious occupation.

Like much of the western world, Newfoundland suffered a severe economic downturn in the last quarter of the nineteenth century. By the 1880s, the standard of living on the island had plummeted, largely because fish prices hit a fifty-year low. The colony was soon in serious financial difficulty and on "Black Monday," December 10, 1894, there was a bank crash. Many of Newfoundland's oldest firms disappeared overnight, thousands of people lost their jobs, and bread riots broke out in the capital.

The collapse of the fishery was exacerbated by record low catch-rates and declining markets. By 1909, Norway had supplanted Newfoundland as the world's biggest exporter of salt fish. Changing technology also took a toll on the Newfoundland fishery. Refrigeration fed a new demand for high-quality fresh and frozen fish. The Boston Fresh Fish Pier opened in 1915, but Newfoundland was slow to adjust to new appetites in the fish-eating public. With soft markets for salt fish, and low prices, Newfoundland's economy continued to stagnate. By 1914, the public debt stood at $30 million. By 1934, the economy had totally collapsed, New-foundland lost her Dominion status, and Britain took over the day-to-day affairs of her bankrupt former colony.

While the Commission of Government struggled to come up with solutions to Newfoundland's chronic economic problems, a revolution was underway in the fishing industry. In 1906, the first French steam trawlers appeared in the deep-sea fishery. These remarkable vessels with their enormous nets eliminated the need for bait, and made it impossible for the fishing schooners, with their longline technology, to compete. By 1909, the French had thirty steam trawlers fishing on the Grand Banks. The Norwegians were quick to imitate the French, retiring their schooners in favour of the new steam trawlers.

In one fell technological swoop, the spectre of fish pirates from distant countries making off with the major part of Newfoundland cod was on everyone's mind. A 1901 editorial in the St. John's *Trade Review* had predicted that if Newfoundland did not rethink her fishing effort "European fishermen will come over and carry off our fish from under our nose."

This was not the first or the last technological blow to the Newfoundland fishery, or to the cod that swam the Grand Banks. While Newfoundland's competitors were modernizing and coop-erating, her own merchants were scrambling to take immediate profits, competing among themselves, and trying to hang on to the old ways. Except for a brief attempt to regulate the sale of salt fish with export and price controls in 1920, her merchants would not cooperate. If there was a shortage, they sent poorly cured fish to market in order to get there first. There was no standard grading of fish until the government imposed controls in the late 1930s, and Newfoundland was left with the less profitable markets in Brazil and the West Indies. In the Great Depression, Newfound-land's markets collapsed.

During the first half of the twentieth century the inshore was the most important cod fishery in Newfoundland. France and Newfoundland caught about 90 per cent of the fish, and Canada, the U.S.A., Portugal, and Spain caught the remaining 10 per cent offshore. The government encouraged the development of the frozen fish industry, and by the time Newfoundland joined Canada in 1949, fresh and frozen fish exports accounted for about a third of the value of all fish production.

The beginning of the end of the northern cod arrived in 1954 in the form of the British ship the *Fairtry*. The three-million-dollar vessel was the first factory-freezer trawler in the world. These huge stern trawlers, complete with on-board processing plants, enabled their owners to triple their cod catch. Even with annual operating costs of $4.5 million apiece, their enormous processing capacity, up to 600 tonnes of fish per day, made them floating gold mines. No matter how deep the fish, or how far away, these ocean-going omnivores could find and catch them in dizzying numbers.

From a distance, the ships look like oceanliners, the largest of them nearly four hundred feet long. They can fish around the clock, seven days a week, fifty-two weeks a year, in all but the worst weather. Even with the Atlantic boiling under a force ten gale (winds of 55 to 63 mph), factory freezers can fish the edge of the Hamilton Bank 120 miles east of the Labrador coast, trailing nets whose gaping mouths could swallow the Statue of Liberty. Powerful lights illuminate the vessel's working decks, green-over-white when the ship is fishing, red-over-white if it is winching in its catch.

Despite their bad-weather capabilities, the specialized function of these vessels, as well as their sheer mass, some over 3,500 tonnes, means that their skippers sometimes face daunting choices. The consequences of ordering a halt to fishing can be catastrophic, particularly if there are several tonnes of fish shifting on the trawl deck in heavy seas and the captain can't "round up," or put the vessel's bow into the wind.

On the factory deck below, the huge volumes of water used to process the catch can slosh with enough force to aggravate the rolling of the ship. The captain of a factory freezer must trim his ballast according to the amount of fish he takes on board, or his ship may capsize trying to turn into the wind in a storm.

The view from the bridge of one of these behemoths is pure science fiction: two huge winches slowly haul in a mile and two-thirds of three-and-three-quarter inch steel cables, which are attached to the gigantic trawl net. The deckhands take up their posts ready to receive the net, while the second mate expertly manipulates the switches and levers on the console that control the winches. The strain of hauling the net can cause the great ship to slide backwards, its 5,000-horsepower diesel engines no match for the mass of fish bulging in its trawl, or the leviathan drag of the ocean.

Tape marks on the tow-lines indicate the last few feet of the trawl that must be retrieved inch by inch, each delicate, hydraulic tug timed to coincide with the rise and fall of the ocean. The huge, oval-shaped doors that keep the mouth of the trawl open when the vessel is fishing are hauled up and locked in place. A chance encounter with those doors, each weighing 2,100 kilograms, can break hands, arms, or backs for the careless or unlucky.

After a few moments, the cables running from the doors to the net are wound in and the "cod end" or tip of the net appears in the ship's wake. It looks like a shallow-broaching whale but there are fish heads and tails sticking through the mesh at freakish angles. Fulmars and kittiwakes wheel above the net, knowing that they will soon be sharing in the catch.

The crew works frantically to bring in the tubular section that runs between the mouth of the trawl and the cod end. The net is so long, three times the length of the working deck, that it has to be laid down in a zigzag pattern when dragged on board. Thirty minutes after the winches first begin to groan, the heavy cod end is gingerly drawn up on deck. Safety gates swing shut to close off the loading ramp. Deckhands working astern have sometimes been dragged overboard when waves surge up the ramp in heavy seas.

Nor is the ocean the only danger. Cables and hooks swing to and fro as the fish are brought aboard and huge steel weights called bobbins shift on the deck, sometimes rolling around like giant bowling balls. (The bobbins, at 550 pounds apiece, keep the net snug on the bottom when the vessel is fishing.) Offshore crews develop remarkable timing and balance while working the deck, but no amount of agility or expertise can remove the risk of serious injury.

The catches are immense; the net and rigging are engineered to haul fifty to sixty tonnes of fish at a time. One hundred tonnes of mature cod can be taken in just two hours by these killing machines. The huge trawl is hoisted up and with a sudden *whoosh*, tonnes of cod shoot through the hatches to the factory deck below. Even though the first net is still half full, a second net is set if the vessel has struck a good shoal of fish. If the cod are small or uneven in size, the crew may throw the smaller fish overboard and hope to land larger ones on the next pass, since the factory freezer's processors need fish to be a common size to work at maximum efficiency. This practice is known as high-grading. Most of the discarded fish are dead. In the past, it was not unusual for a vessel to take double the amount of fish needed to make its quota, in order to return home with the largest, most marketable fillets.

While the net is respooled onto a giant reel, the noise on the factory floor is deafening, a combination of shouting, singing, and mechanical squeals and groans from hell. If the haul is good, fish are everywhere – in the hatchways, sorting pens, on the catwalks and deck. Cod are loaded on conveyer belts that lead to the Baader filleting machines. Once each fish is filleted and skinned, it is hand-trimmed and packed into seven- to eleven-kilogram blocks, frozen, and stored. On shore, these blocks will be cut into fish sticks or fish burgers. The by-catch of wolffish, turbot, or redfish must be hand-cleaned, separated, and forwarded by conveyor belt to a wooden cutting table. The offal and so-called trash fish are sent to the fish-meal factory on a lower deck. On an average day, ninety tonnes of whole fish will be processed and countless other tonnes wasted.

If a vessel from a particular fleet hits a "hot spot," her captain will call in sister ships to work the shoal. As many as fifty factory-freezers will converge on the same location, fishing non-stop until nothing is left. This is called "pulse fishing," and very little is left to luck. Electronic fish-finders, echographs, and, in the case of the Russians, even mini-subs, are used to locate shoals of fish. The newest sonar devices can scan the ocean two miles in advance of a working trawler.

Nor are captains above eavesdropping on the competition's radio to pick up good fishing locations. Complete radio silence is considered bad form on the high seas and is usually interpreted as the telltale sign of a huge fish find. Other vessels steam over to a silent competitor's location with their binoculars glued to its stern ramp; if fish are being hauled aboard, they quickly set their trawls.

The deep-sea fishery is the closest thing to a gold rush that the ocean has to offer.

The U.S.S.R. watched the construction of the *Fairtry* with great interest. Before the vessel was launched at the Aberdeen Shipyard, the shipbuilding firm of J. Lewis and Son received a tender from the Soviets for twenty-four trawlers of the same design. The Russians also requested a set of the ship's plans to "study" the technical specifications of the ship, a euphemism for copying its design. Between 1954 and 1956, the Soviet Union had twenty-four factory-freezer trawlers built in Kiel, West Germany. Christened "Pushkin"-class vessels, they were remarkably similar to the *Fairtry*.

Soviet trade representatives had already started to buy distant-water side-trawlers in Great Britain in 1951. By the mid-fifties, they had one of the best long-distant fleets in the world. Just twenty years later, there was an armada of 900 large factory trawlers on the high seas, 400 of them belonging to the U.S.S.R. The world's most productive fishing nation, Japan, had 125, Spain, 75, West Germany, 50, France and Britain, 40 apiece. As expensive as they were, strong demand for fish and high prices, coupled with declining stocks in the home waters of these nations, made the huge vessels economically viable. They all had one thing in common: an insatiable appetite for fish.

In 1961, the Spanish government decided to expand its fishing fleet because of a projected protein shortage at home. The construction of factory trawlers in northern Spain almost equalled the shipbuilding frenzy in the Soviet Union; in just four years, only the U.S.S.R. and Japan had larger fleets than Spain. The Spanish factory-fishing effort initially targeted rich hake stocks off South Africa, but Spain was already well known on the Grand Banks as one of the world's most rapacious fishing nations. Measured by gross catch, Spanish "pair trawlers" fished very successfully in the northwest Atlantic. In 1968, seventy-two pairs caught 99 per cent of the record 341,000-tonne Spanish catch, roughly 16 per cent of Spain's estimated world landings that year.

Harvesting with pair trawlers takes great skill on the part of the two captains, who must execute what is, in effect, hi-tech synchronized fishing in which the gold medal is a mother lode of fish. The huge net is slung between two trawlers, travelling side by side. The pull of the ships keeps the mouth of the net open so that the heavy doors that perform the same function on a conventional fishing vessel are not needed. This saves horsepower when hauling the net, so more hydraulic pressure can be applied to winching up heavier loads of fish. The two ships herd the desired fish into the half-mile span between them, and in a single haul they can bring in 180 tonnes of fish, triple the maximum trawl capacity of most factory freezers.

The men process the catch under the main deck, standing waist-deep in fish. The cod is split, gutted, and after the spine is removed, washed and salted. (Dried cod is still a highly prized delicacy in Spain.) Other species – yellowtail flounder, pollock, redfish, or haddock – are simply thrown overboard because there are no freezing units on pair trawlers. The usual ratio of total catch to cod is three to one. In other words, three-quarters of the catch from pair trawlers is wasted. Crews from other vessels often shook their fists at the Spanish fishermen as they steamed through the dead, discarded fish left in the wake of working pair trawlers. The Spanish were not overly concerned by what they saw as envy of their fishing prowess. Besides, dumping at sea was as common as under-reporting of catches; today's finger-pointers were tomorrow's culprits. Better than most nations, the Spanish knew that the game was fishing for dollars, not fish. A pair of trawlers can accommodate 1,100 tonnes of fish in their holds, representing a gross value of over two million dollars. With expenses ranging from $500,000 to $700,000 per voyage, which can last up to six months, the return on investment is more than enough to balance the ill will of competitors and a little name-calling. As one Spanish skipper put it, "Everybody's doing it. We just do it a little better than the rest of them."

The skipper was right. Every country has always prosecuted the fishery to the maximum of its technology. Baited or unbaited iron hooks of the early 1500s gave way by the late 1700s to multi-hooked line trawls which were hauled on board by hand winches. The trawl lines increased from thirty to forty pieces by the 1820s, then to ninety pieces by the 1870s, a time of true innovation. Stronger steel hooks replaced iron hooks, and lighter but equally strong cotton lines replaced traditional hemp.

There was the same innovation in small-boat technology, with lighter, more manageable dories replacing the heavy "shallops" used in the French trawl fishery on the Banks. Inshore, the fishery was revolutionized by the introduction of the cod trap.

Seine nets had been used for cod in the French shore fishery from the 1500s to the end of the nineteenth century. (Two boats with the seine stretched between them circle the cod, gradually tightening the net until it is packed tightly with fish.) By the 1840s, as well as cod seines, Newfoundlanders were using a primitive form of gill-net. Weighted on the bottom, the gill-net settles on the seabed. Held upright by floats, it becomes, in effect, a mesh fence in which swimming fish become lodged. The net can easily be shifted from place to place as the fish move. It must be hauled every day to maintain a top quality product, and the fish must be gutted, washed, and iced on board to remain firm. By the 1960s, the cotton gill-net had given way to nylon nets and then to the almost indestructible monofiliament nets, virtually replacing trawl lines in the inshore fishery.

In 1899, the first side-trawler steamed out of a Newfoundland port to fish on the Grand Banks. Ten years later, some inshore vessels turned to mechanical propulsion. The size of the steam trawlers increased in the 1920s and 1930s, until they were replaced by the first diesel-powered vessels in the 1930s. As it turned out, the fast, sail-powered Grand Banks schooners of the late nineteenth century were well suited to the installation of an engine aft of midships.

Significant as it was, none of the older technology affected fish stocks as much as the factory-freezers, pulling trawls that could catch 600 tonnes of fish in a single day. The newer classes of Soviet trawlers, the Super-Atlantiks, were even able to fish Antarctic waters for cod and krill, the preferred food of penguins and whales, in an environment once believed to be too hostile to exploit. Fishing to the maximum of the technology now meant fishing everywhere until nothing was left.

The hourly catch-rate with factory trawlers outstripped conventional side-trawlers by 50 per cent. From 1954 to 1960, the French and Portuguese catches on the Grand Banks alone amounted to as much as 50 per cent of the Canadian catch. Then came the high-impact Spanish fishing effort. By 1959, there were seventy-eight Spanish vessels fishing in pairs on the Banks; ten years later, double that number. Until 1960, Spain kept pace with the catches of France and Portugal. But from 1961 to 1972, the country that had co-discovered the Grand Banks exceeded the catch of both nations, taking over 200,000 metric tonnes of fish for eleven straight years.

The catch-rates told the story as well as anything. For four centuries, catches of northern cod had increased gradually with improving fishing technology, peaking in 1910 at about 300,000 tonnes. For the next fifty years, catches levelled off to between 150,000 and 200,000 tonnes. But by the 1960s, there were stunning increases, culminating in the killer year of 1968 when a staggering 810,000 tonnes of northern cod were taken, and that was only the reported catch. A remarkable watershed had been reached. For the first time in four and a half centuries of continuous fishing on the Banks, more fish was taken offshore than inshore.

By 1971, several Spanish factory trawlers had quit the Gulf of Mexico and the Caribbean because the wide variety of species precluded the efficient processing of the catch. Their destination was the northwest Atlantic and the Grand Banks, where rich stocks of cod and herring were ideal for the huge onboard processors. At the time, these stocks were so plentiful that they accounted for a staggering 40 per cent of the total global fishery. There was no more powerful fish magnet on earth than the teeming waters off Newfoundland.

One of the driving forces behind the over-capitalization of these long-distance fishing fleets was a sense that the ocean's bounty was inexhaustible. Dr. Milner B. Schaefer, director of the world-renowned Scripps Oceanographic Institute in California, concluded in the 1960s that world fishery production could sustain a fishing effort of 200 million tonnes a year, an estimate thought to be conservative because it didn't include the growing production of aquaculture.

Many experts agreed in principle, but set lower estimates. In 1960, the United Nations Food and Agricultural Organization (FAO), Fisheries Division, predicted that fishermen could take as much as sixty million tonnes of fish a year "without impairing the viability of stocks or drawing on new resources." The fishing nations were listening, and the sixty-million tonne world-catch level was reached in 1974, six years earlier than the FAO's prediction. Much of that prodigious effort took place in the western hemisphere. That year, there were 1,076 European and Communist Bloc vessels fishing in North American waters. All told, they caught 2,176,000 tonnes of fish, triple the Atlantic Canadian catch of a resource that was sitting on Canada's doorstep.

It took a mere twenty years after the launch of the *Fairtry* for factory trawlers to dominate the world fishery completely. After being relatively stable for centuries, global landings tripled in the twenty years between 1950 and 1970, from twenty to sixty million tonnes. For the first time in history, vessels could steam anywhere in the world and fish night and day, targeting the exact location where individual stocks were known to be in a particular season. The best catch-rates were recorded when the fish were taken on their spawning grounds, as they routinely were around the world.

It was believed at the time that the Labrador cod massed under the edge of the ice before spawning because the water was warmer near the rim of the continental shelf. Although captains knew that the fish should be given a chance to reproduce, they were also aware that the cod dispersed after spawning into smaller schools that were less economic to fish. So their fishing trips were timed to coincide with the great spawning congregations, a practice they justified with brutal pragmatism: If they didn't take the fish, then some other protein-hungry nation would. And when fish stocks were wiped out, as the Labrador cod stocks were by East German factory-freezers in the 1960s, the armada merely targeted someone else's coast and moved on. In the boom years of the distant-water fleets, international controls were either non-existent or ignored.

Newfoundland was slow to respond to the fishing revolution taking place under her very nose. But what appeared to be a lack of initiative was in fact a deliberate attempt to temper the boom and bust of an economy built on the vagaries of the fishery. In a province bedevilled by chronic unemployment and poor fishing wages, successive Newfoundland governments tried to develop a resource-based industry that would give Newfoundlanders an alternative to spending their entire lives on the water. In 1895, an iron mine was opened on Bell Island just outside St. John's, followed over the next thirty years by lead and zinc mines in Buchans, and a fluorspar mine in St. Lawrence. Grand Falls, the first Newfoundland community to be built out of sight of the sea, got a newsprint mill in 1905, and twenty years later, a British company built a newsprint plant in Corner Brook.

As Newfoundland's economy diversified, the importance of the fishery declined. In 1921, fish represented 70 per cent of the value of annual exports from Newfoundland; ten years later, it was less than 38 per cent. By 1930, Newfoundland was catching only about 40 per cent of the fish taken in her traditional fishing grounds, the balance going to foreigners.

The requirements of a world at war gave Newfoundland a brief but dramatic respite from the hard work of breaking her one-industry obsession. Money poured into the Newfoundland economy during the Second World War as 19,000 Newfoundlanders found work in the construction and maintenance of huge military bases at Gander, Goose Bay, and Argentia.

A second transforming wave came with Confederation in 1949, a political phenomenon that forever changed work patterns in the outports. The average family allowance as part of the Canadian federation was now nearly $200 a year. In 1957, Jack Pickersgill became a Newfoundland hero when he introduced a special fishermen's unemployment insurance program designed to reflect the reality of the seasonal fishery. In the first year alone, payments to fishermen who had worked a minimum of ten weeks of the year in the inshore totalled $1,759,000; just two years later, that payment had doubled. It has since become the backbone of an entire way of life.

Premier Joseph Smallwood did his best to turn Newfoundlanders away from the fishery, advising them to "burn their boats" in a famous and hotly disputed speech. He resettled hundreds of outport residents in urban centres across the island and spent $30 million in an attempt to build a manufacturing sector. But a succession of carpetbaggers from John C. Doyle to John Shaheen did little more for the people than pillage their resources and leave them with enormous debts. One after another, Smallwood's grandiose projects failed: the linerboard mill at Stephenville, the oil refinery at Come by Chance, the chocolate factory, everything but Canada's steadfast financial support.

Canada's new fisheries policy for Newfoundland was based on

fresh and frozen fish for the American market. Where Newfoundland had once sold a single product, salt cod, to several international customers, she now sold a single product, frozen fish, to one. This dangerous dependency produced the usual results. When the American market was saturated with fish in 1955, a depression settled over the Newfoundland fishery as deep as any Grand Banks fog.

Newfoundland's old identity had been lost, but it would, as always, be the sea that restored and reshaped it. A new fishery was in the making. Still, it was not until the 1960s that Newfoundlanders fished in waters deeper than 91.5 metres, while the Russians were already setting their nets at 1,500 metres.

The modern fishery was a place in which Newfoundlanders had to make their way all over again. It was a terrifying place. The factory-freezer trawlers were doing to the oceans of the world what clear-cutting was doing to its forests. For all their technological wizardry and the remarkable skill it took to operate them, they had reduced many stocks to the vanishing point in less than twenty years at sea. They took spawning and immature fish, discarding what they didn't want, and misreported catches to take more than they were entitled to under their quotas. Since fish intermingle, their trawling dragged up every creature on the bottom, including species already under low quotas. Although regulations required that the fish be sorted and returned to the water quickly, the high seas was a place where you almost never had to look into the sheriff's eyes. Virtually all of the returned fish were dead or dying before they hit the water, crushed by the changes in pressure as they were pulled up from the depths, or by the weight of fish in the net, or suffocated in the cod end of the trawl when their gills were squeezed shut.

The bottom line of these high-tech killing machines was a statistic almost too hellish to contemplate. Drs. Jeffrey Hutchings and Ransom Myers, two of Canada's top fisheries scientists, have estimated that about 8 million tonnes of northern cod were caught between 1500 and 1750, representing twenty-five to forty cod generations, which were able to adapt to growing fishing pressures. By comparison, another 8 million tonnes were caught between 1960 and 1975, the heyday of the factory-freezer trawler, when there were two hundred factory-freezers on the Grand Banks. That shockingly brief fifteen-year period encompassed only one or two generations of cod, leaving no time for the stock to adapt. The catch-rates remained the same, but the hidden reality was that the once incredible stocks were shrinking to the point where the fish could be wiped out.

By 1974 the stocks were in desperate shape, and governments worldwide responded with massive subsidies that merely led to improved gear and ever more efficient fish-killing.

The unthinkable was at hand: Like a sorcerer's apprentice, we were on the verge of using the black magic of technology to make a desert of the sea.

3

LICENSED TO KILL

The destruction of the northern cod was not a one-act play, but a pageant of greed that went on for decades before the curtain finally came down. At every step of the way, Cassandra wailed, but no one listened.

Between 1956, when the first factory-freezer arrived on the Grand Banks, and 1977, when Canada's 200-mile limit closed the barn door after the horse was gone, inshore cod catches in Newfoundland plummeted by two-thirds. There was no mystery; most of the fish was being taken offshore before it could migrate into coastal waters. For most fishermen who went to sea in boats up to sixty-five feet long (the conventional definition of inshore to midshore vessels), the fishery was as marginal an occupation as it had ever been. It was the unemployment insurance cheques from Ottawa that was the most significant catch in many of Atlantic Canada's outports and villages.

Inshore fishermen were entitled to expect Ottawa's financial support. They had watched in anger and impotence while foreign trawlers and factory ships pillaged Newfoundland's fishing grounds. They saw the niceties of international law grossly violated. Foreign trawlers frequently trespassed inside Canada's three-mile limit, ripping up inshore gear in their relentless pursuit of fish. They weren't overly concerned about being arrested, since Canada's sole patrol vessel on that coast was too small to go out on windy days, as the St. John's *Evening Telegram* wryly reported in 1967. Dissatisfied with the fair-weather enforcement of the Department of Fisheries, many longliner captains chose to stay ashore rather than risk losing their expensive gear to marauding foreign fleets.

But not all of the stock damage in Newfoundland had been done by the world's distant-water fishing fleets. Between 1917 and 1954, long before the *Fairtry* hauled her first trawl, inshore catches of northern cod had already declined from 335,000 tonnes to 180,000 tonnes. Although not nearly as obvious as innovations in the offshore, the inshore fishery had experienced steady technical improvements to its gear that dramatically increased its killing power and put even greater pressure on declining stocks. For hundreds of years, the traditional fishery had operated from small boats, usually less than thirty feet long, that fished within sight of land. They could not put to sea in bad weather or stow big catches because their holds lacked refrigeration. In the inshore sector, vessel size was a built-in guarantee of conservation.

But in 1951, trap boats and longliners made their appearance in Newfoundland. Ten years later, longliners were fishing the nearshore shoals that inshore fishermen had previously been unable to harvest because of the distances involved. For the northern cod, there was no place to swim, no place to hide.

Mechanized net hauling, baiting, and setting of line trawls, more efficient cod traps, radar, satellite navigation, and echo sounders theoretically allowed inshore skippers to take more fish in the few months of the year they could operate than ever before. But there was a paradox. Despite more efficient gear, and larger vessels that allowed them to venture out to more distant fishing grounds, catches did not increase. Even the appearance of continued traditional landings was deceptive. The inshore was in fact catching fewer fish per unit of effort. In other words, it now required a much greater fishing effort to take the same number of fish. The new technology was merely allowing inshore fishermen to catch almost all of the fish that managed to escape the offshore slaughter.

Occasionally, the new technology led to fishing practices as destructive in their own way as the monstrous excesses of the factory-freezers. Gill-nets, for example, caught almost everything that swam into them, including the large, spawning mother cod. If these nets were lost in a storm, they could "ghost fish" for years, since they were no longer made of biodegradable cotton, but of material that never dissolves in seawater.

At the same time as the gross number of fish was steadily declining, the number of inshore fishermen was on the rise. Governments had always treated the fishery as the employer of last resort in Atlantic Canada. A confidential 1970 memorandum to the federal cabinet that sought to outline a plan for the economic rationalization of Canada's fisheries stated: "The main objective of government policy has been to maximize employment in Canada's commercial fisheries." The department kept pumping out licences with little regard for the marine environment or the state of the stocks. In 1976, Canada had about forty thousand registered fishing vessels, 95 per cent of them under twenty-five gross tonnes, on its east and west coasts. All of them fished within a day of their home port. The inshore fishery was getting to be a very crowded place.

Unemployment insurance was one of the prime reasons that the number of fishermen dramatically increased at a time when the stocks were actually in decline. Even though they are self-employed, fishermen have been able to collect UI (now EI – employment insurance), since 1957. From the beginning, qualifying for UI has been a financial priority of the small-boat operator. The regulations are complex, but for most of the program's existence fishermen have been able to collect UI from November to May if they worked ten weeks in the inshore fishery.

Newfoundlanders recognized a good thing when they saw it. By 1964, just seven years after fishermen's UI was introduced, and with no increase in the general population, there was a 33 per cent increase in the number of inshore fishermen. During this same period, the inshore catch of northern cod per fishermen fell by 50 per cent.

Between 1956 and 1968, total landings of groundfish had risen from about 540,000 to 1,473,000 tonnes, an increase of about 175 per cent. Most of the increase was northern cod in zone 2J3KL, which runs from southern Labrador to the Avalon Peninsula. Dr. Leslie Harris of Memorial University in St. John's attributes the beginning of the end for the northern cod to the excesses of the foreign fleet during this period.

"I think that the first great assault on the northern cod, the one from which that stock has never really recovered, was almost totally a foreign assault," he says. "This was back in 1968, 1969, and '70 when the Germans first, and then subsequently other East Europeans, developed the technology to allow them to fish in deep water and ice-infested waters. This was the first assault on a pristine cod population, the Hamilton Bank stock. This was the first time it was fished during spawning."

The 2J3KL cod was the single most important stock for Newfoundland, accounting for 80 to 90 per cent of the total groundfish catch in the inshore fishery. In 1968, a record 810,014 tonnes of northern cod were harvested, but as the offshore trawlers did their deadly work, the results began showing up inshore. Between 1959 and 1974, the inshore harvests of 2J3KL cod declined dramatically from 160,000 tonnes to a mere 35,000 tonnes. Stocks were heading towards a collapse and people began to bail out of a dying fishery. In 1960 there were about 10,337 inshore fishermen in 2J3KL; by 1972, that number had dwindled to 6,592.

At the same time, fish prices weakened in the United States and the Middle East oil crisis drove up the cost of going fishing. By 1974, the Atlantic groundfish industry was in crisis, logging one of the poorest fishing years on record. The offshore harvest reached 338,000 tonnes (roughly ten times the inshore catch), just 57 per cent of the 657,000-tonne TAC for northern cod. Fishermen's nets were beginning to provide better data on what was going on in the ocean than sophisticated mathematical projections.

The fishing establishment resisted the bad news. At a May 1975 meeting of the Fisheries Council of Canada, an organization of fish-plant owners, one marine biologist insisted that 2J3KL cod was not being overfished according to official regulatory criteria; at the same meeting, an assistant deputy minister in the Department of the Environment described the Atlantic groundfish industry as being in "a very deep crisis."

By June 1975, the International Commission for the Northwest Atlantic Fishery (ICNAF) assessment committee responsible for the 2J3KL stock finally admitted that its earlier projections had been mistaken and reduced the TAC by half; 300,000 tonnes for 1976. Fish companies were incensed, complaining bitterly that they couldn't make it through the fishing season with such paltry quotas. In order to prevent industry-wide bankruptcies, the federal government set up a special aid program which eventually cost taxpayers $150 million. It would be the first of several huge bailout programs made necessary by misguided optimism about the state of the stocks.

Throughout this period both Ottawa and St. John's continued to look to the fishery to solve chronic unemployment on the East Coast. Between 1970 and 1981, the federal government subsidized the construction of replacement fishing vessels to the tune of 35 per cent, a policy that encouraged an aggressive expansion of the inshore sector. The provincial Department of Fisheries in Newfoundland offered a 30 per cent fishing-gear subsidy to help small-boat fishermen acquire the latest technology. Coupled with full tax exemptions for fuel and equipment used at sea, it was a powerful incentive for more Newfoundlanders to join the fish-force.

The result was astonishing but predictable. In 1975, there were 13,736 registered inshore fishermen in Newfoundland: by 1980, that number had ballooned to 33,640. There wasn't a politician in the land who was prepared to accept the consequences of restricting entry to the fishery.

The fishing grounds were overcrowded in the summer season and the collision of fishing technologies became a source of bitter conflict. Domestic inshore trawlers often repeated the excesses of their foreign counterparts, using superior technology to take a disproportionate share of the stock. Gill-netters complained that their catches were too low and that their gear was regularly destroyed by trawlers or trap fishermen. They responded by increasing the number of nets in the water to catch the same amount of fish. When that failed to increase their catch, they began applying for otter-trawler licences themselves. Although Ottawa tried to restrict entry to this fishery, unions and the provincial government exerted political pressure. New licences were grudgingly granted, but granted all the same. By the early 1980s, not long after the former gill-netters got into the lucrative trawler fishery, another tremor went through the industry: there was a critical shortage of fish in some key inshore fishing grounds.

The unconscionable expansion of the fishery at the expense of disappearing fish stocks was made possible by the way the industry is regulated in Canada. Fishermen operate in a byzantine environment where the federal and provincial governments lock horns for political rather than fishery reasons, which in turn pits inshore against offshore interests, province against province, and even community against community.

At the heart of the political collision is a single, destructive fact. Although Ottawa owns all the fish, the provinces are responsible for fish processing. Since both levels of government use the fishery for political advantage, the industry frequently comes down to a game of bureaucratic blackmail. If the province, for example, licenses new fish-plants in outport Newfoundland, as it did in expectation of a fishing boom after Canada declared its 200-mile zone in 1977, Ottawa comes under great pressure to increase the inshore quota to supply the plants with fish. If the minister refuses to allocate more fish, the result is a vote shortage at the next federal election; if he submits to the blackmail, the stock suffers. In the early 1980s that is exactly what happened. In 1982, scrambling to react to the crisis in the water, federal regulations were tightened to discourage the expansion of the inshore fishery. For once, the provincial government followed suit, terminating its disastrous gear-replacement subsidies. The fishery was not yielding the returns everyone had hoped for, and the industry sank into its worse crisis in a hundred years, just when the country was hit with killer interest rates.

Hooked on the myth of the ocean's inexhaustible bounty, bureaucrats devised a federal fisheries policy that was skewed by incompatible visions of what the industry should be: a social fishery that employed and subsidized thousands of Canadians, or a big business that ran on the principles of economic viability and the demands of the market. Under successive federal governments, the economics of the fishing industry were balanced against the reality that most inshore fishermen in the Newfoundland industry can't make enough money to survive. With few or no local employment alternatives, and forced migration an unpopular last resort, politicians tended to let a bad situation get even worse. In the 1980s, without anyone noticing, the DFO's mandate underwent a sea change. It became a specialized social welfare department in which the biology of fish and the conservation of stocks were often afterthoughts.

While the trawls and nets worked the crowded sea, international developments were having a profound affect on the fishery. After the Second World War, American President Harry Truman claimed ownership of seabed resources out to the edge of the continental shelf off the coasts of the United States. Several South American countries followed suit, claiming ownership of their territorial seas to a distance of two hundred miles offshore. The First United Nations Law of the Sea conference was held in Geneva in 1958. The conventions it passed formally recognized what several states had already declared unilaterally: the right of coastal states to seabed resources such as minerals and hydrocarbons and sedentary fishery resources on their continental shelves. The right to so-called finfish resources remained unresolved.

A second Law of the Sea conference was held in 1960 with virtually no results. Canada failed to win recognition of her territorial sea to six miles, and couldn't persuade other fishing nations to accept an exclusive Canadian fishing zone six miles beyond her territorial sea. As long as the international community bickered about control over fish resources, management of stocks was impossible.

In 1949, the Americans and a few West European nations fishing in the northwest Atlantic established ICNAF. The purpose of the body was to manage the Atlantic fisheries at their so-called maximum sustainable yield. Although ICNAF had the power to advise its members on conservation under the terms of its convention, the organization concentrated on collecting scientific data and proposing regulations on such matters as the mesh size of commercial nets.

As early as 1965, ICNAF was voicing concerns about overfishing and the need for quotas. Nothing was done until national quotas were set for haddock and American plaice in 1969. By 1972, other quotas had been established, including one for northern cod. But commerce so completely overshadowed conservation that the total allowable catch for 1973 and 1974 was in excess of the maximum sustainable yield.

It hardly mattered. Stocks off Newfoundland had been so depleted by then that the actual harvest was far below the established TACs; fishermen were able to land only slightly more than half of what they were allowed to catch in zone 2J3KL, the richest fishing grounds on the Grand Banks.

In 1964, the Canadian government enacted the Territorial Sea and Fishing Zones Act, which unilaterally established a nine-mile "privacy fence" beyond the three-mile limit. In 1970, an amendment to the act combined the two zones into a twelve-mile territorial sea. The act also transformed the Gulf of St. Lawrence into an exclusive Canadian fishing zone. These unilateral moves upset Canada's international trading partners, including the United States, who wanted to preserve the freedom of the high seas for their distant-water fishing fleets.

While the Americans complained about Canada's privatization of her coastal waters, Washington was under mounting pressure at home to do the same thing. Although American coastal states such as California had pushed the U.S. Congress for jurisdiction over near-shore waters for years, both the Nixon and Ford administrations had resisted. They wanted to protect the legal position of America's long-distance fishing fleet and weren't anxious to set a precedent that would lead to successful prosecutions of U.S. vessels fishing in international waters. In the end, though, American legislators had to bow to international trends in law of the sea.

As the competition for fish increased, it was inevitable that individual countries would move to protect their own stocks. With the Americans and the Mexicans moving unilaterally to an extended fisheries jurisdiction, Canada could wait no longer. On June 4, 1976, Canada's minister for external affairs announced in the House of Commons that Canada too would unilaterally establish a 200-mile Exclusive Economic Zone (EEZ) off our coasts as of January 1, 1977. The next day, the *Globe and Mail* quoted the minister as saying that the poor state of fish stocks and the future of our coastal communities "made this action imperative."

The announcement was met with euphoria in Atlantic Canada. Newfoundland's minister of fisheries, Walter Carter, was ecstatic. He told the *Globe* that he believed the stocks could be rebuilt and that Newfoundland fishermen would cooperate, even if quotas had to be temporarily slashed in the rebuilding phase.

Just as the new zone was being declared, there was a boom in the Newfoundland fishery. Cod landings were the highest they had been in five years and prices skyrocketed. The jubilation in Atlantic Canada ignored some stubborn facts. Even with reduced fishing by the foreign fleets, there was still serious domestic overcapacity. Yet, instead of reducing or freezing the size of our fishing effort, the federal government permitted further expansion.

Ironically, it was foreign fishing nations that first benefited from Canada's 200-mile zone. Since 95 per cent of Canadian fishing boats were not large enough to operate in the new EEZ, joint ventures were set up with foreign fishing nations such as West Germany. Under the terms of these deals, a German factory-freezer trawler would contract to take 600 tonnes of frozen cod blocks to a Canadian processor in Newfoundland, and in return, kept 300 tonnes for its home market.

In October 1978, a new fisheries organization was created to replace ICNAF: the Northwest Atlantic Fisheries Organization (NAFO). Fisheries regulations on the Nose and Tail of the Grand Banks, as well as the Flemish Cap, would be the responsibility of NAFO, which started to function on January 1, 1979.

It wasn't long before conservation became NAFO's most pressing problem. Until the fish shortages of the early 1970s, the foreign fleets were not interested in pelagic fish (which live near the surface of the water) such as caplin, because it was a "low-value species." But the fish-hungry Soviet fleet discovered that caplin had great value as the raw material for fish meal. No one stopped to consider that caplin was also the favourite food of cod. Even though every fishermen in rubber boots, including the captains of the factory-freezer trawlers, knew that the entire inshore fishery was based on the cod following the caplin into shallow water every spring, Canada gave the U.S.S.R. a 266,320-tonne quota of offshore spawning caplin in 1978.

It was a disastrous mistake that showed how little we knew, or cared, about ocean ecology. The small silver fish, which looks like a freshwater smelt, spawns at the southeast shoals on the edge of the Grand Banks, although most spawning occurs on or near pebbly beaches. Word that the caplin are running was a welcome sign of spring in Newfoundland. Outports celebrated the arrival of the "caplin scull" with "scoffs" and parties, knowing that the cod would soon be following their favourite food inshore. The caplin massed just off the island's rocky beaches, where they could be scooped up in buckets for local frying pans. Marine biologists believed that the inshore and offshore caplin were two separate stocks, but no one really knew for sure. As the offshore catches increased (300,000 tonnes were caught in 1974 alone), outport fishermen observed that the caplin weren't coming ashore in nearly the same numbers.

The Russians waited anxiously for the run of Canadian caplin in 1978. Their own government had severely restricted the caplin catch in Soviet waters, closing it altogether in some places, because the stock had collapsed from overfishing. Canada's largesse must have seemed puzzling. Everyone knew that if you fished caplin too heavily, the cod would eventually begin to starve and cannibalize each other, just as they had in the Barents Sea. With their own waters fished out, the Soviets sent forty fishing vessels to the north-west Atlantic, twenty-five of them to the Newfoundland zone. But in 1978, Nature had the last, grim laugh. With the Russians, Japanese, and Norwegians all poised to snatch their quota of Canadian caplin, the magical silver fish failed to appear in either the inshore or offshore. After just three years of aggressive overfishing, the crucial caplin stocks had all but disappeared.

Outraged at the collapse of this crucially important fish, the *Daily News* in St. John's called for a ban on all foreign fishing of caplin. Fishery Products Ltd. was opposed to the idea because it had shore-based caplin reduction plants, which were being supplied with fish by vessels from Iceland, as part of a joint venture. The company appealed to the industry's standard stalling tactic to protect its investment – a call for more research. One scientist who was consulted by the companies reassured people that fluctuations in the caplin stock were normal and blamed cold water for delaying that year's spawning season. But by mid-summer, when the caplin still had not appeared, even the president of Fishery Products Ltd. realized with a shudder that the stock had been wiped out.

Arthur May, then director of resource management for Fisheries Canada, the precursor to the DFO, demanded to know what the foreign trawlers just outside the 200-mile zone were doing while they waited for the caplin. ICNAF had died and, as NAFO had not yet come into effect, there were no international controls on fishing on the high seas. What was happening was an outdoor abattoir operation without limits. The foreign fleets were taking as much fish as they could to fill their holds, but the pickings were getting slim. Underutilized species such as scad and blue whiting, once considered junk fish for fish meal, were now taken for the table in an experimental fishery by the British. Consumers ultimately rejected them because of their dark flesh.

Although northern cod in the 2J3KL zone was the worst casualty of overfishing in the 1970s, it was by no means the only one. The crisis was nearly as deep on the southern Grand Banks in the NAFO area known as 3NO. During the twenty years it had been exploited prior to 1977, the cod stock in the area had been ravaged by Spanish pair trawlers. In the mid-sixties, the harvest had exceeded 220,000 tonnes; by 1977, it was reduced to just 17,600 tonnes.

What was left of the stock did not move inshore, but migrated to the Tail of the Banks outside the new 200-mile zone. In 1979, Canada announced that only two Spanish pair trawlers would be allowed inside the 200-mile zone. Nevertheless, nearly all the Spanish pairs showed up in 1980 planning to fish the Flemish Cap and other international fishing grounds with straddling stocks. Canada ordered them off on the basis that Spain was not a member of NAFO, threatening to force the vessels into St. John's for inspections. The southern Banks cod stock was in such terrible shape that NAFO decided that a moratorium on cod was necessary for the 1980 season.

As an non-NAFO member, Spain promptly announced that she wouldn't recognize the moratorium and continued fishing outside Canada's 200-mile zone. Only when Ottawa threatened to ban all Spanish trawlers from Atlantic Canadian ports did the vessels withdraw. Overnight, trawlers flying the flags of non-NAFO, South American countries, began to hunt the endangered 3NO cod just outside the 200-mile zone. These vessels bore an uncanny resemblance to the Spanish trawlers that had just retreated from the Banks. Under existing international law, there was nothing Ottawa could do about these flag-of-convenience fish pirates, or so the bureaucrats who ran the show at the DFO believed.

Canada's fisheries policy was a nightmare from which the country was having difficulty awakening. In the two decades before Ottawa established the 200-mile limit, Canadian fleets had taken only a small portion of 3NO cod, most of it as by-catch. The largest share was taken by Spain. Concerned about just how much fish was being wasted by the Spanish, the fisheries department chartered a pair of Spanish trawlers and went fishing. To everyone's horror, it was discovered that over 45 per cent of the total catch was flounder – all of it was dumped.

A tragedy was in the making on the Grand Banks. By 1981, not even the most selfish politician or malleable mandarin could deny it. The East Coast fishery needed to be rescued.

Ottawa sent a mathematician with a puckish smile and a flair for political fixing to do the job. Had Michael Kirby, whose roots were in Newfoundland, understood the problem that awaited him, he might have stuck to simpler matters like patriating the constitution.

4

THE CHEQUEBOOK MESSIAH

The job of the government task force created on January 8, 1982, by Prime Minister Pierre Trudeau was to recommend "how to achieve and maintain a viable Atlantic fishing industry, with due consideration for the overall economic and social development of the Atlantic provinces." In other words, Michael Kirby, Trudeau's youthful secretary to the cabinet on federal–provincial relations, and the deputy clerk of the Privy Council, was being asked the familiar question about the East Coast fishery: could we have our fish and eat them too?

Whatever the answer, it was clear that the status quo couldn't continue. Even before the Newfoundland fishery crisis of the early 1980s, government expenditures on the bloated industry were already out of control. The federal government spent just under $106 million in Newfoundland in 1980–81, the province another $19 million, a pretty penny for just one of five provinces involved in the Atlantic fishery. During the 1980s, an estimated $8 billion of government money would be spent on the Atlantic fishery, roughly half of it on unemployment insurance. The industry was a basket-case looking for a psychiatrist, and in the journal *Marine Policy* William E. Shrank offered the diagnosis that set out Kirby's task: "Perhaps the fundamental administrative problem is that the Department of Fisheries and Oceans (DFO) has suffered from policy schizophrenia, never being able to determine whether its chief goal is to set and implement policy for the fishery as a viable industry or whether it is to maximize employment and save non-viable rural communities."

Kirby wasn't the only one to feel the social pressures to retain the overcapacity in the industry in the name of preserving hundreds of small communities established by the cod fishery centuries ago. Everyone on the task force knew that these communities would fight tooth and nail to keep their boats afloat, their plants open, and to force Ottawa to keep the benefits flowing.

The subsidies had been enormous in a business infamous for its violent ups and downs. Although 1973, for example, had been one of the most profitable years ever for the East Coast fishery, the very next year, all of Atlantic Canada's major fishing companies were facing bankruptcy. The federal government had to provide $170 million in emergency aid to keep the industry from collapsing. The large fishing companies processed fish bought from independent inshore fishermen as well as that fish caught offshore by their own trawlers.

The policy that Michael Kirby was asked to reconsider had been created by Roméo LeBlanc, Trudeau's political godfather. In 1974 LeBlanc had set out his key policies for one of the government's most difficult portfolios: control of the resource through the establishment of a 200-mile limit; higher incomes for fishermen; conservation in the new economic zone to rebuild stocks; and more government say in how the industry was managed. LeBlanc cautioned against over-expansion in the fishery, pointing to quality improvements and a coordinated marketing effort as the ways to get a greater return on the resource. The New Brunswick politician was clearly biased in favour of inshore fishermen, knowing as he did from his own constituents that they couldn't travel as far to fish as the offshore fleets and that their communities would disappear if the deep-sea trawlers took the bulk of each year's quota.

Ignoring LeBlanc's wise words about conservation, both the provinces and the large companies pushed for massive expansion of the fleet and the processing sector from 1976 to 1980. They aggressively pursued foreign investment, factory-freezers, and more wet-fish trawlers to cash in on the expected bonanza of priority access inside the new 200-mile limit. Both Nova Scotia and Newfoundland cranked up public relations campaigns that urged large-scale fleet development. A worried LeBlanc noted that the industry stakeholders wanted to spend $900 million on new, ice-strengthened fishing vessels – a staggering figure that was three times the landed value of Canada's entire fishery. Idle shipyards may have welcomed the work, but in Ottawa's view, the last thing the industry needed was more capacity.

LeBlanc resisted the industry's political pressure and continued to oppose fleet expansion. But the juggernaut was gathering momentum. When the new 200-mile zone finally came into effect in 1977, both H. B. Nickerson and National Sea Products, which owned both processing plants and their own trawlers, used newspaper ads to push for immediate expansion of the offshore fleets. The Halifax *Chronicle-Herald* supported the two Nova Scotian companies with editorials that stirred up the gold-rush mentality that was taking hold in the industry. The foreigners were finally gone and now it was Canada's turn to reap the benefits.

In speech after speech, LeBlanc insisted that the best way to develop the industry was to increase the supply of fish through prudent conservation policies. After all, why would anyone want to build huge new killing capacity in the form of factory-freezers and modern stern trawlers, when the existing, subsidized fleets were unable to make a profit?

Ottawa was growing alarmed at the amount of public money that was being poured into the fishery without bringing lasting improvement either to the lives of ordinary fishermen or to the balance sheets of the big companies. Although fishermen's incomes increased modestly between 1974 and 1978, they were still well below the Canadian average. During the same period, the federal government had authorized a total of $205 million in "special assistance" to the fishing industry, in addition to the already massive public spending through regular programs. Roméo LeBlanc told the Fisheries Council of Canada (FCC), "If money talks, it has long shouted out the federal commitment to fisheries."

The battery of special aid packages was so rich that it frequently brought the total federal expenditures for the industry within range of the landed value of the entire Canadian fishery, turning the industry into a vast zero-sum game. Millions of extra dollars were needed in 1976, for example, when LeBlanc and his Liberal colleagues extended the period in which Atlantic fishermen could collect benefits in areas of particularly high unemployment.

Despite LeBlanc's interest in conservation, his guiding principle was very different from the traditional departmental goal of stock management to protect the fish. He wanted to use the federal government's power to end instability and low wages in the troubled industry and tip the scales in favour of the small fisherman. In the end, his very compassion added to the problem by allowing more boats in the water at a time when stocks were declining. Although Ottawa froze entry into the offshore sector in 1975 (the big companies could only build replacement vessels to keep their fleets at existing strength), it was a "warm" freeze for the inshore sector, where hundreds of news licences were issued. When the freeze on groundfish licences finally came in 1978, it didn't apply to long-liners, trap boats, or smaller vessels. In 1979, an election year, the "freeze" was liberally relaxed.

Fleet expansion wasn't the only issue that had LeBlanc and the big fish companies banging heads. The minister was unenthusiastic about so-called joint ventures with foreign companies. The problem was that Canada didn't have enough vessels that could get through the ice to fish the distant sectors of the 200-mile zone, where the foreign fleets had been fishing for years. But that didn't stop LeBlanc from telling a Dalhousie University audience in Halifax that "Canadian fish, wherever possible, should be caught by Canadian fishermen." He was suspicious of Canadian companies entering into what he called "cosy deals" with foreign companies, which would get control of the fish supply in return for cheap working capital. If that happened, the main purpose of declaring a 200-mile limit would be nullified. (Ironically, it was LeBlanc's decision to keep the foreigners out of Canada's 200-mile zone that led distant-water fleets to overfish migratory stocks on the Nose and Tail of the Grand Banks and the Flemish Cap.)

LeBlanc was equally firm with the provinces. Like warlords guarding their turf, the provinces were noisily laying claim to the fish off their respective shores. LeBlanc insisted that fish stocks were a national asset and that there must be a national policy to manage them. The management goals would be larger than the issues of corporate gain or provincial boundaries, because fish were a common property resource. Some stocks, such as the Atlantic salmon, migrated through the waters of five provinces. If the federal government handed those five provinces knives to divide up the fisheries in the Gulf of St. Lawrence, the minister said, "I am afraid the knives might end up in each other."

LeBlanc never missed a chance to emphasize that extending offshore control to two hundred miles didn't mean that there would be a new race for the riches among Canadian provinces. The total allowable catch had to go down and stay down for a number of years if stocks were to improve. Properly understood, January 1, 1977, would not be the first day of a gigantic fishing derby, but a day to mark the end of the overfishing binge that had driven stocks to their lowest point in thirty years.

Despite his many insights into the fishery, Roméo LeBlanc's bias toward the inshore sector angered other industry stakeholders. The minister wanted "a decent life" for fishermen, which he thought they could realize if they had a say in the price they received for their fish. To the dismay of processors, LeBlanc not only urged fishermen to organize, but also offered them the expertise of his departmental officials and provided arm's-length funding for the Atlantic region's Eastern Fishermen's Federation. As he told an Antigonish audience in July 1978, he would have failed in his mandate if, by the time he left the fisheries portfolio, there were still groups of fishermen who felt intimidated by plant owners, bureaucrats, or, for that matter, federal ministers like himself.

LeBlanc made it clear that the government had proclaimed the 200-mile limit principally for the benefit of the inshore. The key to the success of the industry was to make sure that the inshore got a greater and more reliable share of the overall resource. "No one wants to add the 200-mile zone to the list of broken hopes," LeBlanc told an FCC audience in May 1978. To ensure the health of the Canadian fishery there would have to be more government involvement than with other industries because, he said, "a common property resource will never take care of itself."

In the winter of 1974–75, the federal fisheries department had examined the chronically troubled fishing industry. The results were published in 1976 as "Policy for Canada's Commercial Fisheries." The report concluded that instability and low incomes, which characterized the industry, actually preceded the twenty years of foreign overfishing that had damaged fish stocks. No one was surprised when the inquiry concluded that the entire East Coast fishery was a "crippled, uncoordinated giant."

LeBlanc did his best to restore the giant to health. One of his lasting contributions was the promotion of a joint effort in marketing. In 1975, he told the FCC, "Get rid of the idea of fish being cheap raw material, and of the idea that you can make up marketing loss by transferring it back to the primary level [the fishermen]." His formula for success was simple: a high-quality product at a price people could afford, with a coordinated marketing effort to encourage the industry to develop new products.

LeBlanc had put his finger on a sore spot. For decades, Canadian fishermen had concentrated on traditional stocks and ignored other species such as silver hake, which the Russians were catching like there was no tomorrow. (Fishing silver hake requires a freezer trawler, since the catch spoils quickly.) European fishermen boxed and iced herring and sold it for as much as $300 a tonne: their Canadian counterparts sold the same species for fish meal at

$30 a tonne. As LeBlanc pointed out, the value of the Newfound-land inshore catch could be substantially raised without catching a single extra cod, simply by improving the quality of the product.

LeBlanc was ready to put taxpayers' money where his mouth was. In a series of meetings between government and representatives of the inshore in 1977, fishermen recommended a refrigerated container system that would speed the delivery of fish from the ocean to the market. The federal government coughed up half of the cost of ice-making equipment to cut spoilage losses, which amounted to a staggering $25 million a year.

Rather than have the owner of every small processing company make an annual pilgrimage to see buyers, LeBlanc encouraged them to mount a joint marketing effort. After all, Canada's major fishing competitors, Norway, Iceland, and Poland, competed against other nations in the marketplace, not each other. In 1978, fifty eastern companies formed the Canadian Association of Fish Exporters (CAFE) to share market intelligence and promotion.

But for all of LeBlanc's enlightened policies, by the early 1980s, the giant was once again crippled and more uncoordinated than ever.

The latest crisis in the Atlantic fishery began with a new round of corporate begging. In November 1981, two of the four major processing companies on the East Coast came to the federal government asking for money. Most of the trawler-based processing sector was in trouble, and some of the firms would not survive without refinancing. "If they were forced out of business, the effect on fishermen, plant workers, communities, indeed the Atlantic economy, would be devastating," one federal official said. Ottawa decided it would have to put new equity into the firms to avoid laying economic waste to an entire region of the country.

Twice before, in 1968 and again in 1974, the federal government had provided substantial assistance to the processing companies. This time, rather than fund another short-term bailout, Ottawa wanted a long-term solution. Prime Minister Trudeau set up an ad hoc cabinet committee, which in 1982 created the Task Force on

Atlantic Fisheries to study the problems of the fishing industry and to come up with permanent solutions. Michael Kirby was at its helm.

The first part of Kirby's mandate was to advise the government on the policies it should implement to establish a healthy fishery in the future. The task force was also to recommend how best to deal with specific requests for financial help from The Lake Group of St. John's, Newfoundland, and H. B. Nickerson & Sons Ltd. of North Sydney, Nova Scotia. By November 1982, Fishery Products Ltd. of St. John's also had its hand out for federal assistance. Kirby was told that any decision on financial assistance had to be consistent with the long-term policy solutions he proposed. While the task force received submissions from ninety groups and individuals and held about 135 meetings in forty-three different fishing communities, a series of intricate negotiations between the companies, the Bank of Nova Scotia, the provincial governments involved, and the federal government went on behind closed doors.

The task force operated by conducting detailed studies of three major areas of concern: fishermen's incomes on the East Coast; a revenue and cost survey of the groundfish processing plants in the Atlantic region; and an analysis of potential world markets for Canadian fish. The three studies were the most extensive of their kind ever carried out on the Atlantic fishery and established a solid fact-base without parallel in an industry that has literally been studied to death.

Kirby quickly took the measure of the way things were. Newfoundland and Nova Scotia were the two major groundfish harvesting provinces. In 1981, 779,000 tonnes of groundfish were landed in the Atlantic region. This was processed into 270,000 tonnes of product worth $705 million. (About 35 to 40 per cent of a fish is flesh, the rest is skin, bone, and offal.) Approximately 60 per cent of the catch was either frozen as fillets or in blocks to be cut into fish sticks. About 25 per cent of the catch was salt cod sold to Spain, Portugal, the Caribbean, and South America. Only 10 per cent of the Canadian catch was sold as fresh fillets, and the rest was trucked to New England as gutted, whole, fresh fish. Canadians themselves ate only about 20 per cent of their own fish and the rest was exported, 57 per cent of it to the United States.

Kirby found that the number of licensed fishermen in the Atlantic region had risen from 36,500 in 1974 to about 53,000 in 1981, an increase of 45 per cent. The processing sector had increased its freezing capacity by two and a half times during the same period. It was clear to the task force that the expansion in plant capacity and in the numbers of fishermen, based on the expectation of increased catches after 1977, was dangerously excessive.

Kirby was also struck by the "us versus them" mentality in the fishery, a collision of interests that boiled down to a competition for fish allocations among the provinces, and also between the inshore and offshore fleets. Typically, the deep-sea sector wanted a year-round supply of fish in order to keep processing plants at work full-time. Larger allocations to the seasonal, inshore fishermen stymied the trawler-owners' interest.

The big companies also argued that trawlers were necessary to exploit the offshore stocks of redfish and flounder that could never be harvested in commercial numbers by inshore technology. It would be foolish, the big companies argued, to give more fish to the inefficient inshore at a time when Canada's major competitor, Iceland, was also turning to trawlers.

Kirby was keenly interested in the employment figures and found that over 62,000 jobs were located in 1,339 small communities that were totally dependent on the fishery. In 1981, 48,434 personal commercial fishing licences were issued in the Atlantic region, but only about half of them went to full-time fishermen. The task force concluded that there were about 27,800 bona fide fishermen in the Maritimes who actually used their licences in 1981. On average, after expenses were deducted, the full-time fisherman earned about $12,000 – the rural poverty line in 1981 for a household of four. The problem was clear. These bona fide fishermen were sharing the harvest with too many marginal fishermen.

The task force found wide variations in income, with the highest incomes in southwest Nova Scotia and western New Brunswick, the lowest in Newfoundland and Labrador. In southwest Nova Scotia, UI payments made up only 6 per cent of the total income for full-time fishermen; in Newfoundland, that number was 33 per cent. Fishermen were not making enough to pay down their boat loans, and between 1977 and 1982, their indebtedness to fisheries loan boards increased by 400 per cent.

Matters were not much better for plant workers. The Kirby task force concluded that the processing sector created as many jobs and almost as much income as fishing itself. But in 1981 the average income of a fish-plant worker was about $4,500. In the processing sector, costs were rising more rapidly than revenues, consumers couldn't afford expensive fish, and runaway inflation and interest rates greatly increased the cost of doing business. For the hundreds of plants that operated for six months or less each year, costs had skyrocketed 30 per cent. Roméo LeBlanc's prophecy had come to pass. The surge of investment in anticipation of a bonanza from the new 200-mile limit had brought on an industry-wide disaster.

The entire processing sector suffered from the cycle of feast or famine. All of the plants were needed in the summer months to deal with the glut of fish from the inshore fleet during its peak season. But for the rest of the year, there was not enough fish to keep all of them operating. Despite the state of the stocks, a year-round, uniform supply of fish was still believed to be the most effective way to deal with excess capacity in the processing sector.

Ottawa was expected to make turkeys fly. Regardless of how inefficient an operation might be, it was always a major political issue to close a plant in places where there was no alternative employment. Weak businesses were routinely saved from what would be a normal bankruptcy in any other industry. Subsidies were paid to open new plants and paid again whenever over-expansion threatened to close them. There was 50 per cent overcapacity in frozen-fish plants in Newfoundland, 45 per cent in the Maritimes, and 65 per cent in Quebec. "Please consider carefully the wisdom of rapid expansion," LeBlanc cautioned in 1978.

No one listened, and it was difficult for Ottawa to control the situation by itself. In 1979, the Department of Regional Economic Expansion (DREE) refused to finance a new plant in Jackson's Arm, Newfoundland, on the grounds that there was already a DREE-funded plant in the same community. According to the DFO, there was not enough fish to warrant a second plant. It was built anyway, with a licence from the Newfoundland government and financing from the Royal Bank. The second plant operated at 12 per cent capacity in 1980, and at 28 per cent in 1981, before closing that same year.

For all its problems, Canada was the world's biggest exporter of seafood, with about 80 per cent of its fish shipped to foreign markets. In 1981, the U.S.A. took 52 per cent, Europe and Japan 10 per cent each by value of the Canadian catch. Iceland specialized in selling to the expensive "white tablecloth" market and franchised restaurants such as Long John Silver, which were willing to pay more for high quality fish and a guaranteed daily supply. The tiny country captured 75 per cent of the top-quality frozen-fish market in the U.S.A., fetching cod prices that were 15 to 30 per cent higher than the average price for Canadian fillets. Less than 20 per cent of Atlantic Canada's fish made it to the top-quality markets that paid the highest prices. Canada's place in the American market was the middle-quality, moderately priced product. When fish prices went up, Canada's customers switched to chicken or cheaper fish such as South American hake or Alaskan pollock.

In his public pronouncements, Kirby said that he wanted to foster an Atlantic fishing industry that was economically viable at least to the extent that it would be able to survive downturns with a normal rate of business failures and without further government bailouts. He wanted an industry that was labour-intensive, but there was a crucial qualifier that signalled the direction in which our national fisheries policy was headed: "Employment in the Atlantic fishing industry should be maximized subject to the constraint that those employed receive a reasonable income as a result of fishery-related activities, including fishery-related income transfer payments."

Kirby suggested a program for income supplements that would eventually replace UI in areas where the inshore fishing season was short. His idea was to reward improved fishing practices with a bonus system. For delivering better quality fish, fishermen could earn cash credits to be collected in the off-season, a plan that squared with Roméo LeBlanc's desire to raise incomes in the inshore sector while improving the industry's competitiveness abroad.

Almost everyone Kirby consulted urged changes to the existing unemployment insurance regulations for fishermen, so that benefits would be calculated on the best ten weeks of fishing, rather than the last ten weeks. The existing regulations had discouraged fishing in the later, off-peak season when catches declined. This had hurt fish-plant workers, who had nothing to process when the men stopped fishing after the peak season. Kirby also suggested that fishermen who worked exclusively during the winter season be allowed to qualify for benefits. Offsetting this new group of qualifiers, he recommended removing benefits from the scourge of the industry, those who fished for less than six weeks and then drew unemployment for the maximum period the law allowed.

In the drive for higher quality Canadian fish, Kirby recommended both dockside and final-product grading. He wanted mandatory bleeding, gutting, washing, and icing of the catch at sea, and the use of hook and line gear, which produced a better quality catch than nets or traps. This government initiative would be backed up by an education program for fishermen and plant workers promoting the benefits of producing a higher quality product. If all these things were done, Kirby observed, grades and labelling could be used as selling tools to break into new markets.

"From the very beginning of the industry in Canada," Kirby wrote, "fish products have often been considered as commodities to be produced rather than goods to be consumed, as a source of livelihood and not as a delicate and perishable food on a distant table." The Newfoundland practice of "forking" fish when unloading a vessel was unacceptable, Kirby said. Now that choice cod fillets cost more than prime cuts of beef, consumers wouldn't accept damaged product.

But quality could not be increased by imposing higher standards on fishermen alone. Kirby also recommended the licensing of fish exporters. Under Kirby's proposal, the minister could pull the licence of any plant that violated quality regulations. Processors had repeatedly emphasized the need for improved quality of fish, but were generally opposed to licensing exporters and final-product quality labels. They blamed poor quality on the fishermen, yet 40 per cent of the cod blocks rejected by large American buyers had left the plant with bones still in the fish.

There were also severe problems at the administrative level of the industry. Competing interests made consultation and decision-making extremely difficult. The DFO itself was sometimes seen as "secretive and arbitrary," making its binding decisions without adequate advice from fishermen and processors. Provincial governments felt that Ottawa treated them like glorified interest groups, not fundamentally different from offshore companies or inshore fishermen. Kirby recommended more efficient and less expensive consultation among the industry's stakeholders to develop policy and resolve conflicts. He also thought that scientific material should be interpreted for the public, and that fish biologists and fishermen should have formal contact.

If the first objective of Ottawa's brave new fisheries policy was an economically viable industry, the second was maximized employment based on a reasonable income for fishermen and plant workers. When you cut through the rhetoric, that meant that the number of people employed in the fishery should decline over time. Kirby believed that the institution of "quota licences" would gradually reduce the number of fishermen, who would sell their licences when they left the fishery or retired. The task force also acknowledged that some of the least efficient fish plants would have to close, which would further reduce the number of people employed in the fishery. While downsizing would not be without pain, the incomes of those who remained in the industry would go up. Although Kirby talked about the need for downsizing, nowhere in his exhaustive report, released in December 1982, did he ever mention the optimum number of fishermen or plant workers in Atlantic Canada. In government reports as in all things, he who tells too much truth hangs himself.

The third objective of the task force, Canadianization of the industry, would depend on how successful the stakeholders were in attracting new investment from government and the private sector. To make the industry more appealing, Ottawa would have to resist the temptation of gaining access to foreign markets for manufactured goods by trading allocations of fish within our 200-mile zone, a practice many fishermen believed had wiped out the once rich Newfoundland squid fishery.

The degree of mistrust and downright animosity between fishermen, processors, and the provincial and federal governments made cooperation almost impossible. The federal government blamed excess capacity in the processing sector on greedy plant operators and provincial governments that licensed and financed more and more plants with cheap loans in order to extort more of the overall quota. The provinces blamed Ottawa for the same problem, insisting that they could do a much better job of setting quotas if only the federal government would surrender, or at least share, jurisdiction over harvesting policies. The fishermen blamed government for not understanding their difficult occupation and processors who never paid enough for their catch. As one insider said, "Everyone was so busy blaming everyone else that they forgot to look in the mirror."

Instead of easing suspicions between the governments involved in the rescue of Atlantic Canada's deep-sea fishery, the Kirby task force exacerbated them. Newfoundland premier Brian Peckford was extremely proprietary about the northern cod stock, which he claimed was of far greater, long-term significance than the exciting Hibernia oil find on the Grand Banks. Peckford wanted inshore fishermen and processing plants on the east coast of New-foundland to have first call on stocks in 2J3KL, the richest NAFO sector of them all. Other Canadian trawlers should fall in behind Newfoundland-based trawler fleets, as the fishermen with the least claim to the resource. Although Peckford's idea of how to appor-tion northern cod was a big political hit in Newfoundland, it was a provocation to out-of-province trawler owners, who had been repeatedly told by Roméo LeBlanc that Canada's fish stocks were a national resource.

When he realized that Ottawa was contemplating a serious downsizing of the Newfoundland processing sector, Peckford began attacking Kirby's "raw economics" approach to restructuring the industry and insisted on an "all plants open" policy. Without such an assurance from Ottawa, the province whose industry was being saved would not cooperate in the rescue.

Despite pressure from St. John's, Kirby continued to champion a new deep-sea fishery that would be self-sufficient and viable in the long term. But the foxy bureaucrat would not go so far as to say that plants had to close. Instead, he suggested that if the closure of an uneconomic fish plant meant the death of a community, then governments, not the new fish companies, should pay to keep the plant afloat.

Having deftly hit the ball back into Peckford's court, Ottawa decided to go it alone. In a surprise press conference, the federal government announced that it would unilaterally restructure Newfoundland's bankrupt fish processors without the support of the provincial government. Pierre De Bané, the new fisheries min-ister, told a shocked Memorial Day gathering of journalists in St. John's in 1983 that Ottawa would kick in $75 million to create a single new company out of the assets of three financially troubled Newfoundland firms: Fishery Products Ltd., the Lake Group, and John Penny and Sons Ltd. All creditors would be paid in full and the new company, Fishery Products International, would become the second-largest fish processor in the world. All told, it would operate fifteen plants in Newfoundland and employ 16,000 people. Ottawa would be the majority shareholder, with the Bank of Nova Scotia, the Canada Development Corporation (CDC), and private interests taking a minority position.

The standard political grousing accompanied the shocking news. De Bané accused Premier Peckford of making a "totally false statement" when he publicly suggested that Ottawa planned to close six deep-sea trawler plants on Newfoundland's south coast. But Newfoundland fisheries minister Jim Morgan had indeed signed a deal with Ottawa on May 17, 1983, agreeing to merge certain inefficient operations at Burin and Grand Bank with other plants at Marystown and Fortune and to permanently close another operation in St. Lawrence.

Roasted by Peckford for his momentary political lapse, Morgan hotly denied agreeing to the closure of the Grand Bank or Burin plants, referring to Ottawa's claim as "rubbish and hogwash." Even though Ottawa was armed with a study showing that Newfoundland's new fish company would lose $50 million over five years if it ran the two aging plants at Burin and Grand Bank, Peckford overruled his own minister's memorandum of understanding with Kirby. In Newfoundland, you never lost many votes when politics triumphed over unpleasant financial reality.

The assets of Fishery Products Ltd. were purchased in October 1983 from the CDC. The new fish company would be owned 60 per cent by Ottawa, 25 per cent by Newfoundland, and 15 per cent by the Bank of Nova Scotia. Talks with the CDC had been like white-collar guerrilla warfare at times, degenerating at one point into mutual lawsuits. Purchase of the company was made possible only when the Bank of Nova Scotia called Fishery Product's huge and unpayable loan. Michael Kirby knew how to play hardball.

Negotiations had been equally sticky with the Bank of Nova Scotia, which at one point wanted $70 million more for its help in restructuring the Atlantic fishery than Ottawa was willing to pay. Throughout the difficult negotiations, the bank believed it could get more out of bankrupting the companies than saving them.

George Hitchman, the man charged with putting the bank's horrendous fisheries account in order, commented to federal negotiators about the financial gulf between them: "It's too much to flip for, boys."

In the end, no other private investors could be found to invest in the bail-out, and government and the bank became buyers of last resort. In a single week, $145 million of federal revenues were expended to bail out the largest industry on the East Coast: $75 million in Newfoundland and $70 million in Nova Scotia. The provinces kicked in $60 million in non-cash help by converting previously held debt to equity in the new firms. The Bank of Nova Scotia kicked in $100 million, including the conversion of $44.1 million of old debt to equity in the new companies.

In Nova Scotia, two major fish companies, Nickerson and National Sea, were also in trouble. De Bané and his shell-shocked officials negotiated a merger of the two giants into the largest fish company in the world. De Bané would later say that restructuring this sector of the fishery, with its two years of political infighting, corporate intrigue, and often brutal backroom negotiations, was the hardest thing he had ever done in politics. The man who had cut the deal, Michael Kirby, agreed that rescuing the Atlantic fishery "was much more difficult than the constitutional stuff."

When Pierre De Bané released the Kirby Report, he trumpeted loud and clear the dread message that Brian Peckford hadn't wanted to hear: the era of the free lunch in the troubled industry was over. "The restructuring negotiations are aimed at putting the companies back on a healthy footing and the federal government is prepared to make a substantial contribution to ensure that this happens. But once this has been done, once the industry is economically viable again, we do not want the industry to rely on government handouts again, and again, and again. We believe that the potential viability of the industry is great enough that this can happen. And we believe that it should happen."

Michael Kirby summed up his essential analysis of the fishery:

there was no doubt that the industry was in "deep trouble." He went on to blame the 1982 crisis in the Atlantic fishery on three things: the unbridled optimism that followed the 1977 declaration of the 200-mile limit, which led to over-extension by fishermen and processors just when the general economy went into recession; resistance to change in a tradition-bound industry, where custom often superseded sound business practice; and mediocre fish quality and plant management made worse by poor product marketing. Kirby also cited the political malaise over the fishery, where constant bickering between the governments and the stakeholders produced a climate that "inhibits change, shelters the less efficient, and leads participants to pick sides and fight for turf."

Turning the corner in Atlantic Canada was not a cheap proposition. The estimated cost to the federal government of implementing the recommendations of the Kirby task force over the next five years was $198 million. The money would come in the form of $120 million in total annual operating expenditures for the big fish companies and another $78 million for capital grants. Twenty-eight million dollars would be set aside for generic promotion of Canadian fish products. Amendments to the UI program would cost $50 million over five years, and $11 million was earmarked for implementing dockside and final-product grading to improve the quality of fish. This funding did not include federal financial assistance to the processing sector, which was still being negotiated.

Kirby blamed all of the industry's stakeholders for failing to adapt to new conditions. "Everyone – fishermen, processors, and governments – has fallen into a rut of applying Band-Aid solutions to problems that require deep corrective surgery," he wrote. There had been three major crises in the industry in the past fifteen years. If the industry continued to go through periods of boom and bust, the result would be social chaos for the people of Atlantic Canada. Hundreds of scattered communities depended on the fishery for their very existence, but Kirby, like Pierre De Bané, made clear that the day of unrestricted federal subsidies was coming to a close. "Preserving jobs in those rural communities is of fundamental importance. . . . At the same time, we have to recognize that permanent, unlimited public subsidies are simply not available to preserve every job in every community that now depends on the fishery. Those communities cannot expect to be supported in perpetuity by the Canadian taxpayer; they need an economically viable industry to support them."

This was something that they had never had. In their study of the fish plants, the task force had uncovered "a puzzling and discouraging record of poor productivity which seems to have persisted for at least the last ten years." Kirby recommended that as a condition of federal financial assistance, every plant had to agree to a productivity improvement program. Keeping those plants supplied with fish was more complicated. The task force agreed that it had to figure out a way to spread the processing of the catch throughout the year, to supply resource-short plants, and finally, to increase plant efficiency by having them operate full-time. As difficult as all that might be, at least it seemed possible, given the growth in cod stocks projected by DFO scientists. The minister believed the northern cod stocks were being well managed, and the TAC was projected to be at least 380,000 tonnes by 1987.

Kirby understood that the fundamental problem in the harvesting sector of the East Coast fishery was rooted in the fact that the resource was a common property. Ecologist Garret Hardin described the "tragedy of the commons" in *Science* magazine in 1968: "Picture a pasture open to all. It is to be expected that each herdsman will try to keep as many cattle as possible on the commons. . . . The rational herdsman concludes that the only sensible course for him to pursue is to add another animal to his herd. And another, and another. . . . But this is the conclusion reached by each and every rational herdsman sharing a commons. Therein is the tragedy. Each man is locked into a system that compels him to increase his herd without limit – in a world that is limited. Ruin is the destination toward which all men rush, each pursuing his own best interest in a society that believes in the freedom of the commons. Freedom in a commons brings ruin to all."

Hardin's "ruin" was premised on the logic of greed rather than cooperation. Rational fishermen invested in bigger, more powerful boats in an effort to get more of the limited quota of fish before their competitors did. The ensuing free-for-all created more expensive fishing capacity for the same amount of quota, driving up costs just as incomes went down. As governments tried to administer the common property resource for the benefit of all, individual fishermen became ingenious at getting around regulations aimed at protecting the resource. When Ottawa placed restrictions on the length of vessels, hoping to limit their carrying capacity, wily fishermen built boats with wider beams. The same rugged individualism that prided itself on finding ways around government regulations was causing resource disasters all around the world.

For all its intelligence and breadth of analysis, the Kirby task force thought of everything in the troubled industry but the fish. Kirby's own words best capture the enormity of Ottawa's speculative blunder about the health of the northern cod stock: "Although the industry has many problems, a shortage of fish is not one of them. By 1987, the groundfish harvest should reach 1.1 million tonnes, an increase of about 370,000 over 1981. . . . Almost all the increase will be confined to one species – cod. And about 70 per cent of the growth in the harvest will take place off the northeast coast of Newfoundland and Labrador. . . . Northern cod constitutes the fastest growing stock of groundfish off Canada's east coast."

The mandarin had spoken. Now it was the turn of men whose knowledge of the fishery was gained at the stern of their boats to show the Ottawa establishment just how wrong it was.

5

BAD NEWS BEARERS

As the 1980s progressed, inshore fishermen could see with their own eyes that the cod stocks were not nearly as healthy as the DFO would have everyone believe. Much of the cod caught inshore was too small to process as salt fish, and older skippers recalled a time when the cod in their traps were twice as big.

By the fall of 1986, the newly formed Newfoundland Inshore Fisheries Association (NIFA) was so concerned about the condition of the northern cod stock that it funded an independent technical audit of the DFO's method of stock assessment. With the active cooperation of DFO personnel, three independent biologists from Memorial University in St. John's, Drs. Derek Keats, Don Steele, and John Green, reviewed the department's science. The Keats Report raised some alarming questions. The Memorial scientists concluded that the 1986 DFO stock assessment had seriously over-estimated the size of the northern cod stock. (The 1986 TAC was set at 266,000 tonnes.) The report also concluded that there was a connection between poor inshore catches and massive offshore landings – something inshore fishermen had been trying to tell dismissive federal bureaucrats for years.

Keats, Steele, and Green pointed out that the commercial catch-rates on trawlers, which Ottawa used to fine-tune DFO assessments, were misleading. Catch-rates could be excellent even when the stock was in decline, because the deep-sea fleet had simply improved its technology or was trawling more in concentrated schools of fish. But their warning didn't stop the Canadian Atlantic Fisheries Scientific Advisory Committee (CAFSAC), the organization that provided scientific advice to the DFO, from concluding that the northern cod stock was in fact growing. When the inshore fishery failed in 1986, CAFSAC blamed environmental factors – cold water temperatures and uneven caplin distribution – rather than its assessment of the stock.

CAFSAC had been established in 1977 as a forum for scientific debate and for the development of biological advice to the DFO for resource management. The steering committee was made up of a chairman; the directors of the science branches at headquarters and the Gulf, Scotia-Fundy, Newfoundland, and Quebec regions of the DFO; the chairpersons of seven subcommittees; a DFO economist; and four outside experts.

Nearly as startling as their findings was the fact that Keats and his colleagues had used the DFO's own data to arrive at their conclusions. If the three-month study was correct, inshore fishermen had been right all along, and the DFO was burying its collective head in the sand. The state of denial in Ottawa reached all the way to the top.

In 1995, former fisheries minister John Fraser admitted that he knew in 1985 "from anecdotal information that the size of the cod was coming down steadily." He called his people together and said, "We have got some kind of problem here." Some denied there was any trouble because the total tonnage of the catch was constant. Others talked about cold water. Fraser conceded, "There were signs which we did not act upon." Soon afterwards, Fraser was forced to resign over the "tainted tuna" scandal.

After reading the controversial Keats Report, federal fisheries minister Tom Siddon, who had taken over the portfolio, and his senior science director, William Doubleday, met with Keats in Ottawa. Keats says that science wasn't the main thing on the minister's mind. "The minister's team was more concerned with my age and formal credentials than with the facts, which were never addressed in the meeting we held with them." The Keats Report had met with derision from the senior DFO management group in Ottawa, and the alarming possibility that stocks were being severely overfished was officially, at least, ignored.

Concerns about conservation of fish stocks had led to the development of the concept of what is known as $F_{0.1}$. Under this arbitrary measure, two out of every ten fish in a cod stock are taken each year, leaving those that do not die from natural causes to spawn and grow. Canada adopted $F_{0.1}$ as its fisheries management standard when the 200-mile zone was declared in 1977.

Although DFO scientists had held to $F_{0.1}$ in setting quotas for northern cod, that would not bring about the intended conservation result if they had overestimated the size of the stock. Departmental scientists believed that the spawning biomass of northern cod would reach 1.2 million tonnes by 1985 (the low range for a projected recovery to 1.8 million tonnes after the devastation of foreign overfishing). They based TAC recommendations on that number, even though a 1986 study done by the DFO's own scientists, Rice and Evans, estimated that the spawning stock had only reached 0.5 million tonnes as late as 1984. It boiled down to a catastrophic possibility: Canada may have been harvesting northern cod at much higher fish mortality rates than federal scientists believed. Instead of taking 20 per cent of the available stock, fishermen may have been taking 40 per cent or even 60 per cent for several years running.

Spooked by poor catches in the inshore fishery, CAFSAC finally reviewed the management and status of the northern cod stock. Although they concluded that "catch levels advised have been higher than they should have been," the group of scientists took the paradoxical position that DFO's stock assessment of northern cod was nevertheless sound. Somewhere in the grey zone between the bureaucrats and the politicians, science had become politics, and the state of the northern cod was being viewed through rose-coloured glasses.

In October 1986, the DFO held meetings in St. John's to find out why inshore catch-rates had declined so dramatically since the beginning of the decade. A month after those meetings, Dr. George Winters, the head of the Pelagic Fish, Shellfish, and Marine Mammals division of the Newfoundland Region of the DFO, presented a paper with an exotic reference to Ottawa's stock assessment of the northern cod. The title of Winters's paper was "Aide memoire on 2J3KL assessment: Non Gratum Anus Rodentum?" Translated, the Latin subtitle said that the DFO's stock assessment "wasn't worth a rat's ass."

Winters was uneasy about the way the DFO had arrived at its estimates for northern cod. After looking at the department's report on 2J3KL cod, he wrote, "Not only is its train of thought inconsistent, but quite often there are no passengers on it." He argued that the department relied too heavily on catch-rates from commercial trawlers to fine-tune federal stock assessments. These could be viewed as showing that cod had actually increased in abundance more than threefold from the late 1970s! Winters saw things from a wider and more sinister perspective. He concluded that recent failures in the inshore fishery could be explained by heavy over-fishing of the northern cod stock offshore, based on bad scientific advice for prudent TAC levels.

Winters was one of the first people inside the DFO to suggest that the department's abundance estimates were dead wrong. His paper was never published as a DFO research document, and few people outside the department knew of its existence until 1997. Shortly after he submitted it, Winters' report, among others, was considered by CAFSAC at a meeting in St. John's on November 14, 1986.

CAFSAC's groundfish subcommittee, made up of senior DFO scientists, arrived at their stock assessments after studying various working papers presented to the group. Its steering committee then prepared advisory documents, which became the primary source of information for the Atlantic Groundfish Advisory Committee (AGAC). AGAC then made quota recommendations to senior managers in the DFO.

CAFSAC produced "Advisory Document 86/25," a document marked by striking internal inconsistencies. On the one hand, it projected that the biomass for northern cod would continue to increase after 1987, and that there was "no reason to suppose that the decline in inshore catch after 1982 reflected a decline in the overall stock biomass." Yet a page later, the same document notes, "In retrospect, the catch levels advised have been higher than they should have been." Although the stock had increased since the mid-1970s, "actual fishing mortalities have turned out to be higher than target levels."

It is a truism of fish management that stock analysis becomes more accurate the further back you go, because more information about each year-class of cod is drawn from fishing mortality rates. A graph in the CAFSAC report showed that the TAC for northern cod from 1977 to 1985 had been at least twice as high as it should have been if the goal was to allow 80 per cent of the fish to escape. The DFO had erroneously believed it was setting the TAC at the $F_{0.1}$ level. The CAFSAC document stated very clearly that there was tremendous uncertainty over the current estimates of abundance for northern cod and acknowledged that Ottawa had been seriously underestimating fishing mortality rates.

The document, published in early December 1986, left readers with the sense that something was terribly wrong with the northern cod fishery. But as with the Winters Report, few people knew the advisory document existed, including many of DFO's own scientists. Eighteen key stock assessment questions raised in the report were quietly shelved. Shortly after publication of "Advisory Document 86/25," the fall 1986 research survey results came in. They indicated a huge abundance of northern cod. Biologist Jeff Hutchings later said that DFO scientists should have acknowledged there was no biological means for the stock to have increased as much as the research survey suggest it had from 1985 to 1986. Instead, the DFO accepted the 1986 data at face value.

Twenty years earlier, Wilfred Templeman, a pioneer fish biologist, had warned in his ground-breaking work, "Marine Resources of Newfoundland," that dense schools of cod that gathered to spawn in the deep, warmer waters of the bank would decline under heavy fishing. They would concentrate in a smaller and smaller area and there would still be good offshore trawling in the winter and spring until the stock was greatly reduced. Catches might even go up with improved technology, as the stocks headed for oblivion. In Templeman's view, this was exactly what had happened to the once rich haddock stocks on the southern Grand Banks before they utterly disappeared.

The logs of commercial trawlers showed that their catch-rates for cod had been going up through the early 1980s, though the data from Ottawa's research surveys had shown a "flattening" or declining trend. In 1986, the commercial and survey data actually matched, persuading some DFO officials that results from the deep-sea fleet were a sound indicator of the stock's health. But there were still few fish inshore. Pressured by inshore fishermen's groups and a supportive media, Tom Siddon was finally forced to take action.

In August 1987, the minister appointed a commission to study the northern cod stock. Siddon selected five independent scientists with excellent reputations. Two were from Canada and two from England, including the renowned Dr. John Pope. The chairman was another star of the scientific community, Dr. Dayton "Lee" Alverson from Seattle, Washington. Since fishermen were concerned that the northern cod were not migrating inshore in traditional numbers, and even more ominous, that the fish that were showing up were small and deformed, Siddon wanted Alverson to verify the anecdotal evidence of fishermen, identify a cause, and recommend a solution.

On November 19, 1987, the Task Group on Newfoundland Inshore Fisheries (TGNIF) submitted its report to Tom Siddon.

Alverson and his colleagues reported that from the beginning of the offshore trawler fishery in the early 1950s, the inshore catch had steadily declined. In the 1920s, it had stood at 300,000 tonnes. By 1959, that number had nearly been cut in half, while the offshore catch reached 200,000 tonnes. In 1968, the offshore took 708,000 tonnes and the inshore just 101,000 tonnes. Six years later, the off-shore catch had been reduced to 337,000 tonnes, while inshore landings dwindled to a meagre 35,000 tonnes.

In Alverson's opinion, the DFO had simply gotten its numbers tragically wrong. When he was later asked by the author how Ottawa could have made such a huge mistake in assessing the size of the northern cod stock, Alverson said that the problem had been caused by errors in interpretation of some of the survey informa-tion, compounded by reliance on a faulty mathematical model. "That error was magnified to some extent because it took several years to find it and by then the stocks were on the downturn. I think it came as a shock to all of the fishermen and some of the scientists."

Alverson's analysis came down to this: for several years, fishermen had been catching the very year-classes of fish that scientists had been counting on to grow the stock, exactly as Keats had suspected. Asked who was to blame for the prodigious blunder, Alverson pointed to the people who owned and managed the resource on behalf of all Canadians. "You have to blame it on the government, who've been reticent to make effective and timely decisions."

In noting that other factors might account for poor inshore landings, the Alverson Report demonstrated how little scientists really knew about the biology and habits of the living creatures they presumed to manage. Alverson suggested that, although the northern cod had been treated as a single stock, it may, in fact, be several, separate stocks. After a cod-tagging program was started in 1962, scientists realized that the Labrador–Newfoundland cod stock had several substocks, some of which mingled in summer and separated again in winter. Circumstantial evidence indicated that cod returned to the same grounds each winter and summer, and there was likely never a complete separation of stocks.

Alverson cautioned that until the northern cod's spawning pattern was more clearly understood, it would be prudent to consider each major offshore spawning group as a separate management unit. He even reported that, according to tagging studies, some cod remain in deep coastal bays close to the shore all year and may never migrate to the offshore at all. In that case, heavy inshore fishing may also have been a factor in the decline of the northern cod.

The DFO was particularly taken with another possibility the task force raised. Was it possible that unusually cold water temperatures accounted for much of the reduction of the inshore catch in 1984–85? Alverson noted the contemporary belief that cod reproduce in winter and spring along the deep slopes off the Labrador and northeastern Newfoundland shelf. They then migrate inshore in the early summer, feeding on caplin and other small fish and invertebrates. If the cold-water column (the CIL or "cold intermediate layer") extends to the ocean bottom, cod may not move inshore at all, either because they, or their favourite food, prefer temperatures above zero degrees Celsius. In other words, the absent cod might be trapped in pockets of warmer water rather than fished out.

There was a reason to give the theory serious consideration. The Labrador current flows southward off the coast of Labrador and northeast Newfoundland. The volume and temperature of the CIL in the current varies from season to season, as well as from year to year. From 1978 to 1985, inshore cod catches varied directly with the minimum core temperatures of the CIL and inversely with its volume. In layman's terms, the larger and colder the flow, the smaller the inshore catch. In 1984 and 1985, the volume of the CIL was extremely high. But if cold water had kept the cod from Newfoundland's bays, why hadn't they returned in 1986, when water temperatures returned to near normal levels?

No one knew. Until they did, it would be an exercise in mysticism as much as management to come up with an annual fishing plan for the most valuable fish stock in the Atlantic. Given all the uncertainties, Alverson recommended new measures to help the beleaguered species make a comeback in zone 2J3KL. Even if "the recent decline in catch does not appear atypical of similar declines in past years," Alverson wrote, "there are grounds for concern about the volume of catches and the size of the fish in the inshore fisheries."

Alverson's report was the first time government concerns about the health of the northern cod stock were made public. The report had at least partially confirmed the findings of the Keats report, the Winters paper, and the 1986 CAFSAC report. The DFO now knew that fish might be dying at twice the rate they had used in previous calculations to set the TAC. But belief in the ocean's inexhaustible bounty continued to bedazzle Ottawa. Despite Alverson's recommendation that the 1988 TAC be pegged at 1987 levels as a "minimum" management response, the DFO raised the 1988 quota of northern cod by 10,000 tonnes, setting it at 266,000 tonnes. There could be no clearer indication that the government's socioeconomic concerns in the fishery continued to override worries about the general health of the northern cod stock.

A year later, the first shock wave of what would become the Great Cod Disaster struck Newfoundland. In December 1988, DFO scientists informed the minister that the 1989 TAC for northern cod should be no more than 125,000 tonnes, assuming that it was still a departmental goal to fish at $F_{0.1}$. It was a stunning reversal of advice. If Siddon took the advice, it would mean more than a 50 per cent cut to the existing TAC of 266,000 tonnes and widespread social chaos on the East Coast. In 1988, the inshore allocation alone had been 125,000 tonnes, but if the inshore got the entire TAC that DFO scientists were now advising for 1989, the offshore fishery would be virtually cancelled, throwing thousands of fish-plant workers and trawlermen out of work. Without enough northern cod, the large fish companies, National Sea Products and Fishery Products International, would once again be facing bankruptcy.

Ottawa played for time. Usually the DFO sets its TAC for the following year just before Christmas; the 1989 TAC wasn't set until

December 30, 1988. Siddon announced a provisional TAC of 266,000 tonnes, claiming he was waiting for further scientific advice. The annual stock assessment was delayed until January 1989.

In the meantime, four options were secretly given to the minister: 125,000, 133,000, 200,000, or 233,000 tonnes of northern cod. CAFSAC now knew that from as early as 1981, East Coast fishermen had been fishing at over twice the $F_{0.1}$ level for northern cod. If Canada wanted to fish at $F_{0.1}$, which was still official DFO policy, then the TAC would have to be slashed in half. But the department and its minister were sitting on a political time bomb that could only be defused by opting for the high range of the options suggested by DFO scientists.

In the end, that's exactly what Ottawa did. Accompanied by Newfoundland's cabinet minister, John Crosbie, Tom Siddon held a press conference in St. John's on February 8, 1989, to announce a modest cut in the northern cod quota from 266,000 to 235,000 tonnes. Crosbie told the audience, "We are dealing with thousands of human beings, who live and breathe and eat and need jobs." And vote. He and Siddon had decided that the social and economic consequences of going to a quota of 125,000 tonnes, to be divided between the inshore and offshore, were simply too devastating. Besides, the scientists had been wrong before. How did the politicians know that they weren't wrong now?

In the wake of the politicians, William Doubleday, acting assistant deputy minister, science, tried to explain the new realities of the fishery to a gape-jawed public. He told the news media that the size and growth rate of the northern cod stock had been overestimated for the past five or six years. Stocks were being fished at double the rate that DFO scientists had predicted, which meant a mortality rate of at least 40 per cent for several consecutive seasons. Responding to that information, John Crosbie later said that Doubleday had told both him and Tom Siddon that one year of fishing at 235,000 tonnes "does not constitute any biological danger to the stock."

At a major fisheries conference almost ten years later, Doubleday appeared to confirm Crosbie's versions of events. He was asked at what point a scientist should resign when his advice was not followed by a politician. The mathematician turned bureaucrat replied "[I've] never had a situation yet where I felt I should resign because of a decision a minister has taken." Clearly upset by the accusation that he and other senior DFO scientists had purposely bent their scientific advice to fit the government's political agenda, Doubleday told a reporter from the *Globe and Mail*, "We don't mind people saying we made mistakes, but they were honest mistakes. Implicating us in deliberate tampering, well, we find that offensive."

As modest as the 1989 quota cuts were, their impact was immediate, negative, and serious. The offshore industry absorbed most of the losses of northern cod. Fishery Products International (FPI) lost quota in the southern Grand Banks as well, and the new cuts meant that two of the company's fish plants would be closed and at least twelve of its trawlers tied up. The layoffs were the first public sign of a crisis in the industry. Suddenly everyone in Newfoundland was examining the federal government's management of the fishery and, for the first time, questioning DFO science.

The inshore fishermen were bitterly vindicated, and everyone now knew there would be hell to pay. Siddon and Crosbie realized that an independent review of the northern cod stock, including the DFO's scientific advice since 1977, would have to be undertaken. The data collected by the DFO had been kept under lock and key throughout the 1980s, and it wasn't until the Alverson task force that it was opened to other researchers, including some from Siddon's own department. Previously, only a very small group in the DFO had been given access. Others, such as fish biologist Ransom Myers, were not in the loop. "I fought hard to get access to tagging databases because I knew I could infer crucial information on fishing mortality and migration rates. However, I was not allowed access to this data, even though I was a DFO employee and was the best qualified person to do this analysis. This was extremely hard on a personal level, to fight to do your job on what was perhaps the most important issue for Newfoundland. After the collapse of the cod, I did get access to the data, and published three papers. And yes, it did show that fishing mortality was very high. But it was too late."

Although William Doubleday later said that the DFO had acknowledged overfishing as a cause of the collapse as early as 1989, this was certainly not the emphasis of departmental policy. Dr. Scott Parsons was assistant deputy minister, science, at the DFO from 1986 to 1988. He then took a leave to do a PhD at McGill University and write a 763-page book called *Management of Marine Fisheries in Canada*, which was published by the National Research Council in 1993. In it, Parsons lays out the official line: "It appeared that the sudden, unexpected decline in northern cod during 1991 was the result not of high fishing mortality, but rather [of] abnormal environmental conditions . . . which, through mechanisms not yet understood, may have led to an abrupt increase in natural mortality in the early 1990s."

Whatever else it was, the decline was neither sudden nor unexpected: The DFO had known as early as 1986 that the northern cod stock was less than half of what they thought it would be.

Alarmed that something unthinkable may have happened to the northern cod stock, politicians nevertheless wanted more proof of a disaster before turning on the sirens and racing to the rescue. On February 16, 1989, the federal government appointed Dr. Leslie Harris, the president of Memorial University in St. John's and a well-respected historian who knew a great deal about the fishery, to chair the Northern Cod Review Panel. Harris picked two members of Siddon's earlier task force to help him with his work, TGNIF chairman Dr. Lee Alverson and Dr. John Pope.

Tom Siddon wanted an interim report on the situation as soon as possible, including recommendations that could help him assess the reliability of the scientific advice for the 1990 fishing season. Everyone in government hoped that the new projections would be shown to have underestimated the stock. Until DFO scientists told the minister to reduce the TAC in December 1988, the department had been saying that by 1990, the northern cod would support a TAC of 300,000 tonnes.

John Crosbie later said, "I was now faced with what became the greatest challenge of my years in political life. I was now faced with a biological and economic disaster of unprecedented proportions, and as the Newfoundland minister in the government of Canada, which had full responsibility under the Constitution to manage the fisheries, I and the government of Canada would be looked to for the solutions and assistance and had to accept the responsibility for the situation and any blame that attached to it."

Crosbie and Siddon got a measure of relief when the Newfoundland government announced that it would support the 235,000-tonne TAC for 1989. But Premier Brian Peckford insisted that the offshore absorb all of the quota reductions. Cabot Martin, a former Peckford policy guru and head of the Newfoundland Inshore Fisheries Association, agreed. "After all the offshore has put the inshore through," he said, "that would be like a burglar showing up at your door one morning demanding 50 per cent of everything that he couldn't haul away the night before." Ottawa caved in; in the end, the small-boat fishermen were given almost the same quota they had in 1988.

Although he was against the inshore taking any of the quota cut, Martin came out against the 1989 TAC as simply being too high. He argued that, according to the latest scientific assessment, the fishable biomass of northern cod was only 600,000 tonnes; to propose catching 235,000 tonnes of it was madness.

After the new TAC was announced, Martin began to write some powerful columns in support of the inshore fishery for the *Sunday Express*, a weekly St. John's newspaper. The inshore cod trap was "the simplest and cheapest cod harvesting technology known to man," Martin wrote. How then did we "in a blindingly stupendous act of self-denial and technological idiocy, turn our backs on it all and adopt the concept of an offshore trawler fleet?"

What had happened, the fiery lawyer wrote, was connected to

"our almost insatiable appetite for self-denigration." For him, the destruction of the trap fishery hid "some fundamental truths about our attitude towards our past and the rural way of life." And, he fumed, the total mismanagement of the northern cod stock told Newfoundlanders something about the way they had allowed powerful bureaucracies to govern their lives.

To illustrate his point, Martin reminded Newfoundlanders that as far back as 1979, when the large Canadian trawler fleet moved in to fish northern cod, the inshore fishery had stood quietly by, reassured by Ottawa that it would still be "first and foremost" when it came to resource allocation. The DFO had boasted that its management of the resource would produce so much fish that there would be too much for the inshore to catch all by itself. So if the Canadian offshore fleet didn't catch the "surplus" cod, it would have to be given to the same foreigners who had ravaged the stocks in the first place. Ergo, the Canadian offshore fleet needed to catch northern cod.

Martin and NIFA eventually took the federal government to court to try to end the destructive practice of fishing on the spawning grounds. They lost. Despite the obvious logic of NIFA's position, DFO officials claimed that there was no evidence to suggest that fishing on the spawning grounds in any way harmed the stock. This was not because the DFO had studied the question, but rather because no one had ever bothered to do the research. A bumper sticker appeared in St. John's showing two cod in the act of spawning. One of them was saying, "Not tonight dear, trawlers give me a headache."

In the middle of growing panic over the disappearance of the stock, John Crosbie announced on March 31, 1989, that Canada and France had signed a fisheries agreement that would resolve their longstanding boundary dispute off the south coast of Newfoundland.

The "Cod War" between France and England had started in the sixteenth century, when the two nations began to fish off Newfoundland. There were numerous conflicts and treaties over the years, but in 1972 a new Canada–France treaty was drawn up. Canada granted fishing privileges in Canadian waters and France in turn agreed to phase out its fishing effort in the Gulf of St. Lawrence by 1986.

The modern phase of the conflict began in 1977 when both Canada and France declared a 200-mile economic zone, creating a large disputed area off the south coast of Newfoundland that both countries believed might hold Hibernia-style oil reserves as well as rich fish stocks. The problem was obvious. The French islands of St. Pierre and Miquelon are just twelve nautical miles off the south coast of Newfoundland, so France's 200-mile territorial claim encompassed vast areas of NAFO zone 3Ps. Both countries fished the disputed territory, but after 1983 France increased its traditional 15.6 per cent share of the catch by well over 100 per cent. The French demanded four times their traditional quota in 3Ps to settle the dispute, as well as increased quotas in Canadian waters that would more than make up for the catch they lost by leaving the Gulf.

In March 1985, the French sent a warship to patrol zone 3Ps, where French trawlers were catching quadruple the 6,000-tonne quota set by Canada. Then in January 1987, the French factory trawler fleet arrived, raising concerns among worried St. Pierre and Miquelon fishermen that the resource they depended on would soon be wiped out.

The Canada–France fishery dispute had been a serious problem for Crosbie as Newfoundland's federal cabinet representative and the de facto watchdog over the province's fishery interests. After negotiations between the two countries broke down in January 1987, External Affairs had renewed contacts with the French by suggesting that Canada would "significantly increase" French fishery quotas in Canadian waters if France would agree to arbitration on the boundary dispute.

Centuries of international diplomacy had made the French hard bargainers. France didn't want either the Newfoundland government or industry representatives present at the discussions. It even tried, unsuccessfully, to bar DFO representatives from the talks in Paris.

PMO staffer Fred Doucet had assured Crosbie that the Paris meeting was merely "technical" and that Canada's two representatives were not empowered to sign a binding agreement. Despite Doucet's reassurances, the delegation from External Affairs went ahead and signed on the dotted line.

The fuse had been lit and it didn't take long for the bomb to go off. Premier Brian Peckford called an emergency news conference on January 26, 1987, to denounce the secret agreement. Once again, he thundered, the federal government had shown that it was ready to sell out the East Coast fishery in the interests of international trade. For Peckford, the hypocrisy was staggering. The federal government had cut 10,000 tonnes of northern cod from Canada's own offshore fleet in 1987, but was now giving that allocation to France and throwing Canadians out of work. Playing up Ottawa's blunder to the hilt, Liberal firebrand Brian Tobin demanded that the deal be declared null and void and that Fisheries Minister Tom Siddon be fired. He also suggested that if John Crosbie had a trace of integrity, he would resign to protest what had happened to his native province.

Crosbie knew that the consequences of allowing the deal to stand would be ruinous for Conservative MPs in Atlantic Canada in the pending federal election. The Newfoundland caucus was badly shaken by Doucet's apparent duplicity, and Crosbie believed that his own credibility had been severely damaged by External Affairs' backroom deal with the French. He believed that relations with the Peckford government would be utterly destroyed if the deal was allowed to stand. More than anything, though, he was furious that he hadn't been consulted on the most contentious political issue facing the Mulroney government in Atlantic Canada.

Fish suddenly dominated the House of Commons. NDP leader Ed Broadbent asked for an emergency debate, which was convened on the evening of January 28, 1987. The opposition wanted the government to use military force to stop French overfishing in the disputed zone, and there were rumours that more French warships were on their way to 3Ps. John Crosbie called on his own government to apologize to Newfoundland for not consulting the province before signing the deal.

Crosbie's fury was heard in the corridors of power. Since the prime minister was away in Africa, Deputy Prime Minister Don Mazankowski apologized on his behalf to Premier Peckford for not consulting him before concluding the secret deal with France. Peckford flung the apology back in Mazankowski's face and accused Crosbie of betraying his own province for not stopping the agreement. He demanded that Ottawa recall its ambassador to France and close Canadian ports to French ships.

Behind the scenes Crosbie worked to undo the harm of Fred Doucet's Parisian folly. In a February 1987 letter to Mulroney, Crosbie suggested that the agreement be labelled an interim arrangement that called for further negotiations before proceeding to binding arbitration on the 3Ps dispute. "It is absolutely essential," he wrote, "that the Newfoundland people be given the impression that it is their cabinet minister at Ottawa and their federal MPs at Ottawa that they should look to for protection of their interests in the matter of these negotiations with France and with respect to other matters that come under federal jurisdiction. If they continue to have the impression that only Premier Peckford and his government will truly represent their interests then I and my federal colleagues are finished as a political force in Newfoundland."

Crosbie urged Mulroney to tell the French that future dealings in areas outside the fisheries could be discussed only in return for French agreement to abide by Canadian quotas in 3Ps and arbitration on the boundary dispute: "You should make it clear that we are not just going to sacrifice fish in and about Newfoundland and Labrador and the Atlantic provinces in order to get the necessary agreement from France, but that we are prepared to consider sacrificing other Canadian interests if that is necessary. Surely, we have other levers, including the fact that we may be interested in purchasing French submarines or the Airbus or other goods and services from France just as one example."

While Crosbie was controlling damage, Brian Peckford continued to stir the pot. He sought and won the support of other provincial premiers in his fight against Ottawa and was heartened by polls that showed that the cod issue would wipe out any chance the Conservatives had of winning the next federal election.

Even the French residents of St. Pierre and Miquelon were aghast at French overfishing. When the French trawlers *Grande Hermine* and *Dauphin* came into port, the islanders refused to unload their cargoes, knowing that as soon as their holds were empty, the vessels would put to sea for more fish.

Over ten years of negotiations had ended in tatters, but France finally agreed to go to binding arbitration in the spring of 1989. It was the first time in history that a marine dispute had gone to international arbitration under the 1982 Law of the Sea Convention. But the price of French cooperation was steep, and in the opinion of many Newfoundlanders, much too high. France would be given access to fish in Canadian waters, including 2,950 tonnes of precious northern cod, while the tribunal considered the merits of the competing claims. The tribunal had four years to deliberate before making its binding ruling. In the meantime, France would be allowed to take about double the amount of fish it had previously been entitled to under the treaty of 1972 and a subsequent 1984 agreement. Once again, Newfoundland felt that the federal government had sold out provincial interests in the name of international relations.

In May 1989, Dr. Harris and his blue-ribbon panel handed in their interim report, confirming that the northern cod stock was in serious trouble. On May 26, 1989, Crosbie and other federal officials convened a meeting on regional development with Newfoundland's new premier, Clyde Wells. The first item on the agenda was Harris's preliminary findings on the troubled fishery. Trying to ease the sense of panic, Crosbie told the group that the federal government would set up a task force to assess the impact of further TAC reductions, which now seemed inevitable. It was his view that for the 1989 season, at least, the income support measures already in place were adequate. But beyond that, Crosbie said, special measures would likely be needed for a period of five to ten years.

Crosbie reviewed for Wells the federal position on the interim agreement with France. Wells appeared to think it was reasonable, although he expressed concern over the amount of 3Ps cod given to the French. The politicians also discussed foreign overfishing, particularly by the fleets of the EC. Though sympathetic to Wells's frustration, Crosbie balked at trade sanctions. From Ottawa's point of view, various legal strategies and a public relations campaign in EC countries aimed at portraying overfishing as an environmental disaster were the preferred options. More closely in touch with local feeling, Wells was not persuaded. He wanted Ottawa to make the overfishing issue a national priority and urged that the prime minister become involved to show the EC that Canada meant business.

As information from the Harris panel was made available to the industry, East Coast fishermen got a taste of what was to come.

With or without Crosbie's help, cod did become the national issue Clyde Wells wanted it to be when, in December 1989, National Sea Products closed its plant in Canso, Nova Scotia, and another in the federal district of St. John's West, John Crosbie's own riding. On December 18, there was an emergency six-and-a-half-hour debate in the House of Commons on the crisis in the Atlantic fishery. Crosbie defended the 1989 TAC of 235,000 tonnes. He explained that the TAC had to be lowered gradually to minimize the impact of a reduced fishery on communities whose existence depended on cod. As recommended by the Harris panel, the DFO would further trim the TAC in 1990 to 190,000 tonnes.

"I did not believe that we had to slavishly follow the opinions of marine biologists and I was not going to," Crosbie said later. "Their advice was given as guidance, as was the advice from the Harris Task Force. But the cabinet had to live with the social and economic consequences of this resource situation. There was no imperative that said that we had to immediately in one year or two wipe out the whole offshore fishery. As far as I was concerned, that was not on."

Brian Mulroney finally put his oar in the troubled waters, pledging Ottawa's support to needy Atlantic fishermen. Fishing provided 25 per cent of Newfoundland's employment. In 1986, the average income of a Newfoundland fishing family was $19,850. But only 24 per cent of that was from fishing; 30 per cent was from other employment, and a whopping 41 per cent came from UI. It was clear that the fishing industry could not support the number of people who depended on it for a living. Crosbie rejected calls for an all-plants-open policy, a sentimental echo from the Peckford era. "There was no future in having the workforce working only part of the year in subsidized industries. . . . Newfoundland could never be a viable province with subsidized operation of its main industry."

An ugly mood was building among fishermen and fish-plant workers. On January 2, 1990, Tom Siddon, John Crosbie, and Ross Reid, the young MP for St. John's East, held a press conference at the Radisson Plaza Hotel in St. John's to announce the quota for 1990. As the three men entered the main lobby, they were jeered by a crowd of two hundred fish-plant workers, angry because of the impending plant closures brought on by previous TAC reductions. Richard Cashin, the theatrical president of the Fish, Food, and Allied Workers union, shook his finger in Tom Siddon's face and accused him of being the worst federal fisheries minister Newfoundland had ever seen. One unemployed plant worker from Trepassey, a fishing village in Crosbie's own riding, had a special message for his MP: "You'll be gone in the next election, buddy." Another had a far more ominous message: "There will be blood spilled before it closes."

It was a no-win situation for Ottawa. One side criticized the federal government for setting the TAC at too high a level to allow the ravaged stocks to rebuild, the other was furious because the TAC was too low to keep fishermen employed and existing plants open. Cabot Martin summed up the collision between the bottom line and political damage control in his weekly column for the *Sunday Express*: "On one side, the cool calculating corporate world of FPI [Fishery Products International], of Bay Street, stock quotations, quarterly dividends and plant utilization factors. . . . On the other, the hot, messy, scrabbling, smoke-and-mirrors world of politics: the world of ambush and subterfuge; where the main objective of the day is to survive the news conference, to avoid a bad clip on 'The Journal.'"

In the wake of the TAC announcement for 1990, Ottawa got more bad news. Vic Young, the chairman and CEO of FPI, had to deal with a 12,000-tonne drop in his company's allocation of northern cod. Reluctantly, Young announced the closure of fish plants in Trepassey, Grand Bank, and Gaultois on Newfoundland's south coast. Almost 1,200 plant workers and 169 trawlermen would be laid off in the spring of 1990.

It was a bitter pill for John Crosbie. He had managed to get extra quota for FPI by persuading Tom Siddon to set the catch for northern cod at 197,000 tonnes, instead of the 190,000 tonnes recommended by his officials, "in order to try to save one or two of the offshore plants." He felt doublecrossed by Young when FPI decided to close all three anyway.

Fearing that its welfare rolls would be swamped, the Newfoundland government stepped in with an $11.5-million subsidy so that FPI could operate its plants for twenty weeks in 1990 and in 1991. That way, workers could qualify for another year of unemployment benefits from Ottawa. National Sea Products then announced it was closing its plant on the south side of St. John's, also in Crosbie's district, throwing 492 people out of work. Although National Sea was offered $3 million by the provincial government to keep the St. John's plant open for twenty weeks in 1990, the company opted to close. The loss of 7,000 tonnes of its northern cod allocation was simply too much to stay in production.

Crosbie noted bitterly that the companies quickly disappeared from the public scene after announcing their plant closures, leaving the politicians to take the heat. Crosbie, like his father and grandfather before him, made a point of taking the chair next to the woodstove when the heat in the political kitchen went up. He flew to the small island community of Gaultois to offer what comfort he could. In the end, he managed to get a new operator for the idle plant and a small allocation of redfish to keep the community going.

Crosbie next travelled to Trepassey, where a thousand angry residents showed up at a public meeting. They wanted foreign over-fishing stopped and urged Crosbie to extend Canada's economic zone to the edge of the continental shelf. They also wanted Ottawa to stop giving cod allocations to foreign fleets inside our 200-mile limit. They didn't want UI and they didn't want welfare, just enough fish so that they could work year-round. At the end of an emotional meeting, Crosbie was given a standing ovation after he spoke.

Unhappy with the way Vic Young and his board of directors had dealt with the crisis, Crosbie wanted an independent commission of inquiry to look into FPI's claim that they had to close plants permanently, rather than have seasonal or rotating closures that would keep all plants open for part of the year. Crosbie believed the plants were not normal private-sector operators, since the Canadian government had rescued them financially in the past and annually granted them part of a common property resource that belonged to the people of Canada. In Crosbie's mind, that meant that the companies owed more to their employees than pink slips when the going got tough.

No matter how many plants he could keep open, Crosbie knew that Ottawa would still have to craft an assistance program on a massive scale. The program announced to date would only provide $130 million over four years. In Crosbie's view, the government of Canada had to be at least as generous as it had been with western farmers during their recent crop crisis, even though the federal government was in a period of fiscal restraint.

While Ottawa made its plans, the pot was on the boil in New-foundland. On February 9, 1990, five hundred displaced workers from idle plants in Grand Bank, Trepassey, Gaultois, and St. John's took over the main lobby of Confederation Building. Crosbie was

there waiting for them. At the sight of Newfoundland's most powerful federal minister, the angry crowd booed and began a chant of
"Traitor John" when he tried to speak. "You can boo, you can hiss,
and you can jeer," Crosbie roared back, "but I'm going to keep on
doing what I can to help you whether you believe I am or not."

Local union member Linda Hyde called Crosbie and the federal
government wimps for failing to stop foreign overfishing beyond
the 200-mile limit. In trying to explain what the Mulroney government was doing on the diplomatic front, Crosbie asked an
unfortunate rhetorical question: "What would you do? Would you
send out the battleships if you were in power?" He got his answer
in a heartbeat. "Yes!" the angry crowd roared. Undaunted by his
reception, Crosbie mingled with the crowd, where he was buffeted
with demands for his resignation. "What good would that do?"
he asked. Newfoundland would no longer have a strong voice in
cabinet just when someone had to make the case for a federal assistance package.

For a variety of reasons, Crosbie decided to show up at as many
of these meetings as he could. He understood the anger and fear
in his constituents, and his political experience had taught him
that letting people vent their frustration on their MP was part of
the job description. At a more practical level, he knew that the
public uproar created by demonstrating fisheries workers would
help him to get his tight-fisted colleagues in Ottawa to respond to
the crisis generously. Still, it wouldn't be easy. Ottawa was already
sending money to Newfoundland hand over fist. In 1989, the
federal government collected $1.18 billion dollars from New-
foundland and spent $3.74 billion.

On February 21, 1990, John Crosbie received his personal copy of
the final Harris Report, five weeks before it was released to the
public. While the industry held its collective breath, hoping for a
miracle, federal bureaucrats tried to figure out how to spin the
devastating information. As Harris had not had access to data from
the fall 1989 research vessel surveys, word went out that there

were, in fact, two big year-classes of fish, 1986 and 1987, that Harris hadn't known about. According to the unofficial spin, this new information made much of what Harris had to say out of date. But attacking the messenger wasn't as easy as it had been when the Keats Report was dismissed as the work of a scientist still wet behind the ears. Harris was too highly respected, and the evidence produced by his panel too overwhelming, to be talked away by even the most silver-tongued bureaucrat.

Before the report was made public, there was a change at the top of the DFO. On February 22, 1990, Mulroney shuffled his cabinet and appointed Bernard Valcourt, the MP for Madawaska–Victoria in New Brunswick, to the post of minister of fisheries and oceans. The former consumer and corporate affairs minister was one of Mulroney's "golden boys," and distributed patronage on his boss's behalf in Atlantic Canada. Unlike Tom Siddon, who had welcomed Crosbie's input and advice, Valcourt was determined to play his own hand. Crosbie later described his cabinet colleague from New Brunswick as "young, ambitious, and arrogant." His abrasive personality alienated just about everyone with an interest in the fishery. Crosbie realized he could not survive politically by taking a back seat to a new kid with an attitude. Newfoundland's senior minister would still be accountable for the fishery, and that meant having the final say in how Ottawa would deal with the crisis.

Valcourt released the Harris Report on March 30, 1990. For those who had been hoping against hope for a clean bill of health for the fishery, the prognosis was dire: "Even though there was not an immediate threat to the survival of the northern cod stock, recent catch levels simply cannot be maintained without causing a significant and potentially very serious decline in the exploitable and spawning biomass." If the tragic decline of the northern cod was to be stopped, immediate steps had to be taken to grow the size of the spawning biomass. In Harris's opinion, Ottawa's reduced TAC of 190,000 tonnes "may not serve to reverse the trend of a declining spawning stock but rather contribute to further decline."

The Harris panel recommended further reducing the level of the catch, restricting fishing during the spawning season, and decreasing the take of small fish and by-catches by using fishing strategies and specialized gear that would allow juvenile cod to escape. There was real urgency to this last suggestion. One captain the Harris panel interviewed reported that in his tow, for every pound of shrimp (the catch he was after), there were often ten pounds of dead juvenile cod.

Although Harris was keenly aware that a sudden reduction of catch levels "would precipitate social and economic repercussions of a particularly drastic nature," he insisted that a lower TAC for 1991 was imperative: "It should be clear that the longer the delay in facing the brutal reality, the harder and longer will be the road back."

On the issue of how the cod crash had come about, Harris pointed a damning, yet compassionate, finger at the disastrous advice given to managers and politicians by the DFO's science branch. Those scientists, "lulled by false data signals and, to some extent, overconfident of the validity of their predictions, failed to recognize the statistical inadequacies in their bulk biomass model and failed to properly acknowledge and recognize the high risk involved with state-of-stock advice based on relatively short and unreliable data series."

In laying the blame, Harris and his colleagues took into account the enormous difficulty of conducting a fish census in a vast area of the open ocean. The gadoid (cod) section of the DFO's Newfoundland Groundfish Division had fewer than ten scientists to report on 150,000 square kilometres of ocean. Over three-quarters of their effort was directed at stock assessment, and there was little time left to learn the biological mysteries of the cod.

Without that vital knowledge of the stock itself, Harris doubted that the resource could ever be properly managed. He wasn't alone in that opinion. In what Harris described as a rare showing of solidarity in an industry perpetually at cross purposes, he found that "the entire fishing community," including harvesters, processors, and corporations, was disenchanted with the quality of the DFO's scientific advice. Again, Harris was both charitable and chiding: "It is not at all clear that at the time and under the circumstances in question, any other group of scientists would have done much better. . . . Nevertheless, it is possible that if there had not been such a strong emotional and intellectual commitment to the notion that the $F_{o.1}$ strategy was working, the open and increasing scepticism of inshore fishermen might have been recognized as a warning flag demanding more careful attention to areas of recognized weakness in the assessment process."

Harris also had a few words to say on the way DFO scientists made their stock assessments. As several other fishing nations did, Canada took historical catch data and "tuned" them with research vessel population surveys and statistics on CPUE (catch per unit of effort) provided by the commercial fishery. The system was improved in 1989 when the "bulk biomass model" (all ages of fish combined) was replaced by a research vessel survey on an "age-by-age basis." Harris tipped his hat to improvements in the DFO's modelling methodology, but wanted to see an improvement in how the data gathered from research voyages and the commercial fishery was assessed. He suggested adding an inshore CPUE index to the data (only offshore data were used at this point), supplemented by acoustic survey data and environmental indicators of fish abundance. To do this, the DFO would have to improve its computing power. Harris also suggested that the assessments be submitted to rigorous peer review by scientists "not directly involved in departmental processes."

Somehow, mathematical data and models had become more important than the study of the species. Harris wanted these management abstractions to be tuned by biological, behavioural, and environmental facts about the living resource and the ocean. Some action had already been taken to fund additional scientific research projects, including $3 million allocated to the DFO's Science Branch in 1989–90, a sum of money that represented a 45 per cent increase in funding for cod research.

What was needed, according to Harris, was nothing short of a massive research effort that would use the resources of the broader scientific community to understand the life systems of the ocean. "Because the technology we control gives us the power to be utterly destructive," Harris wrote, "we must be all the more aware of the heavy moral responsibilities we bear. Among those responsibilities is that of seeking and acquiring the knowledge that is within our grasp and that will alone enable us to manage as we ought."

Harris believed that as long as the DFO didn't have the answers to a whole range of key questions, the minister should proceed with "extreme caution" while making it a priority to fill in the gaps in the scientific knowledge. In simple terms, Ottawa couldn't manage what it didn't understand. Little was known, for example, about predator/prey relationships in the Atlantic. The anti-sealing movement had closed the seal fishery in 1983 and many fishermen believed that "nature" was now out of balance. They reported to Harris that seals were more numerous along the northeast coast than at any other time in living memory. It is estimated that a single seal consumes a diet equal to about 6 per cent of its own body weight a day. Several million seals, feeding not just on cod, but on the cod's favourite food, caplin, would consume literally millions of tonnes of fish.

As drastic an impact as seals might have on cod stocks, Canadian scientists didn't even know how large the herd had become since the end of the hunt. Whether the seals ate cod or caplin, the result would be the same; pressure on the cod stock. Simple logic dictated that there had to be a large caplin population in order to sustain a large cod population. Preliminary studies done in the Barents Sea, for example, indicated that dramatic decreases in the number of cod, and even the disappearance of some year-classes, was likely caused because the caplin were overfished or taken in large numbers by other predators.

One of the more urgent questions fishermen wanted answered was the effect of continuous fishing on the cod's spawning grounds by offshore trawlers, a practice they believed was the single most important contributor to the decline of the stock. The DFO disagreed, more out of habit than insight. In one of his last acts as minister of fisheries and oceans, Tom Siddon stood up in the House of Commons on February 19, 1990, and told the House that his scientists had advised him that there was no recorded evidence in the scientific literature or the DFO's own research "which stated that fishing on the spawning grounds does measurable damage to the cod stocks." The minister was right, but only because no one had bothered to do the research.

Wilfred Bartlett of the Newfoundland Inshore Fisheries Association gave the fishermen's view: "We don't catch lobster when they are spawning, the season is closed. You are not allowed to catch salmon when they are spawning. They are left alone to spawn. We don't hunt ducks when they are mating. We don't kill moose when they're having their young. But still for all, it seems okay to kill the fish when they are trying to reproduce."

Bartlett's eloquent argument aside, the DFO and Harris argued that the real problem was the killing of too many fish, not *when* the fish were killed. But inshore fishermen remained convinced that if the cod were killed after they were allowed to spawn, enough of their offspring might survive to add to the overall biomass. They argued that before the deep-sea fishery, fishing methods had been essentially passive: fish had to swim inshore, or to the shallow areas of the Banks, to the gear that caught them during their annual migrations. The deep-sea trawlers had sophisticated equipment to track the fish, and the gear to catch it on the spawning grounds in nearly all weather conditions. Making matters worse, the trawlers destroyed the spawning habitat, disrupted the courtship and spawning patterns, and killed the adults before the young could be spawned. What other species, fishermen asked, do we kill during the act of procreation?

On this issue, Harris followed his own advice to government; when you don't know, proceed with caution. He said it was urgent that Ottawa find out more about the spawning and migrating habits of the stock. In the meantime, he wanted the DFO to establish regulations to limit fishing mortality during the spawning period. Whether this was done by reducing the winter offshore catch, or developing gear that spared juvenile fish, such measures ought to improve yields in the long run.

Harris's view of the ecosystem included human beings. As Dr. Arthur May of Fisheries Canada had done ten years earlier, Harris urged governments to "identify in unequivocal terms the socioeconomic and cultural objectives of the Atlantic coast fisheries."

Harris wrote eloquently about the Newfoundlander's attachment to the hundreds of coves and harbours and bays that were "home," even though they might appear inhospitable to outsiders. "After three or four hundred years of occupancy, even a barren, rock-strewn piece of foreshore becomes an infinitely valued piece of property, sanctified by the lives and the striving of a family through many generations. A house that is owned outright and that stands on the site once occupied by one's father, and his father and father's father, becomes a sacred property not to be lightly abandoned."

But as much as he loved his native province, and paid homage to the spirit of the people who had settled it, Harris knew that there were too many fishermen, too many vessels, and too much processing capacity for what was left of the cod stocks after five hundred years of continuous fishing. The right to jig a cod for supper may be ingrained in every Newfoundlander, but Harris recommended that no new licences be issued. He also noted that there was a limit to how far socioeconomic goals could override biological and ecological reality; that limit had been reached with the northern cod. It was now up to Ottawa to say how far it was prepared to go in using the fishery as an employer of last resort.

After months of study, Ottawa accepted twenty-six of Dr. Harris's twenty-nine recommendations for dealing with the crisis in the Atlantic fishery. Remarkably, reducing the TAC wasn't one of them. Although Bernard Valcourt said that he shared Harris's concern about the long-term health of the cod stock, he would not agree to a further reduction in the 1990 northern cod quota. The social and economic consequences were simply too great. It was the worst management decision ever made by a federal fisheries minister, coming as it did at a time when the landings in some communities were only a tenth of what they had been the previous year.

On May 7, 1990, Valcourt and Crosbie announced the Atlantic Fisheries Adjustment Program (AFAP), an emergency package worth $584 million over five years. Some of the money had already been used for short-term aid in areas where fish plants had closed. Some had been spent on improving Canada's pathetic fishery surveillance beyond the 200-mile economic zone. The rest, roughly $426 million, were new funds designed to bring back the decimated stocks and help communities in Atlantic Canada survive during the long and painful rebuilding process. As they wrote the latest cheque for the chronically troubled industry, federal politicians said that a key ingredient of the initiative was to convince people that the old days of working in the fishery just long enough to qualify for UI were over. The words were just as hollow as they had been when Michael Kirby uttered them ten years earlier.

In June 1990, Bernard Valcourt asked Eric Dunne, the senior DFO official in St. John's, to develop an implementation plan for the recommendations regarding conservation, management, harvesting, surveillance, enforcement, and communications in the Harris Report.

It was an empty process. No serious thought was given to reducing the TAC, nor could Dunne find a consensus on a way to eliminate the catch of juvenile fish because of the cost of developing new fishing methods and gear. The federal bureaucrat never actively considered the possibility that the northern cod was on the brink of commercial extinction unless drastic measures were taken. As he put it, "The issue is simple, the solution is not."

The summer of 1990 was a season of finger-pointing and despair in Newfoundland. One of the biggest issues was the fact that

fourteen rather than ten weeks of work were required to qualify for
UI. Given the state of the industry, it was almost impossible to get
a job in the fishery that lasted longer than ten weeks. Fear, insecu-
rity, and rage rolled through the outports. According to the polls,
there were many more cod in the bays than there were votes for the
Mulroney government in Newfoundland. Responding to complaints about the fisheries now took up 70 per cent of John Crosbie's
workload. As the enormity of what was happening hit home,
Crosbie slowly came to the conclusion that it might be necessary for
him to assume the fisheries portfolio if the opportunity arose.

Ottawa's mismanagement of the northern cod wasn't the only political time bomb ticking away in the East Coast fishery. Although Dr.
Harris blamed the federal government for the poor state of the fish
stocks off Newfoundland, he made it clear that Canada would never
be able to manage the fishery without dealing with the chronic
problem of foreign overfishing off its shores. As a first step, he
strongly recommended that Ottawa stop giving quotas to foreign
vessels inside the 200-mile zone for "foreign affairs" reasons.

Harris also wanted Canada to take unilateral action to stop the
far more serious problem of overfishing beyond the 200-mile
zone. He advised that either the entire continental shelf had to be
brought under Canadian management, or there must be an international agreement that would "curb the irresponsible and destructive activities of certain countries" fishing on the Nose and Tail of
the Banks. Only with an agreement on straddling stocks, would it
be possible to implement a management plan within the 200-
mile zone.

Harris felt so strongly about foreign overfishing that he even
wanted Ottawa to think about "participating in the rape of the
'Nose' and 'Tail' of the Banks." He reasoned that a Canadian fishery
in these areas couldn't harm the stocks any more than they were
already being harmed, and if EC profits could be reduced in the
process, they might "repent their intransigence" and remove their

fleets. The otherwise eloquent Dr. Harris was silent on the point of how outdoing the foreign fish pirates would square with Canada's avowed moral commitment to conservation.

Valcourt was not persuaded. He believed that the kind of unilateral solution proposed by the Harris panel was incompatible with the international Law of the Sea and rejected it out of hand. Rather than breaking international law and risking a confrontation with Canada's allies, Crosbie, Valcourt, and Mulroney had been quietly pressuring the EC to stop its gross overfishing on the Nose and Tail of the Banks. The prime minister had raised the issue with EC leaders at the last Economic Summit with some success. Manuel Marin, the vice-president and fisheries commissioner of the EU, was in favour of scientists from both sides of the ocean doing a joint evaluation on the health of the stock. Once both sides could agree on the facts, Marin believed individual EC members would voluntarily reduce their quotas in international waters. The betting in Newfoundland was that he also believed in the tooth fairy.

While the talks dragged on, the stocks continued to dwindle. In the fall of 1990, Canada hosted a conference in St. John's on the problems of coastal states faced by overfishing of straddling stocks beyond their 200-mile zones. If only one thing became clear, it was that overfishing on the high seas was a truly international problem. Dr. Lee Alverson told his audience that 44 of the world's 186 major fish stocks were being overfished because illegal fishing was the only way to keep an overcapitalized distant-water fishery in business.

Three months later, the EC set its own quota for northern cod in international waters at 27,000 tonnes, just 5,000 tonnes less than the quota it had unilaterally established the previous year. Valcourt set the 1991 TAC for northern cod at 190,000 tonnes. It hardly mattered. Fishing flat out with the deadliest gear on the water, fishermen were only able to catch 127,000 tonnes. Ottawa may still have been issuing the press releases, but it was nature that was now setting the TAC.

With the nets of inshore fishermen all but empty, everyone knew one thing: Ottawa may have belatedly come up with a fisheries management plan in which conservation was more than an afterthought, but as long as foreign fleets kept vacuuming the sea beyond the 200-mile limit, the cod would never come back. The foreigners had to be stopped, and Newfoundlanders would soon be looking to one of their own to do it.

6

SKIPPER JOHN

On April 21, 1991, Brian Mulroney shuffled the deck chairs on the *Titanic* of his increasingly unpopular government and John Crosbie finally got his "nightmare job." Crosbie knew that the fishery was Atlantic Canada's most important file: 100,000 jobs, $3.1 billion worth of production, and 20 per cent of the Gross Provincial Product in the region, though just 0.9 per cent of Canada's GDP. More important in the circumstances, the man whose family had made its fortune in fish knew that 1,500 communities depended on harvesting and processing cod for their survival. If the groundfish that accounted for 60 per cent of the landings in Atlantic Canada didn't come back, those people would need someone in Ottawa who understood their plight.

No one had a better idea of what the troubled waters of the fisheries looked like than John Carnell Crosbie. Before running federally in 1976, Crosbie had been fisheries minister in the provincial government of Frank Moores, where he gained firsthand experience of the competing interests he now presided over. Despite the fact that an imminent stock collapse had been added to the usual problems, Crosbie vowed that he would "do the best I could."

Valcourt's eleven stormy months in the portfolio didn't make Crosbie's job any easier. Considered to be on the uncouth side of brash, Valcourt had offended just about everyone during his brief tenure as minister. NIFA president Cabot Martin was one of many dedicated detractors of the pepperpot from New Brunswick. "It's been quite awhile since anyone in Ottawa has managed to break virtually all the basic rules of good fisheries management in one fell swoop," he wrote in one of his columns.

Martin listed Valcourt's many alleged sins: allowing the swash-buckling Newfoundland company, Seafreez, to freeze fish at sea (bypassing shore-based processing), permitting the company to use foreign fishing vessels, and authorizing it to catch 50,000 tonnes of caplin at a time when the stocks were near collapse and the cod that depended on them were on the point of starvation. Inshore fisher-men suspected that the DFO's stock assessments for caplin were as shaky as the ones for northern cod.

Ignoring protests from Newfoundland, Valcourt had also given the Nova Scotia deep-sea company, National Sea Products, enter-prise allocations, a kind of quasi-property right, for northern cod. For his many contributions to Newfoundland's decline, Martin nominated Valcourt for the "Saddam Hussein Award for creative fisheries policy."

Crosbie laughed along with other Newfoundlanders, but he knew that even sharper barbs would soon be coming his way. For now, though, all was hearts and flowers. Even Liberal MPs such as Roger Simmons applauded Crosbie's appointment, partly because they knew their legendary foe was headed into a political meat-grinder. But they also recognized that Crosbie was able, hard-working, and like a dog with a bone when he set his mind on a course of action.

But from the very beginning, Crosbie faced an industry where the mood was not one of cooperation or contrition for past sins, but rather of suspicion, blame-laying, and a withering selfishness over the disposition of the few cod that were left. As Crosbie put it, "There isn't one decision you can take without a major battle going on as to what you should have done. For every winner, there are three losers. That's the fishery."

For all of its national reach, Fisheries and Oceans is one of the least known departments of the federal government. When Crosbie became minister, the DFO employed 6,149 people, 5,045 of them full time. Only a quarter were uniformed, including guardians, inspectors, and ships' officers and crew. It was not many people to manage 244,000 kilometres of one of the longest coastlines in the world. With the declaration of the 200-mile limit, the offshore area accounted for 30 per cent of Canada's total territory.

The DFO was the largest employer of biologists in the public service, and the second largest of research scientists and technicians. More than 2,200 DFO personnel worked as scientists or as scientific support. The department spent 28.8 per cent of its $800-million budget on science, with most of the $219.4 million going in support of fisheries management. Three-quarters of its in-house science and technology budget was spent on the East and West coasts of the country.

Crosbie had inherited a department that was primarily operational. The DFO conducts research, enforces regulations, inspects fish, produces navigational surveys, publishes charts, and manages 2,200 small-craft harbours around the country. But science was clearly the department's essential mission, as one of Crosbie's top officials made clear: "Science is the foundation of everything we do. Fisheries management requires a sound knowledge of fish stocks; habitat management is based on research on the impact of physical and chemical changes on fish habitat." For DFO to fail in its science would mean that the department had failed utterly in its mission.

Unlike most federal departments, the DFO was heavily decentralized, with 89 per cent of its staff working in 7,000 regional offices, labs, field camps, and hatcheries all over the country. Harvest management was divided into science, allocation, and enforcement. Scientific advice determined estimates of stock abundance. The

DFO then set annual predictions of stock abundance, which were used to establish the annual TACs and harvesting rules. It also negotiated the Canadian and foreign shares of allocations and licences, and monitored and enforced quotas. When necessary, it also prosecuted those who broke the rules. But by 1991 the fines had become so minimal, they were a standing joke in the industry, a minor cost of doing business in a common property resource.

On his first day on the job, John Crosbie was briefed about his new department. He was told that the TGNIF study led by Dr. Alverson had confirmed the results of the current assessment, that the northern cod stock had increased substantially since 1976. The decline in inshore catches was due to a combination of factors, including cold water temperature, the availability of caplin offshore as food, and the uneven distribution of offshore fishing. Although Crosbie was informed that the Harris panel had confirmed that the stock status had been overestimated, there was no sense of urgency in the briefing book. One sentence jumps out: "Scientific advice is that lower inshore catch-rates and smaller fish in the inshore fishery in recent years do not indicate stock decline." Despite Deputy Minister Bruce Rawson's spin, the picture that emerged from the secret briefing book he had prepared for Crosbie was ominous.

Rawson flagged a swarm of problems for his new minister, including poor catch-rates, horrendous foreign overfishing, and rising frustration within the industry at Ottawa's inability to do anything about it. One of Crosbie's problems was a renewed demand by Newfoundland that Ottawa give up its exclusive control over the fishery. Newfoundland had traditionally clamoured for a greater provincial role in fisheries management, an argument that packed more of a punch after the stunning decline of the northern cod. Like his advice to cut the TAC for northern cod and unilaterally take control of the offshore beyond two hundred miles, Harris's recommendation for shared fisheries management had been rejected by Bernard Valcourt.

Clyde Wells was undaunted. In January 1991, Newfoundland had released a major report, "The Maloney Inquiry into the Alleged Erosion of the Newfoundland Fishery by Non-Newfoundland Interests." In a way, it was Newfoundland's advance claim for damages if the stocks collapsed. The previous October, Premier Wells had appointed former Newfoundland fisheries minister Aidan Maloney to investigate the decline of the Newfoundland fishery. His report focused on federal policies that gave non-Newfoundland interests access to fish stocks adjacent to the province, as well as DFO enforcement practices, which penalized Newfoundland fishermen while letting others away with poor fishing practices. Maloney called for greater provincial control over fish stocks, and "priority" treatment for Newfoundland in any future NAFO quota increases in 2J3KL. It was the least Ottawa could do, Maloney said, for past discrimination against the province with all the fish.

Wells endorsed the Maloney Report in the final days of 1990, and publicly pressed for federal–provincial "management" of the fishery along the lines of the Offshore Petroleum Board that regulated oil development in Newfoundland waters. Rawson was careful to point out to Crosbie what Wells was after. Wells wanted jurisdiction over the fishery left with the federal government, but day-to-day management shared by a Canada–Newfoundland board. Worried about being excluded from Newfoundland waters, the fishing industry and the remaining Atlantic provinces, led by Nova Scotia, all supported exclusive federal jurisdiction.

It cost nearly a billion dollars a year to run the fishery in Canada, and Crosbie knew that Newfoundland would like nothing better than to dictate the annual quotas to its own advantage, while sticking Ottawa with all the bills. Like Roméo LeBlanc before him, he believed that shared management would lead to endless strife, or what he jokingly referred to as "civil war." He preferred following the letter of Section 91(12) of the Constitution Act of 1982: in tidal waters, the public right to fish is vested in the Crown, and the federal government exercises all powers with respect to harvest management, conservation, and protection.

The issue of shared management was not the biggest problem Crosbie faced. What threatened most was the towering anger building in Newfoundland fishermen as they watched foreign draggers thumbing their noses at Canada's conservation measures while they were either fishing on restricted quotas or forced to stay ashore.

As a lawyer, Crosbie knew that our international fisheries relations were based on the Law of the Sea. Within its 200-mile zone, Canada has the right to establish the TAC and to allocate quotas to the various domestic fleets. But Ottawa also has an obligation to give other states access to fish deemed to be surplus to the harvesting capacity of Canadian fishermen. Accordingly, international cooperation on management and conservation was a complex process of horse-trading that involved still-forming international law and a variety of multilateral institutions. It is not accidental that the fishery has been, and remains, Canada's most contentious foreign affairs issue.

Crosbie had problems with a number of fish pirates in and around Canadian waters, but few ways of dealing with them. Despite being members of the Northwest Atlantic Fisheries Organization (NAFO), the EC permitted its national fleets to fish in international waters at levels far higher than NAFO quotas. They weren't the only culprits.

To diminish the pressure on fish stocks in waters adjacent to Canada's economic zone, Ottawa had adopted what amounted to a cod-and-stick policy. In return for cooperating with the Canadian management plan, countries such as the former U.S.S.R., Cuba, Poland, Japan, Norway, and Denmark received surplus fish allocations within the 200-mile zone, as well as their traditional share of fish in international waters beyond 200.

The problem was that some countries, notably Spain and Portugal, didn't play by the rules. There had also been a dramatic increase in fishing by non-NAFO members and flag-of-convenience vessels outside Canada's 200-mile limit, including the United States, Korea, and Panamanian-registered vessels of uncertain origin. In 1990 alone, Canadian surveillance officers sighted 130 EC vessels in the NAFO area off Newfoundland. Although the fishing effort had increased, the estimated catches remained at 1989 levels, the historic sign that stocks were in decline.

Given the intricacies of international law, taking decisive action wasn't as cut and dried as it sometimes looked. Every time Ottawa was tempted to do something about foreign fishing, a nervous federal mandarin was there to point out the hidden hook. In August 1989, for example, warrants were issued against the masters of two Spanish trawlers for fishing violations committed in Canadian waters. The two trawlers had recently tied up in St. Pierre and Miquelon and could easily have been arrested while crossing the Canadian zone. But fisheries officers did not board the vessels. As one senior DFO official put it, "France would make use of any such incident to support its contention that Canada's interpretation of the Law of the Sea concerning 'innocent passage' threatens access to St. Pierre/Miquelon and therefore St. Pierre/Miquelon must have an area that extends out to the high seas."

The "Perrier Initiative" of the Mulroney government was talk, talk, and more talk. Cabinet ministers raised the subject of over-fishing with their counterparts in the European Community and other NAFO states at every opportunity, and as a result of these diplomatic efforts, Ottawa concluded that its best chance of per-suading the EC to stop overfishing was to offer more fish inside the Canadian zone. It was not a strategy that anyone was anxious to explain to unemployed Canadian fishermen.

Crosbie's first priority as the new minister was to stop foreign overfishing, which meant dealing with the Spanish and Portuguese. He knew firsthand how intractable the Portuguese were on the subject. One of his last acts as Canada's minister for international trade had been to lead a delegation from Newfoundland on a four-day tour of Portugal to meet the prime minister, his minister of fisheries, and local vessel owners. The owners insisted that Canada's problems were not caused by Portuguese overfishing, but by marauding seals and the small-mesh nets used by Newfoundland fishermen.

While accusations and counter-accusations flew, the provocations continued. The EC totally ignored the 1990 NAFO quota of 15,377 tonnes on the Nose and Tail of the Banks, setting its own quota of 60,000 tonnes. According to Canadian surveillance figures, Spain and Portugal then added insult to injury, taking 62,000 and 32,000 tonnes of fish respectively, while Canada desperately begged for compliance with conservation measures. Ottawa's diplomatic effort continued but the countries of the EC simply fished harder than ever.

While foreign fleets pillaged the northern cod, reports from the Gulf of St. Lawrence and the Scotian shelf showed the same drastic decline in fish stocks as on the Grand Banks. Crosbie knew there wasn't much time to come up with answers to the growing crisis.

Just a month before Crosbie took over from Bernard Valcourt, one hundred angry fishermen from the west coast of Newfoundland vandalized the DFO office in Port aux Basques. They were protesting the early closure of their traditional winter cod fishery in zone 3Pn, a step the DFO had taken because too many redfish were being caught as by-catch. When the protestors found the glass doors to the office locked, they kicked them in. Once inside, they threw computers, filing cabinets, and office furniture through the windows. By the time they were done, they had destroyed $100,000 worth of public property. Two days later, federal officials "found" an additional redfish quota and reopened the 3Pn fishery. A month after that, sixty fishermen staged a peaceful protest at the same DFO office, requesting an increase in their cod quota. Bureaucrats responded by adding 300 tonnes of fish to the original quota of 400 tonnes. Storefront bargaining was hard for Ottawa to resist.

Nervous mandarins continued to hope for a miracle. In June 1991, DFO scientists were set to review the assessment of the northern cod stock. The results would be discussed with industry stakeholders at a special meeting of the Atlantic Groundfish Advisory Committee (AGAC) scheduled for July. The DFO promised that the scientific advice for the 1992 fishing season would be finalized in time for the fall 1991 meeting of AGAC. The entire fishing industry held its breath.

Crosbie tried to maintain control of a potentially chaotic situation by doing what he could to ease the desperation of fishermen, companies, and plant workers caught in the cod crisis. He started by rescuing Newfound Resources of St. John's, a consortium of sixteen inshore fish-plant owners who faced bankruptcy because they had lost their northern cod quota. Crosbie's answer was to give the company a shrimp licence. The Nova Scotia Draggers Association immediately attacked the minister for showing favouritism to a firm from his native province.

There were more charges of favouritism at the end of July 1991, when Crosbie announced that the FPI plant at Gaultois would reopen to process redfish. Two hundred and fifty people were hired. But not everyone was as happy as the people of Gaultois. Over eighty Newfoundland fishermen threatened to fish illegally on the Grand Banks after Crosbie turned down their request for additional cod quota in zone 3NO, an area more than two hundred miles south of Newfoundland. The fishermen, who had a legal quota in zone 3L, claimed that the cod had migrated to 3NO because of unusually cold water temperatures. Crosbie rejected their demand. Canada had already agreed to the NAFO fishery management plan in international waters. If Ottawa didn't observe the rules, how could the Spanish or Portuguese be expected to obey them?

Despite stern warnings from Crosbie, the fishermen sailed their longliners from St. John's to 3NO and began to fish. When the skippers returned to port on July 24, 1991, several of them were arrested on Crosbie's orders. It was the right thing to do, but the sight of Canadian fisheries officers arresting Newfoundlanders while foreign vessels continued to pillage the straddling stocks in the same waters appalled the province's fishermen.

Captain Wilfred Bartlett of Brighton, Newfoundland, sailed his sixty-foot longliner to 3NO because it was the only destination left. In his opinion, the issue wasn't legal but moral; he was after Newfoundland fish: "All of a sudden we're not allowed to go and catch it. There's nothing left for us anywhere else. I don't want to go down in 3NO but out of desperation there is nowhere else. . . . What do you do? Do you stay ashore and starve to death? Or do you go and catch what you believe is yours? Or do you leave it there for the foreigners? That's the question."

By September 1991, the St. John's *Evening Telegram* was calling for "gunboat diplomacy" to stop the Spanish and Portuguese from overfishing. Crosbie sent a letter to the editor reminding Newfoundlanders that firing on, or sinking, a foreign vessel on the high seas would be an act of war. Nor did Crosbie believe that trade sanctions were the answer. How could Canada impose sanctions against the EC, with its huge population of 325 million, when it purchased 20 per cent of Newfoundland's and 8 per cent of Canada's exports? Retaliatory sanctions could do a great deal more harm to the Canadian economy than they ever could to the EC's. Crosbie pointed out that a jingoistic call to arms might make the public feel good, but that the people charged with governing the country knew how dangerously irresponsible it was in the real world of global politics.

As Newfoundlanders agitated for action against the foreign fish pirates, FPI announced that its plant at Trepassey would close on September 20, 1991. Six hundred and forty jobs and $14 million in wages were lost in a dozen rural communities around Trepassey with no other employment prospects. The curtain appeared to be coming down on four hundred years of history.

Crosbie briefed Clyde Wells on Ottawa's progress in fighting foreign overfishing at a meeting in St. John's on September 19, 1991. The two men agreed on one thing: the crisis in the fishery was taking on frightening proportions. As many as seven thousand fishery workers in Newfoundland alone would need financial assistance from government. The inshore fishermen had caught little more than half of their allocation, and they believed the federal government that had managed the stock and set the quotas was solely to blame. Exclusive jurisdiction and shared blame was a dog that wouldn't hunt.

In October 1991, in response to the catch failure, Crosbie announced a $40-million assistance package. Three-quarters of the funds would go to Newfoundland. All told, ten thousand fishermen and plant workers in Atlantic Canada would receive cheques from Ottawa. Crosbie blamed the inshore's empty nets on the ice that had remained on the Banks until August, preventing fishermen from getting their gear in the water. But the minister and his officials in the DFO were the only people who believed that Nature and not bad management was responsible for the disappearing stocks.

On October 9, 1991, Dr. Les Harris went on the CBC's fisheries program in St. John's and publicly wondered if the amazingly hardy fish would survive, let alone rebuild. On the same program, Dr. Brian Morrissey, the assistant deputy minister for science at the DFO, said that both the 1990 stock survey and commercial catch results showed that the northern cod stock had grown from the time Harris did his study from about 800,000 tonnes to 1,100,000 tonnes. He estimated the spawning biomass at approximately 270,000 tonnes, or a little smaller than it had been in 1977. Asked why there were no fish on the northeast coast, Morrissey theorized that the stock had moved south into zones 3K and 3L. Ottawa's whistling past the graveyard was getting loud enough to wake the dead. As Dr. Harris said in a later interview, "I think our scientists saw their data from a particular perspective that the stock was growing at the rate they had projected, and the data were sort of made to fit the equation."

In December 1991, when Crosbie announced the 1992 quota for northern cod, he reduced the 190,000-tonne TAC from the previous year by just 5,000 tonnes, noting that he would review the number later against the results of ongoing scientific investigations. Crosbie recalled, "There was no advice indicating at this time that there should be any further reduction. I was advised at this

142 • LAMENT FOR AN OCEAN

date that the northern cod stock was in better shape than it had been several years earlier." The DFO continued to sleepwalk towards the abyss, having apparently convinced the minister that it would all somehow work out in the end.

On November 20, 1991, Premier Wells had asked Ottawa to use military force to stop foreign overfishing on the Nose and Tail of the Banks. Wells also wanted Brian Mulroney to tell the world through organizations such as NAFO and the United Nations that Canada would take unilateral action to protect the stocks. Crosbie considered Wells's request to be "cheap political rhetoric," and offered a warning: "The consequences to Canada of such outrageous, illegal, and belligerent actions in international waters would be incalculable and would affect far more Canadian interests than simply those of the people living in coastal Canada."

But Crosbie was too seasoned a politician not to realize that public opinion in Newfoundland had turned against the Tories. Something had to be done about the fish pirates and done fast. In January 1992, he announced that Canada would press for international support of conservation measures at the UN. With Newfoundland getting more restless by the day, the federal minister set out on a two-week mission that would take him to London, Japan, and Hong Kong, where he hoped to win international support for a peaceful resolution of the overfishing crisis. He was beginning to look a lot like the Neville Chamberlain of the cod crisis.

On January 10, 1992, Crosbie travelled to London where he addressed a Royal Institute of International Affairs conference on international boundaries. Crosbie eloquently described the severe depletion of the fish stocks off Canada's Atlantic coast caused by overfishing, primarily by members of the EC fleet, outside Canada's 200-mile zone. He talked about the importance of developing international law with respect to the straddling stocks and called for international support for the principles established by the Law of the Sea Convention, but not yet ratified, to end their overfishing. Freedom of the high seas, he declared, had to mean more than the right to overfish and pollute.

Crosbie explained that his government was facing mounting pressure for unilateral action outside the 200-mile zone: "Such actions and their possible consequences are something that no state wants to consider. Time is running out for the resources being overfished and for fishing communities that depend on those resources. Tangible progress must be made in 1992 or other options will have to be seriously considered."

Crosbie assured his audience that Canada would continue to pursue all avenues for a solution and wanted only "agreed, equitable, and enforceable rules governing the rights and duties of states." Since 1986, the EC fleets had taken over 400,000 tonnes above NAFO quotas. This had reduced Canada's own offshore fleet by one-third and created great hardship in traditional fishing communities, particularly in Newfoundland. Crosbie invited Spanish and Portuguese delegations to come to Atlantic Canada in March to see for themselves what foreign overfishing had done to the East Coast. The Europeans came and went, and their unrestricted fishing continued unabated.

Although Crosbie wasn't saying it publicly, he was beginning to come around to the view that it was time to get tough with the EC. In response to a request from the prime minister, who asked Crosbie for his views on what the government should do with the balance of its mandate, he sent a letter to Mulroney on January 24, 1992. Crosbie explained that the most sensitive issue in Newfoundland was how to deal with EC overfishing on the Nose and Tail of the Grand Banks.

He noted that the provincial government was pushing hard for Canada to take over custodial management of the disputed area if the issue wasn't resolved by the end of 1992. He told Mulroney that there was "tremendous" public support for the premier's position in Newfoundland. "Our negotiations with the European Community to try to achieve bilateral progress failed," he wrote. And although he still had hopes of achieving some progress on the issue of straddling stocks at the June UN Earth Summit in Rio de Janeiro, he told the prime minister what must happen if Ottawa ran into a diplomatic brick wall. "If there is not considerable improvement in our progress on overfishing with the European Community by the end of 1992, it is difficult to see how we can avoid taking some kind of unilateral action in 1993 to stop the overfishing now endangering the fish stocks of the northwest Atlantic."

The second arm of the Canadian campaign was a legal one, based on "promising ambiguities" in the Law of the Sea convention relating to straddling stocks. Sixteen other countries had now endorsed Canada's position, and all eyes would be on the subject at the Rio Summit. Crosbie liked the idea of having the fishery resolution adopted at the same gathering that would be examining other ecological catastrophes like global warming and the destruction of the Amazon rain forest. Canada intended to call for a conference on high-seas fisheries and a special session of NAFO to get better surveillance outside the 200-mile zone.

Desperate Newfoundland fishermen, meanwhile, were demanding an immediate cut in the cod quota and swift action against foreign fish pirates. Frustrated by what they saw as Ottawa's dithering, they accused Crosbie of not listening to them. "Bunk," he snapped. "I've been listening to them ever since I was elected . . . and I will listen to them, but I'm not going to carry out advice of theirs that I think is wrong. I'm not going to listen to advice that says, oh, reduce the TAC for the northern cod to 125,000 tonnes when there's no scientific advice that says this should be done, or must be done. I'm not going to do something that I think is wrong for Canada."

Crosbie believed that the only people who wanted the TAC cut were representatives of the inshore fishery like Tom Best, who wanted to see the offshore fishery disbanded, despite the prosperity the deep-sea sector had brought to Newfoundland. "Tom Best as an inshore fisherman expects that he will be able to fish and he doesn't seem worried about the fact that all his brethren on fishing trawlers and all those who work in fish plants supplied by the offshore fleet will be closed, and they'll be out of a job."

In a way, Crosbie had it right. But in a bigger way, so did Tom Best.

Tom Best of Petty Harbour, one of the founders of the Newfoundland Inshore Fisheries Association, had been fishing for twenty-six years. What he saw in 1992 was a complete disaster. Eighty per cent of the fish landed in Petty Harbour were under twenty inches long. Ten years earlier, 80 per cent of the catch had been longer than twenty-four inches. Overall landings were down 75 per cent from what they had been a decade earlier, despite the latest technology and a doubled fishing effort.

Best thought that the solution to the fisheries crisis was a five-year moratorium on offshore fishing by both the domestic and foreign fleets. Trawlermen and plant workers who lost their jobs should be compensated, and the inshore fishery should be allowed to continue. "The inshore fishery has been around for four hundred years and we have never, ever done anything to put the fish stocks in the state they are in today. It has all happened in the offshore."

To Best and most inshore fishermen, Ottawa was perpetrating a terrible injustice by making them pay for the sins of big fishing companies. People such as Fishery Products International president Vic Young, with their stock options and executive pension plans, would have secure futures no matter what happened. But inshore fishermen risked permanently losing everything they had because of the excesses of the offshore fleets.

Vic Young's Nova Scotia counterpart, Henry Demone of National Sea Products, thought that Best's suggestion for a five-year moratorium on deep-sea trawlers would have more credibility if the inshore sector wasn't investing in new, middle-distance vessels that could fish as far offshore as seventy miles. In 1987, there had been seventeen middle-distance vessels that caught 1,300 tonnes of cod. By 1990, there were 114 vessels with landings of more than ten times that amount. Demone pointed out that the National Sea offshore fleet was highly regulated, used larger-than-regulation nets for conservation purposes, and landed its catch at

three government-designated landing ports, Lunenburg, Louisbourg, and St. John's. In the interests of prudent fishing practices,
every vessel had a federal observer onboard. By comparison, inshore
boats could land their catch anywhere and were not required to
carry DFO observers.

Despite their defensiveness about offshore fishing practices, the
big companies were as worried as any inshore fisherman about
what was happening to the stocks. And it wasn't just cod. Fishery
Products International had also experienced a shortage of yellowtail flounder and American plaice. Catches for these species had
dropped 30 per cent over the past three years. FPI had been forced
to lay off two thousand workers over the last few seasons because
there had simply been fewer fish to catch. Since 1989, the company
had tied up seventeen of its fifty-five trawlers. In Vic Young's
words, FPI was reducing capacity, because overcapitalization forces
you "to do the wrong thing with the fish stocks."

As troubled as he was by declining stocks in other species, Young
was mortified by the disappearance of the northern cod. For the
first time in history, in 1991 FPI failed to catch any cod in area 2J.
At first, the company thought it was because of ice conditions. But
when FPI trawlers returned to the fishing grounds in the fall, there
were still no cod in 2J. The only place the company found cod was
in 3K, where it managed to catch its quota. But the fish were uniformly small. A terrible possibility presented itself. Was FPI catching the four- and five-year-old fish that the DFO was counting on
to rebuild the stock? Ottawa insisted that the industry could take
180,000 tonnes of northern cod in 1992 without harming the stock.
Asked about the assurances from the DFO, Young replied, "Now, I
can't say if they're right or wrong. I can say I'm very uncomfortable with it. Why? Because I now see that there's no fish in 2J. That
makes everyone very, very uncomfortable."

Young sympathized with John Crosbie's dilemma. He understood that Ottawa had to balance stock conservation with community survival; in times of poor landings, that was a very difficult
balance to achieve. He also thought that the focus of the federal

government should be on the kind of gear that was killing smaller fish, which the small boat's cod trap did as effectively as a trawler's massive nets. Young believed that at least part of the solution was to increase the mesh size in the offshore, which had already been done once, and to ask offshore vessels to withdraw from any area where the catch was undersized.

As for foreign overfishing, Young fumed that what the Spanish and Portuguese were doing was "absolutely unforgivable." Nor did he think John Crosbie's diplomatic efforts would halt their destructive fishing practices. "The only reason he's been unsuccessful is not because he hasn't put the effort in. It's because the Europeans are impervious to that kind of stuff. They don't give a damn."

Young wanted the Canadian government to devise the best possible legal strategy to unilaterally extend fisheries management to cover the straddling stocks. Catastrophe made for strange bedfellows. The head of Newfoundland's fishermen's union, Richard Cashin, for once agreed with the corporate princes. If Canada couldn't get agreement with NAFO countries within six months, Ottawa should move unilaterally to extend jurisdiction beyond two hundred miles.

John Crosbie stuck doggedly to the strategy of diplomacy over gunboats, saying, "Now there isn't another country in the world that will recognize our right to do it. . . . Canada has no more right to it, no more right to decide what should be done there, than 150 other countries in the world. This is the international high seas. If we did it, we would immediately be up against the whole world. We would risk all our other interests by such an act. . . . You're not going to do it unless there's absolutely no alternative."

To an increasing number of Newfoundlanders, the view was taking hold that it was already too late. Liberal MHA John Efford predicted that both sectors of the Newfoundland fishery would close forever if Ottawa didn't act immediately to end foreign overfishing. "The fact is, the fish stocks are near depletion and in one year or two years down the road, there'll be no more fish for anybody to catch."

Efford estimated that at any given time, there were over two hundred vessels fishing just outside Canada's 200-mile limit off Newfoundland. Half of those were factory-freezers that stood eight storeys high. After taking a surveillance flight, Efford remarked that there were so many ships lit up on the Banks that it was like flying over a "floating city" in the middle of the Atlantic. Efford accused the foreign fleets of catching at least five times the NAFO quota and of destroying the spawning and juvenile cod in their relentless pursuit of fish.

Fishermen in outports like Port de Grave were "very frightened people," Efford said. They faced the prospect of losing a lifetime of work building up equity in their boats and gear, assets that would be utterly worthless if the stocks disappeared. Newfoundland itself could not exist without the fishery, except as a shipwreck. "This will become a complete welfare state for the few people who decide or want to live here."

Dr. Les Harris offered his analysis of why Ottawa was so slow to acknowledge a disaster in the making. When the scientists recommended that the quotas be cut in half, they created a terrible dilemma for politicians. The minister now had to tell fishermen and companies who had invested millions of dollars in the industry that they couldn't have any fish. The alternative was to save the fishermen by allowing them to wipe out the stock. But in that case, Harris argued, Ottawa would end up in exactly the same position, except that the cod would be gone. He believed that the only answer was for government to support unemployed fishermen while the cod stock was allowed to rebuild. But unless Ottawa moved decisively, that option would soon be off the table. "It seems to be too big a pill for the politicians to swallow . . . that the species, the survival of the species, is more important when the chips are down than what happens to any number of individual fishermen in a particular year."

With Dr. Harris's pill stuck firmly in his throat, John Crosbie did his best to fight a rearguard action against critics who wanted him to dramatically reduce the northern cod quotas before it was too late. While he tried to focus on foreign overfishing and a federal fish-aid package to deal with continuing catch failures, Crosbie was bombarded by anecdotal evidence that the DFO had been tragically wrong about the fish stocks.

Behind the scenes, Crosbie's officials were telling him that the biomass was better than it had been in 1977, but had only increased threefold rather than fivefold, as DFO scientists had previously predicted. They insisted that the present course would lead to higher catches, although scientists were still examining the fall research surveys. Crosbie knew what that meant: the advice for 1992 could still change. That had happened once before after the Alverson Report was released in 1987, and John Crosbie hadn't been amused.

"I was alarmed, and not only alarmed but I was disgusted, I was enraged, I couldn't even begin to describe how I felt when I heard that particular year . . . the quota for 1989 should be reduced. . . . A huge, I mean incomprehensible, incredible change in the advice. Naturally, I was disgusted beyond all belief."

Though he was privately furious with his DFO scientists for their wildly fluctuating advice, he accepted their latest assurances and refused to consider reducing the quota to 125,000 tonnes "unless there was very convincing scientific evidence that the fish stocks otherwise were going to disappear altogether. And there is no such evidence." DFO scientists had not recommended a TAC reduction to 125,000 tonnes, he insisted, unless they were "giving advice to someone who doesn't get through to me. . . . They haven't done it. And until they do, I'm not even going to consider it."

Asked if the small fish that were being caught inshore signalled the imminent collapse of the northern cod stock, Crosbie claimed that all the big fish were being caught in zone 3NO because cold water had kept the cod from coming in to the northeast coast. (The meandering and sometimes fatally frigid Labrador current can, in fact, freeze a whole population of fish if it overtakes them. At temperatures of minus two degrees Celsius, cod have been hauled up frozen solid in fishermen's nets.) Confronted with the fact that fishermen hadn't even been able to catch the federal quota in the last fishing season, Crosbie observed that the fishery was a very fickle business, as historical catch records showed: "There's always good years and bad years, and there always is going to be." The question was not whether there should be draconian cuts to the cod quota, but "whether you're going to have a rural life in Newfoundland and Labrador or Atlantic Canada, or not. There is no rural economy in Newfoundland outside the fishery."

While he was scolded, advised, and vilified by every Newfoundland reporter with a byline, Crosbie sought a diplomatic solution to what he thought was best presented to the world as an ecological problem. But his hope of embarrassing the Europeans at Rio was fading. Although Canada had sixteen co-sponsors for its resolution to protect straddling stocks, none of them were "major nations," such as Japan, the United Kingdom, or the United States.

On the domestic front, demands were getting shrill for unilateral action against foreign fishermen. Irritated by the constant criticism that Canada was behaving like a wimp, Crosbie reminded his critics that there was another side to the overfishing problem that few Canadians wanted to talk about. "We're no angels here. The fishermen that you hear complaining all over Eastern Canada – many, many of them are guilty of overfishing, discarding, throwing away smaller fish. The fishery in the Gulf [is] almost ruined. The foreigners didn't ruin the fishery in the Gulf. We ruined the fishery in the Gulf."

In contemporary Newfoundland, it is a toss-up as to who is the poet laureate of the inshore fishery, Cabot Martin or Dr. Leslie Harris. In addition to a rich and detailed understanding of the industry, both men have the gift for expressing the deeper cultural underpinnings of cod. For Martin, the cod crisis was much more than an unemployment problem.

"I think that there is a big world problem here," he said in an interview. "It is food. . . . Here in Newfoundland, it means the destruction of a wage economy. In most of the underdeveloped world it means the loss of a source of food for very, very poor people. There's also a historic problem here of not understanding the limits of nature, not understanding environmental risk. They learned in northern Norway the hard way. Do we have to destroy the basis of our society and our culture and our history to learn that lesson?"

Martin compared what was happening in the fishery to people on the edge of a desert chopping down trees to cook their food, knowing full well that the desert would get bigger as a result of their action. In a similar way, both the offshore and inshore fishery were authors of their own demise. "You have this terrible problem of the big companies trying to keep their quarterly dividends up, or their quarterly losses down; and you get the inshore fisherman starting to implement destructive techniques because he is trying to keep bread on the table and he has to try to get his unemployment straightened away for the winter."

Martin believed that everyone in authority had slipped into a state of denial while the sea was being made into a desert. Until people saw the crisis of the northern cod in the same light as the destruction of the Amazon jungle, old-growth forests on Vancouver Island, and whales and seals, the politicians and bureaucrats would maintain the status quo. But a hard rain had begun to fall on the East Coast fishery and there were no easy choices left for leaders like John Crosbie. "To cut the quota means to inflict pain, and most politicians don't want that," Martin said. "So the terrible tendency is not to do anything, to put off making the hard decision."

Martin himself was convinced that the evidence of a terrible crisis was overwhelming. Between 1870 and 1950, people rowed out to their cod traps or fished with hook and line or longlines and landed over 200,000 tonnes of fish every season. In 1991, an improved and far more efficient inshore fishery landed just 35,000 tonnes of cod. "There is no doubt, in any knowledgeable person's mind, that there is a disaster and the disaster is here. . . . You know that politicians have hard responsibilities, but there is a point at which some element of basic truth has got to come through."

Martin blamed the demise of the cod on the corporate–bureaucratic alliance that ran the fishery and Ottawa's unwillingness to recognize the obvious. Even though some unions and fishermen's groups advised the minister, Martin believed that it was the big companies that called the shots. "Basically, if National Sea or FPI don't agree with something, there is no consensus and there is no advice that goes forward. . . . What you've got is nineteenth-century thinking dressed up in modern clothes. It is very much of a 'the ocean is inexhaustible and cannot be harmed' approach, and we go to the end."

The end was now in sight.

7

FISHED OUT

More surveys were done by the DFO's research vessels in the last six months of 1991 than the department had probably done in the last six years. In February 1992, DFO scientists advised Crosbie that there had been a major decline in the number of cod capable of spawning. CAFSAC estimated that the spawning biomass was now only 130,000 tonnes, down from 300,000 tonnes in the previous estimate and a dramatic decline from the 500,000 tonnes estimated by Rice and Evans in 1986. CAFSAC advised that the quota should be cut to 25,000 tonnes for the first half of the year, half of what fishermen caught in the same period in 1991.

On February 28, 1992, Crosbie announced a 35 per cent reduction in the TAC. The new TAC would be 120,000 tonnes, just 7,000 tonnes less than the total Canadian catch in 1991. Fishing as hard as they could, fishermen had only been able to catch 127,000 tonnes, just two-thirds of the 1991 TAC of 190,000 tonnes. Crosbie also announced that there would be no caplin fishery in 1992.

According to Dr. Leslie Harris, "By 1987−88 DFO scientists were convinced that the thing was totally off the rails, and that the fishing mortality was probably up about 50 per cent and maybe even higher than that. It was then, of course, that they recommended a drastic reduction in the TAC, in order to get the fishing mortality back on the rails. Now when John [Crosbie] and others say subsequently they followed our recommendations, they did to a degree, it's true, but they followed them almost three years after they should have been implemented. When the [DFO] scientists first said in 1988 that the TAC should be dropped to 120,000 tonnes and then monitored from then on, the fishing went on as usual, with steady increases for the next two and a half years. By the time our report came out another year had passed, and so the [TAC] reductions that should have been brought about on a much larger biomass were now being applied to a much smaller one, because the spawning biomass had already declined through three years of overfishing."

Crosbie announced a cap of 25,000 tonnes on the amount of northern cod caught in the first half of 1992, in effect stopping winter fishing on the spawning grounds. He also announced that as a precautionary step the trawler harvest of offshore cod during peak spawning periods would be banned until it could be scientifically demonstrated that such harvesting did not harm the stocks. At least thirty trawlers would be tied up and two thousand plant workers laid off.

When CAFSAC submitted its preliminary report on the state of the northern cod in early 1992, Crosbie reviewed it with the fisheries ministers of the four Atlantic provinces, and industry and union representatives at meetings in Ottawa.

CAFSAC based its report on the fall 1991 surveys, the fall landings, data from environmental monitoring, and scientific information collected over the years. It reported a significant reduction in the number of cod aged seven and older but could not give a reason for the disappearance. The most recent assessment had indicated an abrupt decline in the biomass. In setting out its recommendations for the 1991 TAC, CAFSAC had estimated the spawning biomass to be 270,000 tonnes. But now, less than year later, it revised its figures to about 130,000 tonnes. The total biomass of cod aged three and up was revised downward from 1,085,000 tonnes to 704,000 tonnes.

The CAFSAC document noted that the 1991 inshore cod fishery had been the worst since 1976, when only 67,000 tonnes were caught. Fishermen were catching less fish per unit of effort. The offshore catch had declined by 23 per cent, to the lowest point since 1982. Not only were the cod scarce in the Canadian zone, the weight of the fish for their age was generally lower than average. A special effort was made to see if the cod had moved either off the bottom above the fishing gear or into neighbouring divisions due to the extreme ice conditions of 1991. They hadn't.

There was a crisis in the northwest Atlantic fishery that could no longer be ignored.

One of the largest employers in the Atlantic region, the fishery employed 61,000 fishery workers living in 1,300 communities, and involved about 29,000 vessels. Newfoundland and Nova Scotia counted for about 86 per cent of the registered vessels, 78 per cent of the fish landings, and 77 per cent of the value of the catch. Over 30,000 people worked in 1,000 fish processing plants in the five affected provinces. The majority of cod caught was for export, and cod was 25 per cent of total Canadian fish exports.

In Newfoundland there was anger and panic – the fishing industry accounted for 20 per cent of provincial employment. John Crosbie complained that the advice he was getting was inconsistent, making it virtually impossible to manage the fishery.

Estimating the size of the biomass of northern cod is difficult because the fish migrate through vast areas of the ocean. Error can come from the raw data or the statistical methodology. The DFO used a methodology called Virtual Population Analysis (VPA) to do stock assessments. Each year-class (the fish spawned in a certain year) is tracked and the mortality of the year-class is estimated. Natural mortality is assumed to be at about 20 per cent per year but mortality may be affected by a variety of factors such as changes in the ocean temperature, food supply, or the number of predators, or even disease. One of the big problems with VPA is that it takes about five years before scientists know how many fish are in the stock today. They don't know how many young fish there are until they begin to be caught by the commercial fleet.

This estimate is "tuned" or adjusted with the information from test catches done by a research vessel (RV) and the catch per unit of effort (CPUE) recorded by offshore fishing vessels. These tuning indicators are also subject to error. Sometimes they even give conflicting information. If, as Harris pointed out in his report, the RV data show a decline in population, but the commercial catch-rates show an increase, how do scientists handle the conflicting data? An average of the two figures is no solution.

Clyde Wells says that Harris told the DFO that the decline would happen precipitately, that there would be a sudden drop. "His logic was fairly simple. He said, 'Look, just assume that the top of this desk is a school of fish; and this pen is the vessel. As long as it's anywhere on that school of fish, it can catch all the fish you want. And this is what the feds were basing their knowledge on. The offshore vessels are catching all the fish they want. As [the school] shrinks, and the sheet of paper is now the size of the school of fish, the vessel is still catching it. The catch-rates are still the same, even though the quantity of fish are down to 10 per cent. Then the school of fish gets as small as the pencil, and smaller, and suddenly, no fish!' Harris was absolutely right. He told them long before that this was going to happen, and they didn't move!"

The offshore fishing companies made their records readily available to DFO scientists. They saw a point to the collection and evaluation of data, and the DFO scientists were much more comfortable dealing with the companies than with individual inshore fishermen. With one contact in National Sea Products and one in FPI, collecting data from fifty trawlers was much easier than from thousands of inshore fishermen using different gear in hundreds of locations, and who might conceivably resist keeping records since they had little faith in DFO science.

Even if data could be collected from the inshore fishery, the DFO didn't have the resources to analyze it. A fisherman set his traps where his father set his traps and his father before him. His knowledge couldn't be fed into a computer as readily as statistical information from a trawler.

Marine biology is expensive and complex. The northern cod live in an area about 500,000 square miles. Labs, telecommunications equipment, computers, research ships and aircraft are all necessary. Research vessels try to piece together the total picture of the stock by taking fish samples during a half-hour tow at selected depths in a specific area. The fish are counted, weighed, and measured. Sampling is done in the fall and depends on the weather. The estimates and catch per unit effort were used to tune the Virtual Population Analysis, and became the basis for setting quotas.

Until the summer of 1991, National Sea Products catches had been great, according to Henry Demone. After that summer the company realized something was wrong. It showed the DFO its catch results: "We knew what was coming, it was just a matter of when it was coming." The company pulled its trawlers in. Demone sympathized with Crosbie's position: "The scientists said things are great in '88 or '89. Then, all of a sudden, in '89 or '90 they say, 'Oh my God, things are not great, there is a huge problem here.' And you look for information wherever you can find it and say, 'What do we do here? Do we throw thousands of people out of work?' That's not a minor decision.

"With the benefit of hindsight everyone says, 'Oh yeah, sure, you should have closed it down in '89 or '90,' right. But I think very few people would have done that in Crosbie's situation. I think he took a conservative approach, which was to say, let's put the quota down significantly, wait a year, and see what happens."

In his 1994 book *Fishing for Truth*, Alan Finlayson set out to examine the degree to which scientific error had caused the cod crisis, and how scientific rationality collides with bureaucratic reality. Finlayson explained: "Having made large investments in the production of knowledge, and having originally certified it as valid, the institution will not lightly decertify its validity." Having said the stock was healthy, it was "normal" to reject outside claims that the stock was in trouble. Faced with ambiguous data, DFO scientists interpreted them optimistically.

By the time a report about current stock population estimates makes it to the desk of the fisheries minister, Finlayson says, dissent has been smoothed away by the bureaucrats. CAFSAC reconciles the differences in the data and produces an "objective" report. Even though there was often strong disagreement at CAFSAC meetings, the lack of consensus was not included in the reports. One set of advice went forward. The papers of scientists with a different conclusion were quietly filed away and conflicting opinions stayed within the department. The scientific advice is then matched with the management objectives of the department.

Finlayson wrote: "The idea is that managers can select objectives for stock rebuilding, management and exploitation on socioeconomic (or other) grounds, and decide how to weigh the competing needs of biology, economics, [and] community development." The managers set the objectives and the scientists suggest quotas that will give that objective. The minister then sets the yearly quota, and individuals and corporations make their harvesting and processing plans. At least that is how it is supposed to work. One of the problems was that the scientists often did not know what the management objectives were.

Even using the most sophisticated models of prediction available at the time, the margin of error was as much as 50 per cent. As Art May said in an interview, "That is always forgotten by people at the political level who are too busy to read the 200-page analysis, but want to know what the number is, and the number is the quota, and it's 200,000 tonnes, and you forget that it might be 50,000 and it might be 350,000." May made the qualification that he was making the process sound worse than it was. Pick the middle range and, on average, you will be right. But sometimes you're going to be badly wrong.

In 1991, foreign vessels fishing outside the 200-mile limit, in spite of a NAFO moratorium on 3L cod, caught an estimated 47,000 tonnes of the fish, the second-highest catch by foreign countries since 1977. Most of the vessels were from Spain and Portugal. During the spring 1991 survey, it was found that about 10 per cent of the 2J3KL cod biomass was outside the Canadian zone in 3L. Normally it was 5 per cent. Even if Canada did the right thing inside the 200-mile zone, foreign overfishing outside the zone would continue to have devastating effects.

Prime Minister Mulroney met with Premier Wells on March 3, 1992, to discuss northern cod and foreign overfishing. Mulroney said that using the navy was an attractive option, but that Canada had to be prepared to follow through on any threat. At this stage, Mulroney was not inclined to use force. He told Wells there was an ad hoc cabinet committee on northern cod that had been set up to deal with the issues.

Later in the month in New York, Crosbie met with Maurice Strong, who was organizing the Rio Earth Summit. Crosbie was seeking support for a resolution asking for the right of coastal states to manage straddling fish stocks, which would be presented in Rio. Back in Canada, an Opposition motion in the House of Commons moved by Roger Simmons, MP for Burin–St. Georges, called on the government to institute "functional jurisdiction" of the waters on the Nose and Tail of the Banks. The Tories defeated the motion easily by a vote of 91 to 51.

At the end of March 1992, eight Canadian trawlers sailed to the Banks beyond the 200-mile limit to show foreign fishermen how angry they were. The protest had Crosbie's support, and he flew out in a DFO surveillance plane to show his approval. Crosbie appointed then FFAW president Richard Cashin to head up a six-member federal task force. One of its tasks was to recommend an adjustment strategy.

The following month, Crosbie flew to Panama City, where he met Panama's finance minister and persuaded the government to forbid Panamanian-registered vessels from fishing in the NAFO area. Most of these vessels were owned by Spain or Portugal, although some were owned by South Korea. From Panama, Crosbie went to

Cuba to seek support for his resolution at the Rio Earth Summit in June. Cuba, also a member of NAFO, agreed to help. Cuba had allocations of silver hake, an underutilized species, within Canada's 200-mile zone and had always supported Canada on NAFO fisheries issues.

On April 21, 1992, the final day of his visit, Crosbie met with President Fidel Castro for an hour-long discussion of the fishery crisis. Castro was very interested and asked for maps to see exactly where these events were unfolding. He later instructed his fisheries minister to support Canada on the issues he had discussed with Crosbie, and the minister did so at a conference on responsible fishing held in Cancun, Mexico, during the first week of May. Over six hundred delegates attended from sixty-six countries. The consensus reached was that there had to be a UN conference on high-seas fishing, and that the freedom to fish had to be balanced by the obligation to conserve the resource.

Crosbie, Prime Minister Mulroney, Jacques Delors, the president of the EC, and the Portuguese prime minister, Cavaco Silva, met in Ottawa in late April to discuss overfishing. The mood was positive, and they decided that Canada would request a special NAFO scientific council meeting to assess the northern cod stocks just prior to the annual NAFO meeting in June. When the scientists met, they all agreed that the northern cod stocks were in terrible condition, and recommended that the TAC not exceed 50,000 tonnes.

Since the offshore trawlers had already caught that amount, adopting the TAC would mean that the inshore fishermen would not be allowed to catch any fish that year. Crosbie knew as soon as he received the reports that he would have to close the fishery, but to gain time he said his department had to study these new scientific findings. A decision would be made in early July.

The EC promised to stop fishing for cod, American plaice, and yellowtail flounder on the Nose and Tail of the Banks as of June 3, 1992. Everyone, including Crosbie, suspected that the real reason the EC made this gesture was that their boats weren't catching enough fish to pay for expenses.

At the United Nations Conference on Environment and Development, the Earth Summit held in Rio in June 1992, Canada called for more effective conservation measures for the preservation of high-seas fish stocks and stressed the importance of the special interest of coastal states in the conservation of straddling stocks. Arguing that the management of stocks by coastal states must not be jeopardized by the overfishing of long-distance fleets just outside the 200-mile limit, Canada sponsored a resolution calling for a conference on straddling and highly migratory fish stocks. The resolution was approved by all 188 countries attending the Rio conference.

This was a major win for Canada. On June 11 the NTV station in Newfoundland named John Crosbie the newsmaker of the week for his accomplishments in Rio. The station editorialized that it wasn't easy being a fisheries minister when there were no fish, but "John Crosbie fills the thankless portfolio well." Crosbie had put the East Coast crisis on the national agenda and had brought the issue to the world.

Crosbie's deputy minister, Bruce Rawson, and Marie Antoinette Flumium, his assistant deputy minister for policy, would help the minister immeasurably with the social tragedy he faced at home. The minister knew he could not announce a moratorium without having an assistance plan for the people who would be left without income. Crosbie later said, "In all my years of political life this was the most serious political and economic crisis I ever faced."

In February 1992, CAFSAC had said the spawning biomass was 130,000 tonnes. By July 1992 the estimate dropped to between 48,000 and 108,000 tonnes – the lowest number ever observed. Most of the fish that remained in the stock were born in 1986 and 1987, and were too young to spawn. If they were fished, how could the stock rebuild? The northern cod was the single most important fishery in Atlantic Canada. The largest groundfish stock on the East Coast was worth over $700 million to the Canadian economy in 1991. It supported about 31,000 jobs both directly and indirectly, 90 per cent of them in Newfoundland.

Although Crosbie and his officials devised an assistance program quickly, he then had to take it to the Treasury Board and the Department of Finance for funding. The plan also had to be approved by the special cabinet committee. Crosbie had the full support of the prime minister, even though Mulroney was extremely concerned about the deficit, but he was unable to convince the special committee to approve adequate compensation. He warned his colleagues that the offer would be received with hostility.

In Newfoundland everyone was talking about the crisis, and during the month of June the rumours flew. Crosbie had been invited to Bay Bulls to celebrate Canada Day. The minister and his wife, Jane, took their children and grandchildren with them to enjoy the occasion. It was a perfect summer day. As they pulled into town, they noticed several CBC vehicles down by the harbour, where a fisheries patrol vessel was docked. There was a large crowd along the wharf. To a seasoned politician, this was a sign there would be trouble. Canada Day in Bay Bulls did not usually draw such media attention.

As Crosbie made his way along the wharf, people demanded to know if the fishery was going to be closed. Crosbie knew many of them because they were in his district and realized that the jeering and heckling crowd could become dangerous. The CBC carried footage across Canada that night of Crosbie and his family moving through the angry crowd that blamed him for the disaster. At one point the minister turned on a heckler, saying, "I have not removed the goddamn fish from the water." Crosbie knew that the usual platitudes would not work, but he couldn't really blame the protestors. A way of life that had existed for four hundred years was about to end, and suddenly people who had never done anything but fish would no longer be able to make a living.

The next day Crosbie called a news conference at the Radisson Hotel in St. John's. When he and his staff arrived that afternoon there was a huge crowd waiting in the lobby, the overflow spilling into the corridors. Some of the people in the audience had used the excellent bar facilities of the downtown hotel and this fuelled the highly charged atmosphere. Crosbie entered the conference room and started to address the media. Unknown to him, fishermen had been turned away from the room. They were angry. As Crosbie started to speak there was loud knocking on the locked doors. He kept speaking.

Soon the doors began to shake as the fishermen tried to ram their way through. Crosbie carried on, explaining why he was closing the northern cod fishery as of midnight and declaring a moratorium until the spring of 1994 when the stock status would be reviewed. The federal government would provide the fishermen and plant workers affected with $225 a week for ten weeks, while a long-term relief plan was put into place. It was estimated that twenty thousand workers in almost four hundred communities would be affected.

Crosbie had warned his cabinet colleagues that the fishermen would regard the payment with contempt – and he was right. It was far less than they would receive on UI, and even less than some would receive on social assistance. When the devastating news reached the crowd outside the salon they became even rowdier. Security advised Crosbie and his party to leave the hotel before anyone was hurt. Led by the police, Crosbie ran a gauntlet of angry fishermen and plant workers. Cat calls and insults followed him out of the building.

Henry Demone, the president of National Sea Products, watched the coverage of the announcement on television with shock: "The cod closure we kind of expected. It was a question of when, not if. The shock that I got was the reaction to Crosbie in the Radisson Hotel in St. John's that day. I mean, it was violent. It was violent. I think he feared for his life."

For a variety of reasons, Demone had known the closure would happen. "First of all, the scientists did a 180-degree turn on the cod stocks. In the late eighties, there was a time they were optimistic, then they were very pessimistic. Certain sectors of the inshore were complaining of low, low catches, we saw smaller fish size, and we said, 'Hey, even though our catches are still okay, there is reason to be worried here, and we've got to think about what if.' We always do a lot of scenario planning, and so we did the 'what ifs' on the northern cod disappearing. And that helped us get our mind around the question. And then we had good fishing in June of '91. After that it was never the same; and we voluntarily pulled the boats out of the fishery in February of '92."

In a letter to the prime minister on July 6, 1992, Premier Wells called the moratorium "the most significant economic decision that has been taken by the Government of Canada in our history as a Province." He supported the move and agreed that failure to take action "would have further jeopardized the very future of our people and province." However, the compensation fell far short of "what is fair and necessary."

Wells could not endorse the financial package for the fishermen: it had to be revisited immediately. He continued: "Their reaction to the announcement does not come from selfishness or ingratitude. . . . Rather it stems from disbelief that their country and their government, having in forty years so managed the fish stock from which they and their ancestors derived their living for four hundred years as to require that they be prohibited from fishing it in the immediate future, could even for an interim period offer compensation that for many is less than welfare. That, Prime Minister, cannot be the fruits of Canadian citizenship in this province or any other." Wells assured Mulroney that he was writing directly to him not because he lacked confidence in Crosbie – he knew that Crosbie had done the best he could – but because he was "aware of the limitations on an individual cabinet minister and the requirement to fully support cabinet decisions."

The plight of the Newfoundland fishermen and plant workers became a major news event, and people across Canada witnessed their anger and frustration. Their powerful response helped Crosbie in Ottawa while he attempted to negotiate an adequate assistance program. Letters to editors across the country supported the

Newfoundland workers, and criticized the federal government for its handling of the crisis. Richard Cashin said the compensation was unacceptable and suggested the fishermen respond with civil disobedience and keep on fishing.

It had taken eighteen months to negotiate the Atlantic Fisheries Adjustment Program (AFAP) that was already in place. Despite the recession, high unemployment, and the constitutional crisis, it took just two weeks to announce the new program, the Northern Cod Adjustment and Recovery Program (NCARP), which quickly became known as "the package."

Maximum compensation was $406 per week. Those who decided not to take training got the minimum of $225 per week. A plant worker who chose training either inside or outside the fishery could get up to $406, depending on previous earnings. Almost eleven thousand people chose training inside the fishery; only two thousand workers opted for training outside the fishery. Others chose work projects, early retirement, or the minimum compensation. Only a thousand people chose to sell back their licences, a key part of the plan through which the government hoped to cut fishing capacity by half. In John Crosbie's view, only professional full-time fishermen should get a licence in the future. Uncontrolled entry into the fishery had to stop.

By May 1993, about sixteen thousand people in Newfoundland were receiving assistance under the package. In general, people were satisfied with the terms, although there was grumbling from some quarters about having to take training to collect the maximum amount of compensation. What was the point if there were no jobs available? Some people took advantage of the program to upgrade basic skills. One forty-eight-year-old plant worker from St. Mary's had left school with a grade three education, unable to read or write. Under NCARP he learned to do both.

The $484-million NCARP package was so hastily put together that about $6.5 million in overpayments were made to people who didn't qualify. The DFO sent out cheques based on a best guess about who should get the money. Fishermen and plant workers didn't even have to apply to get the funds. There were reports that money was even sent to people who had died. The October 1993 federal election glimmered on the horizon.

A new legal regime had been created at the Third United Nations Conference on the Law of the Sea in 1982. For the first time a qualification had been put on the principle of the "freedom of the high seas." Distant-water fishing nations now had two obligations: to conserve the stocks that straddle coastal state jurisdictions and the high seas; and, to cooperate with adjacent coastal states which had special rights over the stock. Unfortunately there were no enforcement rights and no dispute-resolution mechanism.

In 1986 most NAFO members had agreed that a moratorium should be placed on the cod fishery in 3L outside Canada's 200-mile zone, but the EC, Spain, and Portugal dissented, and the EC unilaterally established a quota for cod far in excess of its traditional share or that set by NAFO. In 1989 NAFO set the cod quota at 13,000 tonnes; the EC set its own quota at 160,000 tonnes, twelve times higher.

Canada had tried hard to negotiate with the EC. A special NAFO meeting was convened in May 1992 to consider five Canadian proposals for new surveillance and control measures: the establishment of an observer program, improved catch reporting, access to fishing records for NAFO inspectors, notice to the NAFO secretariat of fishing plans, and the setting up of a working group to develop a dispute settlement mechanism.

Norway, Denmark, and Japan supported the plan; Russia hesitated, wanting more information. The EC said it did not have authority to endorse any of the proposals, but its delegation agreed to discuss the items which would be on the table at the upcoming NAFO meeting in September 1992. The most controversial issue was the dispute-settlement mechanism.

At the September meeting the EC agreed with other NAFO members not to fish for cod in area 3L. This was closely tied to the moratorium imposed by Canada in July, which had made the

EC appreciate just how serious the depletion of northern cod was. NAFO also agreed to the introduction of a 130-millimetre net size for groundfish and a minimum fish length of 41 centimetres (sixteen inches) for cod. The observer scheme was agreed to in a weakened form – the EC provided the patrol vessel and put its own inspectors on board. If its patrol vessel was not available, then Canadian patrol vessels would carry both Canadian and EC inspectors. During an eighteen-month pilot project, observers would submit a report to their respective national governments, which would evaluate the findings.

Even with inspectors on board there could still be problems. Observers had been put on board foreign ships in Canada's 200-mile zone starting in 1987, but decrees from the Soviet fleet command sometimes clashed with Canadian rules. When they received orders from the fleet command not to discard fish, the Soviet crews tried to conceal the extra catch from the observer, rather than record it in the logbooks and endure the anger of the head of the U.S.S.R. fleet. On occasion, observers' estimates of haddock, cod, and pollock catches exceeded recorded amounts by as much as twenty tonnes.

An internal DFO report on the 1989 observer program on the Scotian shelf said: "At times, it also appeared that old habits from the days of 'pulse fishing' were still alive. . . . Many Soviet captains still sought massive bags of fish with each tow and did not appear to be too perturbed when their vessels could not haul the catch aboard without bursting the cod end nor process the amount of fish aboard in a reasonable time. Losses of ten tonnes or more of fish during haulback were routine yet no captains are observed to reduce effort or take other steps to avoid this unnecessary waste. There was usually a howl of protest from captains and fleet commanders however when suggestions were made that this fish should be treated as discards and counted against the quota."

There was also the possibility that observers would take bribes. A DFO internal audit report on the observer program in the mid-1980s detailed two attempts by foreign captains to offer "gifts" to observers. One was offered $10,000, and the other had $22,000 left at his home by a foreign captain. Fortunately both observers reported the actions to the DFO immediately.

Canada continued to urge the EC not to lodge a complaint about NAFO quotas, which in effect would legally allow them to fish as much as they wanted. In December 1992, the EC members agreed to operate within NAFO quotas, limit the EC catch to 16,000 tonnes in 1993, and not fish for 2J3KL cod in 1993. They also agreed to work at reducing the number of former EC vessels now operating under flags of convenience on the Banks. In return Canada would allow access to its ports by foreign vessels, denied since the mid-1980s, and access to "surplus stocks" in Canadian waters. However, individual countries, such as Spain and Portugal, could still object to NAFO quotas and set their own catch level.

The December 22, 1992, agreement reached between Canadian and EC negotiators now had to be approved by the EC, its member states, and the Canadian government. Some EC members believed that Canada had won too much in the negotiations. In particular, they disliked the implication that Canada now had the right to establish quotas and enforce conservation outside its 200-mile zone. Still, the EC ratified the agreement in January 1994, but by that time the Liberals had come to power in Ottawa and delayed signing the agreement. Many, including Newfoundland Fisheries Minister Walter Carter, argued that there were just too many ways for the EC vessels to get around the proposed agreement.

While the Rio Summit was on, the international tribunal ruled on the Canada–France boundary dispute. Most observers felt the three-to-two ruling gave Canada the edge. France got a twelve-mile territorial sea around St. Pierre and Miquelon, another twelve-mile economic zone to the southwest of the islands, and a narrow ten-and-a-half-mile-wide channel that led out to the high seas for two hundred miles. This meant that France got about 11 per cent of the 3Ps fishing zone, not the 50 per cent it had demanded, as well as about 50 per cent of the Icelandic scallop beds and about 20 per cent of the sea scallop stock.

Under the terms of a 1972 treaty, France was still entitled to fish in Canadian waters; the amount and species of fish had to be decided. Crosbie believed Canada had the right to determine what that would be, based on the health of the fish stocks. There would be no fish for France unless they agreed to manage the resources according to NAFO or Canadian conservation rules in 3Ps – and this included having observers on their vessels. Crosbie's wish list included access to the rich scallop beds around the French islands that the fish plants in Grand Bank depended on to remain open.

Discussions continued into October without much progress. On October 2, 1992, Crosbie made it clear that Canada would use her navy to prevent the French from fishing in Canadian waters, and to confine them to the territory imposed on them by the arbitration panel. The French had been allowed to take about twenty thousand tonnes of fish a year from Canadian waters under an agreement that had expired September 30, 1992.

Crosbie argued that dramatic cuts to this amount were necessary because of the collapse of the cod stocks. The change in the status of the stocks was something the French preferred not to understand. The ruling of the tribunal had in effect created a new straddling stock problem – this time the fish swam back and forth between the Canadian and French zones in 3Ps. A formal agreement about the stocks was not reached until 1995.

In November 1992, CAFSAC recommended drastic cuts in other groundfish quotas for 1993. This included cod in the southern Gulf of St. Lawrence and off the eastern Scotian shelf, as well as the south coast of Newfoundland. The unions wanted the fishery closed and to be given a "package" similar to NCARP rather than have to work under severe quota reductions. On December 18, 1992, Crosbie held a news conference in Halifax to announce cuts of about 60 per cent to the previous quotas. All groundfish stocks – cod, haddock, pollock – were at their lowest levels since the 1970s. The federal government was already spending $500 million to look after fishery workers in Newfoundland, but Crosbie didn't have a compensation package ready yet for the people who would be unemployed due to this latest disaster.

National Sea Products was hit the hardest by the cuts. The company closed its plants in Louisbourg and North Sydney immediately, and work at its Lunenburg plant was reduced to six months a year. Although many of the fishermen affected could still fish, they would not catch enough to qualify for UI. Many plant workers would not qualify either.

The day that Crosbie announced the closure of the northern cod stock was not Henry Demone's worst day. Demone later said, "My worst day was in the fall of '92. Strategically we had dealt with disappearance of the northern cod. We had closed plants, we had sold plants, we had sold off the food service business [fish for hotels, restaurants, institutions]. We had raised cash from all this. We had a healthy retail business. We were just then getting into the idea of more value-added products and products development."

Then Demone's manager in charge of fleet and government relations told him, "Henry, I've just got the scientific research for the Scotian shelf and the Gulf of St. Lawrence, and you will not believe it, but it's more of the same." Demone says, "That was my darkest hour. I thought, 'Oh my God,' I had just dealt with the impossible, right? I was looking forward in the budget to a profitable '93 in spite of all this stuff. And then he says, 'There's more coming, sit tight.'" National Sea's quota dropped by 95 per cent. At its peak in the mid-1980s, the company had caught 300 million pounds of fish. Now its catch would drop to 15 million pounds, just 5 per cent of their previous catch.

Demone said, "I really never imagined that 95 per cent of the fish could disappear. So we never really did sit down and say what would this company look like without any Atlantic Canadian groundfish until the fall of '92, when we got the scientific advice on the Scotian shelf the year after the cod moratorium became official. That's when we said, 'We're going to have to run this company without fish! Oh my God, what are we going to do!'"

Demone laughed, "That really clears the mind, when you are in a situation like that, and allows you to focus."

Crosbie worked diligently for four months to develop a package for the workers who would be left unemployed by the latest round of quota cuts. It was becoming increasingly difficult to get funding while the federal government was committed to deficit reduction. Sympathy in Ottawa was turning to worry about how far government resources could be stretched. But election talk was already in the air. In April 1993, Employment Minister Bernard Valcourt and Crosbie announced a new $191 million program – 7,600 people would get up to $406 a week for a year. But they had to agree to retraining as part of the deal.

In the fall of 1993, the DFO finally imposed a moratorium on the cod fishery off the south coast of Newfoundland and in the Gulf of St. Lawrence. But there is strong evidence that DFO officials knew the stocks should have been closed earlier. Alan Sinclair has been described by his co-workers as an excellent scientist and the kind of man who lies awake at night wondering if his analysis is right, knowing it will affect people's lives. He was also one of the first scientists within the DFO to realize that the cod stocks were in trouble.

On July 2, 1992, Sinclair, the chairman of CAFSAC's groundfish subcommittee, was to have made an overview presentation to the Atlantic Groundfish Advisory Committee (AGAC). The strong message in his overview was that all the cod stocks were in serious trouble, not just the northern cod. Although Sinclair's paper was on the list of the seven intended presentations, it was not delivered, as minutes of the meeting confirm. Sinclair is not sure who made the decision to remove his overview.

Two days earlier, Bruce Rawson, the deputy minister, had announced to his department that the minister was closing the northern cod fishery. He said that it had collapsed due to unusual ecological and environmental conditions. Yet AGAC, the body that gave quota advice to the minister, was denied relevant scientific information about the other endangered cod stocks. Fishing continued in 1992 and 1993. Some scientists later called this the most serious example of how scientific advice was kept from those responsible for making sound management decisions about the fishery.

The fish caught were small, and the discard rates were extremely high, as they had been since the late 1980s. The fishermen knew that if they didn't discard a sixteen-inch cod at sea, the buyers would throw it overboard at the wharf, anyway. Sociologists Craig Palmer and Peter Sinclair did a study of skippers' attitudes after the Gulf moratorium. Their work confirmed that misreporting of catches, discarding, and the use of liners in nets was commonplace. Just about everyone felt he had to fish illegally. One skipper, assured of anonymity, said, "I cheated like the rest of them, but I was forced into it by watching others make more money [by cheating]. We should worry about what's gonna be left for our sons, but when I told one fella [a dragger skipper] this, he just said, 'Fuck them all.'"

A discussion paper entitled "Implications of Resource Crisis for Newfoundland's Fish Processing Sector" was prepared by an ad hoc committee of federal and provincial fisheries department officials and representatives from the fish processing industry in December 1992. It presented a detailed picture of the industry at the time of the collapse.

The processing sector itself had not been included in the Northern Cod Adjustment Recovery Program. The Newfoundland sector consisted of about 240 plants, of which 163 were inshore groundfish plants employing about twenty thousand. These processed groundfish from about thirteen thousand independent vessels. In addition, there were eleven "offshore" plants operated by large seafood firms. Three of these plants were closed in 1990–91.

The processing industry had always gone from boom to bust. During periodic crises it was usually pointed out that the industry needed to improve quality, increase diversification, improve labour productivity, and improve marketing. There were also, as everyone knew, too many plants for the amount of fish. During the early

1970s, the number of processing plants almost doubled, to 109 by 1974. The decline of cod stocks due to foreign overfishing in the mid-1970s had left many of these plants underutilized. But at the time the 200-mile limit was declared in 1977, the DFO had anticipated a recovery in the cod stock and determined that plant capacity was adequate for their TAC predictions.

Art May, now the president of Memorial University, was deputy minister of fisheries from 1982 to January 1, 1986. He insists that the DFO tried to put a brake on expansion in the industry. He said, "The federal government, honest to God, never ever encouraged anybody to develop anything from about 1974. I say that with the certainty of having been in Ottawa myself from about 1973 to 1990, and having been at the centre of most of the argument that the fisheries had to be restrained, not developed." May claimed it was the provinces that pushed for expansion.

He said the federal government was often caught in the middle of competing provinces, "with one aim in mind, and that was to make coastal populations eligible for unemployment insurance and draw hundreds of millions out of the Ottawa treasury into the provincial economy. Very clear. Nobody ever said it, but what else could it be? We ruined the fishery by trying to use it to solve the unemployment problems of the region, and making the fishery 'the employer of last resort.'"

Former premier Clyde Wells insists the primary reason for the catastrophe was federal mismanagement. But Wells also knows his province played a part. He said, "I don't mean to say the province is lily white in it. We've done things. We've promoted building of new plants, increased the number of boats and all that sort of thing, so we contributed to the pressure on the fish stocks. There's no question about that. But even there, don't forget it was done on the basis of federal scientists saying, 'Get more plants, get more boats, you're going to have a TAC of 400,000 tonnes by 1985.' That was the federal line that was followed.

"'If you're not ready, Newfoundland, we're going to be giving it to Nova Scotia or New Brunswick.' And they were doing it at the time! This was surplus to Newfoundland's needs. Newfoundland can't fish this. This is a Canadian resource, we've got to share it. This is the position the feds were arguing at the time."

The number of plants continued to increase, doubling from 109 in 1974 to over 220 by 1981 (167 for groundfish). In the four years from 1983 to 1987, the freezer capacity for groundfish increased by over 40 per cent. Yet a study done by the province on plant capacity for the inshore showed an average plant utilization rate of only 22 per cent by 1990. The processing sector had undergone a major expansion for an anticipated resource growth that had turned into a devastating decline.

When the 1992 moratorium was announced, fish processors owed about $15 million to Crown agencies such as the Federal Business Development Bank. Collection wasn't likely. A Peat Marwick Thorne study found that anywhere from 50 per cent to 70 per cent of the inshore processors would be out of business at the end of the moratorium period. Many of the processors had already spent money to prepare for the 1992 season which was now cancelled. It would cost about $43 million to buy out the non-survivors and remove their licences from the industry. This intervention would remove 40 per cent of the surplus groundfish processing capacity in an orderly way, and in a short period of time. The drawback would be the perception that firms were being closed to eliminate employment opportunities. Communities and fired workers might believe that government money should not be used to decommission plants. One advantage to the intervention would be that it would remove uncertainty. Alternatively, government could do nothing and let the processing sector rationalize itself.

The federal government expected to spend $700 to $800 million under NCARP until the moratorium was lifted in June of 1994. As well as providing income to displaced workers, the government's aim was to restructure the harvesting sector and upgrade skills and education levels in the new professional fishery that would emerge.

The province of Newfoundland had acquired twenty-seven processing plants through business failures and the development initiatives of community groups; the federal government owned three plants; development associations and community councils owned twenty-two plants. In effect, fifty-two plants were owned by the public sector, but almost all of them operated as private-sector firms through lease or lease purchase. The paper "Implications of Resource Crisis for Newfoundland's Fish Processing Sector" concluded that "the principal public policy objective being pursued through public ownership of fish processing plants appears to be generation of insurable UI earnings in areas where these facilities are located." These subsidized plants were also unfair competition to those financed by private investment. The paper recommended either selling the plants to the operators or closing them when their leases expired.

The paper also recommended closing 44 of the 110 groundfish processing plants along the northeast coast and suggested the establishment of an independent agency to regulate the fish processing industry. This would eliminate political influence in licensing decisions, since the minister would no longer be subject to political pressures from his or her constituents.

The discussion paper suggested that for the same reason a separate agency be set up by the provincial government to license processors, and recommended consideration of production quotas for the plants, based on the idea of Enterprise Allocations or Individual Transferable Quotas (ITQs) in the harvesting sector. The DFO had already announced its intention to reform licensing and allocation systems in a November 1991 proposal. Under the new rules, the minister would continue to provide the broad policy framework, and would be responsible for conservation of the resource and set the TAC.

Over 50 per cent of the inshore production capacity would have to be cut to achieve industry stability and viability. The principal cost of restructuring the inshore processing sector would be jobs. Sociologist Doug House, chairman of the Economic Recovery Commission, said his work suggested that there were 10,000 to 12,000 year-round fishermen in Newfoundland, and an equal number who are marginally employed, who use the industry as a way to get UI. Of the 30,000 people in Newfoundland who eventually ended up on "the package," the majority were part-time fishermen or plant workers.

In an interview with the author just before he retired as premier, Clyde Wells said, "To some degree both governments encouraged the use of the fisheries to create qualification for unemployment insurance. So they can't sit back now and sanctimoniously say, 'Well, those people were pressuring the unemployment system anyway. They shouldn't have been doing [it].' They were induced! They were shown methods by governments as to how to do it! In some cases fish plants and make-work projects would hire workers for a certain number of weeks and then lay off those workers and hire others, so that they'd all have qualification for unemployment insurance. This was done with the approbation and knowledge of both the federal and provincial governments."

According to Wells the rationale was: "It was the easier way to cope with the political problem of unemployment. This was an acceptable way of life for the people who were receiving it, because it gave them a fairly good quality of life."

Looking back on the crisis, after he retired from politics, John Crosbie said in an interview, "Rural Newfoundland totally abuses the system, not for any reason of a love for the traditional fishery but simply because it fits best into their incomes, and into what they will earn, what they will get on UI. Rural Newfoundland is completely dominated by the unemployment insurance system, completely and utterly dominated, every facet of life. There's no one in Newfoundland who thinks it's immoral or improper to screw the government or to defraud the UI. It's astounding!"

On November 5, 1992, Premier Wells wrote to Prime Minister Mulroney thanking him for agreeing to meet on November 23. Wells wanted to discuss the province's recently developed strategic economic plan and seek the prime minister's support for implementation of the plan.

According to Wells, Newfoundland's old problems of an inadequate transportation infrastructure, lack of diversification in the economy, and small manufacturing capacity had to be overcome, as did the lack of policy coordination between the federal and provincial governments with respect to the management of the Newfoundland fishery.

Wells wanted Mulroney's support for joint fisheries management, a Canada–Newfoundland fisheries board to plan, develop, and manage the fishery. He wrote, "To this end we may wish to signal our mutual commitment to this task by mandating our relevant Ministers to take direct and personal responsibility for this initiative on our behalf." It appeared that Wells was attempting an end run around John Crosbie, who was adamantly opposed to joint management.

In Wells's opinion the discussions with the prime minister went well, and he wrote to Mulroney again on January 15, 1993, saying, "I am not aware of any Prime Minister in the forty-three years that Newfoundland has been a province of Canada who has given a stronger commitment than 'to fully engage the federal government at the most senior decision-making level in responding to the economic needs of Newfoundland and Labrador.' For that I express my personal appreciation, and the gratitude of the people of Newfoundland and Labrador."

Negotiations between the federal and provincial governments on NCARP issues continued to go smoothly, although there were difficult questions about retraining. Who would pay if the training lasted beyond the moratorium period? What if someone wanted to go to university?

The province recognized the need to reduce capacity in the processing sector. The Peat Marwick study had shown that even under the most optimistic projections 53 per cent of plants would not likely survive the northern cod moratorium. Key industry players agreed. A significant number of the weaker firms had depended on loan-guarantee support in the past to survive, and that was no longer a viable option. The province would probably have to absorb the loss of $15-20 million in loan guarantees when the plants closed. Large groundfish production plants had already closed in St. John's, Trepassey, Burin, and Grand Bank. Plants in Catalina, Ramea, Burgeo, Harbour Breton, St. Anthony, Charleston, Twillingate, and Bonavista all faced an uncertain future.

Although the province had not put it in writing, the federal deputy minister of fisheries and oceans, Bruce Rawson, sent a memo to Crosbie on March 1, 1993, indicating that the province had committed to a reduction target of 50 per cent of processing capacity during an Ottawa meeting early in 1993. But given the current public environment, the deputy minister advised that publicizing the reduction target would lead to a strong reaction from industry, fishermen, and plant workers. Rawson advised a low-key approach, and suggested seeking confirmation from the Newfoundland government of their verbal commitment to the reduction target. Asking for a written confirmation would test the resolve of the province.

Readers of the *Evening Telegram* in St. John's selected Crosbie as 1992 newsmaker of the year. He had beaten rival Clyde Wells by a ratio of five to one. The man who had shut down a four hundred-year-old fishery and arranged to pay people up to $406 a week not to fish was the most newsworthy man in Newfoundland. The year 1992 was the hardest of a political career famous for its tremendous battles. Crosbie decided to retire in June 1993.

He said later, "Only one thing could have been worse than holding the job of federal fisheries minister in 1992, and that was not holding the job."

The number of registered fishermen in Newfoundland had fallen from 35,000 in 1981 to about 25,000 in 1991, but the number of people actively fishing had remained constant at between 15,000 and 20,000 over that decade. By the same year there were more vessels under thirty-five feet than there had been in 1976. To cover costs, an extra $140 million had to be added to "the package" before it expired on May 15, 1994. NCARP included early retirement incentives, retraining, and licence buy-outs, which it was hoped would help to achieve the goal of an economically viable fishery.

Having a policy and making it work were two very different things. People had their homes, their communities, and for the most part a deeply satisfying way of life, living close to nature and the ocean. They had extended families and friends they had known all their lives. Where else could you buy a house for a few thousand dollars, or bag a moose that could keep a family for months, or cut down free fuel that would keep you warm all winter? "The package" covered moving expenses, but most people didn't want to move. Some of those who did, returned.

In 1993–94 about 15,037 Newfoundlanders moved out of the province, but over 10,000 people moved to Newfoundland. The net population drop of 4,496 was the steepest in eight years, but obviously many felt it was better to be unemployed at home with the support of family and friends, rather than alone in Toronto or Calgary or Vancouver.

Premier Wells described what the moratorium meant to his province: "The impact has at least three characteristics. There is the personal impact on the individual financially, and impairment of the ability to provide the wherewithal to live. There's the social and psychological impact of being in that situation in a small remote community, with no apparent hope, nothing to look forward to, no alternative. There's the worse thing, no alternative. If you could point to something else being available, it's a manageable problem; but when you impose it with no alternative, not only the financial, but the social and psychological impact is devastating. Those are the two impacts on the individual and on the community. The third impact is the impact overall on the economy of the province."

Even when he was campaigning to be Liberal leader in Newfoundland, Wells had taken the position that Newfoundland had to stop its dependence on Ottawa. "Quite apart from what it means to our own self-respect and dignity as people, Ottawa can't continue this forever and we're going to be in a disastrous situation if they stop it! And then where do we go? So we've got to change our economy. That was the whole focus. That's why we moved in the way in which we did. What I didn't know was that the fisheries would be the disaster, so quickly, that it was."

After Wells took office he had set about reducing expenditures and gave the province its first balanced budget in thirty-seven years. The Liberals tried to make the business climate friendlier by lowering business tax rates to attract investment, but what was really needed in the province after the collapse was the equivalent of a Marshall Plan. Wells tried to explain the crisis in terms that Ontarians could understand. "How would Ontario react if the federal government issued a edict that the entire automobile industry of Ontario was closed, all its parts-manufacturing and tires?" It was a disaster in a province that already had the highest unemployment in the country. The only thing that compared to it, according to Wells, was the impact of the Great Depression when fish prices collapsed. But at least in those days you could go out and jig enough fish to eat. "Now you can't even do that," said the former premier. "If the fish don't return, the Newfoundland that we've known can't continue."

8

THE OSLO OPTION

At the same time that DFO scientists were completing their autumn 1989 surveys and advising Canada's minister of fisheries that the northern cod stocks were in trouble, an almost identical fisheries crisis struck Norway. Cod lived in Norway's coastal waters and in the Barents Sea, where the warm Gulf Stream meets icy polar currents, creating a near perfect marine environment for Europe's most important fish. Even though Norway's central coast lies above northern Labrador, the Gulf Stream tempers its climate and winter temperatures hover around the freezing mark.

In October 1989, Norwegians were stunned by the news that fall research surveys showed cod stocks in the Barents Sea were the lowest they had been in over a hundred years of record-keeping. Some Norwegian scientists advised that only 90,000 tonnes could be safely taken from the stock, a shocking number considering that recent predictions had been for a quota of 800,000 tonnes in 1990. Like their Newfoundland counterparts, fishermen in the rural settlements already knew that something was drastically wrong. The fish they were catching had large heads and thin bodies, a sign that the cod were starving. The bureaucracy discounted this anecdotal data until their own work convinced them that Norway was facing a fisheries disaster. When the scientific information leaked out to the press, there was genuine panic, with some experts predicting that both the cod stocks and the country's fish-dependent northern economy would collapse.

The Norwegian government faced a hard decision. Its coastal fishermen had a more or less unregulated fishery with no quotas, unlike its deep-sea fleet, which had been under quota and licensing regulations since the mid-1970s. When scientists told the Norwegian politicians that there had to be severe quota cuts, the politicians acted immediately and backed the cuts, despite a firestorm of criticism from their constituents. The total Barents Sea quota, which Norway shared with Russia, was set at 120,000 tonnes for 1990. The Norwegian share of the quota was slashed to 113,000 tonnes. For some fishermen, the new quotas meant their catch would drop by 83 per cent. Oslo also immediately implemented policies to reduce the number of cod fishermen and vessels.

As it had in Newfoundland, cod (*torsk,* as the fish is known in Norway) had played a vital role in the country's settlement and rural life. The Norwegian fishery dates back more than a thousand years to the time when the Vikings ruled the northern seas, ranging all the way to L'Anse aux Meadows on Newfoundland's Great Northern Peninsula. Eighty per cent of Norwegians lived within six miles of the coast, and there were more than eight hundred fishing communities and about twenty-five thousand fishermen in the industry. There were also ten thousand fish-plant workers, half of them women. If the Barents Sea stock collapsed, the small coastal communities that depended on it would cease to exist.

Norway had seen many crises in its fishery over the years, but this one was the most dire. In the early 1980s, Norwegian scientists believed that their cod stocks were so healthy that the 1986 TAC was set at 400,000 tonnes. That year the coastal fishermen started to notice that the fish were small and too young to have spawned. A year earlier, some scientists had begun to worry about their earlier estimates of abundance, and quotas were lowered dramatically both in late 1986 and 1987. In 1986, the caplin fishery was closed, a ban that lasted four years to help the stock to recover. By 1988, the evidence of the cod's demise frightened even the most optimistic scientist and bureaucrat; in mid-1988, the cod quota was further reduced.

At the time, very little was known about the relationship between cod and caplin. So-called multi-species research, the study of interactions between species, was a new discipline for marine researchers all over the world. After looking at the cod's preferred food, Norwegian scientists developed a striking theory to account for the stock collapse. They believed that rich year-classes of two- and three-year-old cod had eaten over a million tonnes of caplin at the same time as the commercial fishery was heavily fishing the same stock. The result was a sudden and total collapse of the caplin biomass. With the caplin gone, the rich year-classes of cod that scientists had calculated would enrich the fishery began eating each other.

With no caplin to feed on, predatory seals turned to cod, further unbalancing the ecological system of the Barents Sea. The ocean temperature had also changed. Scientists believe this sparked stock collapses in the coastal waters of other North Atlantic countries. The Russians, the Icelanders, the northern countries of the EC, and the Faeroe Islanders all felt the disaster that was engulfing the Norwegian fishery.

From January to the end of March, mature cod migrate from their summer feeding grounds in the Barents Sea to spawn near the Lofoten Islands off the northern coast of Norway, above the Arctic circle. Coastal fishermen fished the Lofoten spawning grounds with hook and line, because draggers were banned from the cod's spawning grounds. For several years in the late 1980s the coastal fishermen had experienced poor fishing.

By 1989 the situation was so bad that the Tromsø branch of the Norwegian Fishermen's Association demanded a moratorium on fishing in the Barents Sea. Other branches of the NFA insisted that Norwegian factory trawlers be banned, but the trawling companies resented being painted as the villains of the piece and reminded everyone of how many jobs they created in Norway's processing sector. Besides, they pointed out, there was a more likely villain to the east, the hungry Russian bear with which Norway shared the Barents Sea. The problem was one that any Newfoundland fisherman could understand. Like the Grand Banks, the Barents Sea simply couldn't sustain the overcapacity of the fleets that fished the rich cod stocks. When the stock collapsed, everyone thought the other fellow was to blame.

With much finger-pointing, the collapse of the cod fishery dominated conversation in every part of the country. Help groups held meetings and conferences to deal with emotional fallout from the closure of the fishery, and the Nature Conservancy Association of Norway acquired observer status on the fisheries regulation board. Norwegians, like outport Newfoundlanders, felt that the disappearance of the cod was endangering their entire culture.

Norwegian fishermen are used to yelling into the storm to make themselves heard, and their complaints echoed at every level of government. Politicians and their officials were berated in public meetings and savaged in the many fishermen's newspapers published around the country. But from the very beginning of the crisis, Norwegian politicians knew that there could be no giving in to the protests for short-term political gain. As Norwegian fisheries official Jon Lauritzen told the author, "The main qualification to survive one week as minister of fisheries is that you have to be tough, because it's the most unpopular occupation you could have in Norway."

Despite all the pressure tactics and demonstrations, in January 1990, instead of a winter cod fishery, Norwegians got a moratorium from their government. Coastal Norway almost revolted and tempers flared. People who had fished all their lives were in danger of losing their boats, their homes, and their self-respect because the officials who were supposed to manage the fish had made terrible miscalculations. Thousands of men went from being the captain of their own vessels onto social assistance, as their incomes dropped on average by 30 to 40 per cent.

The government set up an emergency fund in 1990 to help fishermen with loan repayments, but between 1988 and 1991 almost two thousand of them still defaulted. To reduce the pressure on fish stocks, the government paid factory trawlers subsidies to leave Norwegian waters for other fishing grounds. Some of these vessels steamed as far away as New Zealand in search of fishable stocks. All told, the Norwegian government spent $71 million to remove 25 offshore trawlers and 700 coastal boats from the fishery. Grants were also given to communities to diversify their economies, though there were few real alternatives in most northern villages. Although the government spent $1.6 million in emergency aid in 1990 and 1991, it was scarcely enough to soften the blow of the cod collapse, which some people were calling the worst epidemic since the Black Death.

The crisis forced Norwegians to confront the big issues in the fishery. For the first time, they struggled with the questions of what sustainable development really meant and whether the fishery should be open to everyone. Most people quickly realized that to manage the resources in a sustainable way there had to be a reduction in the capacity of the fishing fleet. Transferable quotas were discussed to reduce the overcapacity, and in 1990 vessel quotas were set up for the first time. Opposed by fishermen, vessel quotas were later changed to a TAC for the fleet in some cases. (As of November 1996, Norwegian fish quotas were divided between different types of vessels. Many receive a fixed quota for various species, others are allowed to fish for a maximum quantity within a group quota. When the quota is reached, the fishing stops.)

After three bitter years of hardships, it was clear that the Norwegian government's prompt reaction to the crisis would ensure a happy ending. In 1991, the fishermen began to see large populations of cod along the coast and the cod quota for that year was increased to 128,500 tonnes. Even though the reports on fish populations in the Barents Sea were encouraging, the government proceeded with caution. By the fall of 1992, there appeared to be some solid signs of recovery, including a large number of young fish in the water.

While in Canada, DFO scientists insisted that there was no proven connection between fishing the spawning stocks and the survival of cod fry, Norway banned all fishing on its spawning grounds as soon as the scientists realized the stock was in trouble. Norwegian biologist Odd Nakkem said, "Although it's difficult to find the relation between recruitment and spawning stock, we are convinced that there is such a relation."

In 1992, the spawning biomass of Barents Sea cod stock was bigger than it had been in twenty-five years. Norwegian fishermen could see what appeared to be an abundant cod stock just off the coast and immediately pressured the government to return to the old quotas. Firmly committed to building stable quotas for the future, Oslo resisted a dramatic increase. By 1993, the Norwegian share of the Barents Sea cod quota was 248,000 tonnes, double their 1990 quota, but nowhere near historic levels.

In January 1992, Norway's fisheries minister, Oddrunn Pettersen, talked about the early evidence of a stock collapse in the Barents Sea. "I think there were warning signs, but we didn't have the knowledge to read these signs," she said, "so from the late '80s we have spent a lot of money on research to increase our knowledge, not only on single fishes, but also to learn more about the connection between the different fish and even mammals in the Barents Sea. There were signs, and some of our researchers gave warning, but I don't think they were taken into enough account – and of course, we also overfished. A combination of overfishing and nature brought the collapse in the caplin stock about, and that has dramatic consequences for the cod, which feed on caplin."

Pettersen said that most of the people in the fishing industry simply hadn't believed the early warnings. They thought it was just another cyclical downturn and hoped it would be better next year. But the hard experience of the early 1990s has taught Norwegians never to take a chance with the resource again, and to use scientific advice to devise policies that will leave the fisheries "on the safe side." This was the best defence against what Pettersen believed had really brought on the cod collapse. "There are two reasons why the Barents Sea landed in a sort of catastrophe, or at least an imbalance that was really frightening. One was the lack of knowledge, the other was overfishing, which you could call greed."

Odd Nakkem's analysis could have come out of Cabot Martin's mouth: "We had been overfishing the cod stock for thirty years. It started in the mid-fifties and we had been overfishing up to the late eighties." Nakkem believed that even though there were some large year-classes of fish, there had been a steady reduction in stock size, from about 3.5 or 4 million tonnes to a million tonnes over the thirty-year period. Nakkem said if they had had the information ten years earlier, they would have started reducing the caplin quotas in the early 1980s. "We were two to three years too late," he said.

Oddrunn Pettersen had learned a lesson the hard way. "It is irresponsible of politicians if they don't manage the resource in such a way that it should last not only for our generation, but for generations to come. One has to do what is right as far as your ability is there and try to convince people that what you do is done for the best."

If Norway had not taken decisive action, "It would have been a catastrophe," Pettersen said. "The Barents Sea was in total imbalance and it would have perhaps taken us years to come back to a normal situation."

The comparison between Canada and Norway is striking. Oslo made dramatic cuts in their TACs as soon as they realized that their cod stocks were in trouble in late 1986. By January 1990, there was a full moratorium on their spawning biomass. Despite evidence that northern cod were in trouble on the Grand Banks, Canada continued to fish hard and downplay negative scientific advice. By the time John Crosbie imposed a moratorium in July 1992, the northern cod had all but disappeared.

In 1990 the Northern Cod Science Program (NCSP) was established as part of the response to the recommendations in the Harris Report. Harris later said, "Perhaps the most important long-term result of our panel's work was to create a sense of crisis or urgency so that government was prepared to commit some money to a concentrated effort on trying to understand a little more about the biology and behaviour of these animals." The NCSP was the largest fisheries research program in the Newfoundland region, the first determined effort to understand the ocean ecology where the northern cod lived. In June 1990, the Atlantic Fisheries Adjustment Program committed $33 million over five years to expand fisheries research into several neglected fields.

Until the NCSP was approved, basic marine research in the Newfoundland Region of the DFO had taken a back seat to stock assessment. Over three-quarters of the department's science budget was spent on calculating the biomass and proposed catch levels. Biologists were fish counters rather than scientists employed in researching stock inter-relationships, ocean climate, or the life cycles of the various fish species that interacted. Yet this information was necessary in order to do a proper stock assessment. Now the fish were disappearing, the DFO realized it was essential for scientists to understand their behaviour and environment if the stock was to recover.

In science, hypotheses are set up and then experiments are done to test them. If the experiments don't support the hypotheses, they are thrown out and new ones are set up to be tested. In the early 1980s scientists hypothesized that the cod stock was rebuilding, at the fishing mortality rate of $F_{0.1}$. But when the stock did not rebuild, for some reason the hypothesis was not examined until it was too late. The delay was deadly.

CAFSAC gave its scientific advice collectively. No one person was responsible, and as the fisheries crisis developed there appeared to be no independent criticism or peer review of decisions. Policies such as fishing at $F_{0.1}$ were set down by the DFO, but then not followed, even when their own scientists knew in 1986 that fishing mortality was two or even three times the $F_{o.1}$ rate. Yet John Crosbie, and apparently the ministers before him, believed that the northern cod were being fished at $F_{o.1}$, right up until he had to close the fishery.

In their 1991–92 annual report, the NCSP program published some of their initial findings. Important work had been done in the development of acoustic techniques that would help many areas of fishery research, and oceanographers were collaborating with biologists in researching the effect of ice and cold water conditions on the fish. For the first time, fish behaviour was studied in the context of the currents and water masses that affected the cod's environment.

Prior to the NCSP research, little was known about the life cycle of the northern cod, where and when they spawned or what happened to their eggs and larvae during the critical first few months. Until the NCSP, scientists had no way to assess the abundance of juvenile cod under age three, because they were too small to be taken by the gear used in the annual groundfish surveys and they weren't targeted by the offshore trawlers.

An analysis of cod stomachs was undertaken to see what the fish ate. This research confirmed what the inshore fishermen had known all along, that the cod's favourite food was caplin. When the caplin were scarce, the cod simply ate less rather than turn to other prey.

Researchers wanted to find out about the annual inshore cod migration that hundreds of Newfoundland communities depended on for their existence. New instruments such as high-resolution echo sounders, and computers to interpret the data, made it possible to study migration pathways. Early research indicated that the migrating cod used valleys or corridors of warm water to stay below a large layer of extremely cold water as they swam inshore. This cold intermediate layer (CIL) lay between the seasonally heated upper layer and the warmer bottom layer of the ocean. In 1991, the CIL off Bonavista was 68 per cent larger than normal, although in 1984, when catches were good, it had been almost 100 per cent larger.

NCSP funding also allowed scientists to start analyzing some of the raw data the DFO already had. Since 1933 over 220,000 cod had been tagged, but to be useful the findings had to be converted into a form that could be fed into a computer for analysis. Further tagging may help to clarify how many cod actually migrate inshore after spawning, and whether cod found near shore in the summer also winter in some of the bays, indicating separate inshore stocks.

When biologist Jeffrey Hutchings came to work for the DFO in St. John's in November 1992 as a Natural Sciences and Engineering Research Council fellow, he came with an open mind. What he saw in the department was a tribal society. "It seemed to behave almost as a tribe, as tribal groups. It was group thinking and group action, that's what seemed to govern a lot of things. The assessment practitioners would meet as a group every year and, with like-minded groups, decide on stock status. They would conduct their assessments as a group. And if you got someone from outside of that group analyzing what you've done, I think there was a tendency to downplay or, possibly, discount it."

At the time there were a number of ideas floating around as to why the stock had collapsed: cold water, ice, not enough food, seals. Hutchings said, "And I accepted it! I thought the government must be on the mark here. If they are saying things were unusually cold, I guess they were." He accepted what they were saying until the day he saw the final draft of a paper to be published by the prestigious *Canadian Journal of Fisheries and Aquatic Sciences*. Although the draft paid lip service to the effects of fishing on stock levels, most of the emphasis was on the environment. When he read the manuscript in July 1993, he wasn't convinced that the empirical evidence for the paper's position was there. "They had three main arguments. None of them appeared to stand up upon a careful look at things. I thought to myself, if this is the best evidence there is, it seems pretty flimsy!"

Hutchings and another DFO scientist, Ransom Myers, decided to gather up all the data that had a bearing on the ideas that were floating around. They began looking for graphs, plots, and data summaries that would support the statements made about environmental causes being to blame. They discovered that they just weren't there. "We could not find, and still to this day cannot find, any direct influence of the physical environment on cod survival."

Immediately after the collapse of the cod, the DFO had pushed sudden and drastic environmental changes as the primary cause of the disaster. It was a much more comfortable position than blaming their own mismanagement of the fishery. As a result, two scientific camps emerged within the department – those who blamed the environment for the disaster, and those who blamed overfishing.

Scientists had tried for years to understand the factors that affect recruitment to the fishery, the number of young fish that join the main stock every year, but it was a hopeless task. In an interview, Hutchings said, "We can't do it! We have nothing. There isn't a single predictive explanation in the scientific literature today that will reliably predict recruitment based on any environmental variable you want to pick. The environment undoubtedly affects recruitment, but we can't predict it."

When Hutchings and Myers began to produce work that contradicted the official DFO positions, there was, Hutchings says, "a lot of pressure from Ottawa." But the head of science in the Newfoundland region, Larry Coady, stood his ground when asked by Ottawa if their papers had been put through internal review. Coady had followed government guidelines for how scientific papers were to be published to the letter. According to Hutchings, "For that he was criticized by Ottawa, because what was being published was inconsistent with what the departmental positions were. He actually stood up to Ottawa admirably." Hutchings knows that a minority of his fellow DFO scientists weren't, as he put it, "particularly enamoured with some of the work I've been involved with, because they view it as a personal criticism on top of the criticism they have already received from many quarters. In a sense, I think they are punch drunk. They've taken so much they are just sick of it."

The introduction to the final report of the Northern Cod Science Program released by the DFO in 1996 shows how much the department had been humbled by the collapse of the northern cod. It begins, "Ours is the first generation with the capacity to do real damage in the ocean. Our ability to find and capture fish has outstripped both the ability of many stocks to sustain themselves and our own ability to understand marine ecosystems and our impact upon them. The ocean does not lend itself to easy study. Cold, stormy, dark and deep, hostile to humans without costly systems of life support, the ocean is like space. It demands as much of our budgets as it does of courage and imagination. . . . Yet ignorance is costlier still."

When the NCSP ended in March 1995, over 230 scientific papers reported the work that had been done. The research projects gave scientists a better understanding of the behaviour and growth of cod at different ages, and work was begun on the next step – understanding how changes in the physical environment affect the recruitment and the survival of cod. Unfortunately, funding for fisheries science has been severely cut back even though there is still a lot of work to do.

Before the cod science program, little was known about plankton growth in Canada's Atlantic waters. The complex ocean ecosystem depends on tiny organisms we can't even see called phytoplankton. Winter storms or currents stir up chemical nutrients, such as nitrogen, on the ocean bottom, and when the ice begins to recede in April and the surface water reaches the right temperature, phytoplankton use the energy of the sun to turn these chemicals into living matter, algae. Zooplankton feed on the algae, and small fish and shellfish in turn feed on the zooplankton. The larger fish feed on them. Scientists have now calculated that it takes about ten million tonnes of phytoplankton at the beginning of the food chain to support 10,000 tonnes of cod near the top of the chain. Without the phytoplankton there would be no fish.

In the middle of the food chain, caplin eat the plankton and in turn become the favourite food of predator species. Most caplin spawn and die at age three or four. Since these tiny fish live for such a short time, the survival of each year-class is important. A couple of adverse years in a row can dramatically affect the abundance of the stock, and this in turn affects the health of the species that depend on the caplin for food.

After spawning offshore, the cod come inshore to feed on the spawning caplin. Cod are in their poorest condition at this time, their fat reserves are low after a long winter, and they are exhausted from spawning, but in a normal year they recover quickly after a heavy feed of caplin. Scientists don't yet fully know the role that caplin abundance has on the inshore migration of cod. Do fewer cod migrate inshore if caplin are scarce or do they stay offshore if there are significant juvenile caplin stocks offshore? Inshore fishermen are convinced of a direct and simple relationship: no caplin, no cod.

It is known that cold water affects the timing of the caplin's seasonal cycles. From 1991 to 1993 the caplin spawned three to four weeks later than normal on Conception Bay beaches. Spawning also lasted three to nine weeks, longer than the typical one or two weeks on beaches that were studied earlier. Scientists theorized that colder than normal winter temperatures had delayed and prolonged spawning.

Icelandic and Norwegian scientists are also studying this complex relationship and are sharing their work through the International Council for the Exploration of the Sea (ICES). They've found that in the Barents Sea the condition of cod declines when caplin are scarce, but this is not as clear with the northern cod stock. Offshore surveys have sometimes found few caplin in their usual locations, even when they turned up inshore to spawn in near normal numbers. Indications are that when caplin are scarce, cod grow more slowly and have less body fat, fewer may survive the winter, and those that do don't spawn as successfully. What we do know is that by 1988, when scientists realized the cod stock had declined dramatically, there had also been a decline in caplin.

An examination of the stomachs of cod from 2J and 3K in the early 1990s revealed that the fish weren't eating as much as they normally did, suggesting that food was scarce. Most cod swallow their prey whole, so their food choices are governed by both the size of the cod and the size of their intended meal. The NCSP found that cod up to twelve inches feed on small crustaceans such as shrimp. Cod up to twenty-four inches feed on caplin, sand lance, and Arctic cod. The larger cod go for larger prey, the young ground-fish of various species, including young cod. Experiments have shown that juvenile cod know they are prime targets for cannibal-ism. If a predator cod is near they will flee to a habitat that older cod generally avoid.

Barents Sea studies have shown that cod become more cannibal-istic when caplin are scarce. Newfoundland studies since 1978 reveal that cannibalism rates vary from year to year, but when there is a strong year-class of young cod, more of these are found in the bellies of the older cod, even if caplin appear to be available. Researchers have estimated that a biomass of one million tonnes of cod would eat about two and a half million tonnes of other fish a year.

Fishing on the offshore spawning grounds was one of the most contentious issues in ocean management. Trawler companies did it because it is cost efficient when the stocks are densely packed together, and the fish are in better condition at this point than they will be later in the year. The DFO argued that it wasn't known whether fishing affected the success of the spawning biomass. On February 1990, Fisheries Minister Tom Siddon stood up in the House of Commons and said, "Scientists advise me there is no recorded evidence in the scientific literature or our own research which states that fishing on the spawning grounds does measurable damage to the cod stocks."

DFO managers were insisting even in 1995 that there were no data that proved trawling on spawning stocks contributed to the decline of stock recruitment. The DFO and the trawling companies were closely aligned, and until very recently no one was doing the research to prove the issue conclusively one way or the other. The NCSP funded the first effort to examine the question.

Studies found that younger males finish spawning earlier than the older males, leading scientists to conclude that the loss of older males before the moratorium was imposed may have shortened the length of the spawning season, with possible detrimental effects on recruitment. Scientists also found that prior to spawning cod tended to segregate themselves by sex, and surmised from their studies that the male cod set up territories on the Grand Banks where the females joined them to spawn before returning to deeper water.

In field research, biologists found that a trawl dragged through a school of spawning cod caused a 300-metre-wide "hole" in the school, about four to five times wider than the trawl, as the fish fled to each side. This hole lasted for more than an hour after the trawl had gone. Obviously, the trawl disturbed the spawning behaviour. Cabot Martin noted the blind spot society had when environmental damage was perpetrated by the big fishing companies: "If an oil company went out to the ocean and dragged heavy objects over the ocean bed, twenty-four hours a day, 365 days a year, there would be a public outcry against the destruction of the environment, yet that is exactly what the offshore fishing industry does with its bottom-trawl technology."

In addition to disrupting the spawning behaviour of fish, the trawls disturb the sea floor itself and the life forms that inhabit it. Huge steel bobbins along the lower edge of the trawl and the heavy "doors" rigged to keep the mouth of the trawl open bump along the floor of the ocean. The trawl kills most of the fish it captures and can injure or disturb other bottom dwellers.

These bottom dwellers are the creatures that restore dissolved nutrients to the ocean. The NCSP final report concluded, "Repeated disturbance of these humble structures in the muck of the sea floor may represent a much more fundamental problem than the collapse of any one commercial species." Thanks to the development of new sampling techniques, scientists have discovered that the diversity of species on the ocean floor may rival that of the tropical rain forest.

Jeffrey Hutchings and Ransom Myers, the two young fisheries biologists who rocked the boat within the DFO and continue to do so now that they have left the department, argue that it was over-fishing clear and simple that caused the collapse of what was once the largest cod fishery in the world. In a now famous article in the *Canadian Journal of Fisheries and Aquatic Sciences*, published in 1994, they wrote, "We reject hypotheses that attribute the collapse of the northern cod to environmental change. . . . We conclude that the collapse of the northern cod can be attributed solely to over-exploitation." Hutchings and Myers dismissed the cold-water-temperature theory after demonstrating that there were periods in the nineteenth and early twentieth centuries when the water temperatures were even lower, yet commercial landings averaged about 250,000 tonnes.

The two biologists reported that the biomass of cod able to spawn was 1.6 million tonnes in 1962. Thirty years later, it was estimated to be as low as 22,000 tonnes. Inshore catch rates declined from 1985 to 1991, a period of greatly increased fishing effort. Offshore, even though the overall abundance was dropping dramatically, the fish remained concentrated. But because fishermen were better able both to find and to catch the remaining cod, catch-rates remained high. This contributed to the overestimation of the stock size. Until the stock collapsed in 1992, the official DFO line was that it was increasing.

Hutchings and Myers do not believe temperature or salinity changes had a significant effect on cod recruitment prior to the moratorium, but noted that when mortality is high, the stocks may be less resilient to environmental stresses. Low numbers make the cod more vulnerable to both fishing pressure and environmental changes. The authors concluded these "may significantly increase the probability of extinction of this stock."

For the first time scientists were looking at the entire food web, not at just a single species. Older female cod spawn more eggs over a longer period of time. Since these older fish had virtually disap-peared from the population, the younger cod were doing most of the spawning in a far shorter season. This reduced the likelihood that larvae could start feeding during the peak period of zooplankton abundance.

Jeff Hutchings has written about the need to recognize the value of the fishermen's local knowledge. If the observations of the inshore fishermen had carried more weight when they said that the stocks were declining, perhaps the cod might have been saved. Hutchings argues they can provide a wealth of information about cod biology, distribution, migration, and habitat. He also suggested a ban on offshore fishing of northern cod during the peak spawning period, and the creation of a seasonal Marine Protected Area (MPA). The offshore ban would force a return to traditional fishing patterns – from before the advent of freezer trawlers fishing on the spawning stock in the 1950s – and the MPAs would be easier and cheaper to police than quotas and by-catch limits.

Hutchings suggests that the stock should not be reopened until it has reached the same size it was in the early 1980s, which should permit a sustainable annual harvest of 100,000 to 150,000 tonnes, half of the level of the 1980s. A recovery to the 1960s numbers of 1.5 million tonnes could take decades. Or it may never happen. Since overfishing reduces the cod's ability to withstand other environmental factors like cold water and an imbalance in the food chain, too few fish in the water may mean the commercial stock has in fact reached the vanishing point.

The collapse of the cod stock has focused attention on the young fish. Until the moratorium they were a subject little was known about, although Russian scientists have studied cod eggs and larvae since the 1960s. Russian data suggested that cod spawn mostly on the edge of the continental shelf and that the currents pick up the eggs and distribute them over the Banks. Surprisingly, NCSP studies of research survey data and of egg and larval drift over a five-year period found that cod spawn across the shelf, not just on the edge; and that storms and currents carry the eggs and larvae into the inshore nursery habitat.

The NCSP also found that some inshore juveniles were actually spawned inshore. From DNA testing, it appears that the cod that winter in Trinity Bay are genetically distinct from the northern cod that winter in warmer water offshore. The inshore cod appear to produce an "antifreeze" that governs their ability to winter in cold inshore waters.

It is important that the cod larvae find food quickly once they have hatched, since they can live for only a short time on their yolk sacs. Cod spawn near the bottom but the plankton that larvae need to feed on is near the surface, so the eggs must rise quickly. Studies have shown that eggs rise slowly or not at all when the oxygen content of the ocean or its salinity is low. If the eggs don't reach the surface they die, so salinity and oxygen content can have a great bearing on the survival of a particular year-class. Ice can have a major effect because it decreases salinity as it melts and also because an ice cover diminishes the effect of the wind on the currents, limiting the chance the larvae will be carried to suitable nursery areas.

A mature female cod can produce a million eggs or more when she spawns. Normally she begins to spawn at about age seven, although that age appears to have dropped to five in the last few years. The older, larger spawners tend to produce millions more eggs than the younger fish. Most of the eggs die within a few weeks. By the time the survivors are 2.5 centimetres long, there are only about one hundred cod for every million that were spawned, and only about one egg in a million will reach maturity. By fall, the young cod settle in sea grass or rocks near the shore, where they can hide from predators. Most cod up to age two are found inshore. By age three the young cod join the older fish in deeper, warmer water farther out on the shelf.

Until the work of the NCSP, scientists knew little about the migration patterns of cod. High-resolution echo sounders locate and follow schools of cod as they migrate (the same technology can be used to track and catch them), and scientists have learned that cod stocks spawn over a three- to four-month period that usually starts in late winter in the north and ends in early summer farther south. Acoustics have given us an amazing image of cod behaviour. For ten days the fish remain stationary in a dense mass, within a small area. During the day, several pairs of fish rise in columns above the school, in what is now believed to be spawning behaviour. Over a period of a few weeks almost all of the cod will spawn. The fish then spread out and are joined by the younger cod who have been waiting in the deeper water.

As the school of cod starts its migration the fish rise from the bottom to about 350 metres below the surface, and spread out so they can just see each other. It is now believed this allows the hungry cod to have a wider area to search for prey, at the same time retaining visual contact. Larger fish at the head of the school, scouts, appear to lead the migration. When the scouts veer off for a meal of caplin the whole school follows.

Scientists have theorized that cod form large migrating schools to increase their chance of finding food. Another theory is that the "elders" teach the younger cod the migrating route. When the stock collapsed, these older fish may have been lost. Scientists found a school of migrating cod in the Bonavista corridor in 1992, but in 1993 there were virtually none. The only adult cod were found far to the east and south, on the Nose of the Banks, where the foreign vessels were waiting to scoop them up. In the 1994 acoustic survey no cod were found at the entrance to the Bonavista migration corridor or on the Nose of the Banks. For the first time since the surveys began, no high-density concentrations of adult cod were found, anywhere.

While the scientists were learning the habits of the fish, Canadian politicians tried to figure out how to handle the collapse of the northern cod stock. News of the disaster was helping to focus attention on what was soon to become an international flashpoint. Certain distant-water fishing nations were still refusing to practise conservation measures; they simply moved to other areas when their catches were too low. According to the Marine Resources

Assessment Group, based in London, England, there were over thirty serious fishery disputes in the world by 1994. Multilateral talks without enforcement of conservation and management regulations had not been a success. In every case, the stocks were depleted before the diplomats reached an agreement.

At the UN Conference on Straddling Fish Stocks and Highly Migratory Fish Stocks held in New York July 12–30, 1993, delegates laid out a draft convention with binding undertakings for all parties. For its part, Canada wanted effective conservation and management of stocks on the high seas, an agreement on surveillance, and a dispute-settlement mechanism. John Crosbie had decided not to run in the next election, but he attended the first few days of the session as new prime minister Kim Campbell's personal representative. Canada's new fisheries minister, Crosbie protégé Ross Reid, gave the opening speech. The draft convention was sponsored by Canada, Argentina, Chile, Iceland, and New Zealand, and a negotiating text was tabled at the end of the conference. Two sessions were planned for the spring and summer of 1994 to ready the convention for adoption at the UN General Assembly meeting that fall.

Vic Young of FPI attended the New York conference with the Canadian delegation to lend industry support. Young wrote to Ross Reid, saying, "If we cannot reach some kind of emergency agreement to end foreign fishing then maybe it is time for a show of force (cutting nets for instance) by the Canadian Navy. We have to show the world that while this may be considered a relatively minor situation by the European Community, it is life and death for Newfoundland." While the three-week New York conference on straddling stocks was underway, there were sixty-four foreign groundfish vessels and thirty-seven shrimp vessels fishing just beyond Canada's 200-mile limit. No one knew what kind of by-catches they were taking of cod, yellowtail flounder, and American plaice.

After the 1993 federal election made federal Tories an endangered species, a new player appeared on the national scene who appeared to like Vic Young's advice. On May 10, 1994, the new federal fisheries minister, Brian Tobin, tabled legislation that would allow Canada to arrest any foreign vessel caught fishing illegally outside the 200-mile limit. The Coastal Fisheries Protection Act received swift passage, and fisheries officers could now board vessels on the high seas to conduct searches. The RCMP, the Coast Guard, and the Armed Forces would all be involved in enforcing the law. Ships could be arrested and towed into a Canadian port and their foreign captains fined as much as $500,000 for breaking federal fisheries regulations.

In April 1994, armed Canadian fisheries officers had boarded and arrested the factory-freezer trawler *Kristina Logos*, for illegal fishing on the Grand Banks just beyond the 200-mile zone. In its holds, inspectors found tonnes of small cod, redfish, and flounder that had been taken with undersized nets fitted with a liner. The vessel was flying a Panamanian flag, but its Nova Scotia-based owner had not cancelled its Canadian registration before taking on the new flag of convenience and violating the Fisheries Act in the NAFO-regulated area. The vessel was therefore subject to Canadian law.

The company was found guilty of the fisheries violations on May 21, 1997. Fines and forfeitures could have cost the owner of the ship almost a million dollars. At the sentencing hearing in June, Crown prosecutor Ann Fagan asked that the proceeds from the sale of the ship and its cargo be forfeited to the Crown. (The vessel had been sold at public auction for $605,000 and its one hundred tonnes of fish sold for $58,989.) Fagan also asked for $120,000 in fines and over $100,000 in expenses to be repaid to the DFO for monies spent in seizing and detaining the trawler.

If the judge had agreed with the Crown prosecutor, it would have been a record sentence and a strong message that illegal fishing activity would not be tolerated. Instead, Newfoundland Supreme Court judge David Russell fined the former owner of the ship over $200,000. The Crown could claim recovery of its costs in federal court.

202 • LAMENT FOR AN OCEAN

While many people in the Canadian industry had adopted the new conservation ethic, others were still up to their old tricks. In May 1994, two National Sea Products captains fishing out of Lunenburg, Nova Scotia, were fined $15,000 and $20,000 for discarding cod. They had dumped 22,000 kilograms of cod caught as by-catch while trawling for redfish in the Gulf of St. Lawrence, an area closed to cod fishing. The company was not charged. The previous year, another National Sea captain had been caught fitting his regulation nets with a smaller liner and fined $15,000. Charges against the company were dropped because fisheries officers believed the captain was operating without his employer's knowledge.

In June 1994, DFO scientists presented a report to the Fisheries Resource Conservation Council (FRCC), which had replaced CAFSAC. The report confirmed what everyone feared. Despite the moratorium, the northern cod stocks had continued to decline. According to the 1993 survey estimate, the biomass was only 3 per cent of what it had been in 1990, and the scientists could not say what had caused the catastrophic decline. The bad news about the northern cod weighed heavily on everyone in the industry.

Former Newfoundland fisheries minister Walter Carter described the emotional impact: "The spring of the year in Newfoundland was always a time of jubilation, a time of hope, promise, of activity. After a long, hard winter, the men were out getting their boats ready and getting their nets ready, mending their wharves and their flakes, getting ready for the big harvest. That's not there any more. Come spring now, men have nothing to do. Men who would normally be down on the stage with their friends, doing their thing, now have to stay home. What man who's got red blood in his veins could be forced to stay home every morning, when he would normally be on the ocean? These are people who live outdoors and who love the ocean, and long to get back on the ocean."

In Carter's opinion, the real social crisis brought on by the cod collapse has yet to happen. Newfoundland would be "entering the real world" when the last cheque from Ottawa was issued. Asked if the fisherman who was getting a cheque was happy, Carter replied, "No, he's not happy. I guess there are some, 'hangashores' we call them. I'd say the vast majority of Newfoundlanders, who have been forced into that position, are very, very unhappy people. A young man with a family and a house, not knowing what the future holds for him or her, how can they be happy? I mean, they are human beings, they think, and they have feelings. How can they relish the thought of being totally dependent on a government cheque?" Without the northern cod, Carter doubted that most of the coastal communities would survive.

On January 24, 1995, Brian Tobin issued a news release containing more bad news. The northern cod stocks had declined further despite three years of the moratorium. There were virtually no large spawning fish in the areas that were surveyed, and the stock was now estimated to be only 1 per cent of what it had been in 1990. Tobin warned fishery workers that they could not expect to be compensated forever: "It's not good for the heart and soul of any individual to be left in a deep freeze, to be stored away with a minimal income waiting for the fishery to recover. This is soul-destroying stuff."

In an article in the *Sou'wester*, a fishing industry newspaper published in Yarmouth, Nova Scotia, Captain Wilfred Bartlett explained why anyone who had watched what had happened over the last ten years had no trouble understanding why the fishery had collapsed. For years, NIFA had pleaded with the DFO to reduce quotas to save the cod stocks. No one had listened. "John Crosbie was more concerned about jobs than the conservation of the fish stocks," Bartlett wrote. In the fall of 1991, NIFA had asked the DFO not to open the offshore winter fishery until results from the fall scientific cod survey were in; instead, Crosbie had given the offshore dragger companies a quota of 25,000 tonnes of cod. Only when the draggers couldn't find any fish did they tie up. "That's when John Crosbie closed down the Northern cod fishery."

Bartlett believed there were several reasons why the northern cod stocks were still declining. During the first two years of the closure, a lot of fish were being caught and sold on the black market. (You could still get fresh cod in most St. John's restaurants.) In 1994, the minister had been pressured to open up a food fishery, and the foreign fleets continued to take the few remaining fish. But the biggest problem, according to Bartlett, was the enormous number of seals eating the few remaining fish in the ocean. The Canadian Sealers Association sold buttons urging people to "Save Our Cod, Eat a Seal." When cod began to appear in some of Newfoundland's bays, a few fishermen thought that Brian Tobin might be making things sound worse than they were in order to downsize the fishery. Bartlett had a different theory. He believed these were the only fish left.

9

THE BAILOUT BLUES

With fitting pomp and circumstance, Ottawa announced The Atlantic Groundfish Strategy (TAGS) on May 16, 1994. At $1.9 billion, it was the second-largest spending program initiated by the Chrétien government, surpassed only by the national infrastructure program, the glittering lure the Liberals had dangled in front of voters before the 1993 federal election as they trolled for votes. The program replaced NCARP and was to be administered by Human Resources Development Canada (HDRC).

John Crosbie and his officials had originally believed that about twenty thousand people would need income support, but by the time TAGS was put in place, there were nearly forty thousand fishermen and plant workers claiming support throughout Atlantic Canada and Quebec. Income support would continue, but TAGS also had the mandate to reduce capacity in the industry by half – a goal first proposed by the federal fisheries department in 1970.

By the end of its first year, TAGS was $105 million over budget. Earle McCurdy, head of the FFAW, warned that cuts to the TAGS program, changes to UI, and rumoured increases in access and licence fees could spark "a period of turmoil" on the East Coast. McCurdy said he had never seen so much frustration with the federal government in Newfoundland fishing communities during his long union career. "The simple message is that enough is enough and it's time to lay off."

On August 10, 1995, the federal government announced several measures aimed at cutting cost overruns in TAGS. More fishermen than originally anticipated had qualified, and if the program continued to hand out benefits at the present rate there would be a $385 million deficit by 1999 when TAGS was originally set to expire. (Some estimates for cost overruns went as high as $800 million.) In response to union and political pressure, Ottawa decided to address the deficit problem by cutting training programs, administrative budgets, and the amount spent on capacity reduction, rather than cutting income-support payments to the fishermen.

By January 1995, only 3,800 of 30,000 or so Newfoundland fishery workers had signed up for retraining. Those who did tended to be younger and willing to leave their homes to find work. Fifteen thousand fishery workers over the age of forty-five saw no point in retraining or leaving. Only 2 per cent of TAGS clients had applied for relocation assistance. Some fishermen had invested as much as half a million dollars in their homes and businesses, and abandoning them for life in Mississauga was not an uplifting prospect.

Like many federal programs, TAGS sometimes had the opposite effect of what government intended. At their plant in Lunenburg, Nova Scotia, National Sea Products had twenty-five experienced people quit full-time jobs paying $10.38 an hour to go on TAGS. National Sea estimated it cost the company $4,800 for each of these employees in terms of lost productivity and the recruitment and training of replacements. All 650 of the company's plant workers were employed at the time and there were no immediate plans for layoffs.

To qualify for TAGS, a worker needed just two six-week periods of work in the fisheries between 1990 and 1992, and to have met UI requirements from *any* source of income in any two years during the same period. More abuses in the poorly thought-out assistance program became public. Initially, there were no restrictions on TAGS based on income, and there was no cross-checking done by Revenue Canada and the TAGS administrators. That changed after it was reported that TAGS benefits had gone to some P.E.I. crab fishermen who had earned over $200,000 for a few weeks' work. It wasn't until July 1996 that TAGS eligibility was tied to an income ceiling of $26,000. By then, the projected overrun for the program was estimated at almost $500 million.

Some people had actually fished in the same period as they had collected TAGS. Others had been sent both UI and TAGS cheques. A two-week waiting period for TAGS was implemented for an expected savings of $42 million. After fishermen from affected ridings contacted their MPs (including Brian Tobin), this cut was modified. Rather than losing the entire two weeks' payment in November, the cut would now be spread out over twenty weeks.

One of the major aims of the TAGS program was to reduce the size of the fishing industry by 50 per cent. It would be hard to imagine a more miserable planning failure. A January 1995 Price-Waterhouse report on the program revealed that the government had failed in most of its objectives except one, pumping money into the hands of unemployed fishery workers. Under questioning in the Commons during the Turbot War, Human Resources Minister Lloyd Axworthy acknowledged the criticism but blamed the program's shortcomings on the scope of the problem government was up against: "It is a calamity beyond the scope of anything we have faced in this country before. That requires major adjustment and changes."

As of April 1995, 38,000 people had qualified for TAGS and more than 80 per cent of the money went to Newfoundland. No one had yet identified which fishermen would stay in the industry after TAGS ended, despite the fact that identifying a "core group of fishermen" had been one of the guiding principles and selling points for the massive aid package.

The DFO plan to reduce the number of fishermen by buying out their licences was a dismal failure. By October 1995, Ottawa had spent $31 million to purchase 252 groundfish licences, less than

2 per cent of the total capacity on the East Coast. The average buy-out was worth about $121,000 to the licence holder. A second round of purchases was announced for August 1996, but a grand total of only 478 groundfish licences were bought back under TAGS. Originally Ottawa had planned to spend $300 million to buy back about 2,500 licences, but only $96.5 million was spent on reducing capacity, including early retirement benefits to just 333 fishermen.

On August 28, 1995, about fifteen hundred former fishery workers gathered on the wharf in Harbour Grace to protest planned cuts to TAGS and changes to unemployment insurance. Demonstrations were also held in Bonavista, Marystown, Burgeo, Englee, Baie Verte, and St. Anthony. Some protesters threatened to resume fishing if cuts were made to benefits. Earle McCurdy went to Ottawa to protest the cuts, but he got nothing more from Tobin and Axworthy than a promise to see if there was a different way of making the same savings. In some quarters in Newfoundland the FFAW was being criticized for not standing up for the fishery workers. The FFAW had received about $34 million from TAGS to run training centres, sentinel fisheries, and other programs; this, critics said, had silenced it.

Protests against changes in the fishery weren't limited to Newfoundland. On February 15, 1996, a boisterous but peaceful crowd of about three thousand inshore fishermen and their supporters marched through downtown Halifax to protest both the jump in fees and the introduction of individual transferable quotas (ITQs), which they feared would lead to the large fish companies buying up the industry one ITQ at a time. The Halifax protesters held on to a 1.5-kilometre-long rope as they marched through the city, handing out orange ribbons to supporters. Three busloads of protesters had left Cape Breton at 4:00 a.m. in a major blizzard in order to participate. Protesters had been occupying DFO offices in Yarmouth and Barrington Passage for a week, and there were also sit-ins at DFO offices in Sydney, Bridgewater, and Meteghan.

The next day, the protests spread to another DFO office in Digby, Nova Scotia, where fishermen set up an around-the-clock vigil in the parking lot. Earle McCurdy threw the support of the FFAW behind the move. On February 22, the DFO shut down fifteen offices in the Scotia Fundy region as a precaution, because employees felt intimidated by the occupations. The staff were stressed to the point where they couldn't function.

In general, it was the part-time fishermen who protested the loudest, those who fished in the good weather and collected UI in the winter months. They rightly saw that their way of life was being threatened. ITQs likely will eventually eliminate part-time fishermen. Some lobster fishermen, angry at hefty fee hikes, also took part in the protests. The fisheries minister insisted he would not negotiate with the protesters until the DFO offices were vacated. But the DFO had a history of caving in to protests, especially around election time.

In early March 1996, inshore fishermen from the Scotia Fundy region gained some ground after three days of talks with DFO officials. There would be a one-year freeze on the transfer of ITQs, but not an all-out ban. Changes were also made in the definition of who was a "core" fisherman. Small-boat handliners who made a minimum of 75 per cent of their earned income from fishing would now be included in the definition. The minister did not back down on licence-fee increases for 1996, expected to generate $42 million, but he did agree to review and revise the fees if necessary for 1997.

The protest movement in Nova Scotia was not all of the same mind. Historically, longline, handline, and gill-net fishermen rarely agreed on how quotas were to be divided. So when the DFO brought in a plan to promote community management – allowing local committees of fishermen to decide how quotas were allocated – Shelburne County fixed-gear fishermen bickered for over a year about how they would divide their reduced groundfish quotas. Some fishermen wanted a competitive fishery, others wanted ITQs they could buy, sell, or trade. Finally they asked the DFO to settle the dispute.

The DFO resolved matters by reducing preliminary quotas to the fixed-gear fishermen, causing an uproar in Shelburne. The handliners' share dropped about 8 per cent, and the gill-netters' share went up. To some handline fishermen this was proof that the DFO wanted to get rid of handliners altogether – the 8-per-cent drop would mean a loss of $500,000 worth of fish to them. Some said they would fish no matter what the DFO said. "If DFO wants a fight, that's what they are going to get," one fisherman vowed. The divisions in this one sector were typical of the divisions throughout the fishery. Everyone was squabbling for a greater share of a shrinking resource, and everyone believed his demand was entirely reasonable.

Protests continued at DFO offices in Sydney and Antigonish, the Sydney protest lasting forty-four days. The three hundred people who took part ended their sit-in only when the DFO said it would have another look at both the Fisheries Act and the Oceans Act.

Although most of the protests were peaceful, some were violent, especially when out-of-work fishermen saw others making good money in the industry. In April 1994, in Newport, Quebec, on the southeast tip of the Gaspé Peninsula, about two hundred angry former cod fishermen and plant workers attacked five crab-boat captains and their crews as they were preparing their vessels for the start of the crab season in the Gulf of St. Lawrence. The mob kicked and punched Maurice Ouellette, then threw him out of the office at the wintering yard where the boats were stored, forcing the other crab fishermen to leave. The desperate mob wanted crab licences and vowed no boats would leave the harbour unless they got them, even though the crab stocks in the Gulf were already showing signs of being overfished.

HRDC did a review of TAGS in May 1996, although it was not made public until a freedom-of-information request by Canadian Press was granted in January 1997. The report found that the key goal of retraining people for jobs outside the fishery was not met because of the inflexible attitude of some fishermen and plant workers. "Strong community ties, home ownership, and an often unwavering belief that the fish stocks will return present barriers to adjusting TAGS clients out of the groundfishery." Inshore fisherman

Tom Best said that trying to persuade people to take advantage of the retraining opportunities offered by TAGS had been one of the most frustrating experiences of his life. He maintained that as long as the government was going to pay direct compensation to out-of-work Newfoundlanders, they would have no incentive to leave the fishery.

The review reported that there was a strong belief that another program would replace TAGS, despite Brian Tobin having said when he was fisheries minister that the current package was the last the federal government would offer. The report noted that minimum-wage jobs didn't pay as much as TAGS, and that in some communities looking for work was frowned on if you were on TAGS because it could prevent a job going to someone on welfare.

Workers in other fields affected by the moratorium, such as equipment suppliers, were forced onto welfare when their UI ran out. But fishermen were convinced that the federal government was responsible for the crisis. As one fisherman from St. Carol's told a CBC radio panel in January 1995, "The federal government created the mess that we're in, and they're not going to shove training down my throat and push me off the Island. . . . I'm not going off this rock that we're on. I'm holding fast."

By June 1996, there were heavy rumours that Ottawa was going to cut TAGS cheques by as much as 12 per cent in January 1997. Earle McCurdy had a warning for the politicians: "People will go ballistic. That's their bread, butter, and shelter they are tampering with. These are very substantial cuts, and people can't afford it. I'm sick and fed up with them [Ottawa] looking at ways of how they can put the screws to people in the Newfoundland fishery. It's a declaration of war if they do that, and we will respond accordingly with all guns blazing." McCurdy threatened a new round of protests. After all, the protests in August 1995 had worked. Ottawa had backed off cutting incomes by 4 per cent, and found savings by trimming administration costs and training programs.

In December 1995, Tobin had unveiled a new licensing policy that he hoped would shape the industry into a fishery that was both economically viable without massive federal aid and environmentally sustainable. The new professional fisherman would have both a good income and a future; and access to licences would be strictly regulated. The aim was to pare down the estimated 24,600 active fishermen in Atlantic Canada to a core of about 13,250 people, eliminating part-timers. But at the same time the minister announced that "no fisherman will lose his licence" as a result of the new policy. The number of fishermen would decline very slowly.

Core or professional fishermen would head up fishing enterprises that held multiple licences. They would be eligible to receive new inshore or vessel-based licences and be able to transfer them. It was expected that about 5,100 of the 8,100 registered groundfish-licence holders in Newfoundland would meet the core criteria. Regional fishing associations would establish the standards to define who was a core fisher. The principles of historical dependency and adjacency (that those who live closest to a resource have priority access to it) would be maintained.

Easier said than done. One of the problems with the plan according to many fishermen was that nobody really knew what the term "core fishery" meant. The vice-president of the FFAW's Inshore Fishermen's Council said, "It's hazy. It's just something out there floating around." He worried that some genuine fishermen would be overlooked under the federal government's definition. Would a crewman have status?

The DFO also planned to hike "access fees" (licence fees and other charges) to recover part of its costs from the people who benefited from the use of a national resource. The department hoped to recover over $50 million in user fees for 1996–97, substantially more than the $13 million the DFO was currently receiving. Thirty million dollars of this would be collected in Atlantic Canada. The announcement created an uproar, and after a firestorm of protests the amount was reduced to about $42 million. The industry was alerted it would be asked to pay more for services in the future.

Just after Christmas 1995, Premier Clyde Wells announced his decision to return to private life. On January 4, 1996, just eight months after the high-stakes heroics of the Turbot War, Brian Tobin told Prime Minister Chrétien that he was going back to Newfoundland to run for the leadership of the provincial Liberal party. Chosen by acclamation, the popular Tobin was sworn in as premier on January 26. In the subsequent election held a month later, the Liberals won thirty-seven of the forty-eight seats in the Newfoundland legislature, and the Conservative leader lost her own seat. Tobin's easy walk to power really said it all – in the eyes of Newfoundlanders he had done an excellent job as the federal fisheries minister, even though there were no fish.

Fred Mifflin, a former rear admiral who had commanded ten destroyers in the navy, was the fourth Newfoundlander in a row to be given the federal fisheries portfolio. His family had settled in Bonavista in 1780, and he had represented the riding of Bonavista–Trinity–Conception since 1988. But he had been spectacularly silent in Ottawa on major fisheries issues. Wags in Ottawa were asking, "Fred Who?"

Mifflin's first test came in May 1996, when an angry mob of over five hundred crab fishermen threw rocks and bricks, smashing windows at the house and office of New Brunswick's fisheries minister, Bernard Theriault. They were protesting against sharing 20 per cent of their crab quota with inshore cod fishermen.

Mifflin threatened to cancel the crab season if the quota problem wasn't solved. The RCMP riot squad braced for more trouble in northern New Brunswick. The DFO's own reports showed the stocks were declining because they were already being fished to the maximum, but blockades and riots led the federal minister to give out new licences in Cape Breton and the southern Gulf of St. Lawrence. Mifflin was widely perceived as having caved in to political pressure, and people worried that crab would go the way of the cod.

In July 1996, Mifflin again bowed to pressure and made some changes to the DFO's proposed new licensing policy for Newfoundland. He accepted seven out of nine changes demanded by the FFAW, dealing with the professionalization of fishermen, including special circumstances for qualification, and the transfer of licences. The union wanted a commonsense attitude to individual cases. For example, if a fisherman met all the criteria but had one bad year because the fishery in his area had failed, the union felt he should still be given status. Mifflin decided to retain a minimum income level of $5,000 for boats under thirty-five feet and $10,000 for vessels over thirty-five feet, for membership in the core fishery. The bottom line was that more people would remain in the fishery.

Unlike Crosbie and Tobin, who through the sheer force of their personalities put fisheries up high on the federal agenda, Mifflin turned in a lacklustre performance from the start. Both Crosbie and Tobin had pushed hard to achieve the UN agreement on straddling and migratory fish stocks. Canada had been instrumental in negotiating the UN agreement in the wake of the *Estai* incident and had signed it on December 4, 1995, but it took until April 17, 1997, for Mifflin to introduce a bill to implement the agreement in the House of Commons. The bill died before the 1997 election.

During this time, the DFO was in the process of reducing its net spending by 32 per cent over a four-year period ending in 1998–99. Funding levels would drop by $450 million, from $1.4 billion to about $950 million, and the department would lose about 40 per cent of its employees. Of necessity, the fishery of the future had to be more self-reliant, and those who benefitted would have to pay part of the cost of management. The DFO was also in the process of integrating with the Canadian Coast Guard (CCG), a merger that caused morale in the CCG to plummet as low as it was in the DFO. CCG members, accustomed to risking their lives to save people, would now have to be fishery enforcers as well. Given the state of the fishery, it could become the riskiest part of their job.

★

In her keynote address to the World Fisheries Congress in Australia in 1996, Dr. Pamela Mace of the U.S. National Marine Fisheries Service summed up the situation facing coastal fisheries: "In many fisheries, stakeholders cannot even agree on the problem, let alone the solutions. Defining and reconciling objectives pertaining to all dimensions of fisheries (biological, economic, and social) is such a difficult task that it is rarely addressed in a comprehensive and transparent manner. . . . We have enough science, enough technology, enough eloquent, forward-thinking words on paper, enough appreciation of the problems, enough spectacular examples of fishery failures – and enough successes – to know what needs to be done. However, the old saying that recognizing the problem is half the solution does not apply to fisheries. Inertia comes from lack of political will, lack of monetary commitment, and pleas from fish harvesters and others to maintain a way of life that, unfortunately, in many cases is rapidly becoming an anachronism."

Dr. Mace pointed out that when a high number of fishery workers are marginal economically, the result will likely be increased pressure on the scientists to produce optimistic assessments, and challenges to their work if they resist. Managers and governments are also pushed for higher, riskier TACs and generous subsidies to prop up parts of the industry that would not otherwise survive. Conversely, or perhaps, perversely, there is also increased incentive for fishermen to get around fishing regulations aimed at restricting their share of the common property. People want to preserve their way of life and they will hang on as long as they can, hoping that things will improve in the future.

Everyone wants the same thing, an ecologically and socially sustainable fishery. But balancing "objective" scientific knowledge with practical social, economic, and political reality is almost impossible to do. There's always a winner in the power structure. In the end, the ones who call the shots are not the people who count fish, but the ones who garner votes.

In April 1995, scientists learned about what was described as "an unusually high density of cod" in the Smith Sound area of

Trinity Bay, within the range of the northern cod. The stock was estimated to be about 17,000 tonnes. Research scientist Dr. George Rose confirmed that a survey had found a good aggregation of older spawning stock, the largest group of seven- and eight-year-old fish seen on the northeast coast in years. Rose shared everyone's relief at the news, but cautioned, "Right now it's simply a hope."

Eleven months later, Rose, who was the senior chair in fisheries conservation with the Marine Institute at Memorial University, said that the large school of fish did not mean that the stocks had recovered enough to harvest. He had been studying the migration of the northern cod since 1990 and knew that by 1993 there were virtually no cod on the offshore spawning grounds. By then, the only large school of fish was in an area outside the 200-mile limit where the Spanish fleet was fishing without regard for conservation. Rose suggested an intriguing theory: it was possible that part of the northern cod stock had come inshore and stayed there for lack of older fish to lead them back out along the migration routes.

One of the older inshore fishermen from Trinity Bay, Jack Marsh, told reporters that the stock had always been there, but the scientists just hadn't bothered to look earlier. According to Marsh, the fish came in every October and stayed there until the ice broke up the following spring. He claimed there were cod in other areas of Trinity Bay and in Bonavista Bay as well, and that in addition to the stock that came in in the fall, there was a stock, known locally as "trap fish," that chased caplin inshore in June and remained all summer in the area.

Retired fishermen, such as Eldon Froude of Old Perlican, could have told the DFO scientists that all they had to do to find other "discoveries" of northern cod was to steam across the bay to Grates Cove and then to other nearby areas such as Winterton as the cod moved into the bay chasing the spring herring. Fishermen from Marystown to Lord's Cove on the Burin Peninsula also reported an abundance of cod inshore.

The DFO scientists had not been able to do a survey of the

inshore because of a lack of money and manpower. Rose suggested that one remedy would be to increase the sentinel fishery. This is a test fishery done in cooperation with the DFO to see what kind of catches can be made. It incorporates fishermen's knowledge and experience with scientific research. Once the boat ties up and the fish are unloaded, the fishermen measure each cod, determine its sex as they gut it, and check what the fish was eating. They then send the information and their comments on the quality of the fish to DFO scientists. Scientists use data obtained from these catches for their studies to determine the abundance, behaviour, and distribution of the cod.

Until the collapse, information from the inshore fisheries was not used because scientists believed there was no efficient way of gathering or quantifying information that had been passed down from generation to generation. Only now are fishermen's observations on stock, water temperatures, and salinity being fed into computers and analyzed.

As sociologist Barbara Neis pointed out in her 1992 paper, "Fisher's Ecological Knowledge and Stock Assessment in Newfoundland," published in the journal *Newfoundland Studies*, successive generations of inshore fishermen have "harvested" rather than "hunted" the resource because they used fixed gear. Over the years they have developed "important traditional ecological knowledge" and a rich understanding of the relationships between cod movement and abundance, ecological changes, and the interactions of other species. In a way, they were better scientists than the scientists when it came to detecting a catastrophic shift in the health of the stocks.

The corporate model lacked that intuitive insight. Yet the DFO "tuned" its stock assessments with the catch rates of the offshore trawling companies, which had insisted until very late in the day that the stocks were fine. Scientists had overestimated the abundance of the stocks in part because these same companies threw away young fish or by-catch species that were not reported in their landings statistics. Worldwide, the offshore sector discards 27 million tonnes of fish a year from landings of roughly three times that amount.

It was the handline and trap fishermen in Petty Harbour who were among the first to insist that DFO scientific assessments of the northern cod were wrong. Some were sceptical as early as 1983 when they noticed that the fish were getting smaller and that the season that had once stretched from June to November now ran from July to the middle of September.

Neis pointed out that inshore fishermen knew that fish congregate in different places according to their size and that there was a relationship between lunar cycles and the marine ecosystem. A scientist will do a survey at the same time each year in an effort to be consistent, but fishermen know that the rhythms of the lunar cycles affect important events like the spawning of caplin. As Leslie Harris put it, "Fish don't use our calendar."

After the excitement of the Trinity Bay find, the June 1995 offshore research surveys showed no signs of stock recovery for the northern cod. Before returning to provincial politics, Brian Tobin released results showing that the spawning biomass was at its lowest ebb ever. Fishermen suspected that the large and voracious seal herd had slowed the recovery of the groundfish stocks.

The NCSP funded research into the basic biology of harp and hooded seals, as well as into their effect on fish stocks. The large-vessel seal hunt had ended in 1983 because of pressure from animal-rights activists, and by 1990, there were about 3.1 million harp seals and about 400,000 to 450,000 hooded seals. By March 1995, the harp seal population had jumped to between 4.5 and 4.8 million, and predictions were that by the year 2000 there would be 6.2 million of the animals. The seal herds had more than doubled since the hunt was stopped and so had their food consumption, just when the cod stocks were most vulnerable.

The total consumption of fish by harp seals in the northwest Atlantic in 1994 was estimated to be 6.9 million tonnes, up from 3.6 million tonnes in 1981. Forty per cent of that was eaten in

Newfoundland waters, mainly on the northeast coast, the home of the northern cod. Off Newfoundland, only about 3 per cent of the harp seals' diet is Atlantic cod, but given the size of the seal herd, they ate an astonishing 88,000 tonnes of them in 1994. During the last year of the commercial fishery, only 26,000 tonnes of northern cod were taken by Canadian fishermen. One tonne of commercial catch equals about 900 fish, but one tonne of year-old cod is equal to about 38,000 fish, and a tonne of two-year-old cod equals roughly 9,500 fish. Since most of the cod found in the stomachs of examined seals was only a year or two old, the seals were taking a huge number of individual cod to make up that 88,000 tonnes. Fishermen were right when they insisted that seals were hindering the recovery of the northern cod stocks.

Matters were no better in the Gulf of St. Lawrence, where harp seals consumed an estimated 54,000 tonnes of Atlantic cod, bringing their total 1994 consumption to 142,000 tonnes of the endangered species. In the same year, voracious harp seals also ate 620,000 tonnes of caplin in the Newfoundland region. The annual total consumption of caplin and Atlantic cod by seals was way in excess of commercial landings by the Newfoundland fishing fleet in the 1980s. Whether seals eat juvenile cod or the cod's favourite food, they have a profound effect on the food web when their population is high and the fish population is at an all-time low.

A comprehensive sentinel fishery along the entire Newfoundland northeast coast took place during the summer of 1995, involving about three hundred inshore fishermen at a cost of about $7.5 million. Old suspicions festered while everyone waited for the cod to return. Some fishermen grumbled that the government cheques paid to sentinel fishermen had a way of silencing previously outspoken critics of the DFO. Mike Hearn, an inshore fisherman from Petty Harbour, claimed that no one was there to fight their battles any more. Hearn suggested that the DFO had targeted certain outspoken fishermen with federal goodies to keep them quiet.

The sentinel survey program cost $6 million in 1996. On March 14, 1997, Fred Mifflin announced the sentinel survey program for 1997. The DFO hoped to recover part of the cost of the program by selling the fish the program harvested. Fish harvester organizations selected 460 participants who were then trained in data collection. They would stay with the program for a number of years. There were also plans to expand the sentinel fishery to include offshore surveys, where the cod had to be found in numbers if the commercial fishery were ever to reopen.

Ottawa continued to play it safe. The halibut fishery in 3Ps along the south coast had been shut down temporarily in January because its 10 per cent cod by-catch allowance had been exceeded. One skipper said there were a lot of large cod on the Grand Banks, thirty pounds and up. No one in authority rose to the bait. The halibut fishery in 3NO on the southern Grand Banks was temporarily closed at the end of February for vessels between sixty feet and one hundred feet long because fishermen were pulling in more than their allowed 5 per cent by-catch limit for cod.

In the meantime, fish processors in Canada were reaping the benefit of prudent stewardship of the cod stock in Norway. Almost 100 per cent of the high-quality cod being processed in fish plants in Atlantic Canada came from the Barents Sea. In 1997, the cod quota in the Barents Sea was set at a staggering 850,000 tonnes. Norway was collecting the dividends of taking swift action in the 1980s to protect its stock, and Canada was paying the price for keeping the fishery open. The world's second-largest exporter of seafood products was now importing its raw material from a major competitor.

IO

ONE STEP FORWARD,
TWO STEPS BACK

In the spring of 1996, a Portuguese fish company, Impormarisco, purchased and reopened Diamond Industries, an idle fish plant in Sandy Cove on the Northern Peninsula of Newfoundland. The firm was prepared to process whatever the fishermen brought in. The new owners planned to sell in the lucrative European market, where the quality of fish demanded was very different than in North America. Europe consumes 33 per cent of total world seafood imports, and is a logical market for Newfoundland and Labrador. The company had already sent live lobsters to test the market, and to see if the creatures survived the journey. Impormarisco planned to process turbot, caplin, lumpfish roe, herring, and even salt cod if they could get fish from the Barents Sea. They renovated the plant to make it more efficient, installing more cold storage so they could sell when market conditions were best.

The plant is a good example of the type of niche processing that can be done in Newfoundland. Small, smart, flexible, linked to fishermen in the community, the company processes what is available, and wastes nothing, trucking in product if necessary. Above all it has market connections for a high-end product. It is part of the effort in Newfoundland to overcome the province's old reputation for low-quality, high-volume fish, and establish a new one for added-value, upscale products.

This wasn't the only good news on the East Coast.

In early 1996, Newfoundland's fisheries, food, and agriculture minister, Bud Hulan, told a St. John's Board of Trade business seminar that the outlook for Newfoundland's fishery was excellent despite the demolition of the groundfish industry and the demise of the cod. The 1995 value of crab, shrimp, lobster, clams, turbot, herring, and other fish was $300 million, the highest landed value in the province's history. The export value of seafood products topped $500 million, up $50 million from the year before.

Shellfish were now the most important species in the Newfoundland fishery. Sea urchins for the Japanese sushi market and rock and toad crabs were some of the new species being exploited. International trade in seaweed products was now worth a staggering $3.5 billion, and the province had three species of kelp in abundance along the south coast that could be harvested.

It was the same story in Nova Scotia. Although certain communities were beggared by the groundfish crisis, landings of other species hit a record high, mainly due to buoyant lobster, scallop, and crab prices. In 1994, two years after the start of the northern cod moratorium, revenues from fish landings were $498 million, a 7 per cent increase over the previous year. Processing increased that figure by another $500 million, pumping a billion dollars into the provincial economy. Two years later, Nova Scotia seafood exports totalled a record $799.4 million, a slight increase over 1995 figures. For all the bleating from the East, some people were still making a great deal of money from the fishery.

But behind these rosy numbers lurked some deeply troubling facts. The processing capacity in Atlantic Canada remained about four times higher than landings justified. A bevy of industry analysts agreed that overcapacity was really a way of getting UI funds into the depressed region. Everyone, including governments, was part of the scheme. Plants would operate for peak periods, employing as many people in the community as they could, who would go on UI for the rest of the year.

The Newfoundland government rejected the option of buying out excess capacity because the province couldn't afford it. Although everyone knows capacity has to be reduced, no one seems to be able to agree just how to do it, despite government studies and a lot of industry input. In March 1997, the new Newfoundland fisheries and aquaculture minister, John Efford, announced a new licensing framework for Newfoundland's restructured processing sector. Central to the restructuring were core multi-species plants that had an average annual production of 1,000 tonnes of groundfish from 1987 to 1991. With the development of quality assurance controls from the dock to the plants, and restrictions on the export of unprocessed fish, the industry was headed in an entirely new direction from its historical place in the fishery. The plants would be licensed to process all species but crab and shrimp from zone 4R off the west coast. Plants without core status could continue to operate with existing licences, or expand through licence transfers.

Of the 212 plants in the province licensed for primary processing, 99 have freezing capacity for groundfish. Under the new regulations non-core plants not currently licensed for freezing will not be given freezing authority, although they can combine their capacity with plants that do have freezing licences.

Another troubling fact was the state of the shellfish industry. While the total groundfish revenues for Newfoundland fishermen had collapsed from about $155 million in 1989 to only $26 million in 1996, shellfish revenues for crab, shrimp, and lobster had jumped from $51 million to $192 million during the same period. The harvesting and processing of crab provided work for 7,000 people, and many crab fishermen cleared $100,000 for about eight weeks' work.

With so much money to be made, dissension had grown in the industry over the issue of crab licences and quotas, and many more Newfoundlanders were going after crab. In 1995 there were 1,200 crab fishermen, in 1996 there were 2,800. Those who took part got less money of course, but more people were eligible for UI.

Unfortunately the new entrants set out for the crab grounds just as prices dropped because of competition from the Russian and Alaskan fisheries, and the Japanese recession.

In 1995, the landed value for all species of crab in Newfoundland was about $181 million, but in 1996 it had dropped to $84 million, even though actual crab landings were up and more people were working in the industry. In 1997, Newfoundland processors were offering less than 75 cents a pound for crab, about a quarter of the price just two years before. When processors tried to explain market conditions and give the reasons why they could not pay 1996 prices, the fishermen walked out of the meeting and 96 per cent of them voted to strike. They complained that crab buyers were trying to pass "the entire burden of the market onto the shoulders of fishermen."

On April 24, 1997, just three days before the election call, 150 inshore fishermen who held temporary crab permits gathered in St. John's to send a strong message to Fred Mifflin. They were not happy with their crab allocations. Two weeks earlier, Mifflin had announced the 1997–98 snow crab management plan for Newfoundland and Labrador. The minister had increased the total quota by 15 per cent to a record 44,315 tonnes. A 42 per cent increase in quota was given to temporary permit holders (their quota increased from 4,160 tonnes in 1996 to 5,895 tonnes in 1997 and 1998). As Gerard Ryan of Ferryland said, "We got a resource that's at our doorstep and we're told we are not allowed a half decent quota to stick her down until the cod comes back. TAGS will be cut off in 1998, and we got to have revenue."

The increase in quota for temporary permit holders fishing from boats under thirty-five feet broke down to less than 8,000 pounds per boat, a quota the fishermen grumbled was hardly worth gearing up for. They demanded 20,000 to 25,000 tonnes per boat. Ryan said, "We've been fighting over crumbs for years and we are not fighting over crumbs any more." Their small boats could not fish farther than twenty miles offshore, and they wanted larger boats kept out of their twenty-mile zone, since crab allocations on paper were useless if the larger boats came in and cleaned out the crab close to the shore. One of the fishermen summed things up neatly: "We want our share of fish, and that's the bottom line."

On May 27, 1997, over three hundred crab fishermen from around the province came to St. John's for a rally. The protesters marched to the Confederation Building to register their anger over regulations that prevented them from exporting their catch to plants outside the province for better prices. The regulations had been put in place to keep processing jobs in the province.

Provincial fisheries minister John Efford met with the angry group in the lobby of Confederation Building. They threatened to close down every fishery in the province if they didn't get the answer they wanted. Over shouts from the crowd, the minister reminded the group that there were 6,000 crab plant workers in the province who would be at his doorstep protesting and blocking the crab as it was loaded on the trucks, if he lifted the regulation. Percolating under the crab protest was anger about user-fee increases by the DFO. One crab fisherman had paid $250 for a licence in 1993, now he was faced with paying about $10,000 for licence fees, observer coverage, and dockside monitoring.

On June 3, the day after the federal election, Efford announced that he would temporarily lift the ban on exporting unprocessed crab for thirty days. The next day, protesters, angry that the restriction would be lifted for only thirty days, and that outside buyers could only purchase the crab through a local fish buyer, chased Efford out of Mary Queen of Peace Hall in St. John's, where he was attempting to explain to five hundred fishermen why he had lifted the restriction. When a fisherman tried to get up on stage to address the crowd while the minister was speaking, he was pulled back by a police officer and the other fishermen rushed to his aid.

Efford was escorted to a waiting car by the officers and driven to safety. The mob turned its attention to rocking a police car, which they tried to prevent from leaving. When police used pepper spray in an attempt to disperse the crowd, the fishermen hurled rocks, injuring one of the officers.

A tentative deal wasn't struck until July 11, when Premier Tobin stepped in and urged processors and fishermen to come to an agreement before Newfoundland lost its entire 1997 crab fishery. It was the first time in his eighteen-year political career that Tobin had jumped into the middle of a collective bargaining process. He didn't ever intend to do it again, but there were too many jobs at risk and just too much money on the table. Crab fishermen finally dropped their pots in the water almost five weeks late; they had to fish until the end of October to get the full quota. As the season progressed, Japanese markets declined further as crab from Alaska, Russia, and Greenland hit the market.

After the collapse of the cod stocks there was increased pressure not only on crab but also on other stocks from fishermen trying to earn a living.

The northern shrimp fishery is relatively new to Canada, having been developed in the mid-1970s. Our fleet consists of twelve modern and expensive Canadian-registered factory-freezer trawlers. John Efford wanted to increase jobs by adding shrimp to plants already processing crab and other species. He didn't like the fact that large overseas vessels were catching shrimp and either processing it at sea or abroad. If the quota was going to be increased, the minister wanted it to go to Newfoundland, to people coming off TAGS. No one mentioned that the shrimp fishery is one of the most destructive on the planet. The small-mesh nets used catch everything, including very small fish.

On April 23, 1997, Fred Mifflin flew to Newfoundland to announce that the new shrimp quota would be 59,050 tonnes, a whopping 57 per cent increase. The additional shrimp was expected to generate an extra $75 million in the local economy, and provide work for 1,500 fishermen and plant workers. The total value of the shrimp fishery in 1997 was expected to be about $215 million.

The shrimp fishery is carried out from Davis Strait south to NAFO zone 3K. Shrimp were abundant in part because there were few northern cod to prey on them. Catch-rates for shrimp had increased dramatically after the cod biomass began to decline, yet in almost thirty years we have never caught the shrimp quota.

Henry Demone made an interesting observation: "You cannot catch shrimp in small vessels, bring it in and process it on land and hit high-quality markets. The Japanese will not even have a discussion with you about that. They want frozen-at-sea quality. They want very specific quality standards on a product before they will buy it from you. We basically set up an industrial structure which guaranteed that the new 20,000 tonnes of shrimp are low value, and low margin."

Demone believes no lessons were learned during the latest crisis in the fishery. "You can look at some of the decisions that were made in the crab fishery and in the shrimp fishery, and you can say it's the same mistakes all over again. You know the government is under a lot of pressure from communities. You go back ten years ago and a crab fisherman and a cod fisherman were equal peers in the community. The cod disappears in Canada, the crab disappear in Alaska, the yen doubles in value, and all of a sudden the cod fisherman is on TAGS, and the crab fisherman is making a six-figure income. Now my attitude to that is force him to pay taxes but don't destroy the industry in the process. But [instead] they issue new licences. They bring new people into the business. They put enormous pressure on the resource just when the scientists say, 'We think we are going into a down period for crab.'"

Fishermen who turned to lobster, Atlantic salmon, and scallops have similarly put these species at risk. By January 1997, conservationists were cautioning there would soon be a crisis in the entire East Coast lobster fishery. There are signs that there may be a region-wide collapse comparable to what happened to the cod stocks. Landings in the Atlantic region are down 25 per cent since 1992. Catches in southwest Nova Scotia are still good, but that may have more to do with increased fishing effort than healthy stocks. About 85 per cent of marketable lobsters are being fished every year.

There are about 10,000 full-time lobster fishermen in Atlantic Canada, and a lot of poachers. It is the old sad story of taking too much and leaving too little for the stock to regenerate.

In May 1996, the TAC for caplin was reduced by 16 per cent off Newfoundland and in the Gulf of St. Lawrence. Earl Johnson, an inshore fisherman from North Harbour, Placentia Bay, said he would sooner see it cut altogether. For years, fishermen had warned that the caplin couldn't take the fishing pressure they were subjected to, yet a provision that closed the caplin fishery in areas where the fish were smaller than fifty per kilogram in 1995 was lifted by Mifflin. By 1996 the sight of millions of the tiny fish swimming to the shore to spawn in the coves and bays of Newfoundland was a thing of the past. The few fish that made it that year were under-sized and often in poor condition.

In June 1996, the Atlantic Salmon Federation asked Mifflin to shut down the commercial salmon fishery off Labrador immediately. The latest data showed stocks were critically low. The International Council for the Exploration of the Seas, made up of distinguished scientists from both sides of the Atlantic, was so worried about the stock that it called for zero harvest of large salmon off southwest Greenland and North America.

By 1996 scallop stocks had collapsed in the Bay of Fundy. After a period of phenomenal incomes with no conservation measures, the inshore scallopers had fished them out. Catches had declined from a peak of 6,000 tonnes to an unfilled quota of 1,200 tonnes in 1996. It was estimated the catch would be less than half that amount in 1997. Three hundred fishermen and their families depended on scallops for their livelihood; some inshore scallopers were making less than two dollars an hour.

They demanded a portion of the quota that had been given to the offshore scallop fleet in a 1986 deal agreed to by the two sectors. Having challenged the deal in court and lost in July 1996, the inshore fishermen turned to the time-honoured methods of getting their way. Two hundred protesters took to the streets and pitched a large tent in front of the HRDC building in Digby.

In early April 1997 protesters again occupied the Digby HRDC office, and when that didn't seem to get enough attention they also occupied the offices of South West Nova Liberal MP Harry Vernon and the DFO in Yarmouth. The scallopers feared they would lose everything they had worked for all their lives if they didn't get access to more scallops. For many, their only alternative would be welfare when their EI payments ran out in May.

On April 18, 1997, Mifflin sent a letter to the inshore scallopers rejecting their demand for 600 tonnes of scallops from the offshore grounds. Instead, the minister offered them access to 100 tonnes from the midshore, in an area that had not been fished for a decade, and which conservationists wanted protected. The deal was on only if they gave up their occupation of federal offices in Digby and Yarmouth. The protesters ended their sit-ins only after they were promised a meeting with DFO officials.

In January 1997, nearly one hundred offshore scallop fishermen were laid off in Lunenburg, Nova Scotia, by Clearwater Fine Foods, National Sea Products, and FPI. Six draggers were tied up. A deckhand on a scallop boat can make about $70,000–$90,000 in a good year, so the layoffs had a devastating impact on the community. The unemployed scallop fishermen refused to accept the company line that the layoffs were a conservation issue. They saw it as a move to increase company profits by employing fewer fishermen in state-of-the-art vessels that could take just as many scallops. They began showing up at nomination meetings to make sure their situation was turned into an election issue. They would have to stand in line.

On September 18, 1996, Fred Mifflin announced that Newfoundlanders could go fishing the following weekend. The minister's riding covers one of the largest fishery-dependent areas in the country, and he had been under tremendous pressure to allow a "food" fishery. From Friday to Sunday, people could catch up to ten cod a day for their personal use. (A fall 1995 food fishery had been cut short by Brian Tobin because the fish were small and so scarce that people found it difficult to catch their limit. Still, about two thousand tonnes of cod was caught in an eight-day period.)

Officially DFO scientists supported the food fishery in 1996. Scott Parsons, the assistant deputy minister of science at the DFO, said that although there was no hope for a commercial fishery in the near future, he had advised Mifflin that a very limited and tightly controlled food fishery was acceptable. In some of the small communities in Mifflin's riding many people questioned the wisdom of the decision. They were not alone.

An internal memo authored by DFO scientist Peter Shelton, an expert on northern cod who was based in St. John's, referred to the May 1996 stock status report that said stocks were still at an extremely low level and that any schools that existed should be preserved. Shelton wrote, "I was therefore quite dismayed by the report that a recreational food fishery will be allowed because of scientific evidence from the sentinel fishery of an improvement in the status of the cod stock." He continued, "I am disappointed and disheartened that important decisions are being made that disregard the scientific advice from this region." Shelton maintained that the inshore stocks that would be fished, "could hold the key to stock recovery, and therefore must be conserved."

The DFO was focusing a lot of scientific attention on these inshore stocks. Shelton knew from his own work that the 2J3KL cod stock was still at a very low level. There were very few fish over age nine in the population, and even if a strong year-class survived it would be several years before the stock was out of immediate danger.

The Reform Party's fisheries critic, Mike Scott, accused Mifflin of putting politics ahead of scientific advice and claimed that Mifflin's staff was aware of internal DFO concerns but went ahead anyway. Mifflin countered that he had never seen Shelton's memo. "I consult my scientists and they tell me something and I respond to it," he said. "The buck stops with [the senior scientist]. He weighs the information. I can't read every letter that is written to every scientist."

Scott Parsons said the memo gave a false impression that the Newfoundland region of the DFO had advised against a food fishery. He said Mifflin was given the current stock status report and information from the sentinel surveys up to the end of August. The minister had even asked Parsons and William Doubleday, the director general of the DFO's fisheries and oceans science division, to make personal observations of the sentinel surveys in various parts of Newfoundland during the month of August. Doubleday was also an "ex officio" member of the Fisheries Resource Conservation Council. Parsons said, "I advised the minister that a very limited food fishery, tightly controlled to avoid abuses, is unlikely to impede the recovery of inshore stock components. The suggestion or allegation that the minister didn't listen to his scientists or ignored scientific advice is false."

Scott Parsons and William Doubleday have been in charge of DFO science since the mid-1980s. Despite dramatic evidence from their own scientists, the Keats Report, and the Alverson Report that the stocks were being fished twice as hard as everyone believed, it took Parsons and Doubleday two years before they recommended lowering the 1989 TAC.

In 1988, some DFO scientists had recommended drastic cuts in the TAC. Yet according to John Crosbie, Doubleday had said a TAC of 235,000 for 1989 would not endanger the stock. The science bureaucrats had smoothed out dissenting opinions and told the minister what he needed to hear. He, in turn, used "science" to justify what he needed to do politically.

For the 1996 food fishery, 13,000 to 15,000 people were expected to get out their handlines and angling rods, and it was thought the catch would be between 500 and 750 tonnes. Jiggers were not permitted. Newfoundlanders headed out to the coves and bays in anything that would float. The fish were generally in good condition, although, as in 1995, it took a long time to catch the limit in most areas. Over a six-day period (a second weekend of fishing was added) there were about 21,944 vessels on the water. An estimated 1,230 tonnes of cod were caught.

The decision to have a recreational fishery outraged Earle McCurdy, who accused Mifflin of trying to buy votes: "It's a case of too much politics and not enough common sense. I'm disgusted with the whole crowd of them, federal and provincial, for clamouring for this thing when we haven't even got enough fish – or we're told we haven't got enough fish – to have a commercial fishery."

The food fishery was announced just one day after new EI rules were tabled in the House of Commons for self-employed fishermen. A sceptic might wonder if the two events were related.

On October 3, 1996, Mifflin tabled the federal government's new fisheries legislation in the House of Commons, the first overhaul of the act since the days of Queen Victoria. The legislation had sparked a great deal of protest when it was introduced by Brian Tobin ten months earlier and had been allowed to die on the order paper. Like the lofty goals of the Kirby Report fifteen years earlier, the aim of the legislation was long-term stability in the industry. The bill proposed that the fishermen themselves would have a role in the management of the industry through partnership agreements. The DFO would retain overall responsibility for conservation and management, but fishermen would play a role in quota monitoring, data collection, and catch inspections. Hoping to avoid more protests, Mifflin said this time there would be extensive public hearings on the new legislation.

In the same month that the bill was tabled, the International Union for the Conservation of Nature (IUCN) placed the Atlantic cod on its red list, suggesting it was in danger of extinction. Under IUCN criteria, populations that had dropped by at least 20 per cent in ten years were considered vulnerable. A population drop of 50 per cent placed the species on the endangered list. According to the DFO's own assessments, the northern cod stock had dropped by as much as 99 per cent.

The IUCN's World Conservation Congress, held in Montreal during the week of October 14, 1996, attracted two thousand people from around the globe. Prime Minister Chrétien delivered the keynote speech, but behind the scenes there was a fight to get northern cod off the endangered list. In the end, Canada persuaded the Congress to review the criteria for ranking marine species, and got the IUCN to include a caveat saying a 20 per cent decline may not always be evidence of the threat of extinction for marine species.

Fisheries Minister Mifflin insisted that Atlantic cod were not at risk of extinction, despite the IUCN red list. An October 11, 1996, DFO press release stated, "The Minister noted the encouraging results from the sentinel surveys for cod throughout Atlantic Canada this year." Scott Parsons said, "While the populations of Atlantic cod are low, this species is far from being endangered and the current extensive recovery plan, which includes moratoria on fishing for most stocks, has arrested the declines and set the stage for recovery." Parsons insisted the IUCN criteria for the red list were "fundamentally flawed and require revision," and that fluctuations were quite normal for marine species.

Six months later, in April 1997, the Committee on the Status of Endangered Wildlife in Canada (COSEWIC) updated its annual list of endangered or vulnerable plants and animals, adding 15 new species for a total of 291. The Atlantic cod was not among them. COSEWIC is composed of both government and independent experts and is supposed to operate at arm's length from the government, much like the FRCC. Species on its annual list are designated to get special protection. By mandate, the process is supposed to be strictly scientific, not political, but its advice carries no legal weight, since cabinet has to approve the list it produces. According to an article by Pauline Comeau in the July 1997 issue of *Canadian Geographic*, the DFO had intervened to prevent COSEWIC from listing cod as an endangered species.

Comeau reported that a three-year study commissioned by the committee and carried out by fish ecologist Dr. Kim Bell of Memorial University had concluded that cod should be placed on the list. Using both Environment Canada and COSEWIC guidelines, the cod were endangered. Comeau told the press that William

Rowat, deputy minister of fisheries, sent letters to senior officials in provincial fisheries departments and natural resources departments in an effort to discredit Bell's study.

Five years after the Earth Summit in Rio, the Sierra Club of Canada did a report on Canada's progress. It gave the federal government a D for protecting marine biodiversity and criticized the DFO for blocking effective endangered-species legislation, lobbying international scientists to remove the northern cod from the IUCN red list, preventing COSEWIC from listing Atlantic cod as an endangered species, and opening the food fishery in Newfoundland just before the 1997 election. The report minced no words: "This pattern of irresponsible decision-making, placing the survival of a species at risk, borders on the criminal."

While people were voting in the February 1996 election that brought Brian Tobin's Liberals to power in Newfoundland, there were twelve EU trawlers on the Nose and Tail of the Grand Banks (eleven Spanish ships and one Portuguese). There was also an Estonian vessel trawling for redfish, and a Japanese trawler fishing for the same turbot as the Spanish. Things had definitely improved. At the height of the Turbot War a year earlier, there had been almost fifty trawlers working the stocks. But observers on board each vessel and tough inspections had made it much more difficult to cheat, so it was no longer economic to send as many ships to the overdrawn Banks.

At the end of the war, Canada had traded the EU a greater share of the turbot quota for the right to put observers on all ships. (In 1996, Canada had only 3,000 tonnes of the 20,000-tonne NAFO quota, compared to 11,000 tonnes for the EU, which prompted Newfoundland MP George Baker to muse over who had really won the Turbot War.) Relations between Canada and Spain had been strained since the *Estai* incident, although the two nations had jointly sponsored a resolution to halt the deterioration of global fish stocks for the sake of future generations at a week-long Inter-Parliamentary Union conference in Istanbul, Turkey, in April 1996.

Over six hundred representatives from 118 countries unanimously adopted a twenty-four-point resolution urging governments to ratify international conventions that would preserve fish stocks.

But when Canada and the EU had begun negotiations for closer trade, political, and security links, a month earlier, Spain had requested an important caveat: EU negotiators must be bound by the wishes of individual states during the talks. Both Spain and Portugal would be vocal. The cooperation pact was supposed to be signed in Lisbon on December 3, 1996, at the biennial meeting of the Organization for Security and Co-operation in Europe, but at the end of November, Spain threw several obstacles in the way and negotiations stalled. Spain wanted a "clear commitment" that Canada would not seize ships suspected of overfishing outside its 200-mile limit.

In September 1996, NAFO held its annual meeting, this time in St. Petersburg, Russia. On September 16, Fred Mifflin announced that NAFO had taken the important step of recognizing that Canada should determine the TAC for northern cod, both inside and outside the 200-mile zone, until the year 2005. Foreign catches would be limited to a maximum of 5 per cent of the TAC, and fished outside the zone. The minister crowed, "This decision effectively commits NAFO members to continue to honour the northern cod moratorium and prevents the buildup of foreign effort on the Nose of the Grand Banks that could jeopardize the rebuilding of the northern cod stock. Northern cod is the lifeblood of hundreds of coastal communities in Atlantic Canada, especially in Newfoundland and Labrador."

Even Emma Bonino, the feisty fisheries chief of the EU, was being a conservationist. In October 1996 she recommended a 40 per cent reduction in catches, smaller fleets, and a $4.7-billion program to retire or retrain EU fishermen. Bonino claimed that only these measures could prevent "the law of the jungle" from destroying Western Europe's fishery. The EU nations recognized there was a problem, but as usual, there was no consensus about how it could be solved. In December 1996, the EU fisheries ministers struck an agreement to set up a satellite system to track vessels. The new system, to be in operation by mid-1998, will allow conservation officials to identify vessels and record their location and activities. The technology promises to be a lot less expensive than building and manning fisheries protection vessels.

Conventional monitoring on the Grand Banks has been working since Canada signed an agreement with the EU in June 1995. In the eighteen months after the agreement, there were only four known violations, compared to fifty-eight in 1994. Two of the latest violations were for using undersized nets, the same infraction that sparked the *Estai* incident. The other two were for misreporting catches.

In March 1997, a Spanish trawler was kicked off the Grand Banks when it was caught lying about how much turbot it had taken just outside the 200-mile limit. Mifflin announced on March 10 that the *Hermanos Handon IV* would not be able to return to NAFO-patrolled waters until 1998. NAFO inspectors from the EU had reacted quickly when Canadian inspectors boarded the ship. The fisheries agreement with the EU was working.

The 1996 Atlantic Groundfish Stock Status Report released on June 27, 1996, said the cod stocks were still fragile but that the decline seemed to have stopped. It noted that individual fish were healthier, but there was no abundance of young fish. The report was presented to the FRCC, and the FRCC advisory panel in turn gave its advice to Fred Mifflin and prepared an annual report after holding public consultations in September. FRCC chairman Fred Woodman told reporters that some FRCC members were disappointed at the recruitment levels. They had hoped there would have been more young fish.

"If I was a fisherman," Woodman said, "I'd have such a pain in my stomach that I wouldn't know what to do next. We do seem to have a good spawning component, which seems to be mature fish in Smith Sound, Trinity Bay, which we hope are going to be protected and left alone to spawn." Woodman also said, "What we have to be careful of is that we must not yield to pressure that we have to open the fishery when we're not ready. We could do irreparable damage to a very fragile stock that's out there."

Fishermen on Newfoundland's south coast and in the Gulf of St. Lawrence were arguing that the cod stocks were strong enough to support a limited commercial catch in their areas. Sentinel fisheries had high catch-rates, by-catches of cod were high, and acoustic surveys had recorded some large schools of fish. The FRCC moved cautiously, holding public consultations with scientists and fishermen in July about reopening certain inshore areas.

In October, the FRCC released its 1997 recommendations for the forty-seven Atlantic groundfish stocks. In "Building the Bridge: 1997 Conservation Requirements for Atlantic Ground-fish," Fred Woodman noted that there was strong pressure from fishermen for a 20,000-tonne TAC for 3Ps cod, "to give fishermen what they need to make a living." The report pointed out that scientific reports, sentinel fisheries data, and anecdotal information often presented differing interpretations of the health of the stocks. The fishermen reported an abundance of inshore cod that were in good condition, as did the sentinel fishermen, leading them to conclude that the stock was making a recovery. Yet the 1996 DFO stock status report indicated an average 1990 year-class and no strong year-classes after that date. Despite a moratorium since 1993, the 1996 RV estimate was only "slightly higher" than the 1994 RV survey, which had shown the offshore stock was at its lowest level since 1978. "In some cases, such as 3Ps, it is not clear if enough information will be available in the foreseeable future to answer all concerns about the state of the stock," Woodman wrote. The most recent stock status report for 3Ps had stated: "A re-opening of the offshore fishery is not supported by trawl survey data. Given the uncertainties and the lack of firm conclusion on current stock size in the inshore, it would be necessary to get more positive signs before considering a re-opening of the fixed-gear fishery at historical levels. There is an unquantified risk of over-exploitation."

Nevertheless, on October 24, 1996, Woodman and his FRCC panel recommended that 3Ps (off the south coast of Newfoundland) be reopened for a commercial fishery in 1997 with a TAC of 10,000 tonnes. The FRCC also recommended "the cautious and prudent low-level re-openings" of commercial cod fisheries in 4RS3Pn (northern Gulf of St. Lawrence) and 4TVn (southern Gulf of St. Lawrence and Sydney Bight). A TAC of 6,000 tonnes was given to both these fisheries despite stock status reports that said the biomass levels remained low and that recruitment was poor. When some industry observers expressed the hope that this was "not a political ploy to appease people," Woodman insisted that the council's recommendation "has nothing to do with politics." The news about the recommended openings of certain fisheries was released to the media, just after the important World Conservation Congress meeting in Montreal, where Canada lobbied so hard to get cod off the endangered species list.

Many believed the FRCC had succumbed to political pressure, and there was widespread criticism of the report. Mifflin decided to delay making the decision until after the industry submitted its conservation harvesting plans, which would supposedly protect the stocks from accidental over-exploitation.

There were many good aspects to the FRCC report. It called for enforcement of small-fish protocols, gear that would let small fish escape, firm sanctions against dumping and discarding, area closures to protect juvenile and spawning congregations, improved surveillance and monitoring, and increased penalties for those caught cheating. The suggested reopenings just didn't fit the tenor of the rest of the report, nor did they satisfy the FRCC's own criteria for reopening a fishery. Something else jumped out of the report. The FRCC recommended that there be no recreational or food fishery in areas still under a moratorium. This was an interesting recommendation, since Scott Parsons had earlier denied that Mifflin had opened the September food fishery against his department's scientific advice.

On April 17, 1997, just days before the election call, Mifflin announced his decision to reopen the cod fishery along the south and west coasts of Newfoundland. This was not the northern cod, and the quotas of 10,000 tonnes for the south coast (3Ps) and 6,000 tonnes for the Gulf (4RS3Pn) were conservative compared to the boom years, but the joy at the prospect of getting back on the water in May was infectious. There were predictions that up to seven thousand fishermen and plant workers would get back to work. Under the terms of the 1994 Canada–France Agreement, France would get 15.6 per cent of the cod TAC in 3Ps and 2.6 per cent in the northern Gulf. Mifflin assured everyone that the fishery would be stopped if there was any indication that conservation measures were not respected, or that the stocks could not sustain the quota level. He insisted the decision "has nothing to do with votes." After taking a few token questions, the minister beat his customary hasty retreat.

The FRCC had also recommended a TAC of 6,000 tonnes for the southern Gulf of St. Lawrence in 4TVn, which borders the Maritime provinces. But a DFO press release said that in 4TVn "the Minister took into account the large number of fishermen who, concerned with conservation, suggested greater caution." What the minister didn't say was that a formal risk analysis by some concerned scientists showed that if the recommended 6,000 tonnes of cod were harvested in 1997 there was a 50 to 60 per cent probability that the biomass of reproductive cod would decline. No such risk analyses were done for the two areas that were opened.

Fish ecologist Dr. Kim Bell, who had recommended that cod be put on the endangered-species list, said, "I can only hope that they know something I don't know. If they don't, it's a big mistake." Even fisheries scientists such as George Rose at Memorial University, who supported the reopening of the stocks, worried that not enough monitoring would be in place to assure that the fishery proceeded as planned. Unfortunately there was a fine old tradition in Newfoundland of ignoring DFO rules if you could get away with it. No one knew if the catch-rates would hold up under a commercial fishery. Earle McCurdy supported the reopening. "There's some who would wait until doomsday until they get some guarantee that no matter what you do it can't possibly harm the stocks," he said. "Unfortunately, we'll never live to see that kind of guarantee. At any time, reopening is a leap of faith."

There was one other problem that was almost overlooked in the rush to get back on the water: markets. No major U.S. chains used Canadian cod any more. Prior to the moratorium McDonald's had purchased about twenty-six million pounds of cod a year. Since Barents Sea cod was abundant and of high quality, and there was now market competition from other species such as catfish from the southern U.S. and Alaskan pollock, cod prices were actually 10 to 20 per cent lower than when the Newfoundland fishery had closed in 1992. Would there be markets for the Newfoundland cod? Would the fish be caught and not sold? During the five-year hiatus, only three companies had stayed active in the cod market: FPI, National Sea, and, in a small way, Clearwater, at its plant in Glace Bay. To get back into the business, companies that had closed their plants five years earlier would have to catch up on processing technology as well as re-establish their markets.

Ransom Myers, until recently one of DFO's top scientists, and now Killam Chair of Ocean Studies at Dalhousie University, told the *Globe and Mail* that the stocks were still at a very low level, and that there was no scientific basis for reopening the fishery. Myers thought the opening was a political decision that could delay the recovery of the stock. He told another reporter, "The collapse of the cod stocks in Eastern Canada has been an economic and ecological disaster. . . . The reopening of the fishery at this point makes it very clear that nothing has been learned."

On April 18, 1997, Fred Woodman appeared on the TV program "@discovery.ca." He told the audience that the stocks had stabilized, and had even increased. He said, "We feel quite comfortable" with reopening the cod stocks, adding that the sentinel survey showed new fish and growth in the biomass.

On the same program, Ransom Myers said the decision to reopen the stocks was "an absolutely disastrous decision" that followed a long line of disastrous decisions at the DFO. The DFO's own stock assessment for the cod in the northern Gulf, which was available on the DFO's "Sea Lane" Web site, said: "No strong year-classes have been observed during the survey since 1992," exactly the opposite of what the supposedly independent FRCC was saying. (Right after the show, the previously reliable DFO Web site mysteriously went down, and remained down for a week. When "Sea Lane" finally came back up on May 6, there were no stock status reports, although they were eventually posted in a different location on the Web site.)

11

THE PRICE TAG

In May 1996, Premier Brian Tobin warned that TAGS was facing cost overruns of $300 to $500 million. The DFO had expected 26,000 people to apply, but about 50,000 people had done so and 40,000 had qualified. Tobin asked Ottawa to hold off reducing income payments because financial strain on the TAGS program could be eased by the reopening of a modest cod fishery and more licences for crab.

Tobin inherited a $6.8-billion debt when he took on the job of premier of Newfoundland and Labrador. Seventeen per cent of provincial spending was going just to service the debt, and in 1995 Newfoundland's economy had shrunk by 4 per cent, the only province to register a decline. Before he left office, Premier Wells had tabled a balanced budget for 1995, but it was based largely on one-time revenues. Facing a $290-million deficit for 1996–97, Tobin proposed to borrow $75 million. To raise the rest, he had two choices – cut programs or raise taxes.

In the end, five hundred public employees were laid off by the $3.4-billion budget, including the premier's chauffeur. Municipalities, whose operating grants had been cut by 22 per cent the previous year, took a 10 per cent cut. Twenty boards and agencies were axed, Memorial University had its grant cut, and ministers were told to fly economy class. Residents earning more than $60,000 faced a new surtax. Spending was cut by $140 million, and revenues were increased by $45 million. Even with a $50-million advance on payments from Ottawa, there would be a $45-million deficit for the fiscal year. This was in a province with an official jobless rate of 20 per cent.

The 1997–98 budget was no kinder. Sixteen hundred jobs were cut. Half were in 1997 (including 468 teaching positions), and the other half would be phased out over three years. The government reduced spending by $40 million and still had a deficit of $20 million. Newfoundland's debt as of March 1997 was $6.4 billion – $9.3 billion when unfunded pension liabilities were factored in.

A controversial book by Fred McMahon, a senior policy adviser at the Atlantic Institute for Market Studies, was published in October 1996. It won the $10,000 U.S. Sir Anthony Fisher Memorial Prize for its contribution to the public understanding of the economy. *Looking the Gift Horse in the Mouth: The Impact of Federal Transfers on Atlantic Canada* argued that massive federal subsidies over the last thirty-five years had actually prevented economic growth in Atlantic Canada. McMahon claimed that the transfer cutbacks of the past few years were helping the region by making it more profitable for companies to create marketable products than to pursue government contracts and subsidies. He did acknowledge that withdrawing from such subsidies as those paid to declining industries, and to the unemployed through UI and TAGS, would not be painless.

McMahon's private-enterprise argument was attacked by the Canadian Institute for Research on Regional Development (CIRRD) at the University of Moncton in New Brunswick. CIRRD recrunched the numbers and pronounced McMahon's study "ideological bull." CIRRD economists said the work should not be used in policy debate because it was flawed both conceptually and methodologically.

The C. D. Howe Institute had earlier published *The Rock in a Hard Place: Atlantic Canada and the UI Trap* by Doug May and Alton

Hollett. The authors argue that UI has become an income transfer program rather than the insurance program it was intended to be. But it wasn't doing the job very well. In too many cases more money was paid to higher income earners than lower income ones.

In 1993, $2.7 billion in UI payments were transferred to the Atlantic region. There is no doubt that UI has reduced poverty in rural Atlantic Canada, but it has done so very inefficiently. Fishing families earning less than $20,000 averaged only half of the income from UI that the top group, earning $80,000 or more, received. One hundred million dollars in UI funds went to families earning over $80,000 a year.

In 1994, over half of the Newfoundlanders who reported a taxable income also collected UI. The $721 million paid to almost 120,000 people was more than the province's annual education budget. Almost half a million dollars was paid to Newfoundlanders earning over $150,000 a year. Twenty Newfoundlanders earned over $250,000 and still collected UI.

May and Hollett argue that one of the most damaging effects of the system is that it encourages young people to drop out of school. Over half of UI recipients in rural Atlantic Canada have grade ten or less. When UI payments were improved in the 1970s there was a marked increase in the number of people entering the fishing industry. Taking a job that doesn't require a formal education, such as fishing or a local make-work project, is made much more attractive by the income that follows from UI. The total incomes of young people aged eighteen to twenty-four who collected UI in 1992 were actually higher than for those in the same age group who didn't collect UI, an average of $12,856 compared to only $8,008.

May and Hollett conclude that UI has not only encouraged too many people to enter the industry but it's also encouraged them to remain in communities where there is a permanent shortage of jobs. Dependence on UI is greatest in outport Newfoundland and in those communities, 78.4 per cent of people receiving UI are repeat users. In 1992, UI payments averaged about 31 per cent of all family income. Repeat use of UI is highest in the fish-harvesting sector. Older seasonal workers have no choice but to resist government changes to the UI rules, because they have made education and lifestyle decisions that make it almost impossible for them to move.

The federal government was gravely concerned about the cost of the unemployment insurance system, and on December 1, 1995, Human Resources Minister Lloyd Axworthy tabled his long-awaited Employment Insurance bill. The federal government was spending about $16 billion a year on UI. As it was phased in over six years, the new legislation would save the government about $2 billion a year. Maximum claims were reduced from fifty to forty-five weeks, and maximum benefits dropped from $448 to $413. Seasonal workers who were repeat users would see their benefits drop by 1 per cent each time they used EI to a floor of 9 per cent less than other claimants. There would also be an hourly-based system for qualification depending on the unemployment statistics in different areas. In a high unemployment area like Cape Breton, a worker would need to have worked 420 hours to qualify. A new worker would have to work 910 hours (twenty-six weeks) before they qualified for EI.

The new legislation passed the House of Commons on May 14, 1996, and went into effect July 1, 1996. Government said the changes were necessary to adjust to the new realities of the present labour market. Critics of the old unemployment insurance system claimed it had weakened the work effort and kept people from moving to find real jobs.

Before the changes came into effect the Atlantic region was paid $2 billion more in UI payments than it paid in premiums.

In September, just before Mifflin announced the opening of the food fishery, new regulations were introduced for self-employed fishermen. In essence, they required fishermen to work longer to qualify for smaller cheques. They had to earn at least $2,500 to collect EI. Ottawa estimated it would save about $33 million a year under the new rules, which were set to come into effect on

January 5, 1997. Newfoundland MP George Baker called the move "an intentional attack by the bureaucrats on fishermen."

According to Statistics Canada, the April 1997 unemployment rate in Newfoundland – 19.1 per cent – was more than double the national average. Many Newfoundlanders are simply waiting for the cod to return. Others are working in "the new fishery," and some are leaving to find work elsewhere. Leaving the Rock is something of a Newfoundland tradition born out of necessity, and perhaps a seafaring tradition. In 1995 more than 18,000 left, but about 10,000 moved back the same year. When school resumed in September 1996, it was estimated there were 107,000 children in class, a drop of about 3,500 from the previous year's enrolment.

Canada's 1996 census revealed a decline in Newfoundland's population for the first time in history, a drop of 2.9 per cent from the 1991 census. In that five-year period a total of 35,000 Newfoundlanders left the province, although enough returned or were born to lower the net loss to about 17,000 people. It was the only Canadian province to show a decline. Only 551,792 people now live in the province, and this could have a significant effect on equalization payments, which are based in part on population. Newfoundland received $900 million in equalization in 1996; a decrease of as much as $50 million in payments would have a profound effect on the economy.

In 1997, high school students from Dover and Hare Bay, small adjacent communities in Bonavista North, did a special class project called "Our Dying Communities." In the 1996 census the communities had a population of 2,300. By the time the student survey was done the population was estimated to be about 1,600. The students compiled a list of 372 people who left between January and June 1997. Some had left after the fishery collapsed in 1992, but since the changes to EI made it harder for people to collect payments, the number of people leaving had increased dramatically.

The students also compiled some interesting information about friends who had graduated from their school, William Mercer Academy, since the moratorium. Since 1992, only 9 per cent had found work in Newfoundland, 42 per cent had left the province, 32 per cent were unemployed, and the other 17 per cent were pursuing post-secondary education.

Unfortunately an estimated 75 per cent of the people who went down the road were the ones who could make the greatest contribution to the new economic realities of the province – educated people aged fifteen to thirty-four. For the most part, they weren't unemployed fishery workers collecting TAGS.

If every disaster has a silver lining, the cod moratorium's is this: Young Newfoundlanders see TAGS and EI as a hopeless dead end and are staying in high school in record numbers. In some rural communities, the graduation rate has jumped to about 85 per cent, and a majority of those students pursue some form of post-secondary education. This is a phenomenal change in a province that until very recently had an illiteracy rate as high as 40 per cent.

On February 21, 1997, about one hundred fishermen occupied the regional Human Resources Development office in St. John's. They wanted Mifflin to back down on plans to terminate TAGS in May 1998, one year earlier than originally planned. One of the protesters, Jim Everard from Petty Harbour, said, "It's just as easy to starve to death within these walls as it is at home." He believed that a lot of TAGS money had been wasted on useless job training programs. Police cleared the office at the end of the day.

The fishermen hoped Buzz Hargrove, head of the Canadian Auto Workers union (CAW), with which the FFAW was affiliated, could help them stop TAGS from ending. On March 5, 1997, Hargrove promised to make TAGS a campaign issue in the expected June 1997 election if government didn't listen to the fishermen's demands. Hargrove flew into St. John's to meet with the FFAW.

The fishermen knew they were going to have a hard battle with what they called the right-wing agenda in Ottawa. Hargrove told reporters that the election would be the union's trump card – it would endorse candidates and parties that promised to make TAGS a priority.

In January, Newfoundland had become the first province to set up a board to certify and register fishermen. The Professional Fish Harvesters Certification Board was the first step towards the goal of a full-time professional fishery, and in order to participate in the commercial fishery a fisherman had to be certified by the board. Fishermen would no longer require a Personal Fisher's Registration issued by the DFO, although they would still need vessel registrations and commercial fishing licences specifying what species they could fish from the DFO. The department mailed out notices to the 20,000 fishermen in Newfoundland and Labrador.

In March, independent fishermen from across Canada met in Halifax to work out a game plan to fight changes to the federal fisheries legislation that they feared would force many of them out of the fishery. (The new federal fisheries bill was undergoing a second reading.) The newly formed Canadian Council of Professional Fish Harvesters (CCPFH) believed they would have greater impact on federal policy with a national organization represented in Ottawa, rather than with dozens of different fishery organizations. The council's newly elected president was Earle McCurdy.

On March 19, about two hundred former fishery workers and their supporters staged another protest at the offices of the department of Human Resources Development Canada in downtown St. John's against cuts to TAGS. Worried officials tried to close the offices to the public, but about forty protesters pushed their way inside before the doors could be locked, and settled in for the night. According to a recent study, HRDC itself was having problems. In 1995, the Liberals had ordered 45,000 civil service jobs cut, 5,000 of them from HRDC, the department charged with helping fishermen and plant workers on TAGS.

The protesters wanted the program to run until May 1999, as was originally planned, and said they would not leave until they got an accounting of how the $1.9-billion TAGS money was spent. They had just learned that $106 million in TAGS funding had gone to 540 training programs, and claimed that this money was wasted because the companies and schools that received it had not used it to retrain people for work outside the fishery. The fishery workers had carried out similar protests at the HRDC offices in February and had met with Fred Mifflin on March 14, but they were unhappy with his answers. One member of the group grumbled, "Mifflin was a joke, he didn't tell us anything."

The two-day occupation ended with the arrest of seven protesters on mischief charges. Warned they would be arrested if they didn't leave, the others had already left earlier in the day. Asked by a reporter if the occupation was worth it, one of the protesters replied, "Sure it was worth it, we got our message out." About forty police officers had come prepared for trouble, with twenty vehicles, a Tactical Response Unit, and police dogs waiting in a van. This show of force was unusual. DFO offices in Nova Scotia had been occupied for weeks, forcing staff to operate from hotels or homes or cars. To some it signalled that government understood the volatility of the situation in Newfoundland.

On March 24, Premier Tobin and Prime Minister Chrétien held an election-style signing ceremony in Ottawa. Newfoundland would get $308 million over the next three years in federal job-training money. The money was not new, it was simply a refund of some of the cash lost when changes were made to the UI system in 1996. The agreement would give money for wage subsidies to employers, job training, and start-up costs for those with viable ideas for self-employment.

As soon as it was announced, the program was compared to the training component of TAGS. Of the 10,000 Newfoundlanders who upgraded or took training under TAGS, about 6,300 were still unemployed as of March 1997. Of the 7,387 TAGS recipients who took an institutional course, 5,870 had no job.

Newfoundland's minister of human resources and employment, Joan Aylward, said that, unlike TAGS, the new program would focus on the individual client. She suggested the jobs to train for were in the fields of information technology, resource-based industries such as offshore oil, and the hospitality industry. Sixteen thousand Newfoundlanders were expected to sign up in 1997.

Demand for the funds was so great that the first year's allotment of $87 million was used up in six months. About 22,000 people received benefits. Welfare and EI clients would qualify, but they wouldn't be penalized if they didn't take training. Unlike past programs, recipients didn't have to have been on EI. They could get training if they had been on at any time in the past three years. The funding was desperately needed. In Newfoundland in 1996, 51,600 people were on welfare, over 5,900 of them for the first time in their lives. There was another new alarming statistic – 21 per cent of those new recipients had some form of post-secondary education.

The day after the new retraining program was announced, Fred Mifflin spoke at a conference in Clarenville, Newfoundland, organized by the Inshore Fishermen's Improvement Committee. The minister told the hundred fishermen in the audience that he hoped to announce definite reopening dates in the very near future. He promised a decision before the end of April so that they could prepare their gear, but warned that because of low quotas, the fishery would really be more of a commercial test fishery.

One fisherman in the audience, Percy Brown of Little Harbour, said, "We have patience with the delay because we would rather not have it opened at all, if it was to be opened in a shambles." Ben Davis, the DFO scientist in charge of the sentinel fishery program in Newfoundland, told the conference that overall catch-rates in the 1996 sentinel survey had improved over those in 1995. He was anxious to see if the sentinel rates in 3Ps held up under a reopened commercial fishery.

The fishermen also wanted to know what was going to happen after TAGS ran out in 1998. Mifflin assured them that the federal cabinet was working on a solution to the problem of TAGS recipients not being considered to have a labour force attachment under the new EI rules. Without it, people coming off TAGS would have to work at least 910 hours or earn $5,500 before being eligible for EI. On May 2, a month before the election, Mifflin announced that temporary changes would be made to EI after the June federal election to enable people coming off TAGS to collect EI when they had worked 420 hours or earned $2,500. The change would last until the end of 1997 and could affect up to 15,000 fishermen and plant employees. Mifflin denied that the promise, which could cost taxpayers up to $6 million, was a campaign goodie.

The next day, Mifflin met with FFAW president Earle McCurdy, CAW president Buzz Hargrove, and three other Newfoundland MPs, Jean Payne, Roger Simmons, and Jerry Byrne. After the meeting, Mifflin hinted that he was trying to convince cabinet to reinstate the final year of the TAGS program. Since an extra $200 million would have to be found to fund the final year, this was a problem, even with an election coming.

Shortly after Mifflin had taken over the department in January 1996, he had posted a message on the DFO Web site: "As minister of fisheries and oceans, I have two priorities – healthy fish stocks and a healthy industry. But we can't have a healthy industry without healthy fish stocks. If we protect the resource, the resource will protect the industry, and the industry will support our fishing families and their communities. But without the unshakable commitment to the principle of sustainable development, the best science in the world is of little use. Unless science comes before political, economic, business, social, or other considerations, fisheries are going to be in trouble."

Canada has always had good fisheries policies on paper. In the pre-election dance of protest and politics, the minister failed to take his own message to heart.

On April 1, 1997, two hundred fishery workers protesting cuts to TAGS entered Confederation Building in St. John's and confronted Premier Brian Tobin. The protesters had been bused in from Bonavista, Carbonear, Harbour Grace, Petty Harbour, and the southern shore. They claimed that TAGS money had been wasted on useless training programs, enough to have kept the income support going until 1999. The mayor of Bonavista, Don Tremblett, who was with the group, said it was time for everyone on TAGS to speak up:

Rural Newfoundland was suffering and the people wanted answers. Tremblett, like the others, wanted an investigation of how the TAGS money was spent. "The word gone across the country is that there is $1.9 billion gone to the fishermen and the plant workers in Newfoundland," he said. "That's not the case. The money has gone to the higher-ups."

A week later there was more trouble in the lobby of Confederation Building while Tobin was meeting with members of HELP. Earle McCurdy and other FFAW members showed up to support HELP's protest against cuts to TAGS. But the organizers of HELP, a protest group backed by another union, didn't want the FFAW's assistance. One of them, Jim Everard, shouted, "We don't want you here. Where were you when we started all of this?"

McCurdy believed Everard had been trying to drum up support for the United Food and Commercial Workers, and win back the membership of inshore fishery workers in the province. Everard denied this. The anger and shouting escalated to the point where McCurdy was hit in the chest before his assailant was held back by fellow HELP supporters.

They demanded McCurdy tell them what happened to the $49 million the FFAW had received from TAGS for retraining. The protest group also insisted that TAGS payments be extended to the original date, and they wanted people who had been cut off reinstated. They also demanded that the new EI rules be scrapped in favour of the old UI system.

An election was coming, and it seemed that everyone but the prime minister knew that it would be called for June 2, 1997. As the party faithful mobilized and the Liberals began to hand out goodies, Tory leader Jean Charest flew to Newfoundland to tell supporters that if elected he would extend TAGS to May 1999. He also promised to give transitional aid to ease workers back into the workforce after TAGS ran out. It was music to the ears of the 2,500 people whose benefits would expire in December 1997. Charest also promised to make changes to the EI program, another hot button in the province. Newfoundlanders eventually gave the Tories three seats in the election.

The protests were obviously having the desired effect on the politicians, even if they weren't pleasing all Newfoundlanders. The same day that Charest was in St. John's drumming up support for the Conservatives, seventy protesting fishery workers closed down the main HRDC office. People trying to find work were angry when they read the "closed" note on the door and went away complaining about "that bloody TAGS bunch."

One of the TAGS protesters told an *Evening Telegram* reporter that HRDC was just trying to turn the public against them. "This office shouldn't be closed. We are not causing any disturbance with anybody. We are not going to break anything up. It's just a dirty, very sneaky tactic to get the public against the TAGS protest."

The month before he left office in June 1993, John Crosbie had announced sweeping reforms of fisheries management at the DFO. Final authority for resource assessments was to be removed from the science branch, everyone's favourite whipping boy for the collapse of the northern cod, and given to the newly created Fisheries Resource Conservation Council (FRCC). The science branch would be advised by and be accountable to the FRCC. The council would include industry representatives, academics, and both DFO and non-DFO scientists.

Its hearings and assessments would be public, unlike those of its predecessor, CAFSAC. That organization had met behind closed doors and sometimes kept controversial assessments secret until politicians decided what to do. The FRCC was designed to open up annual decisions about the fish stocks to public scrutiny and be the conduit between the minister and the science branch, advising the minister on stock assessments and scientific research. There would be public forums to round out the input on TAC recommendations every fall before the minister decided what the Atlantic groundfish plan would be for the following year.

In practice, the DFO's science branch is neither advised by nor accountable to the FRCC. It provides information for the FRCC to use, but the final authority still rests with the DFO and the minister. As for public scrutiny of decisions, news that the 3Ps fishery was going to be opened was leaked to the press by a concerned DFO insider prior to Mifflin's announcement. The scientist felt it was the only way he could express his conservation concerns.

Ransom Myers pointed out there was only one person at the DFO who was authorized to speak to the media after Mifflin's April announcement reopening the stocks. He said that while he was at the DFO "I was routinely censored," and that there were attempts to keep him from publishing certain papers and speaking to the press. Of course, Myers said, scientists have different interpretations of data and differences of opinion, but they should not be prevented from speaking out.

By opening the fishery, the DFO was, in effect, practising Hail Mary management in search of a miracle. Myers has been called the Wayne Gretzky of his field by a former supervisor at the DFO. He had received an official reprimand for telling the *Globe and Mail* in August 1995, "What happened to the fish stocks had nothing to do with the environment, nothing to do with seals. It [was] simply overfishing." This statement was based on research that was being published in respected scientific journals, and it was consistent with conclusions reached at the March 1995 assessment meetings on southern Gulf cod. Yet Myers was told in a memorandum dated September 7, 1995, that: "Your comments, as presented by the media, did not give a balanced perspective on the issue of the status of the cod stocks and were inconsistent with the June 1995 Newfoundland Stock Status report. . . . Your . . . disregard for both departmental policy on communication with the media and the professional opinions of your colleagues warrant the disciplinary action of a written reprimand. In the future, you are expected to respect both the system of primary spokespersons and peer conclusions on matters within your area of expertise."

At an international fisheries conference at Memorial University in October 1995, the buzz had gone around that Myers had been told if he spoke to the media again he would be fired from the DFO. Myers, who worked for the DFO for twelve years, later told an *Ottawa Citizen* reporter that pressure had been put on him "to prevent publication of research that would have shown bureaucrats responsible for disastrous decisions that cost tens of thousands of jobs and billions of dollars."

Myers was not the only scientist to run into problems at the DFO. In 1995, Alan Sinclair, Ransom Myers, and Jeff Hutchings had written a paper entitled "Seal Predation: Is There Evidence of Increased Mortality on Cod?" in which they said that there was no evidence that increased mortality of juvenile cod had led to the closure of several cod fisheries. The decline in adult cod appeared to be simultaneous with juvenile cod. The paper concluded, "The most likely cause of increased adult mortality is fishing," and suggested that the subject needed more study. On August 22, 1997, Myers told Canadian Press reporter Stephen Thorne that the DFO had prevented the scientists from distributing the report at a September 1995 symposium in Dartmouth, Nova Scotia. Myers said, "At first the report was not allowed to be presented verbally or written. Then they reneged and said, 'Okay, you can present it verbally but you can't present any written document at the meeting.'" Five days after the symposium, the director general of fisheries and oceans science, William Doubleday, issued a memo to regional scientists criticizing the work.

Sinclair, the main author, is still with the DFO. He told Thorne, "I was fairly intimidated by the reception that the article received at the time from within the department." A common practice at symposia is that papers are presented and they receive the scrutiny of other scientists from around the world. Because no paper was available, this chance for peer evaluation was lost. After receiving Doubleday's memo, Hutchings wrote to him, saying, "The idea that research . . . cannot be presented in a professional or academic forum simply because it seems at odds with bureaucratic policy will be condemned and ridiculed by the scientific community."

Brian Tobin, who was fisheries minister at the time, told CP that he had no memory of the paper and didn't know if he had ever seen it: "If the suggestion is being made by anybody that I took a paper which was produced and kept it hidden, that is absolutely and totally false." Doubleday acknowledged that the DFO prevented the three scientists from distributing copies of the seal report, but he claimed a later review of their paper supported his view that their data were weak.

In an August 1997 interview with Stephen Thorne, Doubleday said, "I had very sound grounds for the criticism. The peer reviewers subsequently and independently of me came to similar conclusions." As Thorne points out, the peer review was done by the DFO's own scientists, who had been informed about Doubleday's memo criticizing the work. During the normal peer-review process, a paper is presented to scientists inside and outside the DFO for comments and criticisms.

There are almost the same number of people in the fishery as before the moratorium, and Jeff Hutchings believes many fishermen have not changed their attitude towards conservation. Their thinking after TAGS ends will be, "If there's any fish to be had, I'm getting some of it." Hutchings mused, "The reopening of the south coast fishery has me worried that we will be forced to open all of the cod fisheries sooner than we really ought to. What this means in the long run is that if these fisheries are to be sustainable, they will be sustainable at a very low level. People talk about recovery, but recovery to what level? The government is simply not going to wait until the stocks get back to historic levels."

Hutchings has observed that the total fish biomass has remained about the same in the ecosystem. Dogfish and skate have replaced the cod. "Whether or not it is even possible for the species to return to its former level is difficult to say. Perhaps we've changed the community composition, or set in motion those changes which we don't see right now, but might see ten years down the road, such that it won't be possible for the cod to return to its former levels."

On Friday May 9, 1997, Prime Minister Chrétien and his election entourage arrived in Newfoundland to attend the christening of the Hibernia production platform. It should have made for good election coverage, but the FFAW was ready. They had invited Buzz Hargrove of the CAW to St. John's to rouse the troops. The union leaders planned to give Chrétien an earful about cuts to TAGS, EI, and health and education spending, as well as fee hikes for the fishery. Earle McCurdy sent a warning to the prime minister, "If he's not prepared to keep commitments, then he's coming to the wrong place to look for votes."

Five hundred fishery workers stood in the rain and blocked the entrance to the Bull Arm site for two hours, holding the media bus hostage. When asked to move away or risk being arrested by the RCMP, one of the protesters said, "We are fighting for our lives, and it don't make any difference to us now because it's gone too far." They wanted a meeting with Chrétien and his elusive fisheries minister. The workers said they were tired of broken promises, "bullshit," and the bureaucratic shuffle. Chrétien refused to speak to the group, later telling the liberated reporters, "It is the right of all citizens to express their opinions freely and peacefully, but to hold a bus filled with journalists until the prime minister gives in to demands is not acceptable in a democratic society."

Buzz Hargrove was delighted with the attention the incident received, saying, "We sent a strong message here today." He told Newfoundlanders, "We still have a lot of time left before June 2. Demand of the Liberal MPs seeking re-election, and the others seeking office, a commitment to support the workers in the fishery of Newfoundland and Labrador until the fishery is back to health."

Chrétien, Tobin, Mifflin, and the heads of the oil companies involved in Hibernia were flown by helicopter through dense fog for an abbreviated ceremony on the platform. After the protesters left, Tobin told reporters, "We got a black eye courtesy of Mr. Hargrove." Even the rival UFCW called the demonstration an insult to the people who built the Hibernia platform. The president of the UFCW said, "It is unfortunate that the FFAW put their own selfish and political ambitions before the rights of the individuals who built the massive project."

But the fishermen were angry, and the protests got so bad for Mifflin that he had to move his riding headquarters to a secret location. The demonstrations outside his office were so loud that Mifflin's volunteers couldn't hear their phones ringing. Some of those calls were worth money because Mifflin had sent out letters to fish processors in the Atlantic provinces and British Columbia soliciting campaign contributions. A few Atlantic fish companies thought the letter was a joke, others felt the minister had crossed the line in asking them for money. Still, Newfoundland fish-processing companies donated over $21,000 of the $68,503 raised for the minister's campaign. The shrimp-processing companies were especially generous.

On the evening of May 12, 1997, forty-two protesters were arrested and charged with public mischief at Mifflin's offices in St. John's after they refused to clear the building. (A judge later threw out the charges.) The protest had begun in the morning when four hundred fishery workers from Mifflin's riding and the south coast arrived in the provincial capital. After first shutting down the HRDC offices on Water Street they moved over to Mifflin's office.

The demonstrators wanted to meet with the minister and vowed to campaign against him unless he gave either jobs or income support for those about to be cut off TAGS. One of the protesters from Port Union told reporters, "We are sick of seeing our families and friends moving away to the mainland when we have so many resources here in this province. Mifflin and the big companies got to sit down and talk to the little people for a change, the people who are affected, and that's us."

Politicians in electoral heat do peculiar things. Many commentators saw the re-opening of the cod fishery as a crass political move. About 2,800 small boats and 5,500 fishermen were expected to take part in the first commercial cod fishery in Newfoundland since the moratorium closed the south coast and the Gulf in 1993. But while biologists and others worried about the future of the cod stocks, Placentia Bay fishermen were delighted with their catches. The DFO opened their area on May 19, right in the middle of the election campaign. In just three days, the Placentia Bay gill-netters caught their entire 333-tonne quota for the months of May and June. Their fishery would close until July. The cod trap, long-line, and handline fishery continued until their quota was filled.

About eight thousand people in all would have jobs once the plant workers began processing the fish. Fishermen were offered a price of thirty-five cents a pound for cod sixteen to eighteen inches long and fifty cents a pound for cod over eighteen inches. Some observers thought the catches were significantly higher than during the years leading up to the closure. But other people quietly noted that they were lower than those taken from the control sites in the area just a week before the opening. Of course, there were more fishermen taking the fish.

Despite the minister's best efforts to avoid demonstrators, TAGS protesters and the media dogged Mifflin during his campaign, and the crusty ex-admiral blamed the media coverage for his many problems. At a signing ceremony for an agreement to construct a $2.4-million regional community centre in Carbonear on May 22, a group of protesters confronted him and upstaged the event.

Pressed as he made his way to the town hall, Mifflin hinted that the TAGS program might continue until June 1999 if there were sufficient funds left in the program. He promised to hold a stake-holder meeting later in the year to see how long the program would last. "You might not be here after June 2," a woman shouted from the crowd.

Three days before the election, Mifflin repeated that federal fish aid might not end with TAGS in 1998, suggesting it could be fol-lowed by another income-support package. He told the *Evening Telegram* that fishery workers "will not be left high and dry." Mifflin also suggested that a restricted fishery for northern cod might resume in a couple of years, saying that he was encouraged by the stocks that had been observed in certain bays. He planned to ask his officials to take a "special look" at these stocks, and hinted at a possible reopening: "Maybe some kind of a restricted fishery that may be part of the follow-on to TAGS." Mifflin told the reporter, "We're talking about the northern cod zone, but you know how you fellows go crazy when I do things that you accuse me of doing because it's for political reasons, so I have to be very careful."

John Efford, Newfoundland's fisheries minister, had asked Mifflin to look at reopening the offshore northern cod stocks for a test fishery, claiming that the information from offshore research vessels alone was not reliable. He indicated that FPI was willing to conduct an offshore sentinel fishery. Just before the election, Ben Davis, the DFO scientist in charge of the sentinel fishery program, said his department was planning an offshore test fishery for 1997 using small commercial boats up to sixty-five feet, and various gear. Details were being worked out.

Mifflin was re-elected, but it was the fight of his life. He beat NDP candidate Fraser March, who had campaigned on reopening the inshore fishery, by only 570 votes. Tory candidate Randy Dawe made a strong third-place showing with 10,329 votes compared to Mifflin's 12,929. In the 1993 election Mifflin had taken 75 per cent of the votes in his riding.

The day after the election, John Crosbie said that Mifflin's performance as fisheries minister had cost the Liberals several seats in Atlantic Canada. He also predicted that Mifflin would lose the portfolio. Crosbie was right. (Mifflin's wife was the only person who didn't see his appointment to Veterans' Affairs as a demotion.) After strong ministers like Crosbie and Tobin, Mifflin was widely considered to have been ineffective. But not even those ministers could have sold changes to TAGS and EI along with sharp increases in fees.

The Liberals lost three of their seven seats in Newfoundland to the Tories, and their stranglehold on Atlantic Canada was gone. Instead of thirty-one of the region's thirty-two seats, they now held just eleven. No Liberals were elected in Nova Scotia, and the NDP took an astonishing eight seats, including the ones that used to belong to cabinet strongmen David Dingwall and Doug Young.

During the campaign Mifflin had not only reopened the cod fishery on the south and west coasts, but he had also increased quotas for salmon, crab, and shrimps and had hinted that federal aid would continue after TAGS expired. He had even suggested that the northern cod fishery itself would be reopened. The Liberals had behaved as though votes were still more important than fish.

12

FISHING COUSINS

Two-thirds of the world's commercial fish stocks are over-exploited or fished to the edge of commercial extinction. Only 10 per cent of the world's potential fish supply are in international waters but there is intense competition for these resources. Canada may have fired a machine gun across the bow of the *Estai*, but when a Russian coast guard vessel opened fire on Japanese fishing vessels near the Kuril islands off the coast of northern Japan in 1997 two fishermen were injured.

The few productive regions in international waters will continue to be the flashpoint for international disputes. Conservation of important straddling fish stocks is a concern all over the world, whether it is hake and squid on Argentina's Patagonian shelf; orange roughy on the Challenger plateau off New Zealand; tuna in the South Pacific; blue whiting and jack mackerel off the Pacific coasts of Chile and Peru; pollock in the "doughnut hole" in the Bering Sea or in the "peanut hole" in the Sea of Okhotsk; or cod, flounder, and redfish on the Grand Banks outside Canada's 200-mile limit.

Migrating stocks face the same threat from intense competition. Canada's "salmon war" with the world's only superpower promises to end badly for the fish. The Americans are fishing within their own territorial waters, but they are taking fish that were spawned in Canadian rivers, a clear contravention of the 1985 Canada–U.S.A. Pacific Salmon Treaty. The salmon are merely passing through U.S. waters on their way home to spawn.

The salmon has deep cultural significance to both native and non-native inhabitants of British Columbia. A symbol of the beauty and strength of its natural resources, the fish are at the centre of the West Coast ecosystem – food for bears, eagles, and otters, as well as man. Nature has no set rules, times, or areas for the great West Coast salmon runs that occur each year between May and December. But every summer and fall, millions of fish try to make it back to the rivers and lakes where they were born – to spawn, die, and start the great cycle of life again.

Public confrontation with the Americans has rarely ended well for Canadians. The prime minister's slip in front of an open microphone in Madrid in July 1997 captured the essence of the relationship. Chrétien boasted, "I like to stand up to the Americans. It's popular. But you have to be very careful because they're our friends." It may make Canadians feel good to shake a fist at their southern neighbours once in a while on issues such as soft-wood lumber, magazines, or Cuba, but everyone knows that compromise and accommodation are the watchwords of the relationship. Canada desperately wanted the U.S.A. to sign the 1997 treaty banning land mines, but the Americans pulled out at the last minute, spoiling a high point of Foreign Minister Lloyd Axworthy's career.

During a press conference at the UN conference on straddling fish stocks in July 1995, Brian Tobin, who was then Canadian fisheries minister, announced that Canada and the U.S.A. had reached an agreement regarding the mediation of Canada's dispute with Alaska about salmon quotas. The attempt at mediation later collapsed when former New Zealand ambassador Christopher Beebe's non-binding report urging a return to the equity principal was rejected by the U.S.A. Beebe resigned in frustration, and the American interceptions of British Columbia fish continued. (According to an article in the *Ottawa Citizen*, the Beebe report was suppressed by Washington.)

In his opening-day address at the UN conference, Tobin called for public attention to the problem of unequal harvesting of Pacific salmon by Canadian and Alaskan fishermen, even though salmon wasn't on the conference agenda. (The salmon are not in international waters, and the UN draft treaty applied only to fish in international waters.) Canadian scientists said a proper catch by the Alaskans would be 138,000 chinook a year. The Alaskans planned to catch 230,000, and refused to reduce the catch by the 40 per cent Canada requested. Alaska disputed Canadian evidence that deeper cuts were necessary to protect the stock.

Vice-President Al Gore contacted Alaska's governor, Tony Knowles, and asked the state to back Canada's calls for reductions, but Knowles refused. Alaska's commercial fishing lobby is a powerful political force, and the state's senior senator, Ted Stevens, chaired the Senate subcommittee on oceans and fisheries. Under the American system, the state has jurisdiction over fishing. Even though the U.S. federal government heads the negotiations over the Pacific Salmon Treaty, each state involved has a right to veto anything it doesn't agree to. It was a negotiator's nightmare. Different gear types add to the complexity of the salmon dispute; negotiators disagree about everything from the number of fish to which side has the best scientists.

There are five major species and several hundred sub-stocks of Pacific salmon, ranging from the small pink salmon that lives for two years to the great chinook that can live for seven years and weigh as much as thirty kilograms on a fisherman's line. Sixty per cent of all salmon are produced in Canadian rivers, 10 per cent in Alaskan waters, and 30 per cent in Washington and Oregon. When the salmon migrate to the open sea, where they grow to commercial size, they don't carry passports.

When they return, the salmon follow the great sea route that sweeps in from the Aleutian Islands, along the coast of Alaska, down past the Queen Charlotte Islands and Vancouver Island, to the states of Washington and Oregon. Along the way, the salmon branch off to rivers such as the Nass, the Skeena, and the Fraser, finally spawning in hundreds of home streams.

The Pacific Salmon Treaty included a provision intended to divide the catch between each country: "Each party shall conduct its fisheries and salmon enhancement programs so as to: (a) prevent overfishing and provide for optimum production; and (b) provide for each party to receive benefits equivalent to the production of salmon originating in its waters." According to Canada, the U.S.A. was taking more than their fair share of B.C. salmon – 50 per cent more since the treaty was signed in 1985, while the B.C. harvest of fish from American waters had dropped by 25 per cent. Even the U.S.A. figures showed disparity in favour of the Americans.

Portions of the treaty came up for renewal in 1991, but it lapsed in 1992. Talks about a renewed treaty were soon derailed over the crucial question of defining what each nation's share should be. According to Canadian figures, the Americans were catching about $60 to $70 million more salmon a year than they were entitled to take. When talks broke down, both sides fished aggressively.

The original treaty was signed only after fifteen years of negotiations. One of the first commissioners later alleged that the treaty was rushed through by the Mulroney government without an effective dispute-settlement mechanism, just so it could be unveiled at the 1985 Shamrock Summit – Mulroney's first summit with President Ronald Reagan. Disagreements had started the moment the ink was dry, and by 1994 everyone was openly referring to the "salmon wars." That was the year Brian Tobin had announced Canada would fish sockeye aggressively, without regard for American conservation concerns, because Alaska was over-fishing Canadian chinook. It was the fish world's equivalent of mutually assured destruction. By 1994, Canada had cut its quota for chinook by half to try to preserve the stocks, but the salmon had been overfished for twenty years. As well, streams where the salmon spawned had been poisoned by toxic waste, drained for power, or destroyed by clearcut logging.

A 1995 lawsuit against Alaska by Washington, Oregon, and the Northwest Indian bands was joined by Canada. The suit shut down the Alaska run for chinook early, but the Alaskans still caught 175,000 of the salmon. Alaska had replaced scientists on a chinook study with administrators because the government didn't like the scientists' findings. Ironically, the main witness for the successful suit was an Alaskan government scientist.

Canada did not have clean hands, either. In 1994, Tobin had authorized a grab for sockeye from the Fraser River before fishermen from Washington or Oregon could catch them. Everyone got a huge scare that year when the valuable sockeye from the Adams River suddenly went "missing." The Adams was part of the Fraser River watershed and a major sockeye spawning river in the British Columbia interior. Canadian officials later acknowledged that the stock was only hours away from being wiped out completely. Red-faced officials could not explain why an expected 1.3 million salmon had not returned to their spawning grounds.

Former Tory fisheries minister John Fraser chaired an investigation into disappearance of Fraser River salmon stocks in the summer of 1994 for the Fraser River Sockeye Public Review Board. His report was released on March 7, 1995, just two days before the seizure of the *Estai*. One of its key recommendations was that the harvesting of salmon must be on a "conservative, risk aversion basis." But at least 80 per cent of the returning salmon stocks were being taken by the fishery. Fraser's report concluded that errors made by the DFO had almost eliminated the Adams River run. He told a news conference: "We have lost the Atlantic cod, and the public believes it is a national Canadian scandal. The public wonders if the same thing is happening to the salmon." Then Fisheries Minister Brian Tobin pledged that past mistakes would not be repeated, saying, "My department can and will do better."

After the Adams River scare, Tobin planned to shut down the whole Fraser River fishery indefinitely to allow the returning salmon to get upriver to spawn, but intense political pressure persuaded him to agree to a 1995 fishery. Federal scientists suddenly found an extra 700,000 fish. Estimates had originally been for a return of 3.8 million salmon, and this was revised upward to 4.5 million fish. (This was still less than half of the 10.7 million run that had been anticipated earlier in the year.)

DFO salmon co-ordinator Wayne Saito insisted that overfishing had not caused the low numbers. Saito blamed the drop on a combination of warm ocean currents caused by El Niño, voracious mackerel predation on young fish, and "poor ocean survival" of the 1995 run. But all these natural fluctuations had occurred for centuries, and the fish had always multiplied.

After aboriginal and commercial fishermen caught only 536,000 sockeye, Tobin closed the Fraser River run indefinitely. Just 3.3 million fish had showed up, less than the original low estimate of 3.8 million that had led to the first planned closure. Over seven million sockeye had failed to make the spawning run. Little federal help was offered to the affected fishermen and processors. In 1995, fifteen thousand people relied on the West Coast fishery, with about 40 per cent of them receiving UI for most of the year. Tobin and the DFO had a major credibility problem.

The Fraser River was once the greatest salmon-producing river in the world, and more than half of B.C.'s commercial salmon catch came from the river and its tributaries. In 1994, the wholesale sockeye catch alone had been worth $302 million. In 1995, the landed value of sockeye, chinook, and coho salmon together dropped to just $90 million. For the first time in history, the New Brunswick farm salmon industry was worth more than the B.C. wild salmon fishery. Income for West Coast commercial fishermen dropped by 65 per cent.

There were about 4,400 commercial boats in the B.C. salmon fleet. Everyone knew that number had to be reduced, fifteen years of commissions and inquiries had all said the same thing. But no one could agree on how it should be done. The fishing gear was now so efficient that vessels could take in a few hours what had previously taken days. It was not unusual for a good fisherman with modern equipment to make as much as $55,000 for a few hours' work. With such intense fishing power even a brief opening could wipe out a stock.

The B.C. fishermen favoured a phased-in, industry-controlled, voluntary licence-buyback scheme, with government sharing the cost with them. They suggested that they would pay royalties on the salmon they caught, rather than a flat landing fee. The royalties would be used to enhance the resource and reduce the fleet with buybacks. For its part, the DFO suggested area licensing to divide the coast into units that could be managed more easily.

On March 29, 1996, the new fisheries minister, Fred Mifflin, announced a plan to revitalize the West Coast salmon fishery. Conservation would be a top priority. The minister claimed that a 50 per cent reduction in the capacity of the commercial fleet was necessary both to protect the resource and to make the fishery viable. The first step would be voluntary licence retirement, and $80 million would be spent to kickstart the program. The coast would be divided into five areas: two for seiners and three for gill-netters and trollers. A licence would allow the holder to fish one area with one type of gear; if he wanted to fish in another area with another gear type, he would have to buy a licence from another holder. To no one's surprise most fishing-boat owners opposed the plan. Fishermen at the press conference responded with loud jeers. One angry gill-net fisherman confronted the minister, his voice breaking, "I might as well put a match to my boat. . . . Fishermen are having their guts cut out."

Mifflin's announcement came just before what was expected to be the worst salmon fishing season in memory. The numbers of fish returning were anticipated to be so low that much of the fishery would have to be closed. Only 1.5 million salmon were expected to make it back to the Fraser River as it ran through Vancouver. The Fraser fishery was shut down. As many native people relied on salmon as a food source, the DFO allowed a native food fishery, but the commercial industry feared this would be a major conservation risk.

The $80-million buyback program certainly paled when

compared to the $1.9-billion TAGS program on the East Coast. Fleet reduction would mean a loss of at least 3,500 jobs. Yet little compensation was offered to the thousands of fishermen and plant workers who would now be out of work. Capital investment had increased dramatically in the fleet and high operating expenses made it impossible for fishermen to survive on low prices. The resource could no longer sustain a way of life that had once been deeply satisfying to the players.

On April 17, 1996, five hundred people marched through downtown Vancouver to protest the way the federal government planned to reduce the salmon fleet. Mifflin had claimed that his plan was industry-driven, the result of Pacific Policy Roundtable discussions with seventy industry representatives. But some fishermen who sat at the roundtable insisted the recommendations they had made were ignored. Others said that the DFO was doing things backward: Before asking fishermen to sell off their licences, the Pacific Salmon Treaty had to be renegotiated with the U.S.A., then allocations had to be set between commercial, aboriginal, and sport fishermen. Only then would the government and everyone else know where they stood.

In May 1996, angry fishermen blockaded a floatplane set to take off for a fishing lodge on the northern tip of the Queen Charlotte Islands. The protesters were furious that sport fishermen were still allowed to catch one chinook each day, even though a commercial ban was in place.

The next month, B.C. premier Glen Clark gave Ottawa an earful at the First Ministers meeting. Despite federal spending of $241 million a year on the DFO's Pacific Coast operation, the salmon fishery was in shambles. Ottawa had authorized a native fishery of 753,000 fish from the Fraser even though commercial fishing was banned. If native people took their quota it would lead to the lowest escapement levels of sockeye since 1968.

For the 1996 season, Canada wanted the southeast Alaska quota of chinook set at 60,000 fish. Alaska announced the catch would be between 140,000 and 155,000 fish, the lowest limit in years.

Canada and the U.S.A. were still at odds over the number of salmon that originated in each other's rivers. (Scientists are working to identify the different Pacific salmon stocks by their DNA. If they can establish the origin of fish caught at sea then they can also track their migration paths, and manage the harvest of individual stocks better.) Canada continued to insist the Americans were catching about five million more salmon than they were entitled to under the treaty.

While the prized chinook stocks were disappearing at an alarming rate, there were so many pink and chum salmon that they were being ground up and dumped at sea – a tremendous waste of the species. There were no buyers for the fish and prices dropped. The glut was made worse by huge numbers of farm salmon hitting the market just when the wild fish runs peaked. Norway, Chile, and Japan had flooded the international market with farm salmon.

Today over 40 per cent of the world's salmon is produced by aquaculture, and that number is expected to climb to 50 per cent by the turn of the century. In 1996, B.C. produced 34,000 tonnes of wild salmon and about 25,000 tonnes of farm salmon. Conservationists worry about pollution and about farm fish escaping and mixing with the wild stock, but aquaculturalists claim that with careful husbandry there should be no problems.

At the end of February 1997, representatives of all stakeholders in the salmon fishery sat down together in Vancouver for round two of yet another attempt to renew the Pacific Salmon Treaty. Round one had been in Portland, Oregon, a week earlier. The task was to get British Columbia, Alaska, Oregon, Washington, the federal governments of both Canada and the U.S.A., hundreds of aboriginal groups, and thousands of commercial and sport fishermen to agree on a plan to share five species of salmon, which ranged across international borders. Complicating the problem further was the fact that while some species were endangered, others were so abundant they could not be profitably harvested.

There were four teams made up of commercial fishermen, native leaders, sport fishermen, and fishing industry representatives

– thirty-two stakeholders in all, sixteen from each country. Sixty scientists, advisers, negotiators, and lawyers – the same people who had led the negotiations in the past but failed – were there to lend support. The stakeholders would report directly to the top negotiators, Yves Fortier for Canada and Mary Beth West for the U.S.A.

On April 8, 1997, Prime Minister Chrétien was in Washington for talks with President Clinton. The two men reached a number of bilateral agreements during a morning meeting at the White House, but the Pacific salmon fishery, although discussed, was not among them. The stakeholder negotiations continued, and a March 15 deadline was extended to May 9 because there had been some progress, but the talks ultimately failed over the issue of sharing of the resource.

The Canadian election was coming, and on April 16, a deal was announced between B.C. and Ottawa that would give the province more say in managing and conserving salmon stocks. On May 20, talks between the two chief salmon negotiators resumed in Seattle, but the next day Fortier announced he was suspending discussions because he had learned that West did not have authority to make a binding agreement. One former ministerial staffer at Fisheries described the change in ministers from the days of the Turbot War. "In Tobin, we had an energetic guy who could handle a big agenda. In Mifflin, we had a guy who had no energy and couldn't even handle a small agenda. He was interested in parking problems, not solving them. That's why Foreign Affairs was able to take back the fish file on sensitive matters like the salmon wars with the Americans."

Foreign Affairs Minister Lloyd Axworthy announced that Canada would resume negotiations as soon as the U.S.A. was prepared to negotiate in good faith, adding, "We are deeply disappointed that the United States came to these meetings lacking the authority to negotiate." Meanwhile, the DFO was instructed to enforce regulations requiring foreign vessels to contact Canadian authorities when they passed through Canadian waters. If they did not, they would face arrest.

The talks were suspended just twelve days before the June 2 federal election. The core of the dispute was how much U.S.-bound coho salmon Canadians could catch and how much sockeye bound for the Fraser the Americans could catch. The U.S.A. wanted Canada to cut back on fishing American coho stocks until they recovered, but at the same time it also wanted a greater share of Canadian fish.

Four American fishing boats were seized as they passed through Canadian waters after they failed to hail in as they entered Canadian territory. The judge who handed the captains $300 fines commented, "Someone just turned the heat up under you, gentlemen, and you are the pawns." Poking the elephant in this way was designed to get attention, and it did. Regulations requiring American boats to report by radio and stow their fishing gear as they crossed the border had been in effect since June 1996, but they had not been enforced. About six hundred American boats a year take a shortcut through Canadian waters in the Inside Passage on their way to Alaskan fishing grounds.

The elephant was not amused by Canada's antics. U.S. Secretary of State Madeleine Albright called off planned future talks on the Pacific Salmon Treaty after the arrests of the American boats; and Alaska Governor Tony Knowles accused Canada of "gunboat diplomacy."

Although Chrétien had brought the Pacific Salmon Treaty up during his April meeting with President Clinton in Washington, everyone knew it was not a front-burner issue in the American capital. That would soon change. In May, Premier Glen Clark vowed to bar the American navy from access to the weapons-testing site at the Nanoose Bay base north of Nanaimo. The ban would come into effect on August 22. The federal government decried the decision, warning it could spark a damaging trade war or worse. It appeared that Ottawa would rather get tough with B.C. than with the Americans.

Canada has a $30-billion trade surplus with its nearest and dearest trading partner, and in 1996 there was $370 billion in trade between the two countries. Unlike the *Estai* incident, where other EU members, such as Britain, unofficially supported Canada in taking on the Spanish, no one would support the Canadians against the U.S.A. It appeared to be a losing situation no matter what Canada did.

Clark asked the federal government to bring back a $1,500 transit fee for American boats travelling the Inside Passage between Washington and Alaska, a charge briefly levied by Tobin in 1994. Some thought that the transit fee had brought the Americans back to the negotiating table after Vice-President Al Gore exerted his influence on the American stakeholders.

Chrétien raised the issue of the treaty again with Clinton at the G-8 summit in Denver in June. He was told that a deal was difficult because his negotiators needed the approval of the affected states, aboriginal groups, and fishermen before they could strike an agreement. These different interests had to be reconciled before a deal could be made.

Canadian negotiators kept asking for binding arbitration and wanted the White House to override local and state interests because of its international obligation to Canada. But U.S. states do not have to accept binding arbitration. The real question was would the White House anger the powerful Alaskan fishing lobby and state senators, just to please Canada?

The treaty talks had broken down just days before the start of the 1997 salmon season. Both countries then announced plans to fish more aggressively. The Canadian plan seemed to be to take so many fish that American fishermen would regret that the Pacific Salmon Treaty had not been renegotiated, making a mockery of Canada's claim that conservation was our highest priority. On June 26, David Anderson, who had been made fisheries minister just two weeks earlier, the first from B.C. since John Fraser, announced a Canadian quota of almost 24 million salmon. The Fraser River quota was set at 12 million because the 1997 run was expected to be the second highest since 1913 – about 18.2 million fish.

There would be no directed commercial fishery for coho because of "conservation concerns," and certain fishing areas would be closed to protect the coho from being taken as a by-catch. But at the same time as Anderson was saying he would not endanger coho stocks, he was telling B.C. fishermen to maximize their catch of U.S.-bound fish. This could put the salmon at risk of extinction. Both countries set maximum quotas, and as usual it was the fish that suffered. While the U.S.A. was demanding that Canada restrict its coho catch off Vancouver Island, the Americans refused to adopt similar restrictions on the controversial Alaskan fishery.

The salmon war escalated when the Alaskans began targeting Canadian sockeye runs on their way south to spawn. They claimed they were fishing for American pink salmon and getting the sockeye as a by-catch. (Sockeye are worth two dollars per kilo; pink salmon about twelve cents a kilo.) According to the lapsed Pacific Salmon Treaty, the Alaskans were supposed to cap their sockeye fishery at 120,000 fish. Instead they had taken nearly 350,000.

Anderson said the Americans were difficult, stubborn, and "in some respects bullies" during negotiations, but he allowed that "at some point retaliation becomes counterproductive" because the mouse had nothing with which to press the elephant. Other than saying that the U.S.A. had weakened its credibility as a leader in global environmental issues, Canada could do nothing, Anderson claimed.

Nevertheless, Premier Clark continued to push for a tough Canadian stand and took out controversial radio and newspaper ads in Washington State to publish a letter criticizing the Americans for endangering Canadian salmon stocks. A U.S. state department official called Clark's letter unhelpful and "grossly inaccurate." Clark wrote to Chrétien, calling for a joint strategy to counter the Alaskan catches of B.C.-bound salmon. The premier said the situation demanded a national response.

Making matters worse, fewer than expected early Stuart Lakes salmon reached their spawning grounds because of high water levels in the Fraser River. These salmon travel 1,100 kilometres up the Fraser to the lakes without stopping to feed, and high water levels exhaust the fish. Tests on dead female salmon showed they had been unable to spawn. Canadian officials had decided not to reopen the Stuart run because the high water levels would kill at least 10 per cent of the fish, estimated to be about 1.4 million. Washington state fishermen had already taken 25,000 more Stuart-bound sockeye than their usual 80,000. While this was happening, Lloyd Axworthy sent a strongly worded diplomatic note to Washington accusing the Alaskans of violating international laws by taking so much Canadian sockeye. He demanded that Alaska stop its salmon fishery immediately.

On the morning of Saturday, July 19, American boats off Juan de Fuca Strait were spotted intercepting salmon bound for the Fraser river – the early Stuart sockeye run. Outraged, B.C. fishermen retaliated by blockading the Alaskan ferry *Malaspina* in Prince Rupert. Their anger stemmed as much from Ottawa's limp response to American overfishing, as the overfishing itself. Hundreds of fishing boats surrounded the state ferry, which was carrying over three hundred passengers. Although the *Malaspina* was prevented from leaving port, the passengers were allowed to disembark. They spent Saturday night in hotels and reboarded Sunday morning. The Alaskan government obtained a ruling from the federal court of Canada in Vancouver ordering the fishing boats not to interfere with Alaskan ferries. The injunction had little effect on the blockade. The ferry operator suspended further service to Prince Rupert, a business that was worth about $12 million a year to the town's economy.

The fishermen insisted they would not lift the blockade until they talked to Anderson, and Clark's top salmon adviser, Dennis Brown, told reporters that it was "absolutely absurd that the Americans are able to get a court order faster than our fishermen can get a meeting with their minister." Onlookers on the wharf demonstrated their support, and a Vancouver radio station ran a contest for the ten best ways to retaliate against the Americans. The next day, Anderson flew back to the West Coast to attempt to cool down the escalating salmon war.

That night some fishermen began to leave the blockade and move their boats offshore from the hotel where Anderson was meeting protest leaders. The minister told them he would seek cabinet approval to protect the fishermen from possible American lawsuits. He said that he had done everything he could to resolve the dispute but that "retaliation has failed us miserably." U.S. foreign policy had been focused entirely on conflicts in Bosnia and the Middle East, but the blockade soon gained worldwide media attention.

Clark admitted to reporters that he was worried about American retaliation if he shut down U.S. naval testing. But, he said, "There are certain times in a country's life when you have to stand up and exercise your sovereignty, and this is one of those." Both Anderson and Defence Minister Art Eggleton tried to get Clark to withdraw his threat to close the torpedo range. Eggleton said that if Canada broke its treaty over Nanoose Bay, other military treaties could be jeopardized. Clark responded by telling reporters that if the U.S.A. accepted arbitration or returned to the table to settle the dispute, he would withdraw the threat to close the base. During the federal election campaign, Clark said, Anderson and other politicians had supported his threat to close the base. Canadian defence workers at the site were upset by Clark's threat, and the Union of National Defence Employees asked the Supreme Court of British Columbia for an injunction against the closure on August 22. Their writ claimed that the B.C. government had no authority to cancel the lease agreement with the U.S.A. because it was under federal jurisdiction. About ninety jobs were at risk.

Tourist industry representatives let it be known they were unhappy with Clark's fiery defence in the salmon war. They were alarmed that the blockade of the *Malaspina* could have serious implications for B.C. tourism. The president of the Council of Tourism

Associations sent a letter to Prime Minister Chrétien praising him for his "conciliatory approach" to the U.S.A.

Tourism is worth about $7 billion to British Columbia's economy. Much of that money is spent by American visitors. A 1997 government report by Arthur May of Memorial University advised Ottawa that a fish caught in B.C.'s recreational salmon fishery was worth much more to the provincial economy than the same fish caught commercially. A chinook caught by a sport fisherman was worth about $670, but the same fish caught by a commercial fisherman was only worth $26.

The commercial salmon fishery catches about 92 per cent of the fish and is worth about $400 million a year to the province. The sport fishery (mainly chinook and coho) takes about 4 per cent of the salmon but is worth about $600 million a year to the provincial economy. British Columbian native people take the other 4 per cent. The sport fishery also generates six times as many jobs as the commercial fishery. Every year as many as 80,000 to 100,000 salmon fishing licences go to non-resident tourists, who pay as much as $1,000 a day to fly into remote fishing camps.

Premier Clark had tacitly supported the blockade, but in the face of pressure from Ottawa and B.C.'s tourist industry, he agreed it was time to end it. Calls went out to the White House, the U.S. State Department, and the U.S. embassy in Ottawa as senior Canadian officials made it clear that there was a difference between "the acts of some individuals and the Government of Canada." The prime minister's nephew Raymond Chrétien, Canada's ambassador to the U.S.A., promised that the injunction ordering the end of the blockade would be enforced if the fishermen persisted. Ambassador Chrétien telephoned Alaska's powerful Republican senator, Frank Murkowski. After the call, the senator told a press conference that he understood that the fishermen were upset by the unresolved dispute. On July 21, two days after the blockade began, the fishing boats released the Alaskan ferry.

As the *Malaspina* sailed out of the harbour the following morning, Ottawa was searching for a way to make Clark back down on his threat to close the base. Salmon had suddenly become the top issue on the bilateral agenda. Anderson promised to compensate British Columbia's salmon fishermen for fish taken by the Alaskans and to protect the protesters from American lawsuits. Both Canada and the U.S.A. agreed to have "talks about talks." But the tension remained.

A day later, Axworthy and Anderson flew to Washington to meet with senior American officials and senators from the western salmon fishing states. By agreeing to talks about talks, Canada signalled it was giving up its demand that the issue be submitted to binding third-party arbitration. Axworthy publicly accepted the U.S.A.'s position that binding arbitration was "not possible" and expressed his "concern and chagrin" about the blockade during a meeting with Senator Murkowski, but he stopped short of publicly apologizing. Meanwhile, the Senate passed a resolution by a vote of 81 to 19 calling on the president to send the U.S. navy along to protect Alaskan ferries as they passed through Canadian waters.

To lower the temperature of the dispute, it was agreed that two "eminent persons" with direct access to Prime Minister Chrétien and President Clinton would be named as envoys. Ottawa also made it clear that it would not allow Clark to close the military site at Nanoose Bay. When Chrétien spoke on the issue, he said the dispute would be solved more quickly if everyone just calmed down, especially Mr. Clark: "We have to maintain a dialogue. We have to remain on speaking terms with the government of the state that is neighbouring B.C., because they have a lot to say in the solution. We're using the diplomatic way, and I think this is the best way."

Retiring University of British Columbia president David Strangway was the Canadian choice for the new dynamic duo. William Ruckelshaus was selected by the Americans. He was the former head of the U.S. Environmental Protection Agency, briefly served as acting director of the FBI, and was now a Seattle businessman. The envoys were to report by the end of 1997 to both the prime minister and the president.

Clark condemned the decision to place the dispute in the hands of the two men, saying that neither of them had the mandate to negotiate nor to recommend a solution. All they could do was identify areas of agreement and disagreement and set the stage for later substantive talks. The premier stood by his threat to cancel the military lease at Nanoose in late August and accused Ottawa of appeasing the Americans: "This may well be the first time – certainly in my memory – that the Canadian government doesn't stand on the side of Canadians." Clark was not invited to a scheduled meeting in Seattle that week with Anderson and the governors and state senators from Alaska, Oregon, and Washington. The American governors had refused to meet with the bad boy of B.C.

Threats and blockades had failed. The message was clear – the Americans could do whatever they wanted and Canadian politicians were powerless to stop them. The 1997 fishing season continued. When only half the expected number of American sockeye salmon returned to Bristol Bay off Alaska, Alaskan fishermen simply quadrupled their catch of Canadian sockeye to make up for the shortfall. By the end of July, Alaskan fishermen had intercepted almost 500,000 sockeye, worth about $3.5 million.

The heavy American catch left about 30 per cent fewer fish in the important Nass River run in northern B.C. To protect future runs, DFO officials restricted fishing by British Columbian fishermen along the northern coast, threatening their livelihoods even further. Canadian biologists were concerned that the Alaskans were also overfishing steelhead and coho salmon, which were important to the sport-fishing industry.

While the Americans were taking Canadian fish in record numbers, B.C. fishermen were doing the same thing to their stocks – intercepting U.S.A.-bound salmon off the southern tip of Vancouver Island – with Ottawa's approval. The American fleet watched and could do nothing. The only difference in the two countries' rush for spoils was that the Americans took more fish, and the species they took was more valuable. Canada could certainly not claim "the moral high ground," even though Anderson denied the expanded Canadian fishery was an "aggressive" tactic, calling it instead a "vigorous" fishery that would not put coho stocks at risk.

The coho was near commercial extinction in Washington State, primarily because of the damming of the Columbia River for hydro power. The aim of the Canadian action was to get Washington fishermen to exert pressure on their Alaskan counterparts to stop their overfishing, but all it accomplished was to endanger the stocks further. It also turned Canadians into ecological hypocrites. Anderson was in Washington telling the Americans to think of the fish first: "The world looks to the United States for leadership on environmental issues, and the credibility of the U.S. administration is at risk here."

Washington and Oregon, and aboriginal Americans are B.C.'s natural allies in the dispute with Alaskan fishermen, but the fisheries are a state jurisdiction. The affected states, stakeholders, and native people all have to agree before the salmon treaty can be renewed. Each state has a de facto veto over quotas, and this plays into Alaska's hands. Even though Washington, D.C., cannot make Alaska agree to settle the dispute, American solidarity remains. In contrast, in Canada, B.C. and Ottawa are divided and fighting between themselves. Ottawa has been more critical of Glen Clark than of the Americans who are violating the treaty.

Under Mifflin's plan, salmon fishermen were limited to one area unless they bought another expensive licence at a cost of $80,000 to $120,000. The result was that some fishermen were confined to areas where there were few fish. Some small coastal communities in the north depend entirely on the salmon fishery and they are desperate. Since the restrictions came into effect, average incomes for gill-netters have fallen by a third or more, and trollers and seine-net boats make next to nothing.

As much as half of the 800-boat northern fleet faced bankruptcy during the 1997 season, yet the money promised by Mifflin in January for short-term relief had not arrived. Fish plants were operating at about half capacity partly because, after the ferry blockade, they lost the Alaska salmon that was normally packed in B.C. Many packers could not work long enough to qualify for EI. Prices for B.C. sockeye have dropped by about 75 per cent in the last ten years to $1.20 a pound, so to make a living, commercial fishermen must take more and more fish. The competition for the resource is fierce, and thanks to Alaskan overfishing, commercial fishermen along British Columbia's north coast earned an average of only $8,000 during the 1997 season.

The so-called "Canada first" fishery opened on the Fraser River sockeye on August 11, 1997. The aim was simple – to catch as many fish as possible before they reached American waters. Conservationists worried that the all-out assault on the sockeye would endanger the fragile coho stock, taken as a by-catch. In a news release they said the DFO had admitted that seine-net boats would kill at least 63,000 coho. One DFO report was rumoured to say that coho stocks were so weak some runs might not survive, even if no coho were caught. No one would know how much damage had been done until the survivors reached their spawning grounds. By the end of August, it was estimated that Canadian commercial fishermen had caught over seven million Fraser River sockeye, while their American cousins had caught only one million, about 13 per cent of the catch. Dennis Brown wryly observed that the Americans should have taken Canada's offer of 17 per cent of the catch when they had the opportunity.

On August 14, the federal government began legal proceedings to keep the Nanoose Bay weapons range open. Clark immediately announced that he would fight the case, and he accused the federal government of sabotaging B.C.'s attempt to win the salmon war. The premier vehemently denied news reports that he had been looking for a way out of the threatened cancellation without losing face.

On the weekend of August 23, under the cover of darkness, a flotilla of over one hundred British Columbian boats began illegally netting tonnes of salmon on the Fraser River. The fishermen opposed exclusive fishing rights for natives, who fish for food, while they sit idle facing bankruptcy. They refused to allow federal inspectors on board their boats, and drove them back with threats and harassment. Outnumbered, and unable to use larger patrol vessels and helicopters safely in the dark, the DFO officers had to withdraw. Reform MP John Cummins, a former fisherman, took part in the illegal fishing organized by the group calling itself the Fisheries Survival Coalition. Most of the illegal fish was trucked to Seattle and sold to American processors.

At the end of August, the Alaskan government sent out letters stating they intended to arrest the owners of the fishing boats who had blockaded the *Malaspina* if they didn't come up with a $3-million bond to cover damages. Individual boat-owners were given until the end of September to post bonds up to $10,000 or risk having their boats seized by the Americans. After initially promising to seek cabinet approval for aid for the fishermen, at the end of October Anderson said he would not help them. Ottawa was committed to enforcing the law.

After four years of bilateral discussions, Ottawa's diplomacy had failed. The mandarins in the Department of Foreign Affairs had won the battle. Anderson lamely said that Ottawa was seeking international support for its case and that he did not want to "upset the negotiations process" by suing the U.S.A. government for failing to prevent Alaska from overfishing.

On September 8, B.C. launched a lawsuit against the American government and two states for $325 million. The suit claimed that the U.S.A. and the states of Alaska and Washington had violated the Pacific Salmon Treaty by taking too many fish. Two days after the suit was filed in Seattle, Robert Wright resigned from the Pacific Salmon Commission. The veteran Canadian member had been with the commission since 1985. Commenting on why he was resigning, Wright described the DFO as "full of dinosaurs" who were allowing the chinook and coho to be fished to extinction in an attempt to pressure the Americans into a deal. The tactic had failed. Wright had also been an occasional adviser to Premier Clark, but dropped that role because of the province's "ill-conceived lawsuit" against the U.S.A. He said Clark's inflammatory political rhetoric and the lawsuit had worsened an already tense situation.

Wright had built a $70-million sports-fishing business that depended on chinook and coho, and many of his customers were Americans. He accused Clark's advisers, such as Dennis Brown, of being too close to unionized commercial fishermen, and said that the DFO bureaucracy was full of managers who saw the commercial fishermen as the main stakeholders in the salmon industry, but failed to see the importance of fish farming and the sport fishery.

Wright claimed the salmon treaty as it was written was deeply flawed, "doomed from the day of its being signed," because three states and the native people had to agree before an agreement on quotas could be reached with Canada. In Canada, by comparison, the federal government could make a decision even if industry stakeholders disagreed. So, in effect, Canada had to satisfy the demands of four different groups in the U.S.A. – all with different interests. According to the former commissioner, since neither Strangway nor Ruckelshaus had formal power to agree to a solution, their efforts were doomed to failure as well. Wright went so far as to say that neither the Queen nor the Pope would be able to solve the salmon crisis working with the present treaty.

The salmon dispute had all the marks of a typical Canadian fishery dispute: The federal government was warring with a provincial government over an issue with serious international implications. There were disagreements among the fishermen in different sectors, and between the commercial and sport fishermen. There were even disagreements within the DFO. As if that wasn't enough, aboriginal fishing rights added more complications, while environmentalists did their usual dance, and every political party scoured the dispute looking for an edge. Lost in the fracas was the overfished salmon, headed to extinction.

President Bill Clinton knew where his interests lay when he sent a letter to Alaskan senators promising that the U.S.A. would retaliate against further incidents such as the blockade of the Alaskan ferry in July 1997. The letter was written about the same time that Chrétien was on the phone to Clinton urging him to help solve the salmon dispute. So much for Canada's quiet diplomacy. The timing made it clear that the president would press Alaskan politicians for a salmon agreement only when it suited his political needs and his political debts.

On September 24, Senator Pat Carney spoke for a lot of British Columbians when she told Ian Mulgrew of the *Vancouver Sun* that B.C. should renegotiate its relationship with Canada. Carney said, "The lesson of the salmon wars is that B.C. does not count. That's a fact. I think we have to rethink what we want from confederation because the current arrangement is not meeting our needs and the fish war proves that."

The senator said that watching the way the federal government had restructured the fishery on the West Coast, displacing half the fleet and putting as many as seven thousand people out of work, and the way it had handled the fishing dispute with the U.S.A., had changed her from a strong nationalist to a person who believed that B.C. had to rethink its relationship with central Canada. Her office was flooded with calls of support from British Columbians, but her comments set off a media storm in Ottawa and a denunciation from her party leader, Jean Charest. In reaction, Carney said she was tired of the bias shown by "the hysterical central Canadian pig media" and federal politicians. Premier Glen Clark warned that Carney's position should be seen as a wake-up call to the rest of the country. When Intergovernmental Affairs Minister Stéphane Dion asked what salmon had to do with secession, Clark said he showed ignorance of B.C.'s problems: "Salmon has everything to do with national unity because it's a symbol of Ottawa's failure to recognize the unique issues that concern British Columbians." Clark ruled out separation, but said that Carney's statements were "a sign of how deep the feelings of alienation are in British Columbia and I hope [will] send a message to the federal government that they have to take us seriously."

In October 1997, B.C.'s fisheries minister, Corky Evans, attended a meeting of federal and provincial fisheries ministers in St. John's. (Anderson had ignored several previous requests for a meeting, according to Evans.) In a private talk with Anderson, Evans raised the subject of the province's lawsuit against the U.S.A. for violating the Pacific Salmon Treaty. "I asked him to join our court case," Evans says. "He asked me to withdraw our court case." The two men had fundamentally different views: Anderson believed in diplomacy; Evans pointed to four years of failed negotiations. He couldn't help making a comparison to the arrest of the *Estai,* when Canada had stood up for East Coast fishermen against the Spanish. That, Anderson said, was different. The Americans were fishing within their own waters.

The special envoys did their best, but when they reported on January 12, 1998, it was to recommend government-to-government negotiations as a means of breaking the impasse. Glen Clark tempered his praise for the "breakthrough" Ottawa claimed by pointing out that the dispute was now right back where it had started four years earlier.

The Americans had continued to insist on stakeholder negotiations, and Ruckelshaus and Strangway made one last attempt to get the parties talking at a meeting in Seattle on December 19. After a twelve-hour standoff in a private room, no one blinked. The envoys also recommended that the U.S.A. and Canada agree on interim quotas to protect the salmon before the start of the fishing season in 1998. Although they suggested that Canada should get more fish, there was little chance of that happening in a congressional election year. And that wasn't the only reason for questioning the plausibility of what the envoys were recommending, as Clark pointed out: "Do we really believe that commercial salmon fishermen in Seattle will give up fish to us because we will make more salmon available to Washington State's sports fishery?"

But even Clark admitted that the situation was now less volatile thanks to Ruckelshaus and Strangway. In return for a tourism promotion agreement, under which Canada would pump over

$2.7 million into a campaign that would benefit both northern B.C. and Alaska, the state dismissed its $3-million legal claim against B.C. fishermen and their vessels. The fishermen also dropped their counterclaims and agreed to a permanent injunction against further ferry blockades. (The settlement did not affect B.C.'s $325-million lawsuit against Alaska for overfishing, which the province intended to pursue.)

The big shapes, however, remained depressingly unchanged. After delivering a bleak report about Canada's prospects in the talks, the federal government's chief negotiator, Yves Fortier, abruptly quit on February 6, 1998. In a letter to David Anderson and Lloyd Axworthy, Fortier wrote, "Ultimately, after many lengthy and frustrating negotiating sessions, Canada's objectives proved to be unattainable in a negotiating forum in which the U.S. Government considered itself hostage to the demands of various state and tribal jurisdictions."

Fortier saw no hope of a solution unless Washington put federal pressure on recalcitrant Alaskan fishing interests. His resignation sparked fears among fishermen that Ottawa was preparing to cave in and give more salmon to the Americans. Officials in both Foreign Affairs and the DFO adamantly denied that there had been a change in Canada's position, but went out of their way to say that the envoys themselves had called for compromise on both sides.

At the very least, it was a reversal of fortune for the DFO. Under the leadership of the fiery Brian Tobin, the department had wrested the salmon file from mandarins at Foreign Affairs, only to see it handed back to Lloyd Axworthy after the appointment of a weaker fisheries minister. According to a senior DFO manager who worked for both men, "Brian Tobin managed to divide American interests, but Fred Mifflin was nowhere to be seen. He'd run off to his riding and hide for days." Mifflin, the official said, was "looking for ways to park issues, and when Axworthy started flexing muscles over at Foreign Affairs, Freddie saluted." Axworthy hadn't wanted "to provoke the Yanks" in a U.S. election year, and as a result, the salmon file was turned into an exercise of "ragging the puck."

The man who inherited the mess, Fisheries Minister David Anderson, did his best to see the silver lining in the cloud of the failed salmon talks: "You have to remember that the approach taken in the last four years has failed; we've not had an agreement in those four years. This is the first time we've had a high-ranking American official, who happens to be the special representative of the president of the United States, saying that Canada should receive more fish."

When asked about Clark's view that the special envoys had failed to resolve the problem, Anderson bristled. "They were never expected to provide us with an agreement," he said. "They were only asked to give us the type of process that would lead to an agreement. Whether it's enough to come to an agreement, time will tell. The alternative is to throw up your hands, walk away, and say, 'Well, there'll be no fishing.'" Protecting Canadian fishing interests by force, as Tobin had done over the turbot, was not in the play book of David Anderson and the DFO.

13

YES, MINISTER

It is a given of fisheries management that the marine environment is complex, making accurate stock assessment extremely difficult. No one ever has enough data or research to make absolutely accurate predictions, although in the last few years scientists have made huge strides in their knowledge with computerized data bases and new biological research. The Canada Oceans Act finally passed in 1997. It outlines a new ecological approach to marine resource management – a holistic method that invites community input. It will provide the legislative base for a new oceans management regime.

On paper we now have an excellent system. In practice we continue to make the same old mistakes. Although the new act has provisions for the creation of marine protected areas (MPAs), it does not deal with the destructive effect of fishing gear on marine life and habitat, one of the most pressing problems in the fishery. In principle, Canada has adopted a precautionary approach to fisheries management, which includes protecting marine resources and the marine environment, acting more cautiously when information is uncertain, sharing the best scientific information, and adopting ways to deal with risk.

But there are no biological reference points or rules to guide decision-making in applying these precautionary principles. Without them, decisions on stocks will continue to be influenced by social and political factors such as unemployment and elections. Early in 1997, the information the DFO collected on the 3Ps cod was uncertain and contradictory: Research vessel surveys showed there was no increase in offshore stocks, scientists couldn't estimate the fish's biomass, and recruitment of young fish was found to be negligible. Yet the fishery was reopened just before an election.

In the May 1997 issue of the *Canadian Journal of Fisheries and Aquatic Sciences*, published by the National Research Council of Canada, three respected university scientists, Drs. Jeffrey Hutchings, Carl Walters, and Richard Haedrich, published a paper called "Is scientific inquiry incompatible with government information control?" The thesis of the paper was that bureaucratic and political considerations interfered with the ability of scientists to contribute effectively to fisheries management. Politics had intruded upon the dissemination of scientific information and the conduct of science at the DFO, where scientific uncertainties were downplayed and legitimate differences of opinion were left unreported.

The writers called for fisheries scientists to be independent of politics in order to save the resource, saying, "There is an urgent need for public scrutiny of the influence of senior-level bureaucrats in the management of Canada's natural resources." The article stressed that its criticisms were directed at the present system of government-administered science, not at individuals. It did not name names. The authors said that management often based its decisions on scientific documents that failed to show either uncertainties in the data or conflicting hypotheses. "Consensus had to be reached at stock assessment meetings, so differing opinions on the health of a fish stock were not formally acknowledged." The cardinal rule in the public service is this: Only one set of advice goes forward to the minister.

If the research and conclusions presented by such scientists as Keats and Winters had been taken seriously in 1986, the DFO might have exercised caution when setting TACs for the northern cod stock. Hutchings and his co-authors suggest that had the scientific establishment not been tied to politics and government, it would have at least tried to evaluate the concerns raised by the two reports and by Alverson's 1987 report, which had in effect confirmed that the stock was not growing.

Hutchings, Walters, and Haedrich conclude that "constraints imposed by the DFO stifled efforts to undertake, or discuss publicly, such analyses of scientific uncertainty." The constraints took various forms, such as withholding research survey data from DFO scientists who were not formally involved in the annual stock assessment process. "Scientists were also explicitly ordered then, as they are today, not to discuss 'politically sensitive' matters (e.g., the status of fish stocks currently under moratoria) with the public, irrespective of the scientific basis, and publication status, of the scientists' concerns."

While with the DFO, biologist Ransom Myers had been officially reprimanded for talking to the press about his work. Freedom to express a contrary view is essential to good science, but this form of censorship had to have a stifling effect on government scientists. Experts such as Myers who presented contrary views would be forced out, and the remaining scientists would feel obliged to toe the department's line or risk losing their jobs.

The CJFAS paper also asserts that there was bias in some stock status reports, such as the 1995 groundfish stock status report for the Newfoundland region. The document presents changes in the marine environment as the cause of stock declines and gives little weight to overfishing as a possible primary cause. The report obviously did not present a consensus among DFO scientists working in the field.

The Hutchings paper suggested that science and stock assessments for government be conducted by a publicly funded but politically independent institution, and gave as an analogy the judiciary. This new body would report to the fisheries minister but would not be part of the DFO. Assessment documents would include scientific

disagreements about stock status and project the ecological consequences of the various decisions that could be made. All information on stock abundance would be released to the public at the same
time it was presented to the DFO, so the public could evaluate management decisions taken by the minister. In effect, politicians and
bureaucrats would not be able to disregard scientific advice and then
blame the consequences on their scientists.

The writers of the report summarized their conclusions: "The
perceived need for scientific consensus and an 'official' position has
seriously limited the effectiveness of government-based research to
contribute effectively towards an understanding of the collapse of
Atlantic cod. Non-science influences on fisheries research incompatible with normal scientific inquiry include (i) government
denunciation of independent work, (ii) misrepresentation of alternative hypotheses, (iii) interference in scientific conclusions, (iv)
disciplining of scientists who communicated publicly the results of
peer-reviewed research, (v) misrepresentation of the scientific basis
of public reports and government statements."

The article gave an example of "inappropriate government
influence on fisheries science": the 1987 Nechako Settlement
Agreement between the DFO, B.C., and Alcan Aluminum Ltd. At
issue was the rate of water discharged from an Alcan dam on the
Nechako River. The temperature and flow rate affected the salmon
as they spawned on the river, a major tributary of the Fraser River.
Alcan had built a hydro-generating dam on the river, and by 1979
the water flow was only 10 per cent of the natural flow rate. The
DFO obtained a temporary injunction in 1980 requiring Alcan to
increase the flow to about 33 per cent of the natural rate. In 1985,
Alcan petitioned the B.C. Supreme court for a permanent solu-
tion to the discharge rate, and a trial date was set for the end of
March 1987.

A briefing document was given to then fisheries minister Tom
Siddon that suggested two flow rates, a "base" rate and a "preferred"
rate. DFO scientists who had studied the salmon survival rate on
the river suggested the preferred rate or higher if a conservation

target was to be achieved. The minister indicated he did not agree. In a memo dated February 25, 1986, he requested that the flow rate be made "more reasonable." Two days later Siddon's deputy minister, Peter Meyboom, recommended that the DFO revise its pleading to recommend that the lower base flow rate be adopted by Alcan. This was only half the "preferred" rate. Alcan itself wanted a rate that was only about one third of the base rate, or 10 per cent of the natural flow.

The B.C. government pressed for an out-of-court settlement, and there was a four day meeting between representatives of DFO, the B.C. government, and Alcan. The result was an announcement in September 1987 of a flow rate just slightly above what Alcan had requested. This despite the fact that the DFO's own scientists knew that the flow rate would harm the chinook salmon in the river.

A workshop had been held in November 1985 in preparation for the DFO's court case against Alcan. The proceedings, according to Hutchings et al., "marked the first time that scientists began to entertain a suspicion that the Department might not be solely concerned with providing flows that would protect the salmon." The workshop notes failed to document the difference of opinion between scientists and habitat managers, who dealt with industry regularly and started from the point of trying to optimize conditions for the salmon in the limited water, rather than establishing how much water was needed by the fish.

Just prior to the meeting in which the minister of fisheries requested a "more reasonable" flow rate, three scientists who had been members of the DFO's Kemano Task Force had protested in a memo that the views in the report used to brief the minister were substantially different from the views they had offered. In their opinion there had to be a major realignment of the DFO's approach "i.e., away from compromise with industry and towards defining safe conditions for the fish." Significantly there were no research scientists at the meeting when the minister decided to make the pleading "more reasonable." The DFO then proceeded to prepare expert reports that supported the minister's position.

At a meeting in Vancouver in April 1987 the director general instructed staff "to support the minister's position while adhering to the scientific advice." For some scientists it was impossible to do both. One scientist who felt intimidated recalled that it was "pointed out to me that those technical staff who do not support the minister 'must take their game and play elsewhere.'" This was essentially what DFO bureaucrats tried to do on the East Coast as well.

After the B.C. government requested the out-of-court settlement, expert witness statements were no longer needed. Most individuals closely involved with study of the river were excluded from the process or ignored. Hutchings et al. concluded: "The Nechako Settlement Agreement of September 1987 is a poignant example of how government bureaucrats can, and do, interfere with science. Decisions on flow regimes were made and were termed scientifically defensible despite a broad range of scientific opinion to the contrary."

When the project was reviewed in 1994 one of the biologists involved in the original assessment summarised the problems. He said that the minister and his government virtually surrendered to both Alcan and the province: "They did not . . . admit that this was what had been done and chose instead to embark on a program of disinformation. First they had to disavow the existence of credible information contrary to Alcan's view of the impacts of the project. This was accomplished through (1) the suppression of information such as that contained in the Kemano Task Force Report, (2) the intimidation and 'gagging' of employees familiar with the project evaluations done by DFO with respect to the Task Force and the court case to the point that they fear for their jobs."

Dr. David Cook, the out-going editor of the *Canadian Journal of Fisheries and Aquatic Sciences*, wrote an editorial accompanying the article by Hutchings et al. in which he affirmed that the DFO's attempts at censorship went beyond their own scientists and reports. He described two separate occasions when the DFO had tried to influence the journal's content. Cook alleged that in 1988 the DFO tried to have a statement in a peer-reviewed article altered because it would embarrass the department, and in 1994 had attempted to subvert the anonymity of the peer-review process of a paper that upset the department. When Dr. Cook, whose salary was paid by the National Research Council, was contacted by the media he refused to comment on the controversy, saying, "I've been told not to talk to the press, and I'm not going to jeopardize my family's income or my pension to contravene that order."

Dr. William Doubleday, the director general of fisheries and oceans science for the DFO, insisted that the attack in the CJFAS was unjustified and that there were "errors in interpretation." Doubleday has been at the centre of DFO science from the mid-1980s to the present, and he was not the only bureaucrat upset by Cook's scientific journal. William Rowat, the deputy minister of fisheries since 1994, sent an angry letter to Dr. Arthur Carty, the president of the National Research Council, saying, "I am appalled at the unprofessional and unsubstantiated nature of [the journal's] attacks on DFO, its scientists and its managers. These authors have maligned the reputations of hundreds of dedicated, hard-working scientists and managers across the country. These are not scientific papers. These are tabloid journalism of the sort one would not expect to encounter in a scientific journal."

As far as Rowat was concerned, the NRC had allowed two former employees of the DFO, Hutchings and Cook, "a platform from which to launch a personal vendetta against DFO, its scientists and its managers." Dr. Hutchings defended his paper, telling the *Ottawa Citizen*, "This is not an attack on DFO science but [on] how results are filtered up to the minister. . . . We have someone well up in the bureaucracy in a position to alter scientific statements. Bureaucrats and scientists in that department have an overriding responsibility to defend the minister's position."

Dr. Scott Parsons, assistant deputy minister of science at the DFO, challenged Hutchings and the two other authors of the article to a public debate about the management of marine science. Like

Doubleday, Parsons had entrenched his position at the DFO while sixteen fisheries ministers came and went, and from the mid-1980s on he was a powerful bureaucrat at the centre of the department.

Hutchings asked for a time and place. A conference called The Summit of the Sea was coming up in St. John's in September, and an afternoon was set aside for the debate.

In a formal response to a press story about the CJFAS article, Parsons claimed the DFO did not ignore the outside research and warnings of independent scientists. He wrote "The independent reports by Dr. Lee Alverson (Report of the Task Group on Newfoundland Inshore Fishery) in 1987 and Dr. Leslie Harris (Independent Review of the State of the Northern Cod) in 1989–90 were the basis for the management of the fishery in subsequent years." Parsons accused Hutchings, Walters, and Haedrich of being locked in a time warp and "citing and distorting incidents from the 1980s to support their agenda."

Parsons went on to note, "The information concerning northern cod was available to independent panels, led on different occasions by Dr. Lee Alverson and Dr. Leslie Harris. In both instances, these panels reached essentially the same conclusions regarding stock status as had been earlier advanced by DFO scientists." What was truly amazing about Parsons' statement was that he was in effect stating that the DFO knew how bad the state of the stock was prior to the Alverson Report of 1987. If Parsons was now admitting that the DFO had scientific evidence that the stocks were in bad shape as early as 1986, what explanation could there be for the lack of action other than political interference or incompetence?

According to one senior DFO source, Parsons was an introverted man who made up for his social awkwardness by sheer willpower. Recognized by NAFO as a "top-notch negotiator," Parsons was considered to be "extremely insightful." Unlike Doubleday, who was "a very brilliant guy, but lacked the political sensitivity that Parsons had, Parsons knew how to deal with the minister who wanted something he didn't want to do. Doubleday believed that criticism would "blow over"; Parsons took it to heart.

Parsons accused Hutchings and the others of launching "an unprofessional and unsubstantiated attack upon DFO, its scientists and its managers. In doing so, they have maligned the reputations of hundreds of dedicated, hardworking scientists and managers across the country, including many of the world's leading scientists. This article is not a scientific paper. It is science fiction." Parsons did not suggest why three highly respected scientists would risk their careers to do this, or explain why their article had passed peer review. In fact, the three authors had widespread support in the scientific community both inside and outside the DFO.

In an interview that predated the CJFAS article, Leslie Harris gave his opinion about the bureaucratic and political considerations that interfered with the ability of scientists to manage the fishery: "Even in 1988-89, if we had strictly followed the rules then and said, 'Okay, we're going to chop the fishing from 260,000 tonnes down to 120,000,' then that might have saved the day – probably would have saved the day. When we recommended [a cut], we said, 'Look, if you find that this is really too hard to take, if the economy simply cannot absorb that kind of medicine at this time, whether politically, or socially, or economically, then at least do it as quickly as you can within the terms of practical politics and reduce it in two years. Go half way there this year, and go all the way the next.' What they followed was advice to go half way to where they should have gone three years before. So they weren't really following our advice. You really didn't have to read very hard between the lines of our report to find that, in making these recommendations, we were walking on the edge of a precipice. I think that the federal government knew from about 1986-87 onward that the mortality rates were much higher than the figures they had been using showed."

In the wake of the media storm that followed publication of the article, Ransom Myers told the *Ottawa Citizen*, "In my own case, pressure was sometimes brought to bear to prevent publication of research that would have shown bureaucrats responsible for disastrous decisions that cost tens of thousands of jobs and billions of dollars." Myers recalled that Parsons and Doubleday had tried unsuccessfully to keep a paper he wrote entitled "Was an increase in natural mortality responsible for the collapse of northern cod?" from being printed. Myers claimed they wanted to suppress it because the paper showed that overfishing was the cause of the collapse of the northern cod.

Myers said that DFO bureaucrats did manage to suppress an article he co-authored with someone still in the department, which concluded harp seal predation had nothing to do with the cod's collapse. The lead author chose not to deal with intimidation from the department and withdrew the article. Myers also said he was invited to speak at Memorial University in 1988 to explain his early research on cod stocks which showed the stocks were not increasing, contrary to the DFO's claims. Someone else was sent in his place. Someone, he says, "who would give the right answers."

David Schindler, a prize-winning scientist who worked for the DFO for twenty-two years, said he was often reprimanded for publicly discussing research or questioning policy decisions. (He won the $150,000 Stockhold Water Prize for his work in 1991 after he left the DFO.) Schindler told the *Ottawa Citizen*, "There has to be something to buffer the politicians interested in being elected and the bureaucrats interested in being promoted from the scientists who are interested in helping the environment and know what they're doing."

On the June 29, 1997, television program "Sunday Edition," Ransom Myers told host Mike Duffy that unless politicians get independent advice, "then they're going to make the same mistakes that we made with the cod stocks or the salmon stocks and other fish. . . . It's a tragedy, and upper-level bureaucrats who were responsible are still in charge in Ottawa. They're still giving the minister terrible advice." Myers claimed that scientists were being told if they spoke up they would be fired. Even those at universities were being threatened with having their research funding cut. "This atmosphere of fear is really unconscionable in a democracy," he remonstrated.

Gus Etchegary, who has held various management positions at FPI in his forty years with the company, has also called for an independent fisheries research board; one that would assess the health of the stocks and at the same time be free of political interference. Etchegary proposes that the minister should have to abide by the board's recommendations. He blames Ottawa bureaucrats and political considerations in the departments of Foreign Affairs and International Trade for the disaster. Too often in the past, politics had won out over the interests of the industry and the work of the research scientists.

Asked to comment on the CJFAS article, Etchegary told the St. John's *Evening Telegram*, "I'm disappointed that it has taken so long for these university scientists to find the horse thirty years after it was stolen." He reminded readers that in the 1960s and early 1970s there were sometimes six hundred vessels and thirty thousand crew members from sixteen countries fishing off the East Coast. When federal scientists told ICNAF that the fishing had to be cut back, they were ignored, and catches subsequently dropped by as much as 60 per cent. "It is clearly evident what was happening," he said, "yet people in responsible positions kept that information from the public." Etchegary also said the reopening of the Newfoundland cod fishery on the south coast was a mistake.

On June 30, Scott Parsons and William Doubleday threatened to sue the *Ottawa Citizen* for libel unless the paper apologized for its June 27 story saying that they had tried to suppress scientific papers. Ransom Myers was also named in the suit. In a letter to the newspaper, William Rowat vehemently denied that either Dr. Parsons or Dr. Doubleday, both "highly dedicated public servants who had served their country long and well," had tried to suppress publication of Myers' papers. Rowat also denied that the DFO had ever suggested Dr. Cook, the former editor of the CJFAS, not speak to the media.

Some scientists thought the lawsuit was absurd and simply showed how threatened the two bureaucrats were. If the two men hadn't reacted so publicly to both the Hutchings paper and Myers' comments, the controversy might have remained within the DFO, the halls of academia, and various fisheries institutions. Instead, it made the front pages of the *Ottawa Citizen* and the *Globe and Mail*.

David Schindler was astonished at the suit. He told the *Citizen*, "The objective should not be bringing personal defamation suits to court. The objective should be to fix the system." In his opinion the lawsuit was "the worst form of intimidation." Schindler said that during his career at the DFO he had been reprimanded several times for expressing views that the department had not approved. He had once publicly announced that the department was going to stop funding acid rain research, despite having been given a "muzzling order" not to talk about it. "It's almost a tradition in the Canadian civil service to act this way. Every environmental organization in the federal government ought to be scrutinized for the way these suppression and intimidation matters are handled."

If anything, the lawsuit galvanized support for Myers, Hutchings, Walters, and Haedrich. Thirty-seven scientists across the country called for an end to the suppression of the work of government-supported fisheries scientists. They signed a letter to the president of the National Research Council in which they took exception to Rowat's letter attacking the CJFAS article. The scientists said the piece by Hutchings, Walters, and Haedrich was published in the Perspectives section of the journal which had a history of lively debate. As for the accompanying editorial by Dr. Cook, "the opinions of the editor are his own business, and any journal requiring editorial clearance from government bureaucrats would not be worth publishing in."

During the dust-up with scientists, the DFO put up a background piece on its Web site outlining its stock assessment and conservation process. It concluded, "While there is merit in the concept of fully independent and wholly unfettered research, there is also value in science that is integrated to public policy goals because it permits the directing of science to serve a clear public need. This integrated approach is used throughout the federal government in Canada and is the model used for international fisheries science. The integration of DFO science with public needs is what gives it its importance and its relevance – a role grounded in serving Canadians."

A group of federal fisheries scientists who met in August to discuss the criticism in the CJFAS article concluded that government scientists should accept their limited role in policy-making. Bob O'Boyle, the coordinator of the federal fisheries stock assessment review office, said, "It is not up to us to tell the politicians what they should do."

Two scientists at the meeting denied federal scientists were restricted in their right to publish in scientific journals, but admitted that some federal employees were afraid to talk to the media about politically sensitive issues. No wonder; a DFO departmental discipline guide classified infractions into four groups. Horseplay or being late could merit an oral reprimand. Sleeping on the job might get you a written reprimand or one or two days' suspension. If you damaged property or falsified records, you could get a five- to ten-day suspension. Group four infractions might get you fired. They included fraud, assault, drunkenness, and impeding the progress of a voyage. Group four also included "public criticism of the employer."

Ransom Myers had never said that scientists should speak out about political issues, what he had said was that scientists should not have their work misrepresented, censored, or ignored in order to justify political decisions. A June 18, 1997, memo to Newfoundland DFO groundfish personnel states that George Lilly, the acting division head, wishes "to inform staff that you are not to comment on the two articles appearing in the CJFAS regarding DFO science." According to a CP report, this order was supposed to have been issued verbally. A gag order was placed on the gag order.

Gag orders were not a new phenomenon. In 1992, DFO staff, including Larry Coady, the Newfoundland director of science at the time, were told to say nothing to the media if they were asked questions during the closing of the cod fishery. An internal DFO report commissioned by Coady from March 1993 showed that some scientists in the department believed that bureaucrats were distorting scientific findings to suit a political agenda before the cod moratorium. (This report was finally made public in August 1997.) The report contained 184 recommendations developed from non-attributed interviews with DFO staff. It concluded, "Scientific information, specifically the role of the environment, was gruesomely mangled and corrupted to meet political ends."

While scientists were not allowed to speak about the causes of the moratorium, DFO spin doctors were telling the public that cold water and seals, not overfishing, had caused the collapse. Scientists wondered what had happened to their conclusions. The recommendations in the Coady Report included the proposal to separate science from the bureaucracy. Like Hutchings's CJFAS paper, the report had suggested that fisheries science be done at a research institute. It said that the department was preoccupied with its public image at the expense of important scientific research. The department was using precious resources to fund "scouting missions for cod at the expense of planned, valid scientific research."

An article by Stephen Thorne, published on August 21, 1997, reported that current and former DFO employees were claiming that department officials routinely destroyed memos, minutes of meetings, and other records to prevent politically uncomfortable science from becoming public. The information flow was tightly controlled, Thorne wrote, and today it was as bad as or worse than ever. William Doubleday denied the allegation, saying there was a free flow of ideas in the department. He denied knowing of any case where factual information had been suppressed.

One of Thorne's sources at the DFO agreed that "nobody falsified documents." Instead, "they optimized what they had. The politicians and the senior bureaucrats would run away, pick the very best numbers and come out and present them in the very best light. They would hide any negative notions – numbers, information, anything at all that took the gloss off what they presented. Any attempt by anyone on the inside to present a different view was absolutely squashed."

In an interview with Thorne, John Crosbie said that he was unaware of any time in his last ten years in federal politics when a minister had ignored or interfered with science. Conceding that it was "more subtle than that," Crosbie said, "You can't discount the fact there are problems with science fitting into the government structure, and that scientists may feel they have to adopt or adhere to some kind of official departmental, bureaucratic position." He went on to say that there may have been a "collective mindset" that the cod stocks were increasing more rapidly than they were, and certain scientists could have felt an alternate view would hamper their careers.

Bureaucrats don't usually lie outright, but they have been known to cast the appropriate lights and shadows over their information. Everyone at the DFO believed that the cod stocks were growing, despite what the inshore fishermen were saying. When some of their own scientists showed that the DFO had overestimated the size of the cod stock, and underestimated the fishing effort by 100 per cent, officials were still reluctant to change that belief.

The focus of the department had been on counting fish rather than on cod biology. If the mathematical model they relied on to make their annual assessments was shown to be incorrect, the consequences were enormous. As in every bureaucracy from ancient China to the present day, information control became the order of the day. The Winters Report, the 1986 CAFSAC advisory document, and the Keats Report were ignored, and the Alverson Report was downplayed. It took two years for the department to recommend a drastic drop in the TAC.

At the September 1997 Summit of the Sea conference in St. John's, delegates from thirty-seven countries met to discuss how to understand and manage the oceans. John Crosbie gave an unscheduled forty-five-minute speech in which he denied that politicians interfered with scientific research. "I know of no instance where a politician ever directed scientists at a political level what to say." He told the attentive audience that the scientists were guilty of what the Greeks called hubris. "Scientists thought they knew one hell of a lot more than they actually did know."

Referring to the scientific advice that overestimated the abundance of cod while he was minister of fisheries prior to the moratorium, Crosbie said, "There's no minister in the world who can manage the fishery with advice like that." He recalled the scientists had said a TAC of 297,000 tonnes was okay for 1988. If true, the advice contradicted what DFO scientists had known about the state of the stock since 1986. The 1988 TAC had eventually been set at 266,000 tonnes. Crosbie admitted that politicians and bureaucrats had decided to ignore a recommended TAC of 125,000 tonnes in 1989 and had set the TAC at 235,000 tonnes. Crosbie was minister of trade at the time, but was still fully informed about the fishery. He had called the proposed cuts "demented"; in his opinion it was not possible to eliminate that many jobs overnight.

Crosbie said that originally he had thought that science was capable of providing precise and certain knowledge about the state of the stocks, but after he became minister of fisheries in 1991 he found the advice changed throughout the year. Crosbie remains convinced that "whatever the fault was here, it was systemic." The former minister asked the conference to come up with something more substantial than "the usual flapdoodle."

At the conference, Scott Parsons acknowledged that decisions that were not consistent with conservation had been made; the political system had failed to make the necessary changes when the red flag went up. He told the packed room, "It's quite clear that overfishing was the main factor" in the collapse of the cod, although there were other factors. This was not the conclusion he had reached in his 1993 book, which blamed natural factors beyond human control or understanding.

Somehow, Parsons had been converted. There is a certain irony in the fact that the scientists who appear to have got it right – overfishing had caused the collapse – were vilified by the very people in the DFO who got it wrong, men who are still in charge of DFO science and still directing the flow of information to both the public and the present minister.

Parsons told the attentive audience that fishermen, processors, politicians, and scientists had all made mistakes; there was no single cause that could be blamed on any one group. He cautioned, "fisheries management is usually conflict management," and admitted that the fishery rather than the fish had been the first priority. Now everyone had to adopt a new precautionary approach, where conservation came first.

In the past year, Parsons said, he had become increasingly concerned that we may not have learned from our mistakes. With TAGS ending there would be enormous pressure on DFO to reopen the northern cod fishery in 2J3KL. The fishery had reopened on the south and west coasts, but people should not assume the cod stock was rebuilding. "All the evidence points to the contrary," he said. There are "no significant signs of improvement in the great northern cod stocks."

Parsons addressed the Rotary Club of St. John's the same day and called the collapse of the cod stock "a calamity of almost biblical proportions." He repeated that the pressure to reopen the northern cod stock over the next year would be enormous. But that pressure had to be resisted: "If we err, then we must err on the side of the fish and not the fishery." Fishermen along the east and northeast coast were seeing an abundance of cod in the bays, but there was virtually nothing offshore. If the inshore cod were taken, there would be no stock left to replenish the offshore.

Most people expected the September 5 forum on "Fisheries Science in Relation to Fisheries Management" to be the hot event during the Summit of the Sea. The accusation had been made that DFO officials had manipulated scientific research for political purposes, and people wanted to know how the unthinkable had happened. There was an electric buzz in the corridors of the Delta Hotel in St. John's, and Salon A began filling up well before the event. But it turned out that seating Hutchings next to an obviously uncomfortable William Doubleday was the most exciting thing about the forum. Because of the organization of the panel, there was little debate of the specific criticisms raised by the CJFAS paper. Panelists had been given a series of general questions, and the discussions were extremely polite. Doubleday spoke first and talked about the need for fishery science to be a partnership between government, the industry, and academics, of the need to monitor fisheries ecosystems, as well as the need for high quality data to try to get better stock estimates. Teamwork was essential because the work was too complicated for individual scientists.

Doubleday also suggested that data should be validated by those who know the stocks best, the fishermen. Science was only one important element in the decision-making process. What a long way the department had come since the days when the inshore fishermen were ignored. One of the main recommendations of the Hutchings paper had been to have a science body that was at arm's length from the policy branch of the DFO, but Doubleday said he firmly believed that science would be more influential if it continued to be housed by government. He argued there had to be day-to-day contact between scientists and managers. If the scientists were outside the DFO, they may not be at the table when decisions were made. Fisheries Minister Anderson let it be known at the conference that he agreed with his director general of science.

Outside it was raining hard, and gale force winds sent most people in the city scurrying for cover. Jeff Hutchings was the last to speak. His ancestors had come from Sunnyside, Chance Cove, and Spaniards Bay, communities devastated by the cod moratorium. He had joined the DFO as a research fellow shortly after the collapse in 1992 and knew firsthand its effect on people's lives. Low-key, he described the CJFAS paper that had caused such a ruckus as one that raised the issue of how science could best serve the people in the fishery. It had concluded that a reorganization of the relationship, to make scientists more independent, would strengthen the science. And, he suggested, if there were biological risks they should be clearly identified so the public could understand them.

Hutchings had told Stephen Strauss, the science reporter for the *Globe and Mail* that after he realized how strong the reaction to the CJFAS article might be, he had had second thoughts about publishing it. An untenured biology professor at Dalhousie University, Hutchings worried that his research funding could be cut off, as well as future collaboration with DFO scientists who had access to the department's data base. Supported by his fellow scientists who were "almost angry" that he was thinking of pulling the article, he accepted the "moral responsibility" and went ahead with publication.

The first broad forum that could have examined what went wrong contained few answers. Everybody blinked. Instead of an accounting, it turned into a general discussion about how the process could be improved, rather than a raucous debate that cleared the air and answered the burning question of how this tragedy had happened.

Before and during the conference there were repeated calls for an independent inquiry into the collapse of the fishery. On August 18, the Acadian Groundfish Fishermen's association had sent a letter to Prime Minister Chrétien asking for a public inquiry into how DFO policies allowed the cod fishery to collapse. The president of the association, Alyre Gauvin, said that both the public and the prime minister had the right to know what happened: "We can conclude that someone somewhere knew something and we would like to know what they knew."

Gauvin reminded Chrétien that fishermen such as those in his group had known something was wrong well before the moratorium, and had asked the ministry to revise their methods of evaluating and managing the stocks. But nothing had been done. Fishermen were prepared to take their share of the blame, Gauvin wrote, but his group was not convinced that politicians were prepared to do the same.

Just before the new parliament opened in September 1997, the opposition parties also called for an inquiry into the DFO's management of the fishery. On September 22, David Anderson refused the request, saying it would be "a waste of time and money." He admitted that the DFO had made mistakes in the past, but claimed they had been made under the former Conservative government. NDP fisheries critic Peter Stoffer said the real reason Anderson refused to call an inquiry was because he was bowing to his bureaucrats: "There's a whole bureaucracy there that's trying to protect itself." The Professional Institute of the Public Service of Canada supported the call for an inquiry, because of concerns it had that advice given by its members had been ignored or misrepresented by senior managers and politicians in the DFO.

The DFO clearly has not served Canadians well. The collapse of the northern cod stock is one of the most spectacular failures in the history of Canadian government and an ecological disaster of worldwide significance. The social and economic consequences have devastated communities where fishing was not just an occupation but a way of life for hundreds of years.

Thousands of people are unemployed because of DFO decisions, and taxpayers have spent billions of dollars to support them. The great northern cod may never recover from the edge of extinction. The politicians blame the scientists, and the scientists blame the politicians and the bureaucrats. Pacific Coast salmon are being hunted in unconscionable numbers because Ottawa can't resolve its dispute with the U.S.A. The management of federal fisheries has been a costly failure on both coasts.

The DFO now admits it had evidence as early as 1986 that the stocks were being overestimated and overfished. The Auditor General's Report released in October 1997 devoted three chapters to the Atlantic fishery. In Chapter 14 the report said, "It became apparent in 1986 to departmental scientists and external reviewers that a continuing pattern of overestimation of groundfish stocks resulted in a fishing level for northern cod stocks at least double the Department's conservation standard." And Chapter 15 said, "Since 1986, the Department has recognized that the model used to determine the status of most of the key groundfish stocks has consistently overstated their abundance and understated the level of mortality."

Mistakes are still being made. In early July 1997, it took fishermen in the Placentia Bay area of 3Ps only three days to take their
quota of cod for the period July to September. This was the fishery
Mifflin had opened during the election campaign. The fishermen
were pleased to catch large fish, but at the same time troubled by the
absence of small fish, which would indicate the stocks were starting
to rebuild. The FRCC was aware there were few young fish before
they decided to recommend reopening the stocks.

There was another problem. So much cod was caught in those
three days that the processors weren't able to handle the glut. Many
plants had not prepared to process the cod because of the limited
quota or because they were already processing caplin or crab. (Crab
now accounts for half of the Newfoundland fishing industry's
export value. In 1997, it employed about ten thousand people and
will be worth an estimated $150 to $200 million.) Dan Meade had
more cod than his plant in Ship Harbour, Placentia Bay, could
handle. He told the *Evening Telegram*, "I called a number of plants . . .
and none of them could take it. I had to split it, I had to salt it, I
had to do what I could do with it. There is still some I can't get
clear of." Despite the collapse, fish were still being taken even when
they couldn't be processed.

By early August 1997, cod being taken from 4RS3Pn was of
such poor quality that Newfoundland Fisheries Minister John
Efford forbade fish processors to buy cod taken in those zones.
He explained that "continued harvesting of inferior-quality fish
would destroy our markets." It would also affect Newfoundland's
reputation when it came to other seafood products. Efford was
forced to issue the ban because the DFO refused to close the fishery
in 4RS3Pn.

The temporary processing ban went into effect on August 10,
1997, five hundred years to the day that King Henry VII gave John
Cabot ten pounds as a reward for discovering Newfoundland. It had
taken five hundred years to bring the greatest cod stock in the world
to the edge of extinction, and we were still abusing the resource.

On July 29, the FRCC released a report called "The Conservation Framework for Atlantic Canada." It also issued a warning. Chairman Fred Woodman said at a press conference that there was still too much capacity and still too little knowledge about the fish. There would be a new crisis if the fishery was reopened, and this time the crisis would be irreversible. The report called the collapse of the cod "one of the worst social and economic disasters in Canadian history."

Despite spending billions of dollars in the 1990s on programs to reduce fishing capacity, present capacity is now two or three times what is needed should the stocks recover. The report said that reduction is a priority. Increases in fishing capacity had led to political pressure for higher quotas, and these quotas had been "well beyond the natural capacity of the resource." Despite the moratoria, there had been few signs of improvement. Several groundfish stocks were at the lowest levels ever observed by scientists.

The FRCC report called for the protection of nursery and juvenile areas, seasonal closures, and the limiting or banning of fishing technologies that damaged the stocks or their habitat. It also addressed one of the most glaring abuses of the fish stocks: "It is obvious that a decrease in the number of spawners to very low levels must have a negative impact on the future production of new young fish." This obvious fact had never been incorporated in management decisions because there was no "proof" that the link existed. The FRCC report said, "In the future, such links must be assumed. . . . The prudent policy would be to . . . let the spawning process take place in as unhindered a manner as possible." The report admits that the conservation regime of the 1980s had failed to maintain the stocks: "The failure was not due to a lack of suitable goals and principles but, rather, a failure in execution, in a context of difficult environmental conditions."

The introduction of the report said it in a nutshell: "We must address the failures and abuses that led to this path of destruction: overestimation of the biomass; overestimation of recruitment;

failure to recognize environmental changes and their impact on the groundfish fishery; failure of the management system to recognize the impact of technological change; underestimation of foreign overfishing; pressures of our own Canadian industry, which led to misreporting, dumping, discarding, and high-grading; and failure of the political system to make the necessary conservation decisions when the red flags did go up."

Woodman said that the FRCC was reviewing information from the reopened fisheries and would make recommendations to the minister in the fall of 1997 about the 1998 season. Yet the FRCC had recommended the 1997 opening, a move that contradicted their own precautionary guidelines for reopening stocks, and left some dismayed industry observers wondering about political interference yet again. Among them was the Reform Party's fisheries critic, John Duncan, who said the FRCC report illustrated how prevalent political interference was in the fisheries. He was happy with the contents of the report, but saw it as an attempt to rehabilitate the FRCC's tarnished image – the Liberals had wanted the fishery reopened before the election, and the FRCC had obliged by making the recommendation. In effect, the report criticized the very thing that the FRCC did when it recommended reopening the cod stocks.

Another event in July 1997 illustrated how political DFO decisions still were and how ineffective the FRCC really was, despite its fine words. The event slipped by in the summer doldrums with hardly anyone noticing. Federal court judge Douglas Campbell overturned a decision by former fisheries minister Fred Mifflin on the sharing of an increased Canadian turbot quota in Davis Strait. Nunavut Tunngavik Inc. had brought a court challenge against the minister's decision in May 1997.

Canada and Denmark equally shared an 11,000-tonne turbot quota for the area between Baffin Island and Greenland. In April, just before the election call, and without consulting Denmark, Mifflin increased the Canadian share of the turbot quota by 1,100 tonnes. Only 100 tonnes went to the Nunavut region, the rest to other Canadian fishermen. But a land claims agreement had given the Inuit of Nunavut the right to be consulted in the management of the Davis Strait fishery resources, and Judge Campbell specifically blamed Mifflin for increasing the quota despite contrary advice from the Nunavut Wildlife Management Board.

Mifflin had also contravened the advice of his own scientists, who were just as concerned as the Inuit about the high gill-net effort by Newfoundland boats on the spawning turbot stocks. Facing massive discontent in his own Newfoundland riding, Mifflin had ignored the advice of the Inuit, NAFO, and the FRCC, and arbitrarily raised the Canadian quota despite the danger of depleting the turbot stock. Mifflin had even ignored the advice of his own assistant deputy minister of fisheries management, Patrick Chamut. In a memo to Mifflin, Chamut had cautioned: "The Canadian government could be seen as hypocritical by the international community – that the Canadian government exhorts others to share the burden of conservation but is unwilling to do likewise." The memo said that acting unilaterally could be viewed as contrary to both the UN straddling stocks agreement and our new fisheries legislation, and that it could also alienate other NAFO members.

Critics claimed that Canada had risked a war with Spain to protect the turbot stocks, and now the fisheries minister was ignoring expert advice and endangering that same species in order to get himself re-elected. Mifflin's decision was quietly reversed by David Anderson after the Inuit won their case in court. But an extra 287 tonnes had already been caught before the original quota was restored.

On October 14, 1997, the FRCC released its annual report. It included advice to the minister for nine different species, but did not make recommendations on the cod stocks. The new report again recommended that the shared turbot quota be set below 11,000 tonnes. It also said that fishermen must change the way they caught turbot, which had now become "a big fishery." Gill-nets left at great depths for too long led to spoiled turbot, and ghost nets destroyed fish.

Anderson announced the 1998 TAC levels for most groundfish on December 23, 1997, but said that the DFO would conduct a full assessment of the cod stocks, including the results of the reopened fisheries, the sentinel surveys, and the RV surveys, the following month. The FRCC would provide its recommendations to the minister in March 1998. The TAC for turbot would be announced early in the new year – after consultations with the Nunavut Wildlife Management Board.

A two-year pilot observer program carried out by NAFO members after the turbot war was set to expire at the end of 1997. Canada wanted a permanent agreement to ensure that every vessel had an observer on board, and that satellite tracking would be used to prevent overfishing. (About 35 per cent of fishing vessels in the NAFO area were equipped with satellite transponders.) Infractions had dropped dramatically since the program began in 1995. In 1994, Canadian NAFO inspectors had found sixty-three serious infractions, but in 1996 there were only twelve. By the end of August 1997, there had been only three serious infractions. NAFO was still working on a dispute-settlement agreement.

Patrick Chamut headed the Canadian delegation to the NAFO meetings in St. John's in September and won an extension of the observer program for one year. There were plans to make coverage permanent in 1999 after a further review. The seventeen NAFO members also agreed to actions that would make it harder for flag-of-convenience ships to break conservation rules. NAFO accepted moratoria on redfish and witch flounder on the Nose and Tail of the Grand Banks and a continued moratorium on cod. The moratorium on shrimp-trawling on the Nose and Tail would also continue.

But there was some good news for 1998. NAFO decided to allow a small, 4,000-tonne yellowtail flounder fishery on the southern part of the Grand Banks. This fishery had been closed for four years, and Canadian fishermen would get almost all of the quota. There would be no fishing during spawning, or in areas where there were any northern cod. FPI would get 85 per cent of the allocation and the remaining 15 per cent would go to National Sea Products.

The federal government had tabled two new fisheries bills (based on the principles of sustainable development, integrated management, and the precautionary approach) to replace the current Fisheries Act, but the legislation was not passed before the last parliament was dissolved. The department planned to return to cabinet in the autumn of 1997 to confirm its strategy of fishery management reform.

Despite the disasters on two of its coasts, Canada has not yet ratified the United Nations agreement on straddling stocks, even though it had been instrumental in negotiating the agreement after the *Estai* incident. Nor has Canada signed the Law of the Sea Convention, although the Convention has been ratified by 120 states, including its old nemesis, Spain. The government still hasn't made the fishery a priority. The people in power seem to have forgotten that they are responsible for a living resource. As Dr. Leslie Harris put it to the author, "What we are dealing with here is not just a piddling little fishery that keeps half a million people in Newfoundland alive and functioning, not just a little resource which provides a bit of food that could be replaced by a million chickens or something. It is one of the great wonders of the world, one of the great animal populations, which is part of one of the most complex ecosystems that has developed and thrives in a very hostile and difficult part of the ocean. It ought to be one of our glories to protect and preserve."

14

UNCHARTED WATERS

The cod may have been hunted almost to the point of extinction, but unfortunately the human component of the ecosystem in Atlantic Canada has not changed, despite over $3.5 billion spent on special fishery relief programs there in the 1990s. At the end of March 1997 there were still 34,100 people collecting TAGS payments in the Atlantic provinces and Quebec. Seventy-three per cent of the participants do not have a high school education, and 67 per cent are over thirty-five years of age. The majority are married with children, and 42 per cent have at least one other family member collecting TAGS.

On August 15, 1997, the FFAW won the right to sue the federal government for ending TAGS a year early. Justice David Osborn of the Newfoundland Supreme Court refused to grant a federal government motion to throw the case out of court. Lawyers for the union successfully argued that the letters the workers had received from the federal government outlining how much money they would get and for how long were, in effect, a legal contract. Many recipients had taken the letters to their banks as collateral to secure loans.

TAGS has been a dismal failure at reducing the number of people dependent on the fishery. Funds designated for buying out fishermen or retraining were converted to support payments. Even if TAGS had cut the number of fishing licences in half, that would not have reduced capacity by half, as advances in technology since the start of the moratorium have increased fishing capacity for most groundfish. Today's trawlers have nets large enough to envelope twelve 747 airplanes, and can take 200,000 pounds of fish in one set. Longlines can be up to eighty miles long and carry thirty thousand baited hooks.

The large fish-processing companies have adapted well to the cod moratorium and are profitable once again, mostly because of smart management. FPI has transformed itself into a seafood trading company, with almost $665 million in sales in 1996 and $675 million predicted for 1997. In 1996 it made a little over $6.1-million profit, a major achievement considering that it lost over $67 million in 1992, the year of the moratorium. Projected profits for 1997 are $8 million. The company has reduced its active trawlers from forty-seven down to twelve, plus one factory-freezer trawler. Today it employs 3,611 people. If the northern cod ever return, Vic Young, the chairman and CEO of FPI, is content to have inshore fishermen rather than his company catch the stock.

Young told the Summit of the Sea conference in St. John's that we are "living through a societal calamity of our own making." The whole fisheries system had failed, and everyone involved had to ensure it would never happen again. "The world is watching," Young told his audience. The greatest challenge was to leave the fish alone long enough for a healthy recovery. "We all must pull together to do things right. . . . The alternative is unthinkable, and we have just lived through it."

National Sea Products of Nova Scotia reported a year-end profit of $5.6 million in 1995 and $3.5 million in 1996. For the first nine months of 1997 the company showed a net income of over $6 million on sales of almost $206 million. It is projecting $270 million in sales in 1997. Its fleet was reduced from about forty vessels down to five scallop draggers and six groundfish trawlers, two of which were inactive in the summer of 1997.

Henry Demone says: "That was painful financially and emotionally. Before he retired my father was vice-president of the fleet. I was selling off his fleet. There were millions and millions in write-downs to sell these trawlers off at distress prices."

Demone borrowed his management strategies from large companies such as Hewlett Packard and Intel, which reinvent themselves every two or three years through product development. The company learned how to process headed and gutted cod from the Barents Sea, and developed new products that have been successful in the marketplace, despite having to pay twice as much for their raw fish. In 1996 National Sea got almost a quarter of its revenues from new products it had developed, and these are selling well in the U.S.A.

Demone has come to an important conclusion about his company's future direction. He says: "I think from a marketing point of view we see a lot of seafood, not as low-cost raw material for processed food, but as a luxury item. If you are going to have those low catch-rates, it's got to be channelled into high-priced markets: white table-cloth restaurants. Rather than raw material for fish sticks, it will become something you eat when you go out for a nice dinner, like lobster is today."

National Sea Products reduced the number of plants from twelve to three, and the work force of 6,000 down to 1,500, in order to survive. But today those 1,500 people have secure, year-round jobs with benefits and decent incomes. Henry Demone believes the collapse of the fish stocks has been a tragedy for Atlantic Canada but that the most interesting part of the story has yet to come.

A number of people at National Sea left permanent, well-paying jobs to go on TAGS. Some left to get a good education, but according to Demone, "Most people did little to improve themselves. The government has to help people through the transition, but I also think that if you want to change, there're two things that motivate people: fear and desire. There's got to be a little bit of fear there. You can't take all the fear out, and expect people to change.

"The nice emotional thing about TAGS is that it rescued these people financially and put bread on the table," he says. "But it also created a terrible dependency. There was dependency anyway, and this just made it worse. Now there's thousands of people who really think that the government should look after them." Demone believes that people, much like companies, have to evolve, change, or leave: "You need that because the world changes. TAGS, though the original objectives were fine, became, as far as I'm concerned, only income support. None of the other objectives were realized." Like others who watched the fishery, Demone had heard terrible stories about the oversubscription to TAGS. "But you take a generous federal program like this and you put it into a fishing village, where it's administered by a local person, and you can imagine what happens." The Auditor General's Office found an error rate of almost 30 per cent in the eligibility duration rate for Newfoundland. In other regions it was over 35 per cent.

Demone thinks we won't see the true impact of the cod moratorium until TAGS ends: "That is when you will see social unrest, and some serious, serious problems. The reaction of people is going to be, 'Here I sit. It's no better than it was five years ago. The money is gone. I'm in the same position.' There is going to be a lot of anger."

Giving people the impression that TAGS could be extended is a bad idea, according to Demone. "It's kind to people in the short run, but it's cruel to them in the long run, because they are not getting on with their lives. They are not adjusting, they are not dealing with the reality of their lives. There will not be fifty or sixty thousand people working in the cod fishery in Newfoundland. It's not going to happen. Even if the fish were there it couldn't happen, because the world has changed in terms of processing technology and markets. But without fish, it sure as heck won't happen."

Demone is right: federal documents show that the majority of former fisheries workers have done little to adjust to a life without fish. There have been some success stories, such as Isle Madame in Nova Scotia, where half of the TAGS recipients were retrained and work at other jobs, including a telephone call centre set up by an Ontario company. But many former fishery workers expect to collect welfare when the program ends.

At the end of September 1997, the Newfoundland government put the finishing touches on a proposal for a sequel to TAGS. Newfoundland wanted the federal government to put money into tourism, forest products, and information technology, sectors with promise in the province. Brian Tobin told a reporter, "There's recognition that you can't just wave goodbye to twenty-five thousand people with a last paycheque. . . . If you create a program that creates a dependency with no end plan, you can expect the result we got." Tobin is not alone. Many Newfoundlanders quietly worry about civil unrest when people are cut off TAGS. Fear and emotion are running so high that most people are afraid to discuss publicly the changes that are inevitable once TAGS money runs out.

The Auditor General's Report, released October 7, 1997, was scathing in its criticism of TAGS. The report said that instead of restructuring the industry "to make it economically viable and environmentally sustainable," TAGS had encouraged people to stay in the fishery. The level of financial support was also found to be a disincentive to work since it paid more than a minimum-wage job.

The number of people eligible for TAGS was 51 per cent higher than expected. As a result, 76 per cent of the nearly $2 billion spent on TAGS went to income support. (The forecast had been for 36 per cent.) Some people qualified for TAGS, even though they had no historical attachment to the groundfish industry, because at the time of the moratorium they had the good fortune to be working in a fishing enterprise or plant that got at least 25 per cent of its landed value or processing from groundfish. Individuals who processed other species or even did other types of work at such plants were eligible for TAGS. To qualify, workers had to be laid off from a designated groundfish-processing plant. (Some plant owners did not want to be given designated status, because they feared losing employees to TAGS.) As well, in Newfoundland, the DFO did not keep a record of catches for boats smaller than thirty-five feet, so officials could not readily establish if the volume of groundfish catches or the income generated met TAGS criteria.

As the crisis spread beyond northern cod to almost every other groundfish stock, people could not get enough work to qualify for UI, so they stayed on TAGS. Given the choice between a guaranteed regular income on TAGS, and seasonal employment that might not last long enough to get UI, many people opted for the higher income. The average income for participants during the first year of TAGS was $14,721, slightly more than the median annual income for fishing industry workers during the four years that preceded the moratorium. By the end of March 1997, only 0.5 per cent of TAGS participants had voluntarily left the program, a far cry from the 50 per cent that was forecast.

Not surprisingly, the report found that "the deep cultural attachment to the groundfish fishery has been reinforced by several decades of government subsidies. This has resulted in substantial pressure on government to maintain the status quo; that is, to use the fish as a basis for providing income support. Successive governments have provided increasing income support for the people living in the remote coastal communities of Atlantic Canada. This reaction to social pressures has not resulted in an economically viable fishery. In fact, the absence of the fishery has revealed, more clearly than ever before, the substantial reliance on income support by a significant portion of the Atlantic fishing industry. This reliance makes dealing with already complex problems of overcapacity and fisheries management more difficult."

John Efford responded to the report with typical ferocity: "If the auditor general thinks that TAGS has become a way of life, he doesn't know that, if those people had a choice, 99.9 per cent of the individuals affected by the closure of the groundfishery would be working. We have a major problem here in Newfoundland and . . . I'd like to ask the auditor general or somebody, what are people supposed to do, eat rocks?"

Atlantic MPs grilled Auditor General Denis Desautels for two hours during a Commons fisheries committee meeting on October 21, 1997. Some accused him of blaming TAGS problems on fishermen and plant workers when it was the high-tech harvesting methods used by the big fish companies that had led to overcapacity and overfishing. NDP MP Peter Stoffer called for a judicial inquiry into DFO management. Desautels agreed that the DFO should offer an explanation of why the stocks collapsed. Tory Newfoundland MP Bill Mathews asked the $64,000 question. "The real challenge for the government is, what do we do with the people who are not able to make a living from the fishery?" It is a question that successive administrations have been asking for over thirty years.

The fisheries committee decided to travel to Newfoundland and Labrador to get a first-hand account from fishermen. Chairman George Baker, the Liberal MP for Gander–Grand Falls, announced they would report to parliament early in 1998. He told the St. John's *Evening Telegram*, "It will not just be about TAGS. It will be about fisheries policy in general, to suggest changes."

The Commons committee also voted unanimously to launch an investigation into the policies and practices of the DFO. It would investigate allegations that scientists were muzzled and that their work was manipulated to suit a political agenda. It would also examine the decision-making process at the DFO from the point when scientific evidence was presented to the point when quotas were announced. Baker said, "If, in fact, it is true that the scientific advice was not followed regarding, for example, the northern cod, then what we're dealing with is a very, very serious matter." If this was found to be the case then the committee would recommend legislation "to make it illegal for a government to overrule scientific advice." Scientists who testified before the committee would have their rights protected as if they were members of the House of Commons. William Doubleday said witnesses from his department would "cooperate to the extent of their knowledge and ability."

The committee will likely recommend that the science arm of the DFO be removed from the control of the bureaucrats and politicians, and that scientific advice be made public without being filtered through the department. John Duncan, the Reform Party's fisheries critic, has said, "If the public doesn't know what the scientists are really saying, I don't think they can ever have confidence in what the DFO is doing."

On November 6, 1997, William Doubleday appeared before the seventeen-member committee in Ottawa. A DFO insider who knows Doubleday well described him as brilliant but lacking in political sensitivity. He was the "thick-skinned, field-general type" who always believed criticism would blow over. It was a quality he needed during the grilling by the MPs. Gary Lunn, a Reform MP from B.C., told the tough-minded bureaucrat, "You've been a huge player in destroying the Atlantic fishery."

Doubleday denied that he had ever been asked to change any of his data or his interpretations, but added that scientists have only an advisory role. Their advice is not always followed by the politicians. He also denied ever being subjected to a gag order. Nova Scotia MP Peter Stoffer reminded Doubleday that he had not spoken out when Fred Mifflin had increased the turbot quota against the advice of officials in his department. Stoffer also told him that an experienced fisherman with a grade five education "knows more about the fishery than you do." Asked why scientists didn't stand up to bad political decisions, and why he would stay in a department that made the wrong decisions, Doubleday replied, "The world is not perfect."

Eleven meetings were scheduled for Newfoundland, and two each in New Brunswick, Nova Scotia, and Quebec. At the first meeting held in the Tors Cove parish hall on November 27, 1997, inshore fisherman Don Drew spoke for all five hundred people in the room when he said that the moratorium was the result of the federal government having ignored the warnings of the inshore fishermen for years. "We see TAGS as compensation for the mismanagement by the government," he said. Hardly anyone in the hall was under thirty. Most of the young people had already left the region.

Just before the release of the auditor general's report, the federal government did what governments always do when they can't come up with a solution to a difficult problem – they set up another study. Eugene Harrigan, a senior official with the human resources department, was assigned to report on the social and economic implications of the end of TAGS. Harrigan stressed that he had a narrow mandate, to assess what the impact would be on people and communities, not to find solutions to ongoing fishery problems.

Fisheries Minister Anderson repeated in early October 1997 that the federal government would keep its election promise to help workers when TAGS ended, although he offered no details.

The information coming out of Ottawa was contradictory. Anderson's media spokesperson, Athana Mentzelopoulos, said the minister had promised nothing. Human Resources Minister Pierre Pettigrew said a decision on a replacement for TAGS had not been made. A memo from the Prime Minister's Office the same day, sent to aides and MPs, said there would be no replacement for TAGS: "We do not intend to extend, renew, or replace it." The memo shocked and angered people in Newfoundland.

In response, John Efford warned that if there was no alternative to TAGS, many fishermen would start fishing illegally. "When you take the food off their table, they say they have no choice but to go back fishing." Earle McCurdy agreed with Efford. "If the government of Canada thinks they can say, 'sorry, TAGS is over,' and still keep a moratorium in effect, they are dreaming. What they will be doing is announcing a reopening of the fishery. There is absolutely no way that people are just going to be told TAGS is over and you still can't fish." During the week of October 19, 1997, fisheries officers charged seven people with fishing cod illegally along the northeast coast.

Vic Young of FPI told a St. John's Board of Trade luncheon that the federal government must continue to provide help for those affected by the collapse, but as a transition measure. He suggested that a fund should be set up to give fishery workers opportunities outside the fishery: more licence buy-outs, early retirements, training programs for real jobs, and mobility incentives. (All these elements had been part of the original TAGS mandate.) The fund should also support development in coastal communities. Young said that under TAGS fishery workers saw themselves as being in a holding pattern waiting for the fish to return, while the government thought they were somehow adjusting people out of the fishery. "These two concepts passed each other like ships in the night."

Worried about a violent backlash when the program ended, HRDC planned to spend $350,000 to train its office managers in crisis management, according to leaked documents. One of them said, "It is important that the training be ready to deliver in order to avoid an explosion of dangerous situations." It revealed that many employees were fearful as a result of past sit-ins and demonstrations. Some had requested unlisted home telephone numbers, and others took varying routes to work, or left their building only in groups and after dark.

The Newfoundland House of Assembly debated an emergency resolution on November 24, 1997, calling on Pierre Pettigrew to disavow the security move. Beaton Tulk, provincial minister of development and rural renewal, said, "Words cannot describe the deep sense of hurt and insult that all of us feel." Premier Tobin demanded that the minister apologize to the people of Newfoundland: "It is planning for a crisis rather than planning an appropriate response to a very real problem that afflicts thousands of families in this province." Pettigrew agreed to change some of the wording in the proposal, but the plan to train his staff would proceed.

At the start of the FFAW's constitutional convention on December 1, 1997, Earle McCurdy described the "growing mean-spiritedness" in government that the union had had to face in the previous three years. "Newfoundland outports are a tinderbox of frustration because of the way we are being treated," he said. He was astounded that the people who had created the crisis through unfair public policies were surprised when the victims of those policies lashed back.

In response to angry demonstrations and some skilful behind-the-scenes manoeuvring, on December 16, 1997, the deadline for TAGS was extended from May to August, 1998.

The Reform Party believed that any follow-up to TAGS should concentrate on retraining, and that funding should be controlled at the community or provincial level. Their fisheries critic, John Duncan, said, "We believe the long-term solution relies more on the people of Atlantic Canada than on the federal government. . . . Made-in-Ottawa solutions have failed." Duncan was in St. John's responding to Auditor General Denis Desautels's report. The Reform alternative to TAGS included cutting federal taxes in the region to increase consumer spending and encourage business. Reform wanted politics removed from licensing decisions and scientific research separated from political control. The party also supported the expansion of the seal hunt since the market for seal products had the potential to earn coastal communities $100 million a year. Despite constant attacks from powerful animal-rights groups, the sealing industry was growing in Newfoundland. About twenty-three hundred people were employed during the 1997 hunt, bringing in over $20 million.

One of the exhibits in the 1997 Auditor General's Report was a graph showing the changes in fish-processing employment relative to resource availability for the period from 1980 to 1991. In Newfoundland, while the resource declined by almost 20 per cent, the number of processing workers increased by 50 per cent, from 20,000 to over 30,000. At the same time, the average duration of a fish-processing job dropped from eight months in 1980 to just over four months in 1991, long enough for an extra ten thousand people to collect UI.

Income from UI for fishermen has increased substantially over the years. In 1972–73 fishermen received $20.4 million in UI payments. By 1988–89 that figure had risen to over $270 million. In 1981, for every dollar they earned in the fishery, they received forty-three cents in UI benefits. By 1990 that had risen to eighty-one cents. Reliance on UI was the highest in Newfoundland, where in 1981 self-employed fishermen received ninety-six cents in UI for every dollar they earned. By 1990 that number had risen to $1.60. Transfer funds have merely hidden the crisis, and postponed it.

Canada is certainly not the only nation to subsidize its fishing industry. On June 2, 1997, the World Wide Fund for Nature (WWFN) and the UN Environment Program produced a report urging fishing countries to cut subsidies in order to save the fish. When governments pour money into the industry, the oversize fleets wipe out the fish faster than they can reproduce. It is estimated that the world's fishing industry spends U.S. $124 billion every year to produce U.S. $70 billion worth of fish. The difference, $54 billion, is paid for by subsidies in one form or another.

Because the fishery is artificially profitable, people remain in the industry and continue to overinvest in order to get a greater share of a dwindling resource. Claude Martin, the WWFN international director-general, said subsidies send the wrong economic signal to fishermen in depleted fisheries because they create incentives for high levels of fishing. Capacity has increased as productivity has declined in most of the world's oceans.

Particularly vulnerable are those species that congregate to spawn, or those that migrate across national fishing zones. Cod and salmon qualify on both counts. The commercial extinction of species threatens the incomes of millions of people. The study also warned about the destruction of the ocean ecosystems due to destructive fishing practices, and the discarding of as much as 30 million tonnes of undersized or unwanted fish a year, fish that is dumped back in the ocean – dead.

So what is to be done? The experience of other countries raises some radical possibilities. Small-scale fisheries co-operatives have worked well in Japan, and in other parts of the world. Japan is one of our largest markets and is one of the world's leading producers of seafood. Almost half of Japan's national catch by value comes from community-managed coastal fisheries. The value of aquaculture in their inshore production is also increasing.

326 • LAMENT FOR AN OCEAN

Like Newfoundland's outports, Japanese communities are homogeneous with long histories and a common attachment to a local environment that has nurtured people for generations. Communities are given specific fishing rights under the law. They are linked to the upper levels of Japanese national fisheries management through the structure of the co-operative. Conflicts are resolved at frank, loud, and emotional group meetings that end with sake and a snack of dried fish. Perhaps cod tongues and Dominion Ale could serve the same purpose in Newfoundland.

In February 1997, the Senate Standing Committee on Fisheries began examining privatization and quota-licensing in Canada's fisheries. Leslie Burke, director of policy and economic analysis for the DFO in the Maritime region, testified that the experiment with community quotas was in its infancy, but that groups of fishermen had been coming forward to ask for a "local community management board," whose decisions they would agree to abide by as a group. Even though there had been disagreements, the concept was working in the Nova Scotia groundfish industry in seven areas. The boards set plans that take into account the effect of member fishermen on each other. Limitations and constraints on how members operate were voluntarily imposed.

In a recent report called *Beyond Crisis in the Fisheries*, published by the Conservation Council of New Brunswick, the authors argue that Canada should adopt community-based fisheries management in the name of restoring stocks and protecting fishing communities. Ownership of the resource and responsibility for its management within a defined geographic area would be transferred from the federal government to community fisheries boards. These boards would send representatives to a regional fisheries board, which would operate on an ecosystem-wide basis such as the Bay of Fundy or the Gulf of St. Lawrence. Each regional board would establish fishing seasons, close spawning areas, protect habitats, and impose gear restrictions in its area.

In Canada, bickering among fishermen has been a chronic problem. Groups from the same community, even those who use the same gear, can't decide how to divide quotas that everyone believes are too small. But a community co-operative would give a structure for democratic decisions. The co-op would divide the quotas, decide what gear is to be used, monitor conservation and good fishing practices, set up marketing, and resolve the inevitable conflicts. It would also decide the quota share between fixed-gear inshore and mobile-gear middle-distance fleets. Production could be tied to the capacities of fish plants of various sizes. Micro-plants may be the answer in some communities, huge modern plants in others.

Communities and the fishery workers have to be involved in the decisions that affect their lives. Part of a fisherman's special knowledge is intuitive, flexible knowledge. He sees relationships in nature every day when he is on the water, so an interspecies approach to management comes almost naturally to him. The fisherman and the scientist will have to work together in the future. Sentinel fishermen are already gathering data to be used by the scientists, and recently scientists have asked fishermen to help with the design of research surveys.

On October 27, 1997, the first of twelve otter trawlers headed out to the North Atlantic fishing grounds. Onboard were experienced fishermen whom the DFO hoped would be able to find out why there had been no signs of recovery offshore. DFO biologist Ben Davis was hoping that by comparing the situation in 1997 to their historical knowledge of the grounds, they could figure out if the stocks were on the rebound.

The fisherman has learned to be a navigator, a weatherman, and a mechanic, as well as a fish finder, but the formal education and skills levels of those in the fishery have to be increased to allow them to adjust to the new fishery. Regular seminars about good fishing practices, the latest stock conditions, and regulations could be a condition of keeping a licence.

There should be zero-tolerance of high-grading or discarding; everything should be brought in and processed since it will probably die anyway if thrown back. Norway has banned discarding at sea, and Canada must as well. We have to be careful not to overfish alternate species such as skate, monkfish, or winter flounder that were once considered junk fish. Penalties for infractions such as discarding and misreporting of catches ought to be so severe that no one would risk the consequences. Similarly, fishing on spawning stocks must end. Iceland has already ended fishing on spawning grounds, and the FRCC report concludes that it is a sound measure.

In the past, research into fishing technology concentrated on catching more fish, and making more money doing it. Future research will have to go into developing gear that allows small fish to escape and doesn't tear up the ocean floor. Lost gill-nets that "ghost fish" could be equipped with electronic finders.

Adjacency should be a factor in the allocation of quotas, for both fishermen and processing plants. Agreements could be made between communities if one area is willing to sell excess product. Communities could even sell or rent a quota to a large fish company.

Computer technology could play a much larger role in the fishery. There are now laptop computers on the market that can withstand salt spray and there is software for electronic charts and navigational aids, as well as to plan routes and locate traps or buoys. Computers could also be used for instant two-way contact with DFO scientists and managers, either to feed them information or receive the latest stock status reports. They can also be used for up-to-the-minute market information. If prices go down, it is better to leave the fish in the water. The Internet and e-mail could be used to exchange technical information, receive weather reports and communications about world trends in fishery. In August 1997 Stratos Network Research of St. John's was awarded a federal contract in partnership with the Canadian Space Agency to design and develop software that gives ships reliable and affordable access to the Internet and other forms of data communication.

Newfoundland is in the middle of a period of profound change as it adapts to the new world economy. The Food and Agriculture Organization of the UN (FAO) acknowledges that fishing nations, including Canada, have reached the limit of the capture fisheries in the North Atlantic. Hunters of wild fish must now adjust to a high-tech economy based partly on new ocean industries and aquaculture.

Preliminary FAO figures indicate a record total world production of fish in 1995 – 112.3 million tonnes. A major reason for this increase is the phenomenal growth in aquaculture production, one of the fastest-growing food producing sectors in the world. In 1995 the capture fisheries landed about 90.7 million tonnes of fish world-wide. Demand for seafood is growing, but capture fisheries have remained stable at between 85 and 90 million tonnes over the last five years. Aquaculture production rose from 18.6 million tonnes in 1994 to 21.3 million tonnes in 1995. Today almost one quarter of the world's food fish is produced by aquaculture, and the FAO predicts that figure will jump to 35 per cent by the new millennium. Net increases in fish for human consumption in the last few years have been due almost entirely to aquaculture production.

Fish farmers and fishermen exist side by side in Norway. Family members will sometimes own a company that does both. In 1995, 35 per cent of Norway's earnings from seafood exports came from aquaculture, but in Canada fishermen have tended to feel threat-ened by aquaculturalists until very recently.

Henry Demone studies world fishing trends closely and believes that a significant part of his industry's raw material will come from aquaculture in the future: "If you look at protein production in the world, the fishery is the last of the buffalo hunters. And I don't care what you look at, if you go back a hundred years, look at where North Americans got their meat. I'm willing to bet a hundred years ago a lot of it was wild, and now it's very rare to eat wild meat. I don't think fisheries will go to that extreme, but I think each year a higher and higher percentage of the marine products produced in the world will come from aquaculture."

Scientists and other industry experts agree with Demone, largely because they estimate that the demand for fish for human con-sumption will increase 26 per cent by the year 2010. That means that an additional 31 million tonnes will have to be produced over the next decade. Today, aquaculture is worth $40 billion world-wide. If northern cod and other wild stocks disappear, that figure will certainly be much higher.

In Newfoundland, the aquaculture industry has grown phenom-enally since the collapse of the cod stocks. In 1990, the landed value of the capture fisheries was $256,588,693. The farm-gate value of aquaculture products was a mere $6,000. In 1996, the landed value of the capture fisheries was $230,865,058, while the farm-gate value of aquaculture products jumped to $5,249,053. By the time those aquaculture products were marketed they were worth $6.1 million to the Newfoundland economy, almost double their 1995 value. Most of the money came from mussels, steelhead trout, and salmon, although other shellfish and high-value species are being devel-oped. Another dramatic rise in value is expected for 1997.

Newfoundland has about ten thousand kilometres of coastline, and over seven hundred communities that depend on the ocean to survive. About $20 million from the $100-million Canada–Newfoundland Economic Renewal Agreement has been commit-ted to aquaculture. An October 1997 study showed areas suitable for grow-out cages for cod. Fishermen can supplement their incomes by catching small cod and growing them to market size in vast pens. There is little capital investment because the fishermen make their own pens, and can easily learn grow-out techniques. The cod are harvested when prices are high.

Newfoundland's Economic Recovery Commission is headed in the right direction. It is introducing social and cultural reforms to help build a stronger economy. The commission is trying to trans-form a province that depends on natural resources and transfer pay-ments into one that is more knowledge-based and self-sufficient. It has looked at training and education, labour relations, and income support, and steering government toward fostering entrepreneurs, rather than regulating them.

A big boon to the Newfoundland economy is the $6.2-billion Hibernia oil project. It did not save Newfoundland from the devastation of the cod collapse, but it helped. For five years, construction of the gravity-based structure provided almost 4,800 high-paying jobs, and about $2.2 billion of the project's budget was spent in Newfoundland. Critics have called it a multi-billion-dollar make-work project. It's true that only a few people run the rig now that it has started pumping oil, and the jobs are highly specialized.

Although Newfoundland's royalties from Hibernia will replace federal transfer payments, yet-to-be negotiated royalties from other fields will provide a real boost for the province's economy. But fish and oil don't mix unless there are very stringent conservation measures. The province needs money from royalties so badly, there are fears that conservation may be overlooked in the zeal to get much needed cash.

There are spin-off benefits to Hibernia. Some local companies are using the practical experience they gained on Hibernia on other oil projects around the world. It also looks promising for the development of Newfoundland's other oil projects: the $2-billion Terra Nova project and the $1.5-billion White Rose development scheduled for early in the next century.

A high-tech industry connected to the offshore and ocean research is burgeoning. One Newfoundland company, Hi-Point Industries (1991) Ltd., based in Bishop's Falls, has found an excellent way to adapt an old product to a new industry. It sells Oclansorb, a peat-based oil absorbent, around the world. The product was used to help clean up after the *Exxon Valdez* spill, and similar spills in Uruguay and Australia. (It floats, absorbing the oil not the water, and is retrieved easily from the coastline.) The peat has also been used to help clean up oil-contaminated sites in Bosnia and Equador, and the company has had recent orders from Mexico and Japan. Annual sales are now over $1 million. The owner is hoping the product won't have to be used in the Newfoundland offshore industry.

A project with huge potential is the Voisey's Bay nickel, copper, and cobalt find in Labrador, which may eventually employ as many as 2,300 people if the mine goes underground. Surface mining is expected to start in 2000, but it will be several years before the capital costs of developing the mine are paid down and royalties begin.

In August 1997, the Newfoundland government announced it was providing incentives under the Economic Diversification and Growth Enterprise program for a new national telephone call centre. The centre opened in September, and it now employs 210 in jobs paying between eight and ten dollars an hour. There are about twenty call centres in Newfoundland, an industry that is growing at the rate of 20 per cent a year.

The last Beothic Indian died in Newfoundland in 1829. The Great Auk, a large flightless bird that once lived in profusion on Funk Island, was hunted to extinction in 1852. The last Newfoundland wolf died in 1930. Schools of haddock 150 miles long and 25 miles wide once lived on the Grand Banks and the St. Pierre Bank. The Soviets and the Spanish lined up their factory-freezers for miles and took the spawning stock. In five years, the haddock was gone.

Using sophisticated sonar, two commercial and two federal research vessels began the first-ever acoustic survey of inshore 2J3KL cod on October 6, 1997, in St. Mary's Bay. They worked their way around Conception Bay, Trinity Bay, and Bonavista, ending in White Bay in December, a journey of two thousand nautical miles. They found some concentrations of fish, but the overall results were spotty. Bruce Atkinson, the DFO's acting science director in the Newfoundland region, concluded, "The bays are not full of cod, as some people have claimed." Despite a six-year moratorium, the spawning biomass had not increased in either the inshore or the offshore.

At the end of January 1998, Ransom Myers went to St. John's to attend cod stock assessment meetings. Asked for his opinion about what he had learned, he said, "The disaster in the cod fishery is now worse than anyone expected. The survival of juvenile cod has been below average for a decade, and there appears to be neither the political will, nor the conservation ethic, to stop the illegal fishing that continues in Newfoundland. It may be a generation before we see a recovery of the cod. That a five-hundred-year-old industry could be destroyed in fifteen years by a bureaucracy is a tragedy of epic proportions."

About sixty-five thousand years ago, our ancestors carved fish hooks from deer antlers and used them to catch the large, slow-moving catfish along the Congo. Catfish soon disappeared from the great river. Early man fished to the maximum extent of his technology, and his modern descendants continue that devastating tradition with far deadlier gear.

Commenting on the collapse of the cod, Dr. Leslie Harris says, "If I were to look for a single villain, I would look to our known inability to match social policy with technological capacity. We have never in the history of the world been able to amend our social policies quickly enough to keep pace with the speed at which technology grows. And I think that is what happened here. We just became too technologically competent. We became able to kill too easily. We became able to kill everything."

That view was echoed at the Atlantic Vision Conference in October 1997 by Vic Young when he said, "Our strategy to rebuild a sustainable fishery for the future must stand in contradiction to how we have managed the fishery over the last thirty years. As we move forward, we need better science, more conservative management practices, fewer plants, fewer fishermen, fewer trawlers, fewer seals, less political interference, more control over foreign overfishing, and better harvesting technologies and practices."

The federal government released Eugene Harrigan's report on February 10, 1998. It suggested that Ottawa should focus on licence buyouts and early-retirement packages for fishermen, rather than income-subsidy payments. Harrigan believed there was now a consensus in Atlantic Canada that the cod stocks may never return, and many fishery workers would prefer a lump-sum rather than a social assistance cheque every month. Although the report did not list recommendations, it would be used to help the federal government formulate its final response to the cod crisis.

The UN has declared 1998 the International Year of the Ocean to show how essential the oceans are to life on this planet, and to push ocean issues to the forefront of the public agenda. But will individual fishermen respect conservation principles that have been abused for decades? They have learned to navigate around government regulations, and many break the rules if they think they can get away with it. Illegal fishing on the closed stocks still goes on. It is much easier to blame foreigners or governments for mismanagement of the fishery than to take responsibility for being part of the problem. Instead of trying to figure out how he can catch more fish, today's fisherman has to think about fishing smarter for his own sake as well as for the future of the stocks. He has to produce a finer product that fetches a higher price. Sustainable development has to be the overriding rule: we must meet the needs of the present generation without taking away the ability of the next generation to meet its own needs.

Cabot Martin, one of the first people to warn about the destruction of the northern cod stock in the early 1980s, summed up the future for Newfoundland when he said, "We have for far too long blamed our weather, our location, or others for our problems. It's about time we took a long, hard look in the mirror. No society can escape the responsibility for how it lives. And it is in that basic, fundamental way that gaining power over our fisheries is the first essential step to growing up."

15

THE WATERSHED YEAR

"When does fisheries management become mismanagement? Generally I would say that it happens when you become so political in your decisions that you ignore the science and the resource. It happens when you so favour the many clamouring and competing groups that request fishing opportunities that you forget that your primary duty is to protect the resource. You cannot forget that you are a steward of the resource; you are not a person simply allocating resource exploitation opportunities. That is when management would become mismanagement and I think that is clear on both coasts."

These words do not belong to an angry fisherman or to the fisheries critics of Her Majesty's loyal opposition. They were spoken by Canada's fisheries minister, David Anderson, at Senate fisheries committee hearings on November 26, 1998. Whether he intended it or not, David Anderson offered an indictment of the management system he presides over. By his own definition, and despite self-serving claims to the contrary by his senior officials, Canada's fishery has been tragically mismanaged.

On May 21, 1998, Anderson had called a press conference to announce his department's conservation plans for the endangered

West Coast coho stocks. There would be no fishing on the upper Skeena and Thompson River stocks, and only selective fisheries where the by-catch was minimal. There would be no directed coho fisheries. Anderson was throwing down the conservation gauntlet and hoping the Americans would respond favourably to his example.

A month later, Anderson announced his government's 1998 Salmon Management and Coho Recovery Plan, a $400-million strategy that would put limits on all B.C. salmon fishing in order to save the endangered coho. There would be a dramatic increase in efforts to protect and rebuild salmon habitat, the commercial fleet would be restructured and reduced, and people and communities would be helped to decrease dependency on salmon and to find employment outside the fishery. Never before had Ottawa spent that kind of money on the West Coast fishery, and Anderson assured nervous taxpayers that it would be a one-time event.

The minister carefully explained that the program did not mean "no fishing," but rather "fishing in a new way." The salmon fishery of the future would be conservation based, but it would also be humane in the transition period. An early retirement program for older fishermen would help them make a dignified exit from the industry.

Environmental groups such as the Sierra Club of Canada and Greenpeace backed the minister, calling his conservation measures a historic departure in public policy. But everyone realized the measures were only as good as their enforcement. Without 100 per cent monitoring, a fisherman with enough determination could still get away with catching coho.

Although Ottawa dislikes the comparison, the collapse of the northern cod stocks on the East Coast was behind Anderson's historic policies in British Columbia. Previous ministers had put the jobs of fishermen before the survival of fish, but Anderson said repeatedly that the fish had to come first. He knew his decision to close the coho fishery was a big political risk, but one he was willing to take. "Real conservation doesn't come for free," he said.

"There is a price to saving fish and, as a politician, I am willing to pay it."

On June 26, 1998, a one-year salmon agreement was reached with Washington state. Anderson and Washington's governor, Gary Locke, announced a deal in which Canada agreed to reduce its catch of chinook bound for U.S. waters by 50 per cent, and Washington agreed to reduce its catch of coho bound for the Thompson River by 22 per cent.

B.C. fishermen responded to Anderson's measures with anger and protests, but their fury and frustration were muted by a despondency not seen before. Fishermen planned to blockade the Alaska Highway, but cancelled the protest because they couldn't afford the gas to reach the B.C.–Alaska border. As fishermen began the severely restricted 1998 season on July 1, they felt that they had been sold out by the DFO and Ottawa. One protest organizer told the media, "We're seeing the same thing here we saw back east, where the DFO encouraged overcapitalization and bigger boats and that led to the destruction of the cod. We're afraid we're going to see the same thing here."

The Fraser River is reputed to be the world's largest producer of salmon, a distinction once held by the Columbia River before dams destroyed much of the salmon's habitat. On July 3, 1998, Anderson announced a one-year interim agreement with the U.S. on the lucrative Fraser River sockeye fishery. The Americans would be given 24.9 per cent of the catch, which amounted to about 1.2 million of the estimated 5 million salmon to be caught. To spare both the early Stuart Lakes sockeye runs and later runs of upper Thompson coho, the Americans also agreed to restrict their fishing to between July 27 and August 21. It was, at best, a pragmatic solution. Lacking any leverage with the Americans, other than the high moral ground of conservation, Ottawa claimed that it was the best deal it could get. Like most claims in the fishery, it was a half truth. Without an agreement, American fishermen would have had unrestricted access to Canadian sockeye in American waters. When the early Stuart Lakes sockeye returns fell short of preseason estimates, the DFO cancelled the fishery alto-gether. Just what Canada ended up getting in this half-baked bargain remains uncertain.

B.C. Premier Glen Clark called the Anderson deal "a sellout of monumental proportions" that would destroy hundreds of coastal communities in rural British Columbia. "This is not just a bad deal for Canada; frankly, it's an unbelievable sellout of Canadian interests, and it stems from an unwillingness on the part of Canada to stand up to the Americans, to stand up for our sovereignty, for our rights and for conservation principles." Gordon Smith, the former deputy minister of the Department of Foreign Affairs, and now a professor at the University of Victoria, said in a *Globe and Mail* interview, "This is not a great deal," but "the truth is that we are better off because there was nothing more we could do – this is not like squaring off against Spanish fish boats – and the alter-native would be worse."

In the end, Canada and Alaska failed to reach an interim fishing agreement for the 1998 season. Talks had foundered on conflicting interpretations of the scientific data used to evaluate the state of the stocks. Canada called for an independent review of the science, but the Alaskans continued to whistle past the graveyard, acting as if there really wasn't a resource disaster in the making. Canadian fishermen in northern B.C. watched helplessly from the wharf as Alaskan fishermen caught Canadian-bound coho. Glen Clark announced that British Columbia would resume its lawsuit against the United States for overfishing. He also planned to sue the federal government, saying it had abandoned Canadian fishing interests and caved in to the United States' demands. In the heat of the political moment, Clark suggested that Anderson was a "traitor" for negotiating the salmon deal with Washington state. Although Clark grabbed most of the headlines, there was quiet support for Anderson. An Angus Reid poll showed that most of his fellow British Columbians agreed with his decision to close down the coho fishery.

In fact, the fishery was quietly undergoing a revolution of sorts. Farmed salmon is gradually but relentlessly displacing wild salmon in the market. At the Granville Island market wild salmon sold for $6.95 a pound, while farm salmon, which was often fresher and better handled, sold for $4.95 a pound. In 1997, for the first time there was more farm salmon than wild salmon on the B.C. market. The 118 communities that depend on the fishery accounted for less than 1 per cent of the provincial economy. But that didn't lessen the human tragedy unfolding in British Columbia. Just as it was in Newfoundland when the cod collapsed, the burning question was often whether people could make enough to qualify for EI during the winter.

Thrown into this volatile mix was the federal government's policy of allowing aboriginals exclusive fishing rights. B.C. provincial court judge Howard Thomas had ruled in January 1998 that a native-only commercial fishery was illegal, but that didn't stop the DFO from prosecuting Vancouver-area fishermen who had protested the "race-based fishery." Anderson argued that the 1992 Indians-only judicial decision was legal because he, the minister, had the right to allocate fishing rights for broad social and economic purposes. Judge Thomas stayed proceedings against twenty-four protesters on August 7, 1998, the same day that Ottawa unexpectedly announced further major reductions of commercial salmon fishing on the Fraser River. Far fewer fish than expected had made it to the river to spawn. The next day, the DFO also closed sport fishing on the river and "asked" natives to stop fishing for food and ceremonial purposes. Despite the Canadian conservation effort, the Pacific Salmon Commission approved a three-day U.S. fishery of the Fraser River-bound sockeye on August 10, 1998. The pot continued to boil.

On August 14, 1998, the federal government announced it would appeal Judge Thompson's decision that said all federally authorized native-only fisheries were illegal. A Vancouver-area Indian band netted about 18,000 sockeye salmon, weighing five to ten pounds apiece, from the Fraser while it was closed to all other fisheries. The band members had the right to catch fish for their own food and social and ceremonial purposes, but most of the catch was quickly sold to non-natives, including fish-market buyers, who came to the Musqueam reserve to buy the fish for $2.50 a pound. The band's fisheries coordinator claimed that unidentified federal fisheries officers were present while the fish was being sold, an allegation officially denied by the DFO. In the wake of the scandal, one hundred fishermen, led by Reform MP John Cummins, resumed their protest against the native fishery by taking to the Fraser River fishing grounds in their boats.

Special fishing rights for First Nations communities has generated much anger and controversy in British Columbia. Many non-natives objected to a "race-based" fishery, but Anderson believed that their opposition was unfair. As the early Europeans on the coast had bought fish from the Indians, there was a commercial fishery "at contact," which gave the natives pre-existing historical rights. The 1990 Sparrow decision of the Supreme Court of Canada also established that an existing aboriginal right to fish was protected by the Constitution and, after conservation, was the first priority of Canadian fishing policy.

Then the world turned upside down, as it often does in an industry where the predictions come from a scientific crystal ball. On August 19, 1998, the DFO reported a larger than expected salmon run on the Fraser – the estimate was boosted from five million to six million fish. Everyone could resume fishing. The federal fisheries department claimed that unusual water temperatures had made the fish even more unpredictable. Several biologists and conservationists felt that reopening the fishery was a reckless decision – a crass political attempt to appease B.C. fishermen. Anderson's deal with Washington had guaranteed U.S. fishermen one-quarter of the Fraser River sockeye before the cut-off date of August 21, 1998. The one million "extra fish," worth about $15 million, came just at the flashpoint.

Ottawa had closed the fishery to Canadians on Monday, August 17, while they watched the Americans continuing to fish. A day later, the minister gave the green light to sport fishermen, and then on August 21, to the commercial fleet. Twenty-four hours later the Fraser was closed again when it was "discovered" that the weaker, late-summer-run salmon were mingling with the summer-run sockeye. Many fishermen had elected to stay off the DFO's management merry-go-round. Forty per cent of the owners of the province's 3,000 fishing boats had taken a one-year payment of between $6,500 and $10,500, $10 million all told, to stay out of that season's fishery. It was a wise move. The remaining fleet caught less than half of its preseason quota, providing yet another management black eye to the DFO.

The government of British Columbia was furious. Glen Clark announced a provincial inquiry into what he characterized as Ottawa's incompetence and mismanagement of the B.C. fishery. It would be led by management consultant and transplanted former Newfoundland premier Brian Peckford, a man who during his seventeen-year political career had tried to wangle shared jurisdiction of the fishery from Ottawa. David Anderson issued a statement dismissing the inquiry as "yet another unfortunate effort to play politics with fish." It was a laughable comment coming from the master of fish politicking.

Arguing that the outcome of the study had already been dictated by Glen Clark, Anderson said, "It is the same as a judge first declaring a defendant guilty, and then conducting a trial to prove it." The minister would not have this political exercise distract his staff from conserving the resource and restructuring the industry. But there was another and far more basic reason that the DFO would not play ball with Peckford, and David Anderson stated it bluntly: "The provincial government is not responsible for salmon management and conservation – I am." Anderson promised to set up a body called the Pacific Fisheries Resource Conservation Council (modelled on the East Coast's FRCC), to provide arm's-length and independent scientific advice on the state of the stocks and their habitat by September 15, 1998. The announcement couldn't come soon enough. Salmon returning to B.C. rivers were facing the worst conditions on record: Mortality rates were up to ten times the usual 4 to 6 per cent.

In July 1998, the federal government commissioned a study to give an in-depth assessment of the impact of salmon stock declines on B.C. fishing communities. Conducted by G. S. Gislason & Associates, the study also provided advice on community adjustment. The most vulnerable communities were located in the most remote regions of the province and had few economic alternatives. Although Anderson was on record as saying, "My scientists may say what they wish in terms of the scientific opinions that they honestly hold. There is no attempt to control them," the DFO was publicly skewered for releasing a sanitized version of the Gislason Report. The author claimed that the DFO's summary version contained recommendations that he had not made, and that major criticisms of the DFO had been omitted. Although the original report was delivered on September 21, 1998, it was not widely released until February 1999. It estimated that salmon fishing job losses would double to 15,500 by the year 2000, a fact omitted in the DFO summary posted on its Web site. Prior to 1996, there were 26,000 jobs in the commercial and recreational salmon industry. It was estimated that by 2000 only 10,500 jobs would remain.

Gislason reported yet again what people on the West Coast wanted: co-management, with decisions at the DFO and the HRDC made at the ground level, or what he called "bottom-up, locally driven development." They wanted development officers who lived in the communities, cuts in red tape, meaningful consultation, and no assistance money spent on yet another level of government bureaucracy. In short, the time for "consultants, studies, and words" was over. Fishermen wanted action.

On October 14, 1998, Anderson released his "new direction" for Canada's Pacific salmon fisheries. Again, the policy paper made it clear that conservation was the primary objective of his department.

It was also clear that he had been listening to his critics. "The federal government is committed to working with communities to enhance their input into the decision-making process," he said, enhancing his reputation for being a minister who at least said the right things. All sectors of the fishery – First Nations, recreational, and commercial – would use selective harvest measures. After conservation, native requirements for food, social, and ceremonial purposes would have first priority. Supporting and sustaining a vibrant recreational salmon fishery would be a key part of the new salmon management plan, a thrust commercial fishermen claimed pandered to Anderson's friends in the sport fishery.

The commercial fishery would be encouraged to diversify, so it would be less dependent on salmon. Anderson was reading the reports. He quoted from Parzival Copes's study, "Coping with the Coho Salmon Crisis": "The need for reduction in the size of the salmon fishing fleet is beyond dispute." The DFO's goal for fleet reduction was 50 per cent.

Anderson promised that clear and objective information on major issues would be provided to the public for review and feedback. New mechanisms would involve stakeholders in the decision-making process, and increased public involvement would lead to increased understanding and support of federal initiatives. Managers and stakeholders would share the responsibility for sustainable fisheries "including management costs, decisions, and accountability." There would be a structured management and advisory board system to enhance community, regional, and sector-wide input to decision-making. Regional boards could actually "make" decisions in the future, rather than waiting for the next papal bull from Ottawa.

On March 12, 1999, Anderson issued a post-season review of the 1998 West Coast salmon fishery at the Waterfront Centre Hotel in Vancouver. He announced that the coho conservation program he had put in place in 1998 would have to continue for at least two more life cycles since many runs remained endangered. In other words, it would be stone soup for B.C. salmon fishermen for the next six to eight years. More than 250 coho stocks and 60 chinook stocks remained at risk, or on the brink of extinction. His salmon management plan had a single but compelling objective – "put fish first." Anderson called 1998 a "watershed year – a year of significant and fundamental change in fisheries management."

Every day the United States and Canada engage in one billion dollars' worth of trade, and Canadians have learned the Americans are immune to pressure, but open to self-interest. Since late 1998, there have been technical discussions between Canadian and American fisheries managers, including representatives from Alaska, and there was quiet optimism that there would be a break-through in the Pacific Salmon Treaty talks. As with many things in the fishery, acceptance of change comes most swiftly with the recognition of disaster. The fabled Bristol Bay sockeye runs col-lapsed in 1997 and 1998, and scientists at the Alaska Department of Fish and Game said they could not make a prediction for 1999 until the runs came in. In other words, they were fishing in the dark. In 1996, the Bristol Bay salmon fishery was worth $141 million, compared to just $66 million in 1997 and $70 million in 1998. Overall, the value of the Alaskan salmon catch has declined dramatically from $366 million in 1996 to $260 million in 1998. Based on those declining revenue numbers, Governor Knowles declared western Alaska a disaster area in 1998 and offered U.S. $19 million in emergency aid to fishermen and their communities.

Under the Endangered Species Act, the United States spends about $500 million a year to protect and restore salmon habitat in the Pacific Northwest. New ESA listings could push that number to over a billion dollars a year. On March 25, 1999, David Anderson and Lloyd Axworthy released a report by natural resource economist Martin Shaffer which concluded that catch reduction is just as important for the recovery of salmon as in-river programs to restore habitat. Agreements under the Pacific Salmon Treaty are the principal way to achieve those reductions. They are also less costly for governments than habitat restoration. Anderson gave a polite luncheon speech at the Canadian embassy in Washington a month later, saying, "The time has come to step beyond rigid, short-term positions. The situation calls for leadership from everyone involved." On May 27, 1999, the day that Slobodan Milosevic was indicted for war crimes, Lloyd Axworthy and Madeleine Albright met for talks about the war in Kosovo. Over lunch they also discussed the Pacific Salmon Treaty, and a week later a new ten-year agreement was signed. (The Fraser River agreement would last for twelve years.) Anderson made the announcement flanked by state governors and American native leaders, and received rave reviews for the treaty – in the United States. Vice-President Al Gore said, "Today's agreement is integral to our long-term strategy to bring the salmon back." Representatives from B.C. and Canadian aboriginal bands were absent from the press conference, and Vancouver police barred angry fishermen from the room. Fisheries management and science have been cut dramatically within the DFO, but the spin doctors have retained their budget. While the press release hyped "abundance-based management that is more sensitive to conservation requirements," what it really meant was that Canada had abandoned the equity principle, one of the pillars of the treaty – that each country receive the benefits of fish that originate in its own waters. Canada received no compensation for the millions of dollars' worth of salmon the Americans pirated after annexes of the treaty expired in 1992. Now, the harder Canada works at conservation, the more fish the Americans will take.

Alaska will continue to catch our endangered coho that mix with their non-endangered stocks. In 1998, the Alaskans caught over 800,000 endangered B.C. coho, and under the terms of the new treaty, they will be allowed to catch the same number in 1999 if Alaskan abundance forecasts hold. At the same time, endangered chinook and coho runs destined for Washington and Oregon are protected from Canadian fishermen.

The United States agreed to limit its catch of Fraser River sockeye to 16.5 per cent, to be phased in over three years. The DFO trumpeted this as a drop from 24.9 per cent in 1998. But the average annual catch by the Americans from 1989 to 1998 was only 15.6 per cent. Despite the DFO's spin, the United States will be taking a greater percentage of sockeye than they had for the previous decade. They will actually end up taking even more fish, if the stocks improve. Many of the incredibly complex details of the treaty have yet to be worked out, such as how the interest from a proposed $209-million endowment fund will be spent on science and on stock and habitat enhancement in the two countries.

About 240 years ago, a volcano erupted eight hundred kilometres north of Vancouver. According to Nisga'a legend two villages were destroyed, killing an estimated two thousand people. The Nisga'a believed the gods were punishing the tribe for having mistreated spawning salmon. On June 17, 1999, the Chiefs of the Tribal Council representing some of the severely affected communities on the west coast of Vancouver Island appealed to Prime Minister Chrétien to consult with them before he signed the new salmon treaty. Angered that American aboriginal groups had had status at the negotiations while they had been excluded, the chiefs wrote to Chrétien asking for his personal intervention to see that conservation measures were adequate for threatened stocks: "After centuries of sustainable management by our people these fish stocks are threatened by management regimes and international treaties outside our control." The consensus in Ottawa was that even an imperfect deal was an improvement over the chaos of the previous seven years. Chief Larry Baird of the coastal village of Ucluelet said, "Canada appears to have collapsed and accepted a weak deal based on considerations other than the health of salmon stocks my people depend on." Luckily for the DFO, Ottawa rests on the Precambrian Shield.

On the East Coast the ultimate fish story ended on August 29, 1998, or at least it should have. That was the cutoff date for final payments under the jammy but disastrous TAGS program. Until that fateful day, about 25,000 people in Atlantic Canada were still receiving cheques from Ottawa. As usual, politics intervened to extend the bailout, and the underlying problems that made it necessary in the first place.

After many protests and much arm-twisting from former federal fisheries minister, and now Newfoundland premier Brian Tobin, on June 1998, the federal government announced its bailout of the bailout, quickly dubbed TAGS II. In all, a whopping $730 million was allocated "to assist individuals and coastal communities to adjust to opportunities outside the fishery, and to lay the foundation for an economically and environmentally viable, self-reliant fishery." In other words, the latest handout was supposed to do exactly what the original $2-billion TAGS program failed to do.

As of March 1999, the HRDC in Newfoundland and Labrador had received 1,361 applications for early retirement; about 2,000 fishery workers were eligible under the new plan. One-third were fishermen, the rest were plant workers. About $65 million had been set aside for workers still eligible for TAGS between the ages of fifty-five and sixty-five as of December 31, 1998.

Roughly $250 million was earmarked for licence retirement – fishermen who opt for a buy-out have to leave the industry permanently. Core fishermen received an average of $101,500 under the plan, but many people were not happy with this amount. After taxes and repayments to the Fisheries Loan Board, some fishermen reasoned they would be better off keeping their licences. If they made $20,000 on crab, $10,000 fishing another species, and $10,000 from EI, they could gross $40,000 for the year, a comfortable life in a Newfoundland fishing community. About $180 million was set aside for one-time, lump-sum payments ranging from $7,000 to $14,000 for workers who had expected to receive payments until May 1999 under the original TAGS program. There was also $135 million for job training and up to $100 million for that standard phrase of every bailout package, "regional economic development."

TAGS II brought the total spent on "special" East Coast fisheries aid in the last decade to over $4.2 billion. When the stocks collapsed, 2.5 people were working in the fishery for every person in the industry in 1961.

But the fish have fared much worse than the fishermen. Most groundfish stocks are not recovering and several species have declined further despite the sweeping moratorium. Yet dumping and illegal fishing continue, and huge seal herds make the recovery of the northern cod even more unlikely.

Today's limited seal hunt provides important income to about 11,000 Newfoundlanders – in precisely those communities and outports hardest hit by the collapse of the cod fishery. Most of the seals are shot, but the industry is still attacked for bludgeoning cuddly white "baby seals," which have been legally protected since 1987. When Brian Davies, founder of the International Fund for Animal Welfare, was given a $2.5 million payout after he left the organization, sealers saw it as proof that the IFAW was really just a successful business with excellent marketing skills. Donations to the IFAW are reputed to be about $80 million a year, and most of their advertising and revenue is based on the seal hunt. Those are daunting numbers. Newfoundland fisheries minister John Efford says that the IFAW raised six times his entire departmental budget in 1998, and used the money to try to kill a way of life in his province.

Far from being endangered, the population of harp seals has exploded, from under 2 million in the early 1970s to an estimated 5.4 to 6 million since the hunt was curtailed in the early 1980s. A major harp seal population survey was done by the DFO in the spring of 1999, and the results will be known by the end of the year. But John Efford, for one, doesn't have to wait for the DFO's number to conclude that seals are hindering recovery of the cod stocks. Efford makes no bones about what the exploding numbers mean for the Newfoundland fishery: "Now what kind of a fool could believe that six million seals are not impacting on the recovery of the stocks?" A Newfoundlander is not allowed to take a cod for his table, but seals consume millions of juvenile northern cod each year.

In the end, the problem may not be fact, but well-marketed fancy. Efford claims to have been told by a DFO deputy minister, "John, you've got to realize these protest groups are very powerful and they will protest in the EU, and that will impact on trade relations not only with your province, but with all the other provinces of Canada."

In the spring of 1999 the Newfoundland government turned the tables on the animal rights activists. It released a video shot underwater at Big Chance Harbour showing thousands of cod lying on the bottom with their stomachs torn out. Caplin is the main food of the adult cod, and fishermen believe the seals are actually after the caplin in the cod stomachs, and as an additional treat, their livers. The executive director of a marine conservation group funded by the IFAW countered with the bizarre accusation that it was birds, not seals, that had gutted the cod – a statement deemed ridiculous by credible biologists. The DFO's stock status report for 1999 concluded that "predation by seals has been an important source of mortality of cod since the start of the moratorium." The FRCC recommended a cull of half the seal population, and the Commons standing committee on fisheries produced a report in June 1999 calling for a "major reduction" in the harp seal population to protect the cod stocks.

Efford worries that with the fish stocks so fragile and the seal population so high, the whole food chain is in danger if nature sets in a disease. According to veteran sealers, for the last ten years seals have been behaving in strange ways, remaining in bays and coves year-round rather than heading north after mating. They have even been found with kelp in their stomachs when no other food is available. For his efforts to persuade Ottawa that a cull is necessary, Efford has found himself the target of the international animal rights movement. "I get hate mail threatening my person if we go ahead with the seal cull," he says. "Do these threats and hate mail make a difference to me? Not a damn bit of difference in the world. I care more about the communities and about the people of Newfoundland and Labrador than I do about some fanatic sitting down in New York or over in London."

The founder of the Sea Shepherd Conservation Society, who was in California, compared Efford to Nazi propaganda minister Joseph Goebbels: "John Efford has told the lie about seals destroying codfish so often he has begun to believe it himself." Paul Watson offered a $25,000 reward to anyone who could prove that seals were eating the stomachs of cod. Perhaps he should have made another visit to Newfoundland, instead. On Good Friday 1999, hundreds of residents near Summerville, Bonavista Bay, watched in amazement as seals herded thousands of cod towards the shore, ripped into their stomachs, and ate the livers. The stunning event was captured on videotape.

On March 30, 1999, Watson challenged Efford to a debate on the seal hunt, which the minister eagerly accepted. But it may be too late for him to win the battle for the hearts and minds of the world. A big-budget movie based on Watson's book *Ocean Warrior*, with Woody Harrelson cast to play Watson, is planned. Martin Sheen has the role of a photographer onboard the *Sea Shepherd*.

The killing of any animal is a gruesome act. In the slaughterhouse, when cattle are hoisted on hooks, still conscious after their throats are cut, no one sees their agony on the evening news. The hypocrisies don't stop there. A German writer was observed trying to head out to the 1999 hunt dressed in "tight-fitting leather pants." A judge recently rejected an injunction against the slaughter of six million snow geese by the Canadian government because the geese were overbreeding and damaging their Arctic habitat, but the story got relatively little play. With the willing cooperation of the world media, animal rights groups have continued to campaign for a species that is far from endangered, while completely ignoring one of the worst ecological catastrophes in the history of the planet – the destruction of the great northern cod.

In September 1998 there was an index fishery (a commercial test fishery) of 4,000 tonnes in the formerly rich zone 2J3KL, the first commercial fishery on the northern cod stock since the moratorium in 1992. Research survey trawls working offshore in 1998 found abundant shrimp but few cod. An offshore index fishery in zone 3L in November 1998 came up with the same depressing results: no big concentrations of cod in a place where they had once been plentiful. While northern cod have been found in Newfoundland's big bays, there are virtually none on the spawning grounds where the offshore trawlers once fished day and night.

The cod appear to be declining even in the absence of a fishery. Nor have they recovered in the Gulf of St. Lawrence. Even so, fifty frustrated Quebec fishermen seized a Canadian Coast Guard vessel moored off the Gaspé peninsula to pressure for more quota, and two hundred small-boat fishermen in Newfoundland stormed a crab management-plan meeting in February 1999, demanding that their crab quotas be doubled, and that there be a 15,000-tonne commercial cod fishery along the northeast coast in 1999. Now that federal funds have finally dried up, people here must fish, move, or go on welfare.

According to biologist George Winters, who presented a report to the DFO cod stock assessment meeting in March 1999 (just before he retired from the DFO), DNA tests show that offshore and inshore cod stocks are genetically distinct. Winters suggests that rebuilt local inshore populations of cod could be fished, because they aren't going to recolonize the offshore. Winters, who completed an independent cod report for the Fish, Food, and Allied Workers Union, and who is also doing some research for the provincial government on seals, estimates that there may be 100,000 to 200,000 tonnes of northern cod along the east coast, south of White Bay. If true, that would indicate a substantial increase from the previous DFO estimate of about 20,000 tonnes. But when it comes to experts pulling numbers out of hats, no one is taking great comfort from Winters's numbers.

There are still 2,000 inshore fishermen licensed to fish along the northeast coast, and the FFAW feels that the DFO's science branch is too conservative in its quotas, largely because it is overreacting to criticism of its role in the cod collapse. Winters presented his findings during a regional consultation meeting of the FRCC in Clarenville on April 3, 1999. He told the audience that a northern cod fishery of between 35,000 and 40,000 tonnes would not harm the recovery. The five hundred fishermen in the audience gave him a standing ovation.

The DFO's Newfoundland division could be forgiven for holding their applause. Many scientists worry that there is a real risk that recovering stocks can't survive a commercial fishery. The DFO's trawl survey index of biomass in 1997 was the lowest observed since the survey began in 1983, a trend repeated in the most recent surveys. There were few fish older than five, and no indication of any strong year-classes coming along. But that is news few fishermen want to hear. DFO scientist George Lilly was heckled during his presentation at the FRCC meeting. He said some catch-rates from test fisheries were "good to excellent" but there was not enough information to assess the risks of a reopened fishery.

Areas north of White Bay remain desolate. Bruce Atkinson, divisional manager of groundfish for the DFO, estimated inshore cod abundance in the northern cod range to be between 36,000 and 135,000 tonnes – extinction numbers. Tagging showed that some cod were migrating from Placentia Bay on the south coast into zone 3L. Since a cod can swim thirty miles a day, we may even be counting the same fish twice. Genetic studies indicate that this coastal population is not genetically distinct from the cod in 3Ps. Even though offshore stocks are negligible, some fish might follow the traditional migration path from offshore to inshore in the spring and summer. If these fish were taken in a reopened inshore fishery, any hope that the offshore stocks will rebound would disappear. The DFO's 1999 stock status report for northern cod concluded that the prospect for recovery of the offshore cod "appears to be dismal in both the short and medium term," and that "the status of cod in the inshore remains uncertain."

David Anderson was scheduled to announce the 1999 TACs for cod in Newfoundland on May 6. The minister asked the FRCC to delay its recommendation on the northern cod stocks until after a scientific peer review of the analyses presented at the Clarenville FRCC meeting by George Winters. On May 27, 1999, the FRCC recommended a TAC of between six and nine thousand tonnes for the coastal portions of 3L and 3K. In a letter to Anderson, Fred Woodman wrote: "The method we have chosen for setting the TAC for 1999 is regarded by the Council as a default method put forth only due to the unacceptable lack of quantitative data on the coastal biomass. The Council believes it will be impossible to provide future specific TAC recommendations for this stock unless quantitative data are provided on coastal abundance." The FRCC also recommended that the spawning biomass of cod that over-wintered in Smith Sound, Trinity Bay, be closed to all commercial fishing: "This aggregation may be the key to the re-population of this area and perhaps beyond. It is very important that this aggregation be protected by a closure of directed fishing in the Sound." In response, the FFAW announced plans to lobby the minister for a larger quota.

David Anderson reopened the northern cod fishery on June 23, 1999. He announced an inshore quota of nine thousand tonnes to be fished under IQ licences. "The management measures announced today focus on conservation and underline our commitment to a precautionary approach," he said. Contrary to the advice of the FRCC, Smith Sound was opened to resident fishermen. Anderson also decided to allow fishing in zone 2J. Hawke Channel in 2J contains the only known spawning cod on the continental shelf. If the DFO's low abundance estimate of 36,000 tonnes turns out to be correct, 25 per cent of the entire northern cod stock will be taken this year. Even if George Winters's optimistic calculation of a 200,000-tonne biomass is accurate, the "conservation" minister has reopened a stock that contains less fish than we used to catch every year.

Pressure from fishermen is hard to resist. On the south coast of Newfoundland, the commercial cod fishery was doubled to 20,000 tonnes in 1998. At the cod stock assessment meetings held in St. John's in late January 1998, several DFO scientists were very concerned about uncertainties in the data and strenuously cautioned against increasing the quota in zone 3Ps. One scientist vividly expressed his mistrust of the data used to recommend the quota: "You could drive a truck through that work." It was agreed that more analysis was necessary, and a second meeting was held in late February.

The Newfoundland region of the DFO concluded the stock was "rebuilding strongly" and issued a stock status report on February 27 suggesting a 20,000-tonne TAC. That morning the FRCC held the last of its stakeholder meetings in Clarenville, and fishermen in the audience already had copies of the DFO's 1998 3Ps stock status report. Normally, reports for groundfish do not contain a suggested TAC.

It was fisheries mismanagement at its most political. The FRCC is the organization that is supposed to advise the minister on TACs. According to one observer, there was no way the FRCC could recommend a lower quota because fishermen and their union were pushing hard for a 30,000-tonne TAC. It was noted that neither Fred Woodman, nor his vice-chair Jean-Claude Brêthes, appeared very happy at the Clarenville meeting, but the FRCC rubber-stamped the 20,000-tonne quota on March 25. Some scientists felt the 3Ps stock report was overly optimistic, and after e-mails, informal discussions, and a conference call, Mike Sinclair, acting director of science for the Maritime region, sent a memo to ADM Scott Parsons, expressing the concerns of seven Maritime region scientists: "Our concerns remain that the estimates of abundance are unrealistically high. The document does not, in our view, fully express the extreme uncertainty that is integral to this assessment. It presents a view of the resource which is at odds with the status of all the surrounding stocks, and deviates from past assessments of this resource."

Faced with such uncertainty, the scientists suggested the TAC remain at 10,000 tonnes. The 1997 offshore survey in 3Ps was the lowest since 1983, and had been low for four of the last five years.

Stock structure and migrations patterns were also poorly understood, since the cod in 3Ps migrate into other sectors, making it one of the most difficult assessments to make. The fish were also maturing at an earlier age, which could be interpreted as a sign of stress, since this was observed in adjacent cod stocks before they crashed. A zonal assessment meeting was held from May 19 to May 21 to review the assessment. The DFO's Newfoundland region concluded that it wasn't necessary to revise the report. On May 27, 1998, the minister announced a 20,000-tonne quota for 3Ps. Incredibly, it was politics over prudence once again.

The current population biomass in 3Ps is estimated to be 250,000 tonnes, with a spawning biomass of 145,000 tonnes. Fishermen demanded a 40,000-tonne quota for 1999. A risk analysis was carried out for a range of catch options; it showed a 9 per cent risk that the spawning biomass would fall below 100,000 tonnes if there was a catch of 20,000 tonnes in 1999. The 1999 DFO stock status report did not recommend a quota, but Jake Rice, the coordinator of the DFO's Canadian Stock Assessment Secretariat, claims that the 1998 evaluation has proved to be right. He maintains that two surveys and observations from the reopened fishery indicate the spawning biomass is in the historic range of a "healthy stock." The FRCC recommended an increase in the quota to 30,000 tonnes for 1999. Anderson accepted the recommendation.

Cod aren't the only species fishermen are clamouring for; shrimp fishermen are also demanding increases in their quotas. The northern shrimp, which can live for more than eight years, are fished from Davis Strait down to the Gulf of Maine. The 1997 DFO stock status report indicated a high level of shrimp abundance and concluded that the present environment is favourable for shrimp survival. As if by way of afterthought, the writers noted that "beyond the next few years it is not possible to predict how long abundance will last."

At today's fishing levels, not long. Historically northern shrimp were never this abundant, so there have been very few studies done on the species. Biologist Jeff Hutchings has observed that taking 5 or 10 per cent of the estimated biomass may be a safe exploitation level for groundfish, but the safe level of exploitation for shrimp is completely unknown. They are well down the food chain and may affect many more species than a top predator like the cod, which also eat shrimp. Brian Giroux, head of the Scotia Fundy Mobile Gear Fisheries Association, holds a shrimp licence, and he has observed that fishing will be good for four or five years, then go down for seven or eight years, before coming back up again. The decline is beginning in Nova Scotia, and he predicts the same downturn in Newfoundland in three to five years. In fact, one offshore trawlerman who has just returned from fishing for shrimp observed, "We can already see the difference in size in the northern shrimp we're taking. They're already smaller. But when you make $20 million, like our vessel did last year, nobody worries about conservation."

There is not much history to rely on. The first inshore northern shrimp fishery took place in 1997, with landings of about 7,000 tonnes and a value of $12 million. The total landed value of shrimp in Newfoundland that year was over $108 million, surpassing crab, which was worth almost $92 million. In 1998, 250 inshore vessels were given access to 33,000 tonnes of shrimp, and FPI now has the capacity to process 15,000 tonnes of coldwater shrimp annually at its state-of-the art plants in Port Union and Port au Choix. Twelve large trawlers process shrimp at sea. There is 100 per cent observer coverage on the offshore boats, but there are concerns that large quantities of small, less valuable shrimp are being dumped at sea by inshore fishermen because observer coverage inshore is almost nonexistent.

Demand for Canadian shrimp has risen steadily in Europe because suppliers such as Iceland have had to reduce their quotas because of declining stocks. On April 23, 1999, David Anderson increased the TAC for northern shrimp from 84,108 tonnes to 96,540 tonnes. The increase went to shrimp fishing area 6 (SFA6) where the TAC jumped by 27 per cent, with inshore fishermen getting 90 per cent of the increase. From 1989 to 1993 the shrimp TAC in SFA6 ranged from 5,500 to 8,000 tonnes. In 1999 the TAC was set at 58,632 tonnes, a ten-fold increase. Although the stock appears abundant, so did the cod until overfishing wiped out a 400-year-old fishery.

Alarm bells have gone off everywhere but in the DFO and on the busy wharfs of Newfoundland. In his 1999 report, Denis Desautel, the auditor general, raised serious concerns about the way the DFO was managing the lobster, scallop, crab, and shrimp fisheries in Atlantic Canada: "At present, shellfish fishers are enjoying a high level of income compared with fishers who were dependent on groundfish for a living. However, we found problems with the management of the shellfish fisheries that are similar to those of groundfish management and that should be taken seriously."

Desautel noted dramatic increases in harvesting capacity, weak information, and gaps in monitoring the resource, all inconsistent with the precautionary approach to fisheries management and long-term sustainability that David Anderson never fails to mention in his speeches. The TACs were increased for Newfoundland snow crab and northern shrimp in 1998 and 1999 even though there were no stock status reports. Faced with funding cutbacks, the DFO decided to spend its resources doing biological research on the shrimp. Desautel concluded that most shellfish resource decisions were "heavily influenced by social and economic factors." As former fisheries minister John Crosbie has observed, the DFO appears to have learned nothing from the stunning collapse of the cod.

It is clear now that Ottawa's much-vaunted TAGS program has been one of the most costly boondoggles in Canadian history. Although the DFO has spent $85 million to retire 1,300 groundfish licences in order to reduce harvesting capacity, capacity in Newfoundland region has actually increased dramatically since 1997. There are 208 new shrimp trawlers, and 150 enlarged or replaced vessels for fishing snow crab. Many of these vessels were purchased after their owners sold their licences under the TAGS buyout program in the Maritimes and Quebec.

These vessels can easily be redirected to harvest groundfish, and government will be under intense pressure to allocate stocks to satisfy this new capacity. Since the collapse of the cod stocks, there has been a five-fold increase in vessels of this size in Newfoundland. While the other East Coast provinces have bitten the bullet and downsized to run the fishery economically, under Brian Tobin this is not the case in Newfoundland. It has also been noted that "the biggest growth sector in Newfoundland is in recreational vehicles," a reference to the huge amount of public money that has poured into the province.

In his report, Desautels zeroed in on the contradictory goals within the fisheries department. David Anderson has said publicly that his primary mandate is conservation, and that his department does not have the resources or responsibility to manage socioeconomic outcomes. Yet at a strategic planning workshop in October 1998, senior DFO management officials determined that "social and economic considerations do have a role in fishery decisions." This is precisely what this powerful and paternalistic ministry has done – managed a complicated socioeconomic system, but none too well. In that respect, nothing has changed.

Anderson told the Senate fisheries committee, "Canada intends to play a leading role on the international stage to address global marine conservation issues. But we must recognize that we must practise what we preach. As we encourage other nations to promote conservation and the precautionary approach, we must ensure that we address the problems in our own backyard." Yet the DFO still lacks measurable goals and targets for conservation, and management decisions frequently ignore the minister's conservation rhetoric. The DFO wants a fishery that is economically stable and self-reliant and makes ad hoc decisions trying to effect those aims. But Canada still does not have a coherent fisheries policy framework. Over the long term, what do Canadians want, a viable offshore industry, an inshore social fishery, or enough of both to guarantee that Canada will have neither?

The Newfoundland region of the DFO recently started using the Campelen 1800 shrimp trawl for offshore research surveys looking for northern cod because it is better at catching small fish than previous gear. No one mentions that the shrimp fishery, now year-round, will make recovery of the northern cod much more difficult despite the use of sorting grates to avoid by-catch of larger fish. The FRCC has also become concerned about the by-catch of juvenile turbot in shrimp nets since very little is known about the status of the turbot stock. It is ironic that the NAFO moratorium on Grand Banks shrimp continues in order to protect straddling fish stocks while Canada fishes away.

In September 1998, there was formal adoption of 100 per cent observer coverage in the NAFO regulatory area outside our 200-mile zone, an important, and hard-won, outcome of the turbot dispute. On April 20, 1999, the House of Commons gave third reading to Bill C-27, bringing us close to ratifying the U.N. agreement on straddling and highly migratory fish stocks commonly known as the U.N. Fisheries Agreement (UNFA). Thirty nations must ratify the agreement before it comes into force. If the Senate passes the bill, Canada will be number twenty-two.

In December 1998, the International Court of Justice at The Hague ruled that the court had no authority to hear Spain's complaint that Canada's actions during the turbot war violated international law. Premier Tobin called the ruling "a victory for Canada." It was really a victory for the turbot. If Tobin had left the decision to the courts, as many of his hand-wringing colleagues would have preferred, the turbot would be long gone. (Under UNFA, the boarding and inspection of the *Estai* would have been legal.) The turbot has become increasingly important to the Newfoundland fishery. Nunavut wants a greater share of the $45 million worth of turbot caught between Baffin Island and Greenland. Canada's newest territory now gets only 27 per cent of its own turbot, but under the adjacency principle half the Canadian TAC of any fishery is to go to the nearest users. The fishery was explored and developed by offshore companies from Newfoundland, Nova Scotia, and northern Quebec.

The turbot war is still an emotional issue for many Spaniards. The *Estai* has been renamed the *Argos Galicia* and continues to operate out of Vigo. Interestingly, it now flies the Union Jack as it trawls for squid around the Falkland Islands in the South Atlantic. Vigo remains one of the world's largest ports in terms of the landed value of fish, but the size of Spain's own fishing fleet has dropped dramatically since it joined the EU in 1986. This maritime nation once had two hundred vessels searching for cod on the high seas; today it has eighteen. Where Spain's fishing fleet once ranked third in the world, it now comes in seventeenth. Like Canada, Spain lands and processes fish from other nations, rather than relying solely on its own fleet.

The fishery's endless contradictions continue. While groundfish stocks have crashed and taxpayers have spent billions to support laid-off workers for nearly ten years, most people aren't aware that the fishing industry in Canada has enjoyed record sales since the middle of the decade. Canada's export of fish and seafood products was worth over $3 billion in 1997, and $3.2 billion in 1998 – the highest value on record. Canada is the number-one supplier of seafood to the United States. Our neighbours consume 67 per cent of Canada's seafood exports, mostly lobster, shrimp, and crab. Japan is our second-largest market and the EU, with whom Canada nearly went to war over turbot, the third-largest.

Even the offshore industry, decimated by a loss of groundfish for most of the 1990s, has done very well. Profits for Fishery Products International rose to $8.4 million in 1998, up from $8.2 million in 1997, and the company issued its first dividend to shareholders since 1988. The outlook for 1999 looks even better. Today the company is a global seafood enterprise, selling in fifteen countries and buying raw material from over thirty others.

National Sea Products has had a five-year run of increasing profits. The Lunenburg-based company changed its name to High Liner Foods Inc. in 1998 and reported a profit of $10.4 million, up from $8.6 million the year before. But the cost of buying raw fish on the international market has jumped 50 to 65 per cent over the past year. Second- and third-quarter losses are predicted for 1999, with a return to profitability in the fourth quarter. Henry Demone recently stunned the fishing industry when he announced that his company may build two to five new draggers if cod stocks recover off Newfoundland. The large companies have retained a right to their historical quotas if a stock returns to a healthy state.

In the province "hardest hit" by the cod collapse, the wharf has been a busy and prosperous place. In 1998, about 250,000 tonnes of seafood were landed in Newfoundland and Labrador, an increase of 22 per cent over 1997. The landed value was a record $380 million, and the export value was over $700 million, up from almost $600 million the year before. In 1998 there were, according to John Efford, over 30,000 active commercial fishermen and plant workers in Newfoundland, up 6,000 people from 1997 – about the same number of people as when TAGS began.

The industry has become economically stable by diversifying into crab, shrimp, sea urchins, and value-added processing. The largest single contribution to the health of the fishery was made by northern shrimp and crab. Most of the high-quality shrimp is sold in the U.K. and the U.S.A. through FPI. The total landed value of shellfish was about $295 million in 1998.

The province also produced aquaculture products worth $13 million in 1998. Juvenile cod have been captured in 3Ps for cod grow-out projects, a form of sea-ranching in which live cod are held in huge pens and fed to increase their weight. They are then sold when markets are at their peak. In 1998, there were about fifty cod-farming licences in Newfoundland.

In December 1998, Canada got a brand new bureaucrat. David Anderson appointed a commissioner for aquaculture development in recognition of the industry's growing importance in Canada. Wholesale value has increased dramatically from just $7 million in 1984 to $463 million in 1997, over 20 per cent of our total fisheries' landings. These numbers reflect worldwide trends. It is expected that the world population will be 8 billion by the year 2025, and leading experts on the global food supply worry about future shortages.

The FAO estimates that total world fish production reached 121 million tonnes in 1996, over six times what it was in 1950. The landed value of the "capture" fisheries (94.6 million tonnes) was U.S. $85 billion, compared to U.S. $47 billion for aquaculture. Distant-water fishing has declined dramatically since 1990, and markets are beginning to accept cheaper substitutes for highly priced fish such as cod. Capture fisheries continue to level off worldwide as aquaculture production increases.

It is now widely accepted that the world's total fish catch can't increase much more. Twenty-nine per cent of the world's food fish now comes from aquaculture, but it is estimated that global aquaculture production will surpass fish catches within fifty years. Canada must manage this irreversible trend better than it has the wild fishery.

The watchword of the changed fishery will be adjustment. Historically, to maintain employment, Newfoundland produced low-quality, low-priced frozen cod that did nothing to enhance the reputation of Canadian fish. While Iceland became a world leader in the production and marketing of quality cod, quantity, rather than quality, governed most operations in Newfoundland. Since the collapse of the cod stocks there has been a sea-change in the official attitude toward handling and processing. David Anderson believes the key to future success will be high-value niche markets and marketing strategies that exploit the cache of northern fish. Newfoundland Fisheries Minister John Efford now preaches quality with all the fervour of a fundamentalist minister: "Simply put, we want to be number one."

In November 1998, David Anderson appeared before the Senate Standing Committee on Fisheries, which was examining the question of privatization and quota licensing in Canadian fisheries. Would more fishing operators be given IQs, IVQs, ITQs or EAs – the right to harvest a certain quantity of fish annually – as opposed to continuing the old common property free-for-all that had lead to management disasters on both coasts? Privatization of the fisheries has been an issue since the early 1980s and continues to divide fishing communities. In Canada, over 50 per cent of combined landed value on both coasts is now fished under some type of IQ arrangement. After conservation, it is our most important management issue.

Charming and sincere, Anderson stressed that conservation was his first priority, and that giving in to "the inevitable political pressure to subordinate the long-term interests of the fish to short-term opportunity has not worked in the past." He repeated the maxim, "Without fish you do not have fishermen." Anderson's vision for the fishery was one that was "viable, sustainable, and efficiently managed." He said, "We need a fishery that provides a good living for independent professional owner-operators and employees, and one that supports economically healthy coastal communities. It must be a fishery composed of healthy inshore, midshore, and offshore sectors. It must be a fishery that supports a flexible, versatile, and self-reliant industry, largely self-regulating and operating without government subsidies." In short, everything the fishery in Canada is not.

The minister denied that IQs are necessarily a step towards privatization of the fishery. But they are a step in the direction of self-regulation, and although not a prerequisite, a step in the direction of co-management with government. Many small-boat fishermen believe that the DFO has a hidden agenda that favours ITQs. Bureaucrats favour them because they will reduce the number of fishermen at no cost to the government and simplify management for a department that has undergone severe budget cuts.

Anderson claimed that his department was quite willing to have community quotas if the licence-holders supported the concept, although he cautioned that transferring the political pressure to divide the quota from the federal to a local level would not necessarily mean success. The minister had reached the unhappy conclusion that there would always be a level of discontent because of the allocation issue: "The industry has had too many people in it for too long, and it has therefore become very partisan and very political. It is very much an issue of doing-in the other person to satisfy a given community or group. This is my view after eighteen months as minister. I think I have to accept the fact that it is not possible to get that type of industry consensus among fishing groups and fishing communities, or even between provinces. The feeling is that what my neighbour gets is something that is taken away from me. It is a problem that will continue to exist as long as we are in the position of having to restrict fishing efforts, either because of too many fishermen or because of improvements in technology which lead to more intense fish-killing power in the hands of fishermen." He added, "We want to see coastal communities flourish. Coastal communities do not flourish simply because you maintain populations of near-indigent fishermen."

When the Senate committee filed its report on "Privatization and Quota Licensing in Canada's Fisheries" in December 1998, it made some important recommendations after hearing from a wide variety of nationally and internationally recognized authorities. It was the first Senate committee to use video-conferencing, which reduced costs and widened their expertise base to include New Zealand and Iceland, where IQs have been in place for some time. The committee also made transcripts of testimony and background material available on the Internet.

In its list of recommendations, the Senate committee suggested that the issue of privatization and individual quotas should be debated in Parliament, and that no new IQs be given out until the debate had taken place. The DFO also had to issue a "clear, unequivocal, and written" public statement on exactly what the terms meant. To date, the discussion about ITQs has been confined mostly to academics, bureaucrats, and conservative newspaper columnists, but a public resource granted by the Magna Carta in 1215 should not be privatized without a public debate.

The Senate committee urged the DFO to consider the long-term social and economic effects of IQs on coastal communities and to distribute the resource more equitably "to allow small-scale fishers a better opportunity of participating in the fisheries." It also suggested that the DFO stop using New Zealand and Iceland as examples of successful individual quota management systems until the department had listened to the criticisms from those involved. Glowing reports of how well ITQs worked in those countries were, after all, based on information selected and interpreted by the very people who had implemented the systems.

The concept of ITQs was invented by economists. The ITQs work in terms of economic efficiency for governments and ITQ holders, but not for those who don't have them. In countries where ITQs have been in place for some time, there are fewer fishermen and fewer boats. But those who had access to capital bought up a larger share of the stock access. Sometimes that access can bring tremendous returns. A group of eighty-one midshore snow crab licence-holders in New Brunswick, who fish in the southern Gulf of St. Lawrence, is estimated to be worth about $500 million. Not a bad return from a resource that belongs to all Canadians. Some people worry that once privatized, Canada's common-property fishery resources could be controlled or even owned by foreign companies. Theoretically, people fish more responsibly when they "own" the resource; but in practice, ownership is not a panacea: high-grading and discarding of small and low-value fish continues. Fishermen claim the system forces them to dump part of their catch in order to bring the biggest, most valuable fish inshore. Fish don't conform to a business plan, and no one counts the dead fish in the water. Nor will reducing the number of fishermen reduce harvesting capacity, since technological advances will always allow those who stay to catch more fish.

Community quotas are emerging as a major worldwide trend in fisheries management, advocated as a better way to manage stocks and protect employment in a community. A set amount of fish is allocated by government and the quota stays within a geographic area. The system could work equally well for aboriginal communities on the West Coast or small fishing-dependent communities on the East Coast.

Although individual scientists are doing excellent work within the DFO, the science department is still demoralized, according to several marine biologists. The sense of denial of any real role in the cod collapse is regrettably reappearing, as DFO personnel try their hand at revisionist history. The DFO Research Report 98/64, "Considerations on the Demise or Otherwise of Northern Cod," rejects mismanagement as a cause of the collapse: "The hypothesis that the collapse of northern cod was due to undetected increases in fishing mortality beginning in the mid-1980s can be rejected as being inconsistent with nearly all indices of abundance and exploitation, both inshore and offshore. The only plausible hypotheses remaining are catastrophic mortality of idiopathic origin and migration change."

Never has blame in a national disaster been shifted with so pathetic, or demonstrably false, a whimper.

The report goes on to conclude that if the catastrophic mortality did occur, "it was likely most severe in the short period following the abbreviated inshore fishery in 1992." In other words, it wasn't the fault of DFO science managers, but due to sudden and unknown causes, just as the DFO's science ADM Scott Parsons wrote in his government-published book in 1993. George Winters was the co-author of Report 98/64, but he has no problem reconciling it with his "Non Gratum Anus Rodentum?" report of 1986, arguing that the assessment errors had been corrected by the fall of 1988, and that the offshore survey results were accurate after 1989. The cod disappeared "for reasons unknown."

But a report from the Commons fisheries committee in March 1998 directly blamed the DFO for the collapse of the cod and recommended that unnamed "senior DFO personnel who are viewed by the fishing community as being responsible for the crisis" be removed. (Four Liberal members dissented against what they called "witch-hunt justice.") Instead, the Chrétien government removed Newfoundland Liberal MP George Baker, the committee's outspoken chairman.

Computers at the House of Commons printers are programmed to use the gender-neutral term fisher, and rejected the word fisherman three times before finally accepting it for the committees' fifty-eight-page report, as good a measure as there is of just how far the Ottawa mandarins are from the Grand Banks. When the FFAW held a vote on terminology, its female members opted overwhelmingly for "fisherman," rejecting a word already assigned to a forest animal. One woman from La Scie, Newfoundland, drew a standing ovation when she asked the fisheries committee panel to stop using the term. "I won't be referred to as a 'fisher' by no damned bureaucrats or politicians from Ottawa. I'm a fisherman and proud of it." Anderson has begun to use the term fishermen again in very recent speeches.

Scott Parsons, who occupied the key scientific post in the DFO while the cod were disappearing, made a lateral move to become ADM of the oceans sector under the new Oceans Act. He is now in charge of creating programs in the regions. In the cosy world where the same faces keep showing up at councils and conventions, Parsons is also head of ICES, which provides marine scientific advice on the North Atlantic. John Davis, director of science for the Pacific Region since 1986, became acting ADM, science, in October 1998. On April 22, 1999, he was appointed to the position.

William Doubleday remains director general of fisheries and ocean science and continues to be a member of the FRCC, the so-called "arm's-length" body that advises the minister of fisheries and oceans on how to manage our Atlantic fisheries. The minister still appoints the members of the FRCC. Not surprisingly, the body is filled with people who support DFO policies. After Doubleday dismissed Dr. Kim Bell's final report to COSEWIC, in which he had concluded that cod were endangered, Bell said that the process of writing the report had been "like draining a swamp while up to your ass in alligators." Before Bell's report was mailed to members of COSEWIC, "politically sensitive comments" were edited out, and several statements were altered or weakened without the writer's knowledge. There are unconfirmed reports that COSEWIC's non-government scientists may have their voting rights nullified by the environment minister.

Fred Woodman Jr., of Woodman Sea Products in New Harbour, Trinity Bay, got one of the six new crab-processing licences issued by the Newfoundland government in 1998. The company was founded by his father, the chairman of the FRCC. In April 1999, the DFO announced a three-year crab management plan for the Newfoundland region. The quotas for 1999 and 2000 would be over 61,000 tonnes, an 18 per cent increase from the 49,000-tonne quota in 1998. The quota would be reviewed after two years, "because of uncertainty in mid- to long-term snow crab recruitment." Exploratory crab fisheries (with no quotas) would be permitted in new areas. The starting price for large crab jumped from 86 cents per pound in 1998 to $1.38 in 1999.

But not everyone is blinded by the new prosperity the shell fishery has brought to Newfoundland. Biologist Jeff Hutchings is using a grant from the Canadian Foundation for Innovation to fund a groundbreaking study of the effects of trawling on cod. In a recent article in CJFAS, Hutchings and his co-researchers presented evidence of elaborate cod mating rituals that last for days. The males congregate and defend a small territory, while displaying for the females who visit to select a mate. He circles her up to seventeen times, while she decides if he is a worthy match. It seems obvious that trawlers moving through the spawning cod would disrupt this delicate mating process. Population biologist Ransom Myers has a grant from the same organization to study hundreds of different fish stocks in an effort to help scientists predict when stocks will collapse from overfishing. Both scientists remain at Dalhousie University.

In March 1999, at the FAO meeting of fisheries ministers in Rome, Canada's representative gave a keynote address on the issue of overcapacity and called for "concrete actions to bring into force international agreements essential for the conservation and sustainable use of the world's fisheries resources." Canada was the first country to develop its own Code of Conduct for Responsible Fishing Operations, an industry-led initiative that will meet conservation objectives, if implemented. Canada also supports an international plan to limit capacity in the global fleet.

Rather than attend the high-profile FAO meeting in Rome, Anderson chose to address the same issues at a level where he could actually implement them – in his policy statement at the Waterfront Centre Hotel in Vancouver. The changes Anderson has made in the Canadian fishery since becoming minister in June 1997 have put us in the forefront of the international trend towards sustainable fisheries management – at least on paper.

Overfishing, waste, and destructive fishing practices remain rampant worldwide; eleven of the fifteen major fishing areas are in serious decline. Forty-nine of the top fifty countries where fish is the main source of protein are in the developing world. While the FAO was meeting to discuss the international Code of Conduct for Responsible Fisheries in Rome, three children in Kampala, Uganda, died from eating toxic fish. Local fishermen had been pouring poison into Lake Victoria to catch large numbers of fish, which they later marketed.

The International Ocean Institute (IOI), an independent, non-government organization dedicated to studying and preserving the world's oceans, met in Halifax in late 1998 to celebrate the conclusion of the International Year of the Ocean and to discuss the many related problems of ocean and coastal management. The theme of the conference was "The Crisis of Knowledge." One of the IOI's seventeen recommendations was that scientific information should be provided by independent research institutions. Decisions had to be objective, not driven by politics or self-interest.

Jeff Hutchings presented a paper at the conference that proposed the creation of a Science Research Council of Canada, similar to the National Research Council in the United States, which has provided independent scientific advice to government and civilians since 1916.

In his chapter in *Risky Business: Canada's Changing Science-Based Policy and Regulatory Regime*, William Leiss of the School of Policy Studies at Queen's University says that in Canada "there is some serious misalignment in the interplay between science and public policy." He argues that the old pattern of governments doing the scientific work and then applying it to policy choices is obsolete. Scientific advice given and acted upon in secret cannot be challenged by the public. The results of this closed shop, as evidenced in the cod collapse, can be catastrophic.

Leiss believes that fisheries science "was abused over a long period of time as a result of short-sighted economic and political decisions." In his new model, science would be left to independent institutions, and government would be accountable for risk management – honest brokers in controversies played out in public. Humanity no longer has the substantial margin of error it once had in its relationship with natural ecosystems.

The real crisis of knowledge according to the IOI is the cultural and ethical perception of human beings' relationship to nature: "The Western concept of humanity being outside and above nature and of nature being our servant, there to be exploited, has dominated the scientific and industrial revolution and the colonization of the rest of the world." That age is now over, replaced with an ecological world-view that may have arisen too late in the day. It is now accepted that "humans are a part of nature and that, by harming nature, we harm ourselves."

Glossary of Acronyms

AFAP   Atlantic Fisheries Adjustment Program
AGAC   Atlantic Groundfish Advisory Committee
AIMS   Atlantic Institute for Market Studies

CAFE   Canadian Association of Fish Exporters
CAFSAC   Canadian Atlantic Fisheries Scientific Advisory Committee
CCPFH   Canadian Council of Professional Fish Harvesters
CDC   Canada Development Corporation
CFPA   Coastal Fisheries Protection Act
CIRRD   Canadian Institute for Research on Regional Development
CJFAS   Canadian Journal of Fisheries and Aquatic Sciences
COSEWIC   Committee on the Status of Endangered Wildlife in Canada
CPUE   Catch Per Unit Effort (*see Glossary of Terms*)

DFO   Department of Fisheries and Oceans
DREE   Department of Regional Economic Expansion

EA   Enterprise Allocation
EC   European Community
EDGE   Economic Diversification and Growth Enterprise program

EEZ	Exclusive Economic Zone
EU	European Union
FAO	Food and Agriculture Organization of the United Nations
FBDB	Federal Business Development Bank
FCC	Fisheries Council of Canada
FFAW	Fish, Food, and Allied Workers union
FRCC	Fisheries Resource Conservation Council, the successor to CAFSAC
HRDC	Human Resources and Development Canada (formerly the Department of Employment and Immigration)
ICES	International Council for the Exploration of the Sea
ICNAF	International Commission for the Northwest Atlantic Fisheries
ITQ	Individual Transferable Quota
IQ	Individual Quota
IUCN	International Union for the Conservation of Nature
IVQ	Individual Vessel Quota
MPA	Marine Protected Areas
MSY	Maximum Sustainable Yield
NAFO	Northwest Atlantic Fisheries Organization
NCARP	Northern Cod Adjustment and Recovery Program
NCSP	Northern Cod Science Program
NIFA	Newfoundland Inshore Fisheries Association
NRC	National Research Council
NSDA	Nova Scotia Draggers Association
RV	Research Vessel

TAC	Total Allowable Catch
TAGS	The Atlantic Groundfish Strategy
TGNIF	Task Group on Newfoundland Inshore Fisheries
UFCW	United Food and Commercial Workers
UI	Unemployment Insurance (now known as Employment Insurance)
UNCLOS	United Nations Convention on the Law of the Sea
VPA	Virtual Population Analysis
WWFN	World Wide Fund for Nature

Glossary of Terms

2J3KL: Fishing zones 2J, 3K, and 3L off the northeast coast of Newfoundland and Labrador.

Adjacency: The principle that those who live closest to the resource have priority access and benefits.

Biomass: The estimated total weight of all the fish in a stock, including the juveniles. The term is also often used for the biomass of a fishable stock, otherwise known as the "exploitable biomass." The spawning biomass is the total weight of mature fish in the stock.

CIL: The cold intermediate layer of the ocean, which lies between the warmer bottom layer and the seasonally heated upper layer. Although the NCSP used a temperature of $-1.5°$ Celsius to determine CIL, the most commonly used definition today is the volume of water less than zero Celsius.

CPUE: Catch Per Unit Effort: The fish caught by a fixed amount of fishing, e.g., the kilograms of fish caught in a one-hour tow of an otter trawl.

Directed fishery: Fishing for one species only. Other species caught are treated as by-catch or discarded.

Dragger: A vessel equipped with a long cone-shaped net that is dragged along the ocean floor. In many places the word is synonymous with trawler. In Newfoundland the term usually refers to large trawlers longer than sixty-five feet, but in some places it is used to describe a small inshore otter trawler, which usually operates no farther than fifty to eighty miles off the coast.

Enterprise allocation: A fishing quota for a particular stock allocated to a company operating an offshore fleet. The company in effect "owns" the quota and is free to catch its EA whenever it chooses or to transfer it temporarily to another company.

Escapement level: The term used in the salmon fishery for the number of fish that escape being caught and reach the spawning grounds.

Factory-freezer: A ship that is both a trawler and a fish-processing and freezing plant. The largest are about 376 feet long, with half-mile-long nets. Four hundred feet across at the mouth, a net this size could easily swallow the Statue of Liberty.

Fishermen: Although the gender-neutral term "fisher" is now used by academics, journalists, and the DFO, it is a word most people who fish dislike. Even some women who fish prefer to be called fishermen.

Fixed gear: Fishing nets or lines that are fixed in place in the ocean, as opposed to trawlers that pass through the schools of fish. The fish come to the stationary gear, which is checked and emptied frequently. Gill-nets, cod traps, and longlines are all fixed gear.

$F_{0.1}$: Canada bases its TACs on a target fishing mortality of $F_{0.1}$ (pronounced eff oh point one). For most groundfish stocks, this means catching two out of every ten fish each year. The aim is conservation of the stocks, but $F_{0.1}$ has seldom been achieved.

Gadoid: Fish belonging to the cod family.

Ghost nets: Nets that have been lost at sea, but continue to catch and kill fish and other sea life.

Gill-nets: Flat nets that are suspended vertically in the water with lead weights on the bottom and floats on the top. The fish are caught by their gills when they try to pass through the monofilament netting.

Groundfish: Fish that are usually caught near the ocean floor, such as cod, haddock, pollock, redfish, halibut, and flounder.

Handliners: One of the oldest forms of fishing, handlining is still a common method used by the inshore fishery in the Atlantic region. Single baited hooks are used to catch groundfish and other species. The line is hauled onboard by hand and the fish removed.

High-grading: The discarding of smaller or less valuable fish to make room onboard for a more valuable catch. The practice was widespread in both the inshore and the offshore fishery, but is now illegal in most fisheries.

ITQ: Individual Transferable Quota: Right of access to a quota of fish assigned to an individual boat or fishing licence. These quotas are treated as private property and can be bought, sold, or traded.

Landed value: The value of the catch to a fisherman or company when it is landed at the dock.

Longliners: Fishermen who catch cod with long lines bearing thousands of baited hooks which are spread along the ocean floor. The lines used to be hauled onboard manually, but in recent years the baiting and hauling have been mechanized. Some of the lines are eighty miles long and can have 30,000 hooks. Generally the gear is selective, and the fish landed are of a high quality.

Mortality: The death of fish. The proportion of the stock that dies each year is measured as the mortality rate. Fish die from fishing and from natural causes, such as sickness, starvation, and being eaten by larger fish or marine mammals.

Non-targeted fish: Fish caught as a by-catch to the species being hunted.

Northern cod: Cod that live in NAFO zones 2J, 3K, and 3L (known as 2J3KL) off the coast of Newfoundland and Labrador.

Otter trawler: Trawlers with cone-shaped nets that are towed along the ocean floor to catch groundfish. They are named for the rectangular doors, or "otterboards," attached to the cables between the vessel and the net, which keep the mouth of the net open while it is being towed. Fish are trapped in the end of the net, called the "cod end." After a period of towing, the net is winched up and the catch is released on deck for bleeding, gutting, and storage.

Pelagics: Fish that live in the ocean's middle and upper levels.

Pulse fishing: The name given to a particularly destructive form of fishing: If one vessel encountered a large concentration of fish, the rest of the fleet would descend and fish until the entire school was all but wiped out. The practice is now curtailed.

Recruitment: The point at which fish are considered big enough to be caught in the fishery. It also means the number of fish in a year-class that are recruited.

Seiner: A vessel that uses a seine, a vertical net weighted at the bottom and with floats at the top. One end of the net is fastened to the vessel and the other is taken by a small boat or "skiff," so that the net encircles the fish. The bottom of the net is closed like a bag or purse, and the net is winched on board.

Side-trawler: A vessel that allows the trawl net to be set and hauled in from the side. Largely obsolete by the 1970s, they have been replaced by modern stern trawlers, although some were converted to scallop draggers that are still fishing today.

Targeted fishery: See directed fishery, above.

Tonne: A metric tonne is equal to 1,000 kilograms.

Total Allowable Catch: (TAC - pronounced tee ay cee, not tack.) The total tonnage of fish allowed to be caught from a particular stock in a particular year. In Canada, TACs are set by the minister of fisheries and oceans after he receives advice from DFO bureaucrats, advisory committees, and for groundfish, the FRCC.

Trawler: A vessel that fishes with a trawl net, a large, conical, wide-mouthed net that is towed along behind the boat.

Trollers: A small one- or two-person boat that fishes by trolling, or drawing several baited lines strung on outriggers through the water. They are used in the West Coast salmon fishery.

Virtual Population Analysis: One type of Sequential Population Analysis, a mathematical model used by scientists to determine the past history and present abundance of a stock.

Year-class: All of the fish in a stock that were spawned in a particular year, such as 1992. Scientists sometimes also call a particular year-class a cohort.

Index